Paying the Price

PAYING THE PRICE

COLLEGE COSTS, FINANCIAL AID, AND THE BETRAYAL OF THE AMERICAN DREAM

Sara Goldrick-Rab

The University of Chicago Press   *Chicago and London*

The University of Chicago Press, Chicago 60637
The University of Chicago Press, Ltd., London
© 2016 by The University of Chicago
All rights reserved. Published 2016.
Paperback edition 2017
Printed in the United States of America

23 22 21 20 19 18   4 5 6 7

ISBN-13: 978-0-226-40434-9 (cloth)
ISBN-13: 978-0-226-52714-7 (paper)
ISBN-13: 978-0-226-40448-6 (e-book)
DOI: 10.7208/chicago/9780226404486.001.0001

Library of Congress Cataloging-in-Publication Data
Names: Goldrick-Rab, Sara, author. | Anderson, Drew M. | Kinsley, Peter (Educational
policy expert)
Title: Paying the price : college costs, financial aid, and the betrayal of the American
dream / Sara Goldrick-Rab.
Description: Chicago ; London : The University of Chicago Press, 2016. | Includes
bibliographical references and index.
Identifiers: LCCN 2016007474 | ISBN 9780226404349 (cloth : alk. paper) | ISBN
9780226404486 (e-book)
Subjects: LCSH: College costs—Wisconsin. | College costs—Social aspects—United
States. | Student aid—Wisconsin. | Student aid—Social aspects—United States.
| Education, Higher—Economic aspects—United States. | Federal aid to higher
education—United States.
Classification: LCC LB2342.15.W5 G65 2016 | DDC 378.3/809775—dc23 LC record available
at http://lccn.loc.gov/2016007474

♾ This paper meets the requirements of ANSI/NISO Z39.48–1992 (Permanence of Paper).

Isaac Youcha taught me about the transformative power of education, and Geraldine Youcha instilled my love of writing. I dedicate this book to them, and to my children Annie and Conor, with hope for a more equitable and just future.

Contents

Introduction

There is a new economics of college in America. In the past, students and families who worked hard stood a real chance of attaining a college degree, a ticket to the good life. But then the world shifted. Today, the promise of a college degree in exchange for hard work and dedication no longer holds true. Instead, students encounter a price so high that it has changed what it means to attend college.

Unfortunately, many people don't know this. Millions enroll in higher education with plans to work, borrow, and save, only to find that their funds still fall short. Even living on ramen, doubling up with roommates, and working a part-time job isn't enough to make ends meet. Many who start college can't afford to complete their degrees. Others take on huge debt that either they cannot repay or limits their future opportunities. And this is occurring at a time when diplomas matter more than ever.

What happened? Just as Americans decided that college was essential, states began spending less on public higher education and the price of college rose. At the same time, the financial aid system, long intended to make college affordable, failed to keep up with growing student and family need. Student loans became the stopgap. And, to make matters worse, for nearly 80 percent of the public, family income declined.[1]

What does this mean for students facing the new economics in public colleges and universities? How are they managing to make it through higher education today, and where are they falling short? This book is the result of my six-year-long effort to find out. As you will see, the statistics and stories make one thing quite clear: college students are paying a hefty price.

Paying the Price

At dinner tables around the country, families talk about the cost of college. Usually, they speak of tuition and fees, which have been steadily rising over time. The other costs of college, those that come with books and supplies, transportation, housing, and food, have also grown. This is true across public higher education, at two-year and four-year schools alike. As figure 1 shows, between 1974–75 and 2013–14, the cost of attending the nation's community colleges ballooned from just under $6,000 per year (in constant 2012–13 dollars) to almost $9,000 per year. At the four-year colleges and universities, that same thirty-year period saw a more than $10,000 increase. Since the year 2000, community college costs are up by 28 percent, and the cost of attendance at public universities is up by 54 percent.[2]

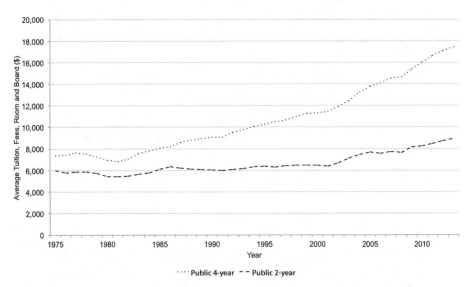

Figure 1. Trends in average tuition, fees, room, and board in the public sector, by college type: 1974–2014. All figures are constant 2012–13 dollars. Room and board for two-year colleges is estimated in the College Board report and figures are in the underlying data provided in the "Download Data" link. Source: adapted from Ma, et al., *Trends in College Pricing: 2015*, table 2: Tuition and Fees and Room and Board over Time.

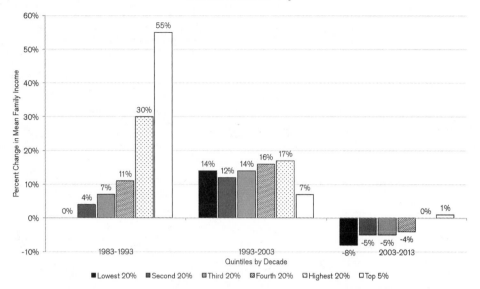

Figure 2. Percentage change in mean family income by quintile: 1983–1993, 1993–2003, and 2003–2013. Income is reported in constant 2013 dollars. Source: adapted from Baum and Ma, *Trends in College Pricing: 2014*, figure 22A: Changes in Family Income over Time.

The rising college prices over the last fifteen years stand in sharp contrast to what happened to family income. While in the 1980s and 1990s, growth in college prices was generally matched by growth in family income, in the current century it was not. Since 2003, the mean family income of all but the very wealthiest 5 percent of Americans fell or stagnated (see figure 2).[3] In 2013, middle-income families earned about $64,000 per year, a decline of 5 percent over the prior decade. Families in the bottom fifth of the income distribution had earnings of about $16,000—down 8 percent.

The financial aid system was built to help with these challenges by offsetting the price of college for financially constrained families, thereby making college affordable. Grants, loans, work-study, and tax credits are—at annual cost of almost $240 billion—supposed to lower the official cost of attendance to a manageable price based on assessed financial need.[4] The centerpiece of these efforts is the Pell Grant Program, which provides a bit less than $6,000 a year to help reduce the price of attendance for the most economically vulnerable

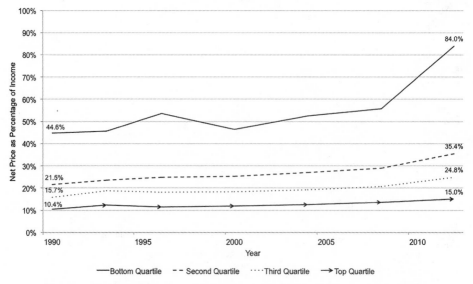

Figure 3. Average net price as a percent of family income, by income quartile: 1990–2012. Net price is the cost of attendance less grant aid faced by the average student across all sectors of higher education. All figures are constant 2012 dollars. In 2012, average family income by quartiles was bottom, $16,311; second, $49,837; third, $89,119; and top, $172,729. Source: adapted from Mortenson, "Financial Barriers to Higher Education by Parental Income and Institutional Level/Control, 1990 to 2012."

students. Soon, nearly ten million people will receive Pell support each year.

But financial aid is falling far short of expectations. Even community college, an institution most think of as free, is no longer actually free for Pell recipients. Consider some bottom-line numbers for low-income families. Students from families earning an average of just $20,000 a year are required to pay at least $8,000 for a year of community college and more than $12,000 a year at a public university.[5] Middle-class families are struggling, too.[6] A year of college at a public university runs a family earning $80,000 a year just over $20,000.[7] That "net price" is the cost after all grants (including the Pell and state and institutional grants) are subtracted from the cost of attending college.

The hard truth is that while financial aid reduces the ever-increasing cost of college, more often than not it still leaves families with unmanageable prices.[8] Figure 3 expresses the average net price of a year of college as a percentage of family income. It depicts substantial growth over time in the burden of paying for college. In 1990, only the poorest quarter of American families had to pay much more than 20 percent of their annual income for higher education. Today, 75 percent of families pay at least that much—after all grants are distributed! And when it comes to the group that this financial aid system was designed to help the most—those families earning an average of $16,000 per year—the net price of college now amounts to a whopping 84 percent of their income.

The consequences of the new economics of college are staggering. When the Pell program began, it was intended to shield recipients from having to take loans. Today nine out of ten Pell recipients graduate with debt.[9] Of the Pell recipients who attend public colleges and universities—fully two-thirds of all Pell recipients—just 48 percent who start college full time complete a degree or certificate of any kind within six years.[10] Of the remaining 52 percent, one in three leaves with a double burden: no credential and an average of $9,000 in student loan debt.[11]

Going to College in the Great Recession

What does it mean for students to confront these prices? In September 2008, just as the Great Recession was getting underway, three thousand students enrolled in the forty-two public colleges and universities across Wisconsin for the very first time. There were just over 5.6 million people living in the state back then, and about 60 percent of working adults had attended college.[12] Wisconsin has been called a "mythical microcosm," and "the most typical state in the nation" because it comes closer than any other to national averages on key measures such as income, education, and neighborhood characteristics.[13] One in four working families had an income under 200 percent of the poverty threshold, and among racial/ethnic minority working families, the fraction was much higher, at 47 percent. Parents who had not attended college led almost half of all working poor families.[14]

These students wanted economic security, so they went to college. They came from all over the state, from small rural towns and suburban communities and from larger cities, including Milwaukee and the state's capitol, Madison. Each showed up for school having completed the Free Application for Federal Student Aid (FAFSA) and secured at least some grant aid, including the Pell Grant. They signed up for at least twelve college credits and began pursuing degrees. My research team got in touch with them and started following their progress.

College costs were rising quickly in Wisconsin's public two-year and four-year colleges and universities, even as employment rates declined during the onslaught of the recession.[15] A private foundation, the Fund for Wisconsin Scholars, was concerned about the implications for educational opportunities in the state and decided to intervene. The creation of its new grant program, aimed at distributing about $5 million a year to students in the forty-two public colleges and universities, made it possible to investigate whether reducing the price of college through financial grants would affect rates of success, including graduation.

Along with economist Douglas N. Harris, I designed and implemented the Wisconsin Scholars Longitudinal Study, which is described in detail in appendix 1. This effort included a robust array of data collection activities, including lengthy surveys accompanied by payments for participation, and legal agreements to collect administrative data from the public colleges and universities and their system offices. I also led a team of graduate students in conducting repeated in-depth in-person interviews with fifty of the three thousand students to help us understand their daily experiences in college. These students attended four universities and two of the technical colleges among the forty-two colleges and universities in the study, and they were among the more than eleven hundred students who had volunteered to meet for interviews. After sorting those volunteers by institution, gender, and race/ethnicity, we selected among them at random. We sought to measure in great detail how and why financial aid enhanced their progress through school, as well as where it fell short.[16]

Our average student was between eighteen and nineteen years of age in 2008 and came from a family with an adjusted gross income of just under $25,000. Their average expected family contribution, which is used by the college to determine the student's financial aid award, was $1,370.[17] Fifty-eight percent of the students were female, and 57 percent of them had parents who had not completed a bachelor's degree (this makes them the first generation to pursue higher education). Almost three in four students identified as non-Hispanic white, with the rest of students identifying as African American (10%), Hispanic (7%), Asian (8%), or another race/ethnicity (4%). They were broadly representative of more than six thousand other undergraduates across the state meeting the same criteria, and with a few exceptions (notably, they were disproportionately white) they were generally representative of the national population of first-time, full-time, on-time Pell Grant recipients attending public institutions. A full description of their characteristics is contained in appendix 1.

The institutions they attended included the thirteen public universities and thirteen two-year branch campuses in the University of Wisconsin (UW) System, long lauded as a leader in public higher education. In addition, students came from across the sixteen public technical colleges that compose the Wisconsin Technical College System, which grants certificates and associate degrees in applied fields. In total, half our students enrolled in either a UW college—a two-year branch campus in the UW System—or a Wisconsin technical college. The other half enrolled in public universities. Appendix 2 contains a detailed description of higher education in Wisconsin.

The students did not know it, but Wisconsin, like many other states, was in the midst of a long period of reducing support for public higher education. Competing priorities and political preferences for tax cuts meant that as college enrollment in the state grew, subsidies on a per-student basis for public colleges and universities fell. For each $1,000 in taxpayer support, the state was spending less and less. When the Pell Grant Program was created in 1972, Wisconsin invested almost fifteen dollars in public higher education per $1,000 of state personal income, but by 2008 it put in just about six dollars.[18] At the same time, while spending grew slowly for the state's need-based grant program, the Wisconsin Higher Education Grant, it covered less and less of the costs of college attendance.[19] That was primarily because public colleges and universities were raising tuition and other costs in order to recover the lost monies from the state.

Had the students in this study begun college in the year they were born, they would not have needed to borrow and simply could have worked at a part-time job year-round to cover college costs. Or, had they borrowed, they could have worked only during the summer and focused entirely on school for the rest of the year. In 1990, an average student from a low-income family in Milwaukee paid roughly $4,500 per year (after grants) to attend that city's public university—but when our students enrolled in 2008, a similarly situated student paid about $7,460.[20] Affording college, even for the poorest students, now required both work and borrowing.

We watched as students came to grips with these financial realities. They started with great expectations. Many were disappointed. Half of them left college without achieving their goals. Less than one in five who entered a public university finished a bachelor's degree in four years.

We documented the extent to which the Fund for Wisconsin Scholars' investment in grants changed those odds of success. Sometimes, the program made a big difference, as the funds helped students avoid working long hours or taking on more debt, making it possible to finish a bachelor's degree in a shorter period of time and with lower debt. For each additional $1,000 received, the percentage of students who completed a bachelor's degree on-time (in four years) went up four points.[21] But more often than not, the $3,500- per-year grants the foundation offered university students, and the $1,800-per-year grants it offered two-year college students, did not change the odds of graduation very much.

This did not mean that money was not important in their lives—it was. Students echoed the words of the Wu-Tang Clan: "Cash rules everything around me."[22] But financial aid is not cash. You can use cash in your wallet or your bank account as you need it. But you can't just go out and buy milk with financial aid dollars. Those who think that financial aid simply transfers money to students who need it are fundamentally wrong. Today's financial aid programs and policies are bureaucratic and complex. Financial aid often falls short—in terms of both how much it pays for and how it is delivered.

Millions of American families wrestle with these struggles in private. Many people continue to believe that financial aid is working to make college affordable, at least for people from low-income families. They are upset about loans but focus mainly on the struggle to repay them, rather than their root cause: the high price of college that makes them necessary in the first place. These misperceptions are understandable, since the changes creating the current mess happened without warning or real discussion and accelerated rapidly during the last decade.

This book is intended to be a wake-up call. It brings the lives of students pursuing college degrees front and center and unveils their financial struggles. Ensuring that the American public has a clear sense of how and why financial aid is failing to get students to graduation will help us find effective solutions. Low-income families are not alone—middle-class families are squeezed too, as the current system often expects more from them than they can give. Outdated policies that are not up to the task of funding a widely accessible, high-quality system of higher education have compromised the ability of hard-working people from all family backgrounds to complete their degrees and left millions in debt, without a degree, and worse off than when they began. Perhaps the best sign of hope we have is that there is growing recognition there is something terribly wrong when so many Americans are falling flat just trying to pay for school.

Overview of the Book

Improving our collective understanding of college affordability takes work—work to look beyond the published figures and media claims and get down to the real experiences of regular Americans. This book is grounded in the lives of six students, whom you will meet in chapter 1. These men and women represent the range of students we studied, and I draw on their experiences throughout the book. I also include the stories of other students, where they help to illustrate particular points. In chapters 2 and 3, I explore today's financial aid system and how it attempts to make college affordable for people without sufficient resources. Tracing changes in the characteristics of Pell recipients over time and contrasting those trends with shifts in the prices they pay for college, I dispel common misperceptions about who gets Pell and why. Then, beginning in chapter 4, the students themselves, who generously shared their time with us over many years, explain how well-intentioned efforts to provide financial aid come up short. My team documented the careful dance involved in cobbling together work and loans and in reducing expenses while ensuring students are equipped for school each day. Chapter 5 reveals what happens when the dance isn't enough, and students face scarcity.

Families often provide the impetus for college enrollment, and how relationships with family members affect and are affected by the act of paying for college is the topic of chapter 6. In chapter 7, I return to the academic side of college life, investigating ways that the new economics of college affects how students pursue their course work and engage in learning activities. A desire to do well in school was shared by nearly every student in our study, but some faced additional challenges. Chapter 8 documents the especially fragile circumstances surrounding the students who attended college in Milwaukee, a city in economic distress, whose public colleges and universities are underresourced and often ill-equipped to ensure that all students graduate.

Finally, in chapter 9 the graduation outcomes of the three thousand students are revealed. After six years, they reached a variety of points in the road. Some graduated, but many did not. Sometimes financial aid was sufficient, and occasionally additional grant support made graduation possible. But often, making ends meet with too little money during the Great Recession left these undergraduates wondering what college was good for. It was meant to provide them a route out of poverty, but for far too many, it left them feeling poorer than ever.

The last chapter of the book describes how we can do better. There are some solutions that are straightforward and could be implemented locally by colleges and universities. Others would require state or federal action. Whenever possible, I reach beyond educational policy solutions to think about other supports that could help more students succeed. The price of college must be lowered much further than the current system allows. Money must be brought to the table—there is no way around it. But how that money is deployed so as to ameliorate the price barrier to college graduation is a matter deserving of national debate.

The bones of the current financial aid system are now more than a half a century old. The GI Bill and its successors, the Truman Commission, the National Defense Education Act, and the Higher Education Act of 1965, were the first steps in the process of ensuring equitable opportunities at the postsecondary level.[23] This book tells the stories of students actually *experiencing* the financial aid system today, and it should give us pause. The evidence points to the need for a more effective system of college financing that works with students in their efforts to obtain college degrees.

There is reason for hope. An improved college financing system could help America create a future where more people can use their own hard work to get ahead. These college successes will get better jobs, contribute more to the common good as taxpayers, and lean on the government less for support throughout their lives. Such a future would be far brighter than the one we face today.

1

Possible Lives

A public debate is raging about the future of financial aid, with experts often trying to blame financial aid recipients rather than the system. Data on their academic performance have been used to question whether they belong in college in the first place. Data on their use of student loans have been used to question their financial literacy and how they live their lives. Data on their degree completion rates have been used to question whether the Pell Grant Program is a waste. Some even ask whether, since college credentials result in increased earnings, we should subsidize college participation for anyone. Let those who can afford it get ahead, while the others remain behind, they argue.[1]

Amid this national furor, students from lower-income families are simply trying to make a better life. In this chapter you'll meet students in the Wisconsin Scholars Longitudinal Study, including the three men and three women who serve as focal points throughout much of the book. But first, let's take a look at the original plans and designs of financial aid and what happened to them over time.

College Then and Now

In the 1960s, when federal financial aid policy was first formulated, the nation was in the midst of a period of economic growth and security, declining poverty, and great social change. Women, African Americans, immigrants, and working-class white people were all clamoring for a shot at middle-class jobs and the American dream, and politicians in Washington wanted to help. From President Lyndon Johnson on down, many policymakers believed that helping people improve their education and skills levels would in turn help the nation. Providing access to higher education was a clear and seemingly fair way to do that.[2]

Passage of the Higher Education Act of 1965 dramatically increased federal investment in higher education and provided grants and loans for students attending public and private colleges. In 1971, the U.S. Senate Subcommittee on Education debated a bill introduced by Senator Claiborne Pell that took things a step further, establishing as a policy of the federal government "the right of every youngster, regardless of his family's financial circumstances, to obtain a postsecondary education." His actions followed those of the Truman Commission, which in 1947 recognized that college costs impeded the nation's ability to double the number of college goers (from 2.3 million in 1947 to 4.6 million by 1960).[3] While that commission took steps to create more affordable institutions of higher education—most critically, the nation's community colleges— Senator Pell and his colleagues believed that it was also important to indirectly subsidize the costs of college. The bill provided $1,200 annually for each student to use as a voucher to lower the amount of tuition they paid at the college or university of their choice.[4] In 1972, the bill passed, and the Pell Grant was born.[5]

The creators of the current federal student aid system knew that college degrees brought real opportunities. The architects of the financial aid system did not, however, envision college as the only route out of poverty. During the same period, Congress invested in jobs programs, a safety net for those left behind, and Head Start for the children of poor families. The emphasis was on college as one option, one possible pathway, and the Pell Grant Program was organized to support that. The grant could be taken to any college or university in the nation participating in the federal student aid program, providing students with a wide range of options, and policymakers hoped that the higher education marketplace would respond by ensuring that opportunities were of the highest quality.[6]

The creation of the financial aid system followed more than a century of investment in public higher education, beginning with the Morrill Act of 1862 and continuing with the GI Bill (1944), the Truman Commission (1947), the National Defense Education Act (1958), and the California Master Plan (1960). By the time the Pell Grant was created in 1972, 80 percent of American college students were enrolled in public colleges and universities.[7] Historian Roger Geiger described the scene this way: "American states poured enormous resources into building public systems of higher education: flagship universities were expanded and outfitted for an extensive research role; teachers colleges grew into regional universities; public urban universities multiplied and grew; and a vast array of community colleges was built."[8] Economists Claudia Goldin and Lawrence Katz have linked these major investments in public education to a growth in human capital that enabled the United States to thrive as a global economic powerhouse.[9] These results would not have occurred if only the wealthiest or even only the highest-achieving students went to college.

Despite these overt commitments to higher education as a public good, not everyone shared Claiborne Pell's vision for how to bring more equality of opportunity into the American system. In fact, the "system" of higher education has never been much of a system at all. It is instead a loose conglomeration of government institutions (at the local, state, and federal levels) and both public and private educational providers that share some similar interests but hold many different ones as well.

Soaring rhetoric about the value of hard work obscures the fact that family money has long been one of the best predictors of college success. In the words of the Truman Commission: "For the great majority of our boys and girls, the kind and amount of education they may hope to attain depends, not on their own abilities, but on the family or community into which they happened to be born or, worse still, on the color of their skin or the religion of their parents."[10]

The children of wealthy families are still most likely to complete college, followed by students from middle-income families. Students from low-income families are the least likely to graduate.[11] Should breaking the link between family income and degree attainment be a public priority supported by taxpayer dollars? In the late 1960s and 1970s, states including California, Florida, Michigan, and North Carolina said yes and invested resources in their public colleges and universities in order to keep the prices charged to students low, while also creating state need-based aid programs to complement the federal Pell.[12] State fiscal support for higher education nearly tripled from $3.56 per $1,000 of state personal income in 1961, to $10.42 in 1979.[13]

Other states disagreed. Massachusetts, New Hampshire, New Jersey, Pennsylvania, and Vermont, among other states, appropriated little money to public colleges and universities and instead relied on private institutions to offer opportunities.[14] Rarely do state expenditures per student come anywhere close to matching the federal investment in the Pell Grant.[15] Even the states that initially spent heavily on public colleges and universities reduced their support as more and more people went to college. Beginning in 1981, state appropriations began to decline, from $10.18 per $1,000 of state personal income in that year to $9.24 in 1990 to $7.52 in 2000 to $6.32 in 2010. Today, the share of state resources invested in higher education is about the same as it was in 1966 (about five dollars for every $1,000 of personal income).[16]

Wisconsin, the focus of this book, is among the states that reduced support to higher education the most.[17] Perhaps this was a reaction to signals that college was now sufficiently accessible— after all, demand was rising—or perhaps competing needs (such as Medicare costs) simply required the funds.[18] Or, as many have argued, disinvestment in higher education may be the direct result of shifts in political priorities.[19] Whatever the case, no federal authority requires that states make college affordable, and tuition and other costs grew rapidly, even at public colleges and universities.[20] Had states been required to maintain a reasonable level of commitment (say, the ten dollars or so per $1,000 of personal income provided in 1981), the total amount states contribute to higher education today would be about $146 billion, instead of the $81 billion contributed in 2015.[21] That commitment would have likely prevented the rapid

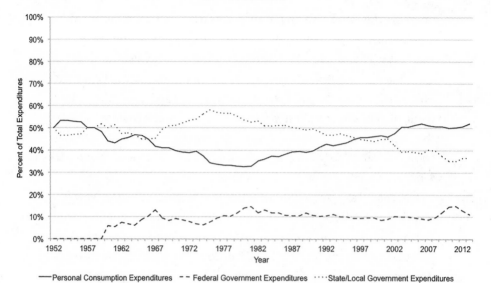

Figure 4. Distribution of revenue sources for financing public and private higher education: 1952 to 2013. Source: adapted from Mortenson, "State Investment and Disinvestment in Higher Education, FY1961 to FY2014."

increases in tuition and fees in public higher education (see fig. 1) that fueled the declining purchasing power of the Pell and the need for so many middle-class families to turn to student loans. As figure 4 illustrates, the federal commitment to higher education has long been smaller but steadier. What has changed is state behavior—and this is what drove changes in the prices paid by individual Americans directly from their wallets (as opposed to collectively, through their taxes).

But the federal financial aid system is virtually silent on the role of colleges and universities in keeping the price of higher education reasonable. It also does little to ensure that the education delivered is high quality, and it says nothing about which colleges should admit which students. It does not mandate that institutions create their own need-based aid programs or direct resources to support economically vulnerable students. There are no requirements that the Pell Grant vouch for a meaningful amount of the cost of attending that college. A college that charges $60,000 a year can receive $5,000 Pell vouchers just as easily as a college that charges $6,000.

The revenues available from the Pell, along with the array of other federal programs under Title IV of the Higher Education Act including student loans, flow into the coffers of colleges and universities without extracting any accountability for keeping costs affordable.[22] For-profit colleges and universities benefit substantially, pocketing billons in federal student aid each year while producing degrees that employers value far less than community college degrees, often equating them with high school diplomas.[23] The rapid growth of federal spending in that sector is one reason why the entire Pell program is being reexamined today.[24] But some nonprofit private colleges and universities, and a few public flagships, benefit as well, making extensive use of Pell Grants even as they construct mammoth endowments worth billions of dollars and hoard opportunities for the wealthiest students.[25]

Over the past fifty years, America built a financial aid system with lofty ambitions and few teeth. That was fine, perhaps, at a time when a college degree was nice but not required. When the Pell program began, Pell Grants subsidized more than 80 percent of the cost of attending the average public university and all of the costs of attending a community college. Things are different now. Today the maximum Pell covers less than one-third of the cost of attending a public four-year college or university and barely 60 percent of the cost of attending a community college. Figures 5 and 6 illustrate the problem. Spending on the Pell program has lagged behind growth in the number of recipients for decades. These trends, along with rising college costs, have resulted in the significant erosion of the Pell purchasing power.

At the same time, economic restructuring and political decision making has rendered higher education the singular option for getting ahead in America. The spectacular dropout examples, like Bill Gates, are, like some exotic, endangered species, vanishingly rare. Today, the American vision of success runs this way: good parenting and hard work leads young adults to college, college attendance (both for young adults and midlife back-to-school students) leads to better jobs, stronger families, happier marriages, and healthier and longer lives. College is supposed to grant entry to (or at least keep

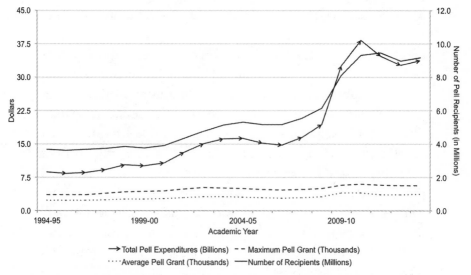

Figure 5. Total Pell expenditures, maximum and average Pell Grant, and number of recipients: 1994–95 to 2013–14. All figures are in constant 2013 dollars. Source: adapted from Baum and Ma, *Trends in Student Aid: 2014*, table 5: Number of Recipients, Total Awards and Aid per Recipient for Federal Aid Programs in Current Dollars and in 2013 Dollars, 1976–77 to 2013–14.

you in) the middle class and certainly more or less guarantee you earn enough money to make ends meet.

If only this were true. Colleges and universities are populated by students and governed by policies—and over time changes in both the students and the policies have altered the meaning of American higher education and limited what our nation's colleges and universities have the capacity to achieve. Against a backdrop of widening inequality in both income and wealth, the number of Americans living in or near poverty has grown. Today 22 percent of the sixty-seven million children in the United States live under the federal poverty level.[26] Many researchers think that the federal poverty level understates the level of income families really need in order to subsist with a modicum of decency.[27] We do far less to support impoverished children and their families than we once did, withholding cash assistance, food stamps, and affordable housing unless or until we are convinced they work hard enough to be "deserving" of help, requiring not only drug tests and jobs of parents, but often frequent reapplications and jumping through multiple bureaucratic hoops as

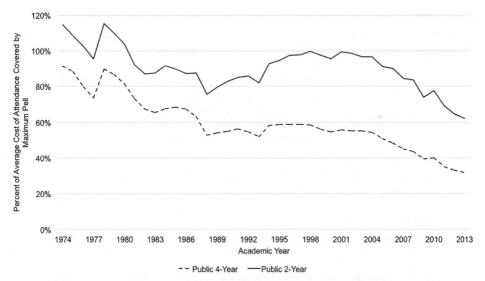

Figure 6. Purchasing power of the Pell Grant at public institutions, by type: 1974–2013. Purchasing power is the percentage of the average cost of attendance covered by the maximum Pell Grant. Source: adapted from Baum and Ma, *Trends in College Pricing: 2014*, table 2A: Tuition and Fees and Room and Board over Time, 1974–75 to 2014–15, Selected Years.

well.[28] At the same time, we pressure their schools and teachers to educate students, regardless of the disadvantages they face in their homes and communities. The K–12 system is required to graduate most students and move them on. What then?

Fifty years ago, many of these students could have gone on to production and manufacturing jobs, often with unions and benefits, and some of them could have made it into the middle class.

Twenty years ago, even, most would have moved straight to the workforce, trying their hand at unstable, low-wage jobs, with some finding their way into more reliable blue-collar work with protections offered by unions. Working-class white men, in particular, continued to find some opportunities that way, even in the post-Reagan era.[29]

Today, those jobs are much harder to find, unions are weaker, and high school graduates are more convinced than ever that their only viable option for a better life is higher education. Higher education is no longer seen as a choice or a luxury—it is viewed as the only available next step and, indeed, the only hope.

Of course, America's hopes for higher education can overstate what college today tends to achieve. Some think that because a college degree brings higher wages, better chances of full-time work, and jobs with benefits, increasing the number of people who attend college can decrease economic inequality. This is a false hope. The social mobility offered by higher education, the opportunity to climb from one rung on the ladder to the next, is not accompanied by any assurance that others higher on the ladder aren't also moving ahead at an even faster rate. There is no guarantee, in other words, that college-educated people from low-income families will not be left behind. And in American higher education, a vicious cycle of exclusion and adaptation in which resources are unequally distributed in ways that preserve privilege helps to ensure that people from lower-class backgrounds stay behind.[30]

The process is quite effective. For people born in the early 1960s, prior to the first Higher Education Act, the odds of bachelor's degree completion (conditional on college entry) for a low-income individual lagged 31 percentage points behind that of a high-income person (see fig. 7). But for those born in the late 1970s, when the financial aid program was in full swing, that gap was 45 percentage points.[31] Despite making some gains in accessing college, the poor are simply running in place.[32]

Furthermore, the average financial benefit of college degrees—the bonus that appears evident when you compare the earnings of a person who holds a bachelor's degree to those of a high school graduate—does not accrue equally for everyone. The returns on investing time and money in college are uneven and unstable since they depend on opportunities in the ever-shifting labor market—a market rife with uncertainty and ongoing change and, too often, discrimination to boot.[33] People who grow up in economically fragile circumstances often continue to live in economically fragile communities, even after they attend college.[34] They are better off than their peers who do not go beyond high school, but they remain far behind most Americans.

All this means that college alone will not conquer inequality. But this doesn't mean we shouldn't be doing more to realize the ideals of meritocracy and equal opportunity that launched the federal

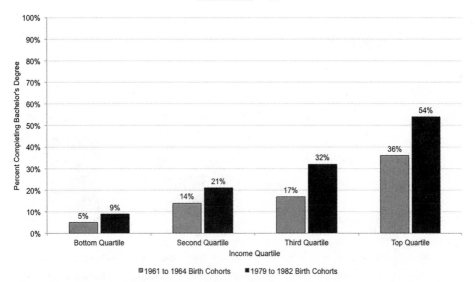

Figure 7. Percentage of students completing bachelor's degree, by income quartile and year of birth. Source: Bailey and Dynarski, "Inequality in Postsecondary Education." Based on data from the *National Longitudinal Survey of Youth*, 1979 and 1997.

Pell program. As figure 8 illustrates, today the likelihood of earning college degrees is still tied to family income.[35] Tracking America's spring 2002 high school sophomores, the U.S. Department of Education found that, among students with similar performance on math tests, students from higher-income backgrounds were vastly more likely to complete college degrees than student from middle-income backgrounds, who were in turn much more likely to graduate than students from low-income backgrounds.

Why is this happening? Students from working- and middle-class families who hit the books in high school and are academically prepared for college are turning away from higher education because they cannot afford it. Those who do make it in the door are leaving without degrees at higher and higher rates. [36] Those who remain in college take longer to finish their degrees, racking up additional debt along the way.[37] This is even truer today than fifty years ago. As members of the Truman Commission wrote, "The democratic community cannot tolerate a society based upon education for the well-to-do alone. If college opportunities are restricted to those

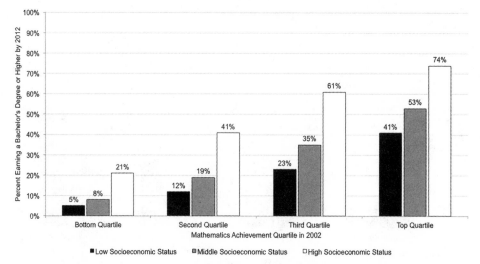

Figure 8. Percent of spring 2002 high school sophomores who earned a bachelor's degree or higher by 2012, by socioeconomic status and math achievement quartile in 2002. Source: adapted from Kena et al., *The Condition of Education 2015*, figure 5.

in the higher income brackets, the way is open to the creation and perpetuation of a class society which has no place in the American way of life."[38]

The "class society" the Truman Commission feared is now very much a reality, and income inequality is starker than it has been at any time since the Gilded Age.[39] The economic successes of the twentieth century were propelled by investments in education. Now the expected benefits of attending college are increasingly outweighed by both the perceived and real costs, especially over the short term. For people from fragile economic circumstances, the short term is the only future they know they have.

Six Grants, Six Lives

The students of the Wisconsin Scholars Longitudinal Study, who entered college in the fall of 2008, were born in 1990. Their young lives were bookended by financial crises. In the years leading up to their birth, America struggled with the aftermath of Black Monday, the 1987 stock market crash, and the collapse of the savings and loan industry. In the summer of 1990, Iraq invaded Kuwait, causing the price of oil to rise, diminishing consumer confidence, and accelerating an economic downturn that became a recession for the next three years. Following that period, however, their childhoods were made easier during a robust period of strong economic growth and job creation. Real family income in Wisconsin grew by almost $14,500 during the 1990s, far more than the national average of $11,600.[40] Prosperity was not felt evenly, however. Male jobless rates rose in Milwaukee during that period, the population there fell, and the city became majority-minority as its white population diminished from 61 percent of the population in 1990 to 40 percent in 2008. In that year, more than one in three children in Wisconsin's major metropolitan city were living in poverty.[41]

As our students walked onto campus in September 2008, Lehman Brothers filed the largest bankruptcy in the history of the United States. While the Great Recession technically lasted only nineteen months, from December 2007 to June 2009, its aftermath is widely considered to have extended for many years. Between October 2008 and August 2010, a national poll found that Americans felt that "education, schooling, and the ability to afford college" was one of the top two most important problems facing the nation.[42] High levels of unemployment persisted through 2014. Other markers of a weak economy lasted as well, including low consumer confidence, rising federal debt, a slide in rates of home ownership, and unemployment's statistical doppelgänger, underemployment, a measure of part-time workers who would like to be full time, highly skilled workers who were working in low-skill or low-pay jobs and the like.

Our students felt that their only hope of getting a decent job and a stable life for their families was to go college. In prior decades, some of them might have found alternatives, going to work in construction or manufacturing jobs or working on a parent's farm. But those jobs had largely disappeared, and so here these students were, pursuing more education to get ahead. The unemployment rate in Wisconsin for high school graduates without a bachelor's degree was 10 percent—two and a half times higher than the rate for bachelor's degree holders. People with bachelor's degrees earned about ten dollars more per hour than their counterparts with high school degrees.[43] Our students seemed to know this. Ninety-one percent felt that education would pay off in higher earnings: they anticipated a median annual earnings increase from completing a bachelor's degree of $20,000. This would, they estimated on surveys, lead them to careers making about $50,000 a year.

TYLER OLSON

Tyler Olson grew up in a small Wisconsin city banked by a river and a lake, in a community where nine in ten residents share his Anglo origins and where families like his were known for their commitment to football, wrestling, and fishing. Tyler's parents were divorced and experienced frequent spells of unemployment. His mother was disabled by a back injury, and in the year before we met Tyler his dad earned less than $10,000 per year. When he was fourteen years old, Tyler started working at Hardee's fast food restaurant. By his senior year of high school he was putting in twenty hours of work each week. Still, Tyler did not consider himself "poor." "We were middle class, or actually the missing class. You know, making just enough to get by and pay the bills and not be considered lower class but not enough to enjoy the life of a middle-class person where you get to go on a vacation or buy your kids nice gifts for Christmas, go to the movies, and hang out with friends bowling. We were stuck in between. We'd get a Green Bay Packers jacket and just be happy."

Like many of our students, Tyler hoped to gain the knowledge and skills in college to eventually open his own business. He did not want to continue working in fast food, in a situation he considered "settling," and he applied to several universities, including the University of Wisconsin–Madison (UW–Madison), the state's flagship.[44] Convinced that an athletic scholarship was the only way for him to pay for college, he looked for a school that would pay him to play football. "I finished high school with a C average. I didn't put forth much effort—I figured if I could play football I didn't need to really try, but I knew I could succeed in college. Not many teachers believed me, but I didn't really care. I finished high school; well, they pretty much graduated me because they didn't want me there anymore. I'm not gonna lie." Tyler said that several football coaches told him "that they would talk to the admissions office for me, and the financial aid office too, since I said my parents don't have much money." When an offer from Madison failed to materialize, he found another public university on the other side of the state that would give him a scholarship, and moved there without a second thought.

Tyler earned a 3.19 GPA in his first semester, but over the winter break he broke his ankle. While treating him, doctors discovered that he had a rare genetic clotting disorder that meant an injury could be life threatening—he could not play contact sports. Tyler needed regular medical attention, and his dad's health insurance did not cover the hospitals near his university. His football days were over. Tyler moved back home and enrolled in the closest university. Without an athletic scholarship, he only had financial aid to depend on, and his future no longer seemed so clear.

NORBERT WEBSTER

Norbert Webster was born outside of Wisconsin, but as a young child he moved north with his family to the reservation of his tribe, the Oneida. Located about ten miles from Green Bay, the reservation was home to a small high school where Norbert eventually became interested in college and in planning for his future. "Our graduating high school class was twenty-six people. . . . I knew everyone's name in my high school and knew a lot about them. It was a really small community." In general, Norbert reported that few students in high school went on to college but that his cohort was an exception. "Our class was always on top of things and we all wanted to go to college. Almost all of my close friends [from high school] are in college now." He was conscious of how that defied common perceptions of Native Americans and felt that people sometimes looked at him with surprise.

In fact, when Norbert began high school he wasn't very interested in college at all—he was interested in sports. He enjoyed wrestling and focused his time and effort on those tournaments, until midway through his freshman year when he was placed on academic probation and his opportunity to wrestle was suspended. "I couldn't participate in two tournaments, which kind of sucked. My brother is a pretty smart kid, he wrestled too, and I talked to him and he told me [to do better]. So I had a little bit of motivation to do better in academics, and then the next semester I made the honor roll. I was also working, so that helped me stay out of trouble." As he moved toward his senior year of high school, Norbert became more focused on school and began to take steps to ensure that he would begin college on the right track. "I knew I wanted to go to college ... I just did not know what I wanted to do, or where to go, but I always knew that I would go to college. It was a no brainer." Every time he heard about opportunities to prepare for college, he seized them. This included taking a college tour: "It helped me get a feel for what college would be like and that helped me with my decision," he said.

Norbert graduated from high school with a 3.09 GPA, having taken the types of rigorous course work that qualified him for an Academic Competitiveness Grant, a special federal program for Pell recipients that provided him an additional $750 a year. He considered several Wisconsin public universities (including UW–Madison, where he was accepted but did not go), deciding instead on the same public university Tyler attended because it was closer to home and boasted a strong mentoring program for Native American students. When he began college, his older brother was enrolled at a technical college, and his younger brother was in middle school.

The vast majority of Norbert's college expenses were covered by an uncommonly generous scholarship provided by the Oneida Nation of Wisconsin, which awarded up to $20,000 per year. This meant that Norbert needed to pay less than $100 for his first year of college.

Norbert wanted to become an accountant. He knew that the Oneida offered good jobs for accountants in its casinos, and this seemed like a smart option. On a survey, he estimated that if he completed a bachelor's degree and went to work he would earn $64,000 a year, and if he didn't complete a degree he'd likely earn just $22,000 a year.

IAN WILLIAMS

There were many reasons why students joined the Wisconsin Scholars Longitudinal Study, which required providing access to their administrative records, participating in surveys, and sometimes sitting for lengthy interviews. Some wanted the money we offered — twenty dollars for a survey or an interview, payable in cash as soon as the survey or interview was done. Others expressed gratitude for the chance to speak about their challenges, and wrote "glad you asked!" in the margins of surveys. Ian Williams met with our team eight times over six years and completed every survey promptly. He explained why: "What I'm hoping to do is speak for the people who don't have this opportunity, people who live in my community, my brothers, my family. . . . I'm going to speak for them, instead of myself."

Ian's low-income community could benefit from more voices like his. Possessing a quick smile and an indelibly positive attitude, Ian is the second youngest of five African American children who grew up on the north side of Milwaukee. Life was not easy coming up in what Ian called a "ghetto-ish type of neighborhood with a lot of violence." His family struggled to pay the bills.

> Sometimes we didn't [have enough to eat] but it was something that we just dealt with because we knew that in the future there was going to be food. We are just going to have to work with what we have, but next week we know there is going to be food in the house. . . . We just divided it amongst us so we didn't get greedy, we knew what to do because we were in that situation so many times. We just divided it amongst each other and let each other know not to eat too much.

Once, Ian's family would have qualified for cash assistance and other income supports, but by the time Ian entered elementary school, Wisconsin governor Tommy Thompson had substantially reduced the availability of such programs. Life in Milwaukee was challenging for Ian and his siblings. He reported, "It was hard for us to get through school because we had so many problems."

During high school Ian participated in after-school programs in order to stay away from trouble on the street. In youth programs, Ian played basketball, took computer classes, and played video games and described that time "as a good experience, instead of just seeing the bad side, you see the good side of the black community." Still, Ian had trouble in school. "I was struggling really badly because I couldn't really concentrate on my work, there were so many class clowns. It was really irritating me and distracted me from my work."

Ian had a vague sense that he wanted to go to college but was not confident that he would make it. "I felt it in my heart that I wanted to go . . . but I don't know for sure. So I kept on feeling like 'Oh, all I'm fixing to do is go through high school,' you know, and that's it. I'm going to get out of high school and have . . . a full-time job paying my mother's bills and everything."

In 2007, Ian graduated from high school. He then spent a year working to save money and finally enrolled in college. "Somehow I managed to stay more focused on my education, and that's why I'm here [in college] right now. . . . I've been through the struggle and it made me stronger." But while his brothers enrolled in a technical college, and his sister attended a for-profit university, Ian went to a public university, where he aimed for a career in finance. His goal was a master's degree in business administration, and his ambitions were much like Tyler's. "Ever since I was younger I've been trying to fulfill the goal of having my own company or something . . . succeeding means accomplishing the goals you set forth, even if you have to go-go-go, even if it has to be going to college—as long as you set your goal at a young age and you accomplish it, that's what succeeding means to me."

Enrolling in college is an achievement where Ian comes from, he said. He was proud of the message his enrollment sent to other people in his community. "They see me going to college and are like, 'Oh, he's doing something positive, he's breaking through the ceiling.' . . . I'm trying to be a positive role model to them and let them know I'm not the only one who can do it."

NIMA CHAUDHARY

When she was young child in Nepal, Nima Chaudhary's experience of grinding poverty was so severe that her parents were often forced to decide which of their children would receive an investment of the "good" food for the day. The family often lacked sufficient clothing as well.

Nima recalls the time when her mother won an immigration lottery, as one of the best and most important moments of her family's life. Nima moved to Wisconsin from Nepal when she was eight years old.

Life in Wisconsin was better for Nima but still difficult. When I met Nima, she was eighteen years old and living in a small two-bedroom apartment with her parents and two older brothers. Her parents shared one bedroom, she got the other, and her brothers slept on couches in the living room. Both brothers were students at UW–Madison, a fact that her parents often boasted about to friends.

A South Asian woman raised by parents with traditional values, Nima was unsure of whether she should go to college. She worried about the costs involved and, particularly, about how those costs measured up relative to the value of her education as a woman. Even though she had done well in high school, earning a solid B average

Table 1. Characteristics of WSLS focal students

	Career Goal	Type of College	High School GPA	No. of Siblings	Race/Ethnicity
Nima Chaudhary	Graphic design	Technical college	3.3	2	Nepalese American
Chloe Johnson	Vet tech	Technical college	2	0	Non-Hispanic white
Tyler Olson	Business	Regional university	2.2	2	Non-Hispanic white
Sophie Schmidt	Christian motivational speaker	Research university	NR	3	Non-Hispanic white
Norbert Webster	Accounting	Regional university	3.1	2	Native American
Ian Williams	Finance	Research university	2.4	4	African American

Source. WSLS data.

Note. All students are Pell recipients and the first in their family to attend college. We do not have Sophie Schmidt's high school GPA, but she was admitted to a selective university.

and an ACT standardized test score of nineteen, she was plagued by doubts. She was almost surprised by her own success. As she explained, "I did not think I would graduate from high school. But I did—and with honors."

She decided to apply to just one college, a nearby technical school. It was the less-expensive option, and she knew she could get in—the school had an open admissions policy. As if by chance, she was enrolled. "I didn't think I was going to college," she told me. "And now I'm in college." Her brothers had helped her complete her financial aid application, and while she wasn't quite sure how she had arrived, she was completely confident that she would complete her degree.

While Nima's brothers focused on majors that would seem to guarantee economic returns (they chose nursing and engineering), Nima planned to study art and become a graphic designer. She felt such a job required an associate degree, and with a degree in hand she expected to earn $20,000 a year—an improvement over the $15,000 a year she anticipated making if she did not attend college. The two-year program of study had a purpose, she explained. "I want to have a good job in art and have enough money to support my family. To have everything paid, all of their bills, and help my parents and my family in Nepal."

SOPHIE SCHMIDT

Most Pell recipients do not come from a background of generational poverty. Some come from middle-class families but don't have either the income stability or the parental support for college that the financial aid system assumes is possible. A study by economists Meta Brown, Karl Scholz, and Ananth Seshadri found that students who weren't receiving the "expected" amount of money from their parents were often hurt by the financial aid system's approach to allocating resources.[45] That is Sophie Schmidt's story.

Sophie was a small-town girl who grew up in a community of just fifteen hundred people composed almost entirely of non-Hispanic white people like herself, and she was excited about college. She was the first person in her immediate family to enroll, yet she reported,

"It was kind of always assumed that after high school I would be going to go to college. This is what I was supposed to do."

When she was very young, Sophie enjoyed a life that included vacations, toys, and the little luxuries that come with middle-class financial stability. But her parents divorced when she was seven years old, and her family's income fell when her father ended his support. The divorce was contentious, and as it progressed Sophie became much closer to her mom, who worked in a factory and as a hair stylist before going to school to become a certified nursing assistant. Her dad began a new life with another family. Her mother also remarried, but that marriage lasted just a short time before also ending in divorce.

When it came time to complete her financial aid application, Sophie's mother was unemployed, and her father was earning $70,424 a year. She was eligible for the federal Pell Grant, but just barely. According to Sophie, her father refused to contribute to her college education despite having a nice home, a new car, and enough time and money to take vacations. In her eyes, he was "cheap"—a "jerk" who would not help her. Intent on making it in spite of him, Sophie applied and was admitted to a selective public university where she would need to borrow or earn almost $16,000 a year to cover costs. With "a plan and a purpose" in mind, aiming to become a Christian motivational speaker after graduation, she went for it. She had worked thirty hours a week while in high school and planned to try to work her way through college.

CHLOE JOHNSON

Like Sophie, Chloe Johnson was born in a small town. Port Edwards is located in central Wisconsin, with a population just under two thousand people. Each year, the town high school graduates about thirty-five students. The community grew up around a papermaking sawmill. In 2008, as Chloe began college, the sawmill closed, resulting in the loss of five hundred jobs.[46]

But by that time, Chloe was living in Fond du Lac with her mother, who moved there along with Chloe's older brother following a divorce. She went to college because that was what was expected of her.

> I didn't know what I was doing, I just knew that you get out of high school and you go to college. That's what you do, and that's what I did. . . . It just feels like you can't get a decent job, you know. I don't want to spend forever—it might be OK for some people but I definitely knew it wasn't for me—working at PetSmart or Kohl's or McDonald's, or something like that for the rest of my life. I just couldn't see myself doing that, and I knew I had to get an education in order to prevent that from happening.

Ever since Chloe was five years old, she had wanted to become a veterinarian. She loved animals and had dogs and a horse growing up. But as she learned more about the responsibilities of being a vet she decided instead to become a veterinary technician to avoid the life-and-death decisions that a vet has to deal with. She enrolled at a technical college, in Wisconsin's only accredited program for the degree she needed. The sticker price for a year of higher education was just over $15,500 a year.

The Truth

Tyler, Ian, Norbert, Nima, Sophie, and Chloe are not composites. While their names have been changed, this book tells their real stories. We spent years getting to know them, meeting with them for interviews, examining their financial aid records and transcripts, and asking them to respond to surveys. They were extraordinarily generous in sharing their lives, and we learned a lot from them. Coming from different ethnic, racial, and family backgrounds, from small towns and big cities, from intense poverty and the middle class, these six young adults have similar stories in two key respects: all tried to attend and succeed in college under financial pressure. And all received at least some help from Uncle Sam in the form of a Pell Grant.

In important ways, their experiences are representative. When they started college, these six students had a great deal in common with the 2,994 other students my team studied. Like Ian, Nima, and Chloe, over half of our students indicated that college costs played an important role in their decision about where to attend college, and like Nima and Ian, just under one in three said they selected a college because it was near their family's home. All six had specific career goals and plans in mind when they started college, as did four in five of the rest of the students. Most of these students felt confident that they were as smart as their college classmates, but like Nima and Ian about one in three had their doubts. Still, none of these six students began college with even an inkling that they could leave college without a degree, nor did the vast majority of the thousands of students we surveyed. In other words, these Pell recipients started college with great expectations.

On one survey we asked the students to rate on a scale of 1–5 their level of the agreement with the statement: "I am willing to sacrifice today so that my life can be better tomorrow." Eighty-one percent of students said that they somewhat (4) or strongly (5) agreed with that statement. They were generally forward-thinking individuals who saw the purpose of those sacrifices. Eighty-six percent also indicated: "I have to do well in college if I want to be a success in life."

Giving for a Change

For decades, studies have shown that family income relates to how students engage in school. We know, for example, that students from families with fewer resources are less likely to feel academically and socially part of campus life. Fewer economic resources often mean a lower likelihood of participating in extracurricular activities, visiting professors during office hours, and spending time on campus. In turn, this results in fewer opportunities to build relationships that could pave the way for social networks yielding greater returns to the college degree.[47] This helps explain why there are large income disparities in who persists past their first year of college and completes degrees.[48] It might be why lower-income students are more often described as "academically adrift."[49]

These observed differences are often attributed to social class writ large, a configuration of economic, cultural, and social resources that come together to create advantages and disadvantages.[50] Too often, however, what students go through in order to pay for college is overlooked, as writers favor more simplistic ways of understanding class differences. Money, they say, is not really what matters. But in reality, money does matter—a lot. What happens in college is not simply a function of students lacking social networks, academic skills, or cultural know-how or having more commitments to work or family. It is rooted in the struggles they endure because they cannot pay for what they need and in the lengths they must go to in order to find money.

John and Tashia Morgridge, graduates of Wauwatosa High School and the University of Wisconsin–Madison, know many young people like the ones in our study. They have been committed to social philanthropy for decades, and their giving has included scholarships at public and private colleges and universities around the state. Over Christmas in 2007, they decided to broaden their investment in Wisconsin, establishing the Fund for Wisconsin Scholars with a gift of $175 million. "Wisconsin's public high schools do an outstanding job of preparing students for higher education. We are committed to helping ensure that higher education is accessible and affordable," Tashia Morgridge said in a press release.[51]

Under the guidance of its board of directors and the hard work of Executive Director Mary Gulbrandsen, the Fund for Wisconsin Scholars now runs the largest private scholarship program in the state. It is second in size only to the state-funded Wisconsin Higher Education Grant. The Wisconsin Scholars Grant (which from now on I will refer to as the WSG) is generous, providing university students with a $1,750 grant per semester for up to ten semesters (fall and/or spring semesters), making the total maximum award $17,500 per student. The grant is transferable among all public colleges and universities in Wisconsin, and the amount increases or decreases if a student changes sectors—for example, if a student moves to a two-year public college, the grant declines to $900 per semester, and vice versa.

All students eligible to receive the Wisconsin Scholars Grant, and therefore all students in this study, met the following criteria:

- Resident of the state of Wisconsin
- Graduated from a Wisconsin public high school no more than three years prior
- Enrolled full time at a Wisconsin public college or university
- Filed a Free Application for Federal Student Aid (FAFSA)
- Pell Grant recipient
- Net price (cost of attendance minus all grants) of at least one dollar

The fund's first group of students, selected from among the three thousand in this study, was first notified that they would receive the grant on October 22, 2008—the second month of their first semester of college. They did not apply for the grant; it was a brand new program, and instead, financial aid officers simply examined their records to identify and nominate eligible students. The names of all eligible students from around the state were submitted to the state's financial aid agency, where a drawing was held to select twelve hundred winners at random.

Those chosen for the grant were then informed of their good fortune. Funds were distributed to their financial aid officers by the end of the term. For most students, the award appeared in their aid package in early December 2008. Subsequent payments arrived by the start of each new semester. Thus, in their first year of college, students received two grant payments (a total of $3,500 or $1,800, depending on the type of college they attended) if they were eligible in both terms.

In order to continue receiving the grant, students had to be enrolled at a Wisconsin public two-year or four-year college or university where they also had to register for a full-time course load. They needed to remain eligible for the Pell Grant, which meant they had to refile their FAFSA and qualify for the Pell based on their family's financial situation, and they had to make "satisfactory academic progress," a specific federal student aid standard discussed in chapter 2.

Wisconsin Scholars Longitudinal Study

The generosity of the Fund for Wisconsin Scholars and the program's use of a drawing to select among eligible students at random created an opportunity to closely examine how philanthropy changes lives. I was consulted about the program during the early stages of the fund's planning process and, soon thereafter, asked if I could study the first group of students they served.

I felt it was important to conduct research on this program for two reasons. First, most studies of financial aid, the nation's primary investment in making college affordable, have a hard time figuring out how aid affects students' performance in college. Students who receive more aid are very different from those who receive less—they tend to come from poorer families, live in neighborhoods with fewer resources, and grow up attending weaker schools. Any of these reasons, or a host of others, could lead to lower graduation rates. Simply comparing the graduation rates of students with more or less financial aid, then, doesn't tell us much. It might even lead us to believe that getting more financial aid *caused* students to drop out of college—a far-fetched hypothesis indeed.

In order to really untangle the impact that the fund's grants would have on students, we needed to compare the outcomes of two groups of students who were identical in every respect except for luck at a particular moment when the drawing was held. Up until that moment, all students eligible for the grant were essentially the same. But then, at random, some were chosen to get the WSG and others were not. That is the point at which their lives diverged, and from then on my team measured their experiences all the way until graduation. We did this for those who got the grant and those who did not. By comparing the results, we were able to determine the effect of the additional grant aid. If paying for college were a challenge, would this make a difference? We wanted to know.

What does it really mean to say that paying for college is difficult?

Under what circumstances do students find it challenging, and when does it feel manageable? Is it about the absolute amount of money held in hand, or are students' perceptions of affordability shaped by other factors? How do they cope with financial challenges? How do these affect school? Does family help out? Since every program, including financial aid, operates in the context of ordinary lives, it was important to understand these factors.

With the generous support of multiple funders and a team including my coinvestigator Douglas N. Harris, we designed a comprehensive study that collected student surveys, interviews, financial aid records and applications, and college transcripts for the next six years. This was an enormously complicated undertaking, and the costs of the study were almost as large as the costs of the grants students received. Even though the students all agreed to participate, the time they committed to the study was substantial. The comments and notes we have received suggest that students understood that participating was a way to make a difference. They wanted to tell their stories.

The various details of how we collected data are contained in appendix 1. We have examined the issues from multiple vantage points, comparing results obtained from quantitative analyses with those gleaned from interviews and often circling back again and again to triangulate sources and look for conflict and congruence. The analytic work has been ongoing since the study began, and the process was iterative—we collected data, analyzed it, wrote, and then began the process over again.

Nima, Chloe, Tyler, Norbert, Ian, and Sophie represent the range of men and women we interviewed over time. While each is unique in his or her own way, they are actually quite typical. Like many Americans, they all identified as "middle class," despite coming from families living well below the median income. They were searching for a better life, a stable job, and some security. Hard work was something they valued, and by finishing high school, completing the FAFSA, and enrolling in college they demonstrated a commitment to a brighter future. They all planned to finish college degrees.

These six individuals were willing and able to walk us through their college journeys, revealing the good, the bad, and the terribly sad. They have added great depth to my thinking about college prices and financial aid and helped me to reimagine the current system. Listening to them will help readers understand why a well-intentioned approach to financing college isn't working as planned, how it harms instead of helps, and how we can do better moving forward.

2

The Cost and Price of a College Education

When American families say "college costs too much," they are usually referring to the *price* they face when paying for college. Most understand that providing a good education costs money. It requires time and effort from high-quality teachers, not to mention books and materials. The majority of costs for undergraduate education are instructional costs, directly related to teaching and learning. These include many of the things we'd expect in an educational experience, items like faculty and staff salaries, libraries, tutoring, computer labs, and academic buildings that house laboratories and classrooms. Student support services, which include academic advising, tutoring, and counseling, also fall into this category.

What is really affecting students and families, especially those enrolled in the public sector, are changes in the price of college—not the cost to institutions of providing education. As the last chapter described, states used to discount more of the costs, passing on a smaller fraction to families. While there have always been large variations from state to state and school to school, a generation ago public colleges and universities received on average about 75 percent of their operating budget from state appropriations. Today that number is closer to 50 percent.[1] As that discount was removed, the price facing an individual person purchasing a college education grew.[2] Moreover, the approach to further discounting that price with financial aid has become ever more complicated. This chapter explains how all of this discounting occurs in public colleges and universities, via the financial aid system.

Cost of Attendance

Every college and university has a sticker price, derived from what it assesses it needs to charge students in order to cover its costs. The official term for it is unfortunate—the "cost of attendance"— since it is really a price. Federal law dictates the components of that cost of attendance, and the items that are included and excluded are critical in determining what students pay.[3] Most importantly, with few exceptions, the total amount of financial aid a person receives cannot exceed the cost of attendance for the school they attend. If aid is to truly make college affordable, the accuracy of that number is extremely important.

The cost of attendance includes tuition and fees, books and supplies, transportation, and other living costs. But it largely excludes a hugely important factor, something economists call the opportunity cost. When students spend time in class, studying and going to and from school, they miss opportunities to do other things. Most obviously, when students choose to go to school instead of working full time, they are passing up short-term wages in the hopes that their investment in college will bring much larger lifetime gains. They would have used those wages to cover living costs (which is why living costs are part of cost of attendance), but also for other basic expenses including those incurred by their families. These are not included in the federal formula.

As table 2 shows, between 1996 and 2012, the average annual cost of attendance for Pell recipients attending community college rose from about $8,500 to nearly $13,000, a 52 percent increase. Similar trends occurred for students attending public universities, where the annual price increased from almost $14,000 in 1996 to nearly $20,000 in 2012.[4]

Surprisingly, tuition and fees are not the biggest price drivers. Most of these increases since 1996 came from the other parts of the cost of attendance: living costs, transportation, books and supplies,

Table 2. Trends in cost of attendance facing Pell recipients in the public sector, by college type: 1996–2012

	1996 ($)	2000 ($)	2004 ($)	2008 ($)	2012 ($)
Community colleges:					
Official cost of attendance	8,503	10,328	11,176	11,907	12,975
Tuition and fees	1,725	1,777	2,082	2,193	2,438
Nontuition costs	8,092	8,550	9,093	9,714	10,538
Public 4-year colleges and universities:					
Official cost of attendance	13,740	14,027	16,495	18,014	19,780
Tuition and fees	4,501	4,407	5,624	6,231	7,045
Nontuition costs	9,697	9,620	10,872	11,783	12,735

Source. National Center for Education Statistics, *National Postsecondary Student Aid Study NPSAS*, 1996, 2000, 2004, 2008, 2012.

Note. The sample is students who began college full time at a public two-year or four-year institution and received a Pell for their first term. Figures are adjusted for inflation and expressed in constant 2012 dollars.

and personal expenses. Between 50 and 80 percent of total sticker prices, and most of the change over time, occurred in those other components.

The debates about the cost of college often dismiss the importance of addressing living costs, suggesting they aren't really educational expenses. But students have to pay for books, food, rent, and gas if they are to have any chance of succeeding in school. Ireland and the United Kingdom recognize and address these needs with "maintenance" grants, and historically the United States has too.[5] Monthly "subsistence" payments for living costs were made to veterans in the original GI Bill, and in the 1940s when veterans reported that the subsistence payments were inadequate, the government responded by increasing them.[6]

Not only are living costs important, trends in these costs are independent of tuition trends and of family and student income trends. When tuition is frozen, these living costs are not—and just as they do for many Americans not attending college, they can outstrip what families can afford. This is one reason why efforts to freeze tuition or reduce tuition to zero often don't succeed in making college affordable. Students can't focus on their studies when they've given up work hours for classes and can't afford to pay their living costs.

Big Spenders or Bad Prices?

Students and parents often say that the price of college is much higher than they expected. Financial aid officers, in contrast, often say that students don't know how to live within their means or that they lack financial literacy.[7] They, along with many politicians, even accuse students of "overborrowing" by taking loans to cover costs they do not face.[8] Who's right?

There is evidence that for many reasons the cost of attendance understates the true cost of attending college. Since the cost of attendance caps the amount a student can borrow, the contention of overborrowing rests on the hypothesis that actual costs are *less* than the stated costs. But, again, consider living costs. The federal government requires colleges to report estimated costs of living on and off campus. While the assumption is often that college students live on campus, in reality 37 percent of undergraduates live at home, and 50 percent live off campus alone or with someone other than family.[9] When completing the FAFSA, students have to indicate where they plan to live during college, and their resulting financial aid package reflects that information. Schools typically provide bigger living cost allowances for students living on campus compared to off campus and allow much more for students living off campus apart from family compared to living with family. But many students don't understand this. Without this information, their decisions about where to live are insufficiently informed—they might prefer to live on campus or live with friends but instead assume that they cannot afford it.[10]

For students living on campus, costs are based on what the university charges for their residence halls. The costs reported by the university could be too low for a number of reasons. For example, many students skip breakfast or lunch because they are in class or at work. But meal plans may only cover food at scheduled times. If students eat at other times, they pay out of pocket. Further, colleges often don't account for, or underestimate, costs for food and housing during winter and spring breaks when school is closed. Our research has substantiated all of these problems.[11]

For off-campus students, estimating costs is more difficult, since university administrations usually don't thoroughly research all the actual costs required to live within a reasonable distance of campus. Still, every institution must provide an estimated cost.

The government gives colleges and universities a great deal of latitude in how they calculate "living cost allowances." They can ask students what it costs to live near campus, survey landlords, look at ads in the newspaper—many types of research are acceptable, and no one checks that the information is valid. While many colleges and universities understand their responsibility to provide students with accurate information, university administrations and admissions and financial aid offices face incentives to look affordable. Raising their cost-of-attendance sticker price may cause a reduction in applications and a slide in national or regional college rankings. In the worst-case scenario, a big increase could also trigger a federal investigation.

Every institution must decide on and report a living cost allowance for students living off campus apart from their family. But they are not required to provide an allowance for students living with family—this includes one in two undergraduates nationwide. Instead, colleges and universities are allowed to assume that students without children of their own will have lower living expenses if they share a residence with their families, and they may use this assumption when creating their financial aid package.[12]

In a recent study that Robert Kelchen of Seton Hall University, Braden Hosch of Stony Brook University, and I conducted, we examined the estimated living costs, trying to understand the implications of this leeway.[13] We looked at variations and inconsistencies in living allowances across colleges and universities in the same region for students living off campus but not at home. We computed a standard measure of living costs that accounted for location-specific differences. Our assumption was that students would live just above the poverty line, and we included estimated costs for students living alone as well as for those living with roommates. Then we compared our measure to the estimates given by each college and university in the nation.

What we found surprised us: at least one-fifth of all institutions provide living allowances at least 20 percent below what we estimated was necessary for a very modest standard of living. Further, colleges located in the same area reported widely varying living costs. For example, colleges in Washington, DC, claimed living costs ranging from $9,387 to $20,342, while in Milwaukee figures ranged from $5,180 to $21,276.

Moreover, the assumption that living at home is free just does not hold true. Students who live with family often incur significant costs. Our studies showed that even when parents pay the family's rent or mortgage, students often pay for significant amounts of food directly out of pocket—and families are sometimes in no position to put any money in those pockets. In fact, sometimes the flow of money is expected to go the other way entirely. In his dissertation research, Peter Kinsley of the University of Wisconsin–Madison found that 13 percent of students in our sample had to regularly provide money to their families while attending college, though among students living at home, that number was 20 percent. In a more recent survey of low- and moderate-income undergraduates attending ten public and private universities in Wisconsin, researchers at the Wisconsin HOPE Lab learned that 55 percent of students were making financial contributions to family, with 17 percent providing at least $200 per year.[14]

The true cost of attendance is understated in several other ways. The most obvious reason for such underestimation is that stated tuition applies only to the upcoming year—and it is likely to change. Annual tuition increases are common across higher education, and in the public sector they are especially unpredictable. Oftentimes, a college or university has to work with an oversight board and the state to determine tuition. At best, the student deciding on a college knows what tuition will be for her first year—beyond that, she has to gamble on her best estimate.

This is a big problem, especially given that the time it takes to earn a degree is increasing. Just 19 percent of full-time students at public universities complete a bachelor's degree in four years and just 5 percent of full-time students at community colleges finish an associate degree in two years. Even a "one-year" certificate takes 84 percent of students more than a year to finish.[15] More students are moving among colleges and universities, searching for a better fit or a better price, often losing college credits in the process.[16] A longer time to degree means more debt, and that debt can rise exponentially as students reach the lifetime limits on grants. This is ironic, since while there are many factors prolonging time to degree, the challenge of paying for college shouldn't be one of them.[17]

Fees are also unpredictable. In many states, student fees are less regulated than tuition and can be used to fund an array of campus programming. Sometimes student fees are even substituted for state appropriations when instructional resources fall short. Robert Kelchen found that, between 1999 and 2012, fees increased faster than tuition, growing by 104 percent at community colleges and 95 percent at public universities.[18] Therefore, like tuition, the prices students are quoted for fees are applicable only to their first year, since fees will likely rise.

In other words, if you go to college and discover that it ends up costing a lot more than you thought, you are not alone.

Inaccurate college prices hurt students. Since each institution's declared cost of attendance determines the top cap for aid eligibility, it affects the distribution of federal, state, and even private aid. If the true price of attendance is higher than the stated cost of attendance, families must make up the difference. Of course, federal and state aid is not designed to help with those costs—since federal and state authorities often don't recognize that those costs exist. In fact, hard-working students who receive outside scholarships may have their federal aid reduced to ensure that their total aid package does not exceed the total cost of attendance. When a college's cost of attendance is too low, these students lose financial aid they might have otherwise received, and badly need, to cover their actual costs of attendance.

Who Needs What?

If the cost-of-attendance sticker price reflects the amount that families and students are asked to pay (or to put together between what they pay out-of-pocket, plus loans, grants, and the like), the next amount that financial aid offices need to calculate is: what can they afford to pay? Students with particularly extensive financial need (or the sorts of talents recognized by scholarship providers) may receive grants and scholarships. The cost left to pay once grants and scholarships are subtracted from the cost of attendance is officially known as the net price. This process, then, begins by assessing "need."

Like virtually any system used to means test individuals to determine eligibility for a government program, the federal needs-analysis process is complicated. Indeed, the process is so complicated it is often unpopular among those who have to administer it and those who are subject to it. It relies on the "federal methodology" and follows a formula that uses data from the FAFSA to target aid to the neediest students. Generally speaking, the formula works such that the more income and assets a family has, the higher the expected family contribution—the amount the analysis finds that they can pay for college.[19]

In practice, determining an expected family contribution involves many imperfect calculations and what amounts to judgment calls. Perhaps most importantly, the analysis does better at sorting between wealthy people and the middle class than it does at delineating between the lower-middle class and the working class. In other words, it was never intended to be, nor is it good at, choosing among people with few resources to decide who is "neediest." That is one reason many students object to it.[20] And of course, once the federal government determines what a family can pay (the expected family contribution), it must be paid—grants are rarely available to cover it. If a student's family cannot or will not pay the entire expected family contribution, the student must come up with the money, usually by taking out loans. This typically isn't enough, since the maximum a student can borrow is $5,500 for the first year of college. In order to pay their expected family contribution families often turn to Parent PLUS Loans, which require a credit check, come with higher market-based interest rates that can fluctuate from year to year, and offer no income-based repayment or pay-as-you-earn options.

For students listed as dependent for financial aid purposes, paren-

Three Key Financial Aid Terms

Cost of attendance (COA): The "sticker price" listed by the college or university for one year of education, including tuition and fees, books and supplies, transportation, and living costs.

Expected family contribution (EFC): The federal government's measure of a family's financial ability to pay for college, determined using information from the Free Application for Federal Student Aid (FAFSA), including income, assets, family size, and the number of children in college. The EFC is used to determine eligibility for the Pell Grant along with other financial aid. The difference between the COA and EFC is called demonstrated need.

Net price: The difference between the COA and all grants and scholarships equals the bottom line cost of college for the student and/or his or her family. It represents the price that must be paid using income, savings, and loans.

tal financial resources determine the expected family contribution. But it is no surprise that many young people cannot access those resources. Parents are not legally required to pay for college, not all contribute as much money as colleges and Uncle Sam say they should, and some contribute no money at all. Young people facing these situations are in a bind. Under federal rules, it is very difficult for a person under age twenty-four to gain independent status so that parental resources do not affect their aid eligibility. They need to get married, have a child, serve in the military, become a ward of the state, or, in rare cases, petition for independence. None of these are necessarily desirable options, and students are frustrated. One young man we interviewed explained:

> I think it's a crock when you're independent, working, and you don't live with your parents or depend on them, but you're still a dependent.[21] That really makes me mad—how they determine how much money you get by how much your parents work, you know what I mean? Like your parents could [make] $100,000 between the two of them, and you don't have a job at all . . . and you have to take on all these loans by yourself. I don't think it's the parents' responsibility to be involved or have to get involved

with how much you're supposed to get from the state or, you know, if you have to pay it back or if you don't have to pay it back. I really don't think that's fair because that makes it sound like the parents have to pay for the college—that doesn't make any sense to me. . . . You're telling me, like, if I just went and got married to someone, then I would be able to get all my schooling paid for, or if I was able to knock up this girl and, you know, be with her then I could get all my schooling paid for? I don't think that really is a good way to put that. You know what I mean? I wish I had a kid to bring to school so I got my schooling paid for.

The survey data we collected suggest that a sizable fraction of students who are expected to contribute financially to college costs do not in fact receive any financial help from their parents. We closely examined the issue by asking the question two different ways in the same survey. Nine percent of students who had an expected family contribution (greater than zero) indicated that they did not receive any financial support from their parents, and 23 percent reported that their parents provided no money for their college education (tuition specifically).

The expected family contribution formula has another major flaw. Many students actually have a negative expected family contribution. Some students from very low-income families were already making essential financial contributions to their family's well-being before going to college. They helped pay the rent, buy food, and cover medical expenses. Those contributions are reduced as students' incomes go down when they decrease their work hours in order to attend college. If we truly accounted for the family financial contributions of these students, they would actually need to be paid to attend college to cover opportunity costs and help keep their families afloat. Instead, the federal rules truncate their negative expected family contribution number to zero, limiting the amount of aid they can receive. This is yet another reason why students feel their aid is insufficient—because aid policies do not accurately reflect their real costs or ability to pay. And it is why aid officers like those we interviewed who adhere to these policies often don't know or understand students' true costs and ability to pay and, as a result, say things like "no matter how much we give them, they want more."

You Hafta FAFSA

In order to determine their expected family contribution and see if they qualify for grants, loans, and work-study programs, students must complete the FAFSA. Before attending college, the messages they receive about this process are—today—fairly clear and consistent. Apply for financial aid. Fill out the FAFSA. It's quick, it's straightforward, and it works. Yet some students do not do it: the most recent data available indicates that 11 percent of undergraduates living below the poverty line, and 15 percent of those living between 100 and 150 percent of the poverty line, had not filed a FAFSA and were therefore not receiving financial aid.[22] Many more do not file a FAFSA and never attend college. In 2014, the White House and the U.S. Department of Education began the Reach Higher initiative, encouraging students to further their educations beyond high school, and First Lady Michelle Obama spoke to students across the country, urging them to complete the FAFSA. These outreach efforts cheerily explain that the process is "free, quick (on average, taking about 20 minutes!), and easy."[23] Mrs. Obama provides a compelling face for this movement, and every student profiled in this book followed her suggestion.

But the FAFSA is a small American bureaucratic tragedy all its own. The stakes are high. Overstatement of assets or income can mean a student will not get aid they're entitled to—while understatement of assets or income could be a form of fraud. There are consequences for incorrectly completing the form. Many FAFSA forms go through a verification process, and if information is inaccurate, disbursement of funds may be substantially delayed—or not occur at all.

To make matters worse, the FAFSA is notoriously onerous and complex to fill out.[24] As a student tweeted: "Why is the financial aid process harder than college itself?"[25] In recent years, the Internal Revenue Service (IRS) and the Department of Education have worked together to smooth the process by allowing students to transfer their IRS data into the FAFSA seamlessly and in real time using the IRS Data Retrieval Tool. But this works best for students who are paying for college on their own. First-time students who depend on their families for support, like nearly all of those in this book, spend a long time gathering information before they can sit down to complete the form. In 2015, the Department of Education estimated that once a student logged into the online application, it took about thirty minutes to complete.[26] But gathering the necessary information can take much longer—it includes the student's Social Security number, the parents' Social Security numbers, federal tax returns, records of untaxed income, plus information on cash, savings and checking account balances, investments, and real estate (except the home in which the student lives) for both the student and their parents.[27]

With all the needed information on hand, does the average FAFSA experience take less than the twenty minutes Mrs. Obama promised? To find out, researchers at the Wisconsin HOPE Lab conducted a survey in fall 2014. Working with a sample of almost 1,110 students who were very similar to those in this study, my team found that over 90 percent said that it took them longer than thirty minutes to complete the FAFSA. Forty-four percent took between thirty minutes and an hour, 29 percent took one to two hours, and almost 20 percent required more than two hours. About one in ten Pell-eligible students found that it took them more than three hours to complete the form, one reason being that it was sometimes very difficult to obtain their parents' information.[28] Some parents don't want to share detailed information about their income and assets with their child (or with their child's would-be college). What happens when a student wants to reduce the price of college attendance by applying for financial aid but can't get the necessary tax information from their parents? One student explained that he needed to "nag and nag" his folks to share their information and was unable to file until they did. Another student described having difficulty getting her parents to provide their data because they didn't understand why it was necessary since they were not helping him pay for college: "I'm a poor student—I work at Subway. I don't make that much money. But he [the financial aid administrator] said if your parents claim you, they have—it's like—an obligation that the state says my parents have to pay for my schooling. And I was like, well, my parents aren't following that obligation."

Most students in this study had help completing their first financial aid application. Just 18 percent of students reported completing the FAFSA alone, although one in three African American students did so. Three in four non-Hispanic white students got help from their parents, compared to two in five African American students, who were twice as likely as white students to receive help from a sibling. One in three students said that the person who helped them complete the FAFSA had not attended college.

The FAFSA is not a one-time experience. The application must be renewed each year, regardless of the student's circumstances. Even those students who remain at the same college year after year, living in the same economic conditions with parents whose jobs do not change must refile. Unfortunately, many students are unaware of this. Nationally, 15–20 percent of first-year Pell Grant recipients in good academic standing do not refile their FAFSA. Refiling rates are particularly low among community college students.[29] Indeed, 15 percent of our students did not refile their FAFSA yet did enroll for a second year of college. Attempting to continue in college without refiling the FAFSA can lead to an unexpected and often substantial increase in a student's cost of attendance, which can then result in dropping out.

Putting the Aid Together

After assessing a student's expected family contribution using data from the FAFSA and comparing this to the institution's cost of attendance, the financial aid office can begin to construct a financial aid package. For many students, the Pell Grant is the centerpiece of the aid package. Students below a certain expected family contribution threshold ($4,041 in the 2008–9 academic year, the year this study began) qualify for a Pell. Students with a zero expected family contribution receive the maximum Pell, which in 2008–9 was $4,731.[30] The maximum increased to $5,550 for 2010–11, and it is now $5,775.

The Pell Grant hardly ever covers the entire difference between the cost of attendance and the expected family contribution. If that were the case, the one trillion dollar student loan industry would be substantially smaller. In practice, when a Pell is awarded but does not cover all of a student's need, financial aid officers turn to other federal grants and then to state grants to fill the gap. When that is not enough, and it often is not, they add loans and work-study funds to the package. They also look for private sources of aid, institutional scholarships, foundation scholarships, and whatever else is available.

In Wisconsin, there is a state need-based grant available to some students. The Wisconsin Higher Education Grant, which receives $100 million per year in taxpayer support, was established by statute in 1965, the same year the landmark Higher Education Act was signed by President Lyndon Johnson.[31] Students can receive the grant for up to ten semesters, and in order to get it, they must enroll at least half time. The Wisconsin Higher Education Grant is means tested and scaled according to the expected family contribution—students in the University of Wisconsin System (UW System), Wisconsin Technical College System, private not-for-profit colleges, and tribal colleges are eligible. On average, a student receives $1,500–$2,500 per year. Like the Pell, the Wisconsin Higher Education Grant's value has been declining. Since 1997, its effective purchasing power (e.g., the average grant amount divided by the cost of attendance) diminished from roughly 10 percent to between 6.19 percent (in the technical college sector) and 7.65 percent (in the private college sector) while it remains 9.44 percent in the UW System. With far fewer students enrolled in the state's two tribal colleges and with lower costs of attendance, the Wisconsin Higher Education Grant has generally covered 11–12 percent of the cost of attendance there during that time.[32]

Many students who are eligible for the Wisconsin Higher Education Grant don't receive it. While statutorily it is an entitlement, as it gets a "sum-sufficient allocation" of funding, this has routinely been suspended in favor of a set limit on funding. Since the total number of eligible students increased faster than the funding limit, there are now more eligible students than funds to support them. To handle this, grants are awarded on a first-come first-served basis using the FAFSA filing date. Each year, a suspension date occurs when funding has been exhausted. After this date, applicants go on a waitlist. The suspension date has moved earlier each year. In 2008–9, the year this study began, more than sixty-two hundred students in UW System and almost twenty-one thousand students in the Wisconsin Technical College System did not receive a Wisconsin Higher Education Grant even though they were eligible. Providing these students with grants would have cost the state another $44 million.[33]

These circumstances mean that most students from economically challenged families face a gap between the aid they are given and the cost of attendance. A fortunate few, however, get enough scholarships to ensure that at least the sticker price is covered. Many of these students are academically talented and have competed for these awards. But unlike their wealthier peers, they cannot keep all that they win. That is because for financial aid recipients, the cost of attendance represents the maximum support a student can receive from any source. If private aid is available, then state or federally supported aid (excluding the Pell) must be removed such that the cost of attendance is not exceeded. This is called displacement, and it can lead to a substantial reduction in the value of a private scholarship, diminishing the positive impact that the donor intended. Here is an example: a student receives a $2,500 private scholarship and the university uses 50 percent of the scholarship to replace institutional grants and 50 percent to replace loans in the financial aid package. The student's net price decreases by $1,250 because part of the private scholarship replaces loans. But the other $1,250 of the scholarship simply displaces the $1,250 in institutional grants. As a result, the overall decrease to the student's net price is only half as much as as much as it could have been. And the student, who thought they would gain $2,500 from the scholarship, often does not know what happened.[34]

This does not happen to students who do not file for financial aid. They may accept all of the outside scholarships they receive, even if they have no financial need and their parents have already covered their cost of attendance. But if students receiving financial aid get more grants than their "demonstrated financial need" allows, then they must ask their school's financial aid administrator for help. The financial aid administrator has authority to adjust the cost of attendance for a specific student, officially known as adjusting their budget. This process, known as professional judgment, is done on a case-by-case basis, is intended only for special circumstances, and requires adequate documentation. For example, if a student faces higher childcare costs or a costly medical situation, the aid administrator might raise the budget to allow a student to take a larger loan. However, while federal law allows this procedure, it is not easy for an aid administrator to execute, and some won't do it because they don't want to increase students' eligibility for loans. Many rules and regulations govern their work, and they often fear that exercising professional judgment too frequently or without sufficient documentation will cause trouble the next time a review of their aid program takes place—if a review goes badly, the school can lose their ability to participate in the federal student aid program. Some aid administrators are also fearful of recourse from the Office of Civil Rights, where students may file a complaint if they did not get the aid they asked for. A request for professional judgment is therefore no simple matter, and it places a burden on both the student and the aid administrator.[35]

These constraints within the financial aid system can make it difficult for philanthropists like the Fund for Wisconsin Scholars to put additional money in the hands of students who need it. As described in the last chapter, the fund selected its recipients in the fall and then sent the money to the schools to distribute. In many cases, students had already had to take out loans in order to pay their bills. When the new grant arrived, particularly at universities where the grant amounted to $3,500, there was not always room for it in the aid package. As a result, sometimes a student offered $3,500 in grant aid effectively received no additional money in hand. Instead, their loans (subsidized first and then unsubsidized) were reduced.[36] While this meant they had less to repay after college, students often didn't understand how their new grant had been used.

If you are confused, you are in good company. We found that students themselves varied in the extent to which they knew and understood what was in their financial aid packages. Every student in the study received a Pell Grant in the first semester of college, but when asked in a survey to report what was in their aid package, one in seven did not mention their Pell. They described feeling uncertain about why they received the amount they did, why they could not get more, and what they needed to do in order to ensure they would keep getting aid. By and large, the students hoped to follow the appropriate rules—but they did not always know what they were.

Following the Rules

There are many rules affecting students' ability to get and keep financial aid. There are forms that must be filled out and signed, filed on time, and verified. Failure to keep up with these requirements can cause delays or even the loss of support. The amount of aid a student gets varies depending on where they attend college, so if they transfer they must reapply. This affects many students each year since today at least one in three students transfer schools at least once.[37] Students have to apply for loans, decide how much of the loan offered to accept, and again, sign forms. They must also meet academic standards, known as satisfactory academic progress, which include both a grade point average requirement and a specified pace of progress (e.g., completing a specified fraction of attempted credits in order to remain on track to earn a degree). Additional rules govern how long a student can receive aid. How much aid they can get varies from semester to semester according to the number of credits they take.

Finally, changes in financial status can invalidate students' needs analysis and jeopardize their aid. To keep the needs analysis accurate, then, students who are working while in school are allowed to earn a certain amount and no more. Critically, they must be careful that their income does not go above that specified level—or they may become ineligible for Pell Grants. But that income ceiling is rarely communicated to the student, and it is nearly impossible to predict, since it depends on an individual's circumstances and often those of their parents.

Table 3. Knowledge of and interaction with financial aid rules

Knowledge of Financial Aid	Percentage
Knew difference between grant and loan	93
Knew that financial aid package might change from year to year	88
Knew that financial aid package might change if student takes time off from school	82
Knew that government loan is a kind of financial aid	81
Knew that financial aid package might change if student transfers schools	81
Knew that student earning more than a certain amount of money will reduce financial aid package	74
Knew difference between subsidized and unsubsidized loan	68
Knew that money a student earns from working during college is used in financial aid calculation	58

Source. WSLS data.

Note. Sample is WSLS students who responded to the first-year survey questions on financial aid rules, *n*= 2,100.

So how many Pell recipients actually understand these rules? In our survey, we were pleasantly surprised to learn that more than nine in ten students could accurately identify the primary differences between grants and loans (see table 3). Four in five knew that transferring colleges and taking time off from college could affect the amount of aid they receive. About seven in ten understood the difference between subsidized and unsubsidized loans and the effects of students' earnings on the amount of financial aid received (e.g., that earning more money could reduce the amount of aid awarded). Still, what students knew about the rules and their impact was neither comprehensive nor universal.

In the fall of 2014, the Wisconsin HOPE Lab examined awareness of the satisfactory academic progress requirements. We surveyed a group of almost eleven hundred students, all of whom had an expected family contribution of less than or equal to $10,314, which is up to 200 percent of the threshold for Pell Grant eligibility, and all of whom would be receiving federal financial aid when they began college for the first time in September. We asked them: "True or False? To continue receiving financial aid each year, students have to maintain a minimum GPA."[38]

Just over one in four students (26%) answered the question incorrectly, indicating "false." They were unaware they had to meet this academic requirement in order to continue receiving federal financial aid (including keeping their loans). The percentages of students who were unaware of satisfactory academic progress requirements was similar across several key demographics, including first-generation college students whose parents do not have bachelor's degrees, continuing generation students with at least one parent with a bachelor's degree, and students from both urban and rural communities across Wisconsin. This may help explain why large numbers of students (including, according to researchers, some 40% at community colleges) lose their Pell grant each year because they do not meet the satisfactory academic progress standards.[39]

The challenges involved with following the rules also affected the implementation of the Fund for Wisconsin Scholars. In order to reinstate a grant after an absence from college, students had to notify their financial aid office, the program's executive director, and submit a written request.[40] Students did not receive regular reminders about the grant's renewal criteria, but the program administrator did send e-mailed communications containing "different messages about eligibility, transferring, good luck with classes, and other general information."[41] But two surveys we administered, one a few months after the program began and the second a year later, showed that barely half of students offered the grant even knew that it was part of their financial aid package. Moreover, 85 percent of students were confused about the grant's satisfactory academic progress requirements regarding grades (same as the Pell—a C average) and enrollment intensity (twelve credits in order to get the grant). Students who were also receiving federal Academic Competitiveness Grants, which required a B average, seem to have mistakenly thought that the WSG also demanded a B average.[42] For students, the many different components of financial aid can all begin to blur together.

Who Owns Aid? Where Does It Come From?

Students report that financial aid helps—but it seldom fully addresses the true costs of college. Many students told us they felt their aid was helpful and that they were grateful, but at the same time they were quick to point out how little it covered. As one put it, "Financial aid needs to step up its game." In a sense, sometimes a grant acts as an increasingly small coupon that entices a student to try college, but at the end of the day leaves them with a bill they can't afford.

This surprises students. For example, one Pell recipient told us that because of her financial aid, "I thought I was set—just to be free and not worry about paying for it, to keep going to school without the cost." But that was her sense only during her first term. She quickly discovered that the amount of aid she received was not enough to provide for meals, and she faced a new challenge—because she was enrolled in college, she thought she was no longer eligible for the federal food assistance program.[43]

When aid does mitigate students' experiences of economic insecurity, it seems to do so partly by reducing feelings of stress. One student told us that it "cleared my worries" and calmed him down. Another described what it felt like to look at her aid package for the first time: "I remember just waiting. Like waiting, waiting, waiting. When is it coming in the mail? And as soon as I got it I looked at the numbers . . . then it added up and I got a total and I had a huge amount of money that was tuition for the whole, um, year."

A few students claim that financial insecurity motivates them. When asked, "How would college be different if you had more money?" a male undergraduate responded: "I'd probably do worse in college, I think . . . if I had a lot of money to spend I wouldn't care about what I was doing." A woman explained to us that she is getting better grades than her sister did in college because school "means more to me because I am paying for it. . . . Paying for college yourself makes you want to go to class, makes you want to do things. I admit if my parents paid for it, I probably wouldn't be as serious about it because I'm not wasting my money, I'm wasting theirs. So I think it makes a lot of difference when you're paying for it."

Another striking gap in what students know about the financial aid they receive is that many of them have no idea where it all comes from—one in seven Pell recipients does not even know they have a Pell! This likely has consequences, since the source of money is an important factor in determining its meaning and how it can be spent. For comparison, think of gifts and remittances from family members. Even though these monies may arrive with no explicit strings attached, recipients often feel constrained in how they may spend them. Thus a birthday check is not supposed to be cashed for groceries. Christmas money is not supposed to be used to pay a gambling debt.[44] In experiments, college students have been shown to discount money they "won" at a higher rate than money they were "owed," suggesting that they valued won money less than "their own" money. People have also been found to be more willing to take risks with money from a windfall gain, a phenomenon known as the "house money effect."[45]

Partly because the sources of financial aid are far from clear, students who receive it often don't fully understand how they are meant to use it.

Doctoral candidate Kaja Rebane of the University of Wisconsin–Madison and I find that students frequently treat financial aid money differently than money obtained from other sources like work and gifts. Since aid appears to move through a variety of actors (e.g., from federal student aid offices in Washington to college coffers, to financial aid officers to students through a complicated packaging and awarding process), students are not exactly sure what financial aid *is*, what kind of money it represents, or to whom it belongs. Students are confused about their available monetary resources and unsure who "owns" the money they receive from financial aid. One man put it this way: "A lot of times I wonder, like, where financial aid comes from. Like who provides it? Where does it go? They say I'm paid for school but I didn't see the money flow . . . and so I don't know where it's coming from or what I'm paying. . . . It's kind of confusing but I'm just going along with it right now."

This is one reason why many Pell recipients refer to grants as "free." Consider this exchange with a woman in her third year of college:

INTERVIEWER: Are there particular components of your package that you think are really much more important?

RESPONDENT: Oh, the grants! The grants [are much more important] because you don't have to pay a cent, so it's like free money. That's huge.

Of course, for taxpayers grants are not free. But this is rarely clarified for the student. When they know the source of grants, as in the case of the Fund for Wisconsin Scholars, students convey gratitude. A recipient expressed her appreciation this way: "I'm just very thankful for financial aid. It helps a lot, a lot, a lot. I don't know who came up with this brilliant idea to just give out money like this but I very much appreciate it. Oh, really. Oh, really."

Another student who received the Fund for Wisconsin Scholars Grant explained that getting it led him to focus even further on his goal: graduation.

INTERVIEWER: Do you have any anxiety around [your financial aid package for next year]?
RESPONDENT: Nope, I'm pretty sure I saved up enough already, and then it tends to work out. I mean that Fund for Wisconsin Scholars [grant] wasn't . . . [pause] . . . I didn't know what the heck that was, and all of a sudden it dropped on my lap, so that helped a lot. . . . I won't take it for granted, that's for sure . . . if I get that much money and I get bad grades, I'm going to feel shitty as hell. . . . I guess in return, I'll graduate. That's the best thing I can do, I guess . . . it's not a loan where you can pay back but at the same time I like and appreciate it. So the only way I can pay it back is to graduate with my bachelor's in criminal justice. That's my goal.

Another student who knew the source of his Pell Grant also noted that he felt the need to act responsibly, saying, "I don't think it's fair to ask the government for money and then spend the money you do have foolishly. That doesn't make sense to me."

All this confusion has other consequences, too. Drawing from a tool chest of potential grants, loans, and work-study programs, financial aid administrators build each student's financial aid package. This process does not always involve the student. While students over the age of eighteen are technically required to sign off on their packages, this occurs via online systems that allow students to easily assent without fully examining or understanding their aid packages. Also, if a student has consented to give their parents access to the information, mom or dad may agree to a package—or part of a package, such as a loan—without the student's knowledge or active consent.

When financial aid administrators exert more control over the aid-packaging process, students report feeling less control over their aid. Students who feel powerless appear to make poorer decisions. When they feel informed, they seem to make more effective choices. For example, an African American woman attending a moderately selective university said that her room and board cost about $4,000 for a term and that she had intentionally asked for a smaller room to reduce her housing costs. In contrast, an East Asian university student said that because she never actually saw her financial aid money, she didn't know how much she had.

Some students contend that because they are not charged with handling their financial aid, they don't learn how to budget and thus are less conscious of where and how their money is spent. That said, we found little to no evidence that students' spending was wasteful. We analyzed budget logs and found that very little money was allocated for entertainment, alcohol, or leisure activities. But not all their decisions were strategic. Students did not always have enough information about their overall financial aid picture to make decisions about, for example, possibly attending less expensive colleges or covering their room and board through on-campus work. In other words, though students with incomplete financial aid data often knew enough to make thoughtful choices from day to day (by trying to shop for less expensive groceries, avoid costly purchases, and so forth), they didn't have the information needed to make larger, big-picture decisions as wisely as they might have done otherwise.

When faced with financial stress, many students turn to their financial aid offices. The professionals who work in these offices have the enormous task of translating federal, state, and institutional policy into action by distributing aid dollars. They are governed by thousands of rules and regulations, and interviews reveal that many feel that they serve multiple masters with vastly differing goals— the federal government, their college president, the boss overseeing their unit, and, of course, students and their families.

But financial aid offices don't have enough staff to provide the in-person support and guidance that could help students better understand their aid packages. For a program that distributes billions of dollars a year, the budget for actually allocating aid is very small. At a large public university attended by many students in this study, the head administrator reported that she had one administrator for every thousand applicants. "We're at a point when the automation in the system has done what it can do and then the rest has to be done on a one-on-one, personal basis," she explained. "But that's very difficult for them [the students] to understand." According to a 2015 national survey of financial aid administrators, while larger institutions tend to have more staff, schools with more than twenty thousand students have an average of twelve administrators.[46] One reason is that operating budgets for financial aid offices have not changed much over time, even though financial aid budgets and the number of applicants has increased substantially. Just under half of financial aid administrators surveyed report that their offices faced a moderate to severe resource shortage in the last five years. [47]

In their first semester of college, nearly 60 percent of our students sought financial aid advising. Remarkably, given the demands on financial aid personnel, 95 percent of those who asked for help received it. Nearly all of those helped found the assistance useful. Students at two-year colleges were more likely to seek help with financial aid compared to students at universities. While resources for financial aid offices vary, students at two-year colleges who sought help were also just as likely to receive it and find it useful as students at public universities.

African American students were especially likely to seek financial aid advising. Nearly three in four African American students reported requesting help, compared to just over half of all non-Hispanic white students. For those who requested help, the odds of receiving it were the same across all racial groups. Students' racial and ethnic characteristics were not associated with whether they found the assistance they received helpful.

The greater rates of help-seeking behavior observed among two-year college students and African American students corresponds to their greater likelihood of knowing whom to contact in their financial aid offices. For example, 73 percent of university students reported having that knowledge, compared to 85 percent of two-year college students.

Financial aid administrators recognize that aid means a lot to the students who receive it, and they often understand the difficulties the system creates. One long-term senior administrator explained:

> There are times when we have to collect documentation for very sensitive issues, say if there's a question as to whether someone's parent is actually living or dead, and you have to collect death certificates. There are those cases where you have to discuss personal issues and discuss sensitive issues that you never would imagine would be part of the financial aid world. It's like being a health care professional, and [an] accountant, a lawyer, and maybe a spiritual counselor all wrapped into one—then you've got your financial aid administrator. You are touching so many different aspects of one's life.

Given these issues, it's no surprise that we found trust hard to come by between financial aid recipients and financial aid offices. Even when students respected an aid administrator and felt grateful for their help, they never felt sure that their support would continue. This lack of trust bled over to other sources of financial aid, including the Fund for Wisconsin Scholars. In the weeks after that program began, we went out to talk with students who would be receiving the award. We were there as researchers from what we then called the Wisconsin Financial Aid Study, not as emissaries of the fund, and the students clearly understood that. On several occasions we learned that people who had received the award letter announcing the new financial support thought that the grant was a "scam." They did not know "where it came from" or "what it was for." The first notable impact we observed was an uptick in their use of the financial aid office, where they went to find out what was going on.

The Payoff

Given these complexities, does financial aid work? Our study is far from the first attempt to answer this question. Efforts to measure the effects of financial aid tend to focus on academic outcomes, since the stated intent of the federal student aid program is to increase the number of Americans who graduate from college. Studies examining the question reach conflicting conclusions about the efficacy of aid, mainly because of the enormous array of differences across studies in the types of financial aid examined, the conditions associated with that aid, how much aid is given (not just in sheer dollars but also in purchasing power), who it is distributed to, and when it is delivered.

For more than forty years, researchers have studied federal grants and state grants, need-based grants, and scholarships distributed based on academic "merit" (usually but not always measured by standardized test scores). They have looked at programs that tell students about their aid before college begins and those that provide support only after students enroll. They have looked at the impact of aid on those who enroll in college, where they attend, what courses they take and how many credits they complete, and of course, whether they finish degrees.

Overall, the results are pretty mushy. The best studies use statistical controls and other techniques to distinguish the independent contribution of the financial aid from the student characteristics that make them eligible for aid. This is very important, since the characteristics that make students eligible for aid often also make them less likely to finish college. In these studies, like those of economists Eric Bettinger, Ben Castleman, and Bridget Long, grants tend to exhibit positive effects.[48] Students with demonstrated economic need who receive grant support from the time they are deciding to attend college are more likely to enroll. They are more apt to attend a bachelor's degree–granting institution and a more selective university rather than a community college, and, perhaps most importantly, they are more likely to finish their degrees.[49]

The more complicated the grant program, the less effective it seems to be, and the evidence on the effects of loans and work-study programs is much less promising than for grants.[50] Later in this book, I will describe what we learned about the students in this study when we were able to measure the impacts of adding additional grant support to their financial aid packages after they had enrolled in college.

But these studies don't paint a full picture of what aid achieves—or fails to achieve—because they look at it too narrowly. There are many ways that financial aid ought to be able to alter the college experience—since many aspects of the experience are clearly affected by financial constraints. Alleviating those constraints should help students focus on school rather than work, reduce stress, and make it more likely that they will be well rested and well fed when they are trying to learn. But what if financial aid fails to reduce many financial constraints—perhaps because it does not provide money in the ways that students need, or it is too little or too late? Financial aid is usually studied as if it was a simple transfer of money, which it is not. The study of financial aid in isolation, therefore, cannot tell us how money and scarcity shape the college experience. Only research on money as it is actually possessed and used by college students can accomplish that.

3
Who Gets Pell?

The college cafeteria was crowded and chaotic on the cloudy October afternoon I first met Chloe Johnson. Students were chatting, speaking over one another, and tapping away on devices while enjoying snacks and each other. I sat at a table in the corner, waiting for her, tape recorder in hand.

When Chloe arrived, she sat down cautiously, but then ventured a casual, "Hey, what's up?" We walked over to buy lunch, looking over the burgers and fries, salads, and shakes, and she pondered her options. She chose a thick fruit smoothie and fries and looked away while I paid the bill. Walking behind her as we returned to the table, I was struck by her very thin body.

As we talked, Chloe barely looked at me, preferring to gaze into her smoothie. She said that she rarely had time to sit and eat these days. I nodded, since as a busy professor and mom, I thought I understood. But as she went on, the sense that I could relate to Chloe quickly disappeared. Her struggle to find time to eat was part of a story full of much bigger sacrifices, ones totally unlike mine.

Tall and pale with bright blue eyes, Chloe spoke rapidly as she talked about animals. She grew up around them and wanted to become expert at their care. She was excited to be the first in her family to attempt college and eager to get started. Since neither she nor her parents ever figured that she would make it to college, they had no savings.

To pay for college, Chloe sold her beloved horse. She had raised him since he was six months old and rode him every day, but he was valued at $1,000, and she needed the money to pay for school. It broke her heart, she said, but she did not have other options. She received two offers for her horse and picked the lower one; while she needed the money, she also needed to know that her friend was going to a good home.

The federal government estimated that Chloe's family could afford to contribute $2,520 a year to her education, and she received an $1,100 Pell Grant, along with a $777 Wisconsin Higher Education Grant. After using the proceeds from her horse toward the expected family contribution and getting help from her parents for the rest, she still needed to come up with more than $10,000 for her first year of college. Her parents were divorced, her father had moved a thousand miles away, and her mother was in a new relationship. So to reduce her expenses, she decided to live with her high school boyfriend in a town forty-five minutes north of school. She took on two jobs and registered for five classes.

Nine Million Chloes

There are a lot of Chloe Johnsons. Over the last twenty years, the number of undergraduates from lower-income families receiving financial support for college from the federal Pell Grant grew from just under four million to more than nine million. Total Pell expenditures are now about $35 billion a year.[1] This creates the impression that the program is increasingly generous, even though neither the maximum nor the average grant has grown significantly over time, especially when compared with college costs.[2] As described earlier, the purchasing power of the grant has declined, which means that it buys less than it used to.

Critics charge that the costs of the Pell are "out of control," the program is under attack, and its recipients have been explicitly compared to "welfare recipients."

So what's the real story? Are we doing students from low-income families a service by funding part of their college expenses or a disservice by giving them false hopes? Is the Pell program a sound financial investment in the nation's future, or is it a wasteful and ineffective program that allows students access to money—perhaps even enticing them to attend college and incur debt—without ensuring that they graduate from college? Do Pell recipients "deserve" the aid they get? Are they helped by it?

As Pell spending has increased and the number of Pell recipients has grown, these questions have become increasingly contentious. A recent NBC headline read, "$2.2 Million in Grants Awarded to Area College Students Who Quit or Failed."[3] "In what may be a national trend, a North Carolina NBC affiliate is reporting the Feds awarded $2.2 million in Pell Grants last year to college students who eventually dropped out or withdrew from classes. The 500 students, who received an average of $4,400, received the grants but ultimately quit school, and it's unlikely any of that money will be repaid."[4]

In 2011, U.S. Representative Denny Rehberg (R-Montana) chaired the House Appropriations Subcommittee on Labor, Health and Human Services, and Education that was tasked with considering the future of the Pell program. In an interview on Blog Talk Radio, he explained: "You can go to college on Pell Grants—maybe I should not be telling anybody this because it's turning out to be the welfare of the 21st century. You can go to school, collect your Pell Grants, get food stamps, low-income energy assistance, section 8 housing, and all of a sudden we find ourselves subsidizing people that don't have to graduate from college. And there ought to be some kind of commitment and endgame."[5]

Rehberg added one final note: a student could "go to school for nine years on Pell Grants and you don't even have to get a degree."[6] Another critic (a professor at the University of California–Irvine) pointed out, "The 9-year entitlement until graduation is almost double the federal mandate for length of welfare."[7] When U.S. Representative Paul Ryan (R-Wisconsin) released his budget proposal in spring 2013, he stated that "welfare spending" was the largest item in the federal budget and classified Pell Grants as a welfare program.[8]

These comments and actions are reminiscent of those made in the 1980s by U.S. Secretary of Education William Bennett and his colleagues, who seized on an anecdotal report of one financial aid recipient driving a Corvette during spring break in Florida to claim widespread abuses existed in the financial aid system.[9] But politicians with axes to grind are not the only ones talking like this. Some financial aid professionals and college faculty also tell stories of "undeserving" Pell recipients. A team of financial aid scholars proposed revising program eligibility, suggesting that many of today's Pell recipients (particularly the 60% of students who are independent for tax purposes, many of whom are parents of young children) would be better served by other programs.[10] A highly regarded scholar at the Brookings Institution, Isabel Sawhill, proposed making the receipt of Pell conditional on "college readiness," so as to "motivate students to work harder in high school" and ensure that dollars are focused on the students "most able to benefit."[11] Such statements are a form of dog-whistle politics, which employs language that is coded, meaning one thing to the general audience while being pejorative to a targeted subgroup.[12]

Some are far less subtle, however. The *Chronicle of Higher Education* reported the following in 2011:

> When a prospective student called her office 15 times in one day to ask when his federal aid would be disbursed, Laurie A. Wolf, executive dean of student services at Des Moines Area Community College, became suspicious. "He'd say things like, 'I want my money,' or 'when can I get my money?'" she said. "Something didn't seem right." She pulled his student-aid record and discovered that he had received aid from seven other colleges. When she requested transcripts, he vanished. The student, she believes, was a "Pell runner," a scam artist who bounces from college to college, staying just long enough to receive a Pell Grant refund. Runners represent a small fraction of the 9.5 million students who received Pell Grants last year, but their numbers appear to be growing, particularly at community colleges, say financial-aid administrators and Educational Department officials. Their fraud costs taxpayers

untold thousands and drives up colleges' default rates when the students take out loans as well.[13]

So today, the U.S. Department of Education is spending time and money investigating so-called Pell runners, people who purportedly find filing a FAFSA and enrolling in college an expedient way to obtain a few thousand dollars.[14]

Like the infamous so-called welfare queens of yore, the Pell runner is a politically powerful concept that has little basis in reality and diverts attention from the real issues. Is there any evidence that there are thousands of such runners, dozens, a handful, or none at all? At least one college president reported that in an effort to stop the Pell runners, his school decided to double tuition—likely a counterproductive move.[15]

When the U.S. Department of Education's Office of the Inspector General examined student aid fraud, it estimated a total fraud loss of about $187 million between 2009 and 2012 for a program that was responsible for almost $758 billion during that time. In other words, the loss rate was about 0.02 percent.[16] In another report, the Office of Management and Budget reported that for the Pell Grant Program, which spent $31.6 billion in the year examined, $0.7 billion was spent in error, a rate of 2.2 percent. By comparison, the error rate for Unemployment Insurance (a $48 Billion a year program) was 11.6 percent; for the National School Lunch Program ($11.5 Billion a year) it was 15.2 percent; and for Supplemental Security Income ($55.4 Billion a year) it was 9.2 percent.[17]

Yet a "law enforcement bulletin" issued by the Federal Bureau of Investigation in 2014 continued to fuel anecdotal reports. A community college public safety officer and an assistant professor claimed their research "showed that an absence of capable guardianship makes the program a target for fraud perpetrated by motivated offenders."[18] The evidence? "The authors interviewed financial aid administrators at several Midwest state colleges and universities who inferred that white-collar crime is moving out of the boardroom and into the classroom as a result of higher education reform." They conclude, without presenting any numerical evidence to describe the magnitude of the situation, that "Pell Grant fraud is widespread" and go on to make the following recommendations: "A compromise might be to disburse financial aid in segments throughout the semester and only to students who attend classes and demonstrate academic progress. The first disbursement would pay for tuition, while subsequent payments would cover incidental expenses. Federal aid would become a quid-pro-quo for academic improvement. More capable guardianship earlier in the admissions process also could help. Stricter admission or academic progress requirements, such as allowing more direct access to financial information by the academic program, could weed out some motivated offenders." Indeed, the prominent research firm MDRC is promoting and evaluating two financial aid innovations—one that makes grant aid conditional on performance, and another that distributes the funds in smaller increments "like a paycheck."[19]

Critics of the Pell point to cash "refunds" as a source of particular concern. Much like critics of welfare, Pell critics worry that cash assistance is too easily wasted. Yet the word "refund" here is inaccurate and politically charged. True, students may receive a check or other cash transfer as a disbursement of their credit balances when those funds exceed institutional charges. But these checks are intended to help students with books, supplies, transportation, and other living expenses—they are not refunds at all.[20]

The comparison between welfare and Pell Grants is apt in an unexpected and troubling way. The nation, we are told, needs to fix the "broken" Pell Grant Program. The recipient of the Pell Grant is a subject who must be governed with ever-increasing rules and regulations.[21] Yet the case for Pell reform is the exact opposite of the case for welfare reform. In the mid-1990s, the key concern driving welfare critics and reformers was the worry that long-term cash benefits to women with young children would breed a cycle of permanent dependency. Pell Grants, in contrast, are based on the idea that higher education is critical to long-term economic success both for individuals and for the nation as a whole—and this has never been truer than it is today. There is no evidence that Pell recipients get "hooked" on college classes, either. They attend just long enough to complete degrees. What is similar between the two programs is that they provide income intended to promote upward mobility and they are attractive targets for budget cuts. Critically, they also serve people from the struggling lower-middle and working classes. In doing so, they risk leaving other hard-working people struggling with economic insecurity feeling that they deserve support but can't get it. This contributes to resentment, a key driver of political attitudes.[22]

Underlying these discussions are highly charged stereotypes of today's Pell recipients. It is easy to think of many of them as impoverished, "nontraditional," racial/ethnic minorities who are unprepared to attend college. These images are grounded in America's history, where thinking about social programs has long been intertwined with racial, class, and gender politics.[23] But many of these images are inaccurate.

Let's look at who actually goes to college. While today on average two-thirds of high school graduates attend college, up from 50 percent in 1975, the fact is that most children from impoverished families still don't attend college.[24] Many never make it past high school graduation.[25] Others never apply to college or stumble when it comes to completing the FAFSA and enrolling in school. Among high school graduates, barely one in two students from families in the bottom fifth of the income distribution enroll in any college, demonstrating how hard it is to even get there. This is a rate that has declined since 2007 when it reached an all-time high of 58 percent.[26]

As table 4 shows, the fraction of undergraduates receiving the Pell Grant has grown dramatically over the last twenty years and particularly since 2008, when the economy weakened during the Great Recession, making more families eligible for the Pell Grant. In 1996, 22 percent of undergraduates received the Pell but by 2012 it was 41 percent. Pell recipients are often called low-income, but in fact the program serves many lower *middle-class* families. To many people, these students appear middle class and refer to themselves as part of the middle class. This is partly because, in recent years, Congress made big changes to rules affecting Pell eligibility.[27] It did so under intense pressure from middle-class families because of rising college

Table 4. Trends in the characteristics of Pell recipients: 1996–2012

	1996	2000	2004	2008	2012
% of undergraduates receiving Pell	22	23	27	28	41
Enrollment:					
% first-time in college	45	45	48	46	45
% enrolled full time (in fall term)	79	81	72	74	74
Fall-term enrollment					
% enrolled full-time	68	69	62	59	59
% enrolled part-time	18	17	25	20	21
% not enrolled	15	15	14	21	20
Age and family:					
Age	22	22	22	21	22
% dependent	58	57	42	42	41
% married	18	21	16	15	15
% with dependent children	40	38	38	37	36
% female	64	63	65	66	62
% neither parent has bachelor's degree	79	74	75	78	76
% with unmarried parents	51	50	53	58	56
Race/ethnicity:					
Non-Hispanic white	52	51	48	46	47
Black	22	22	25	24	24
Hispanic or Latino	17	18	18	20	19
Asian/Pacific Islander	6	5	4	5	5
American Indian/AN	2	1	1	1	1
Native Hawaiian	N/A	1	0	1	0
Other	1	1	2	0	3
More than one race	N/A	N/A	2	3	N/A
Income:					
Median AGI combined ($)	14,902	20,110	17,887	15,994	16,923
AGI as a percentage of poverty line	102	117	124	116	110
≤50% of poverty line	29	19	20	22	28
≤100% of poverty line	55	45	42	45	51
≤150% of poverty line	75	69	65	68	70
≤200% of poverty line	89	86	83	86	85
% on welfare	6	3	2	3	3
Education:					
High school math completed:					
Less than Algebra II	. . .	. . .	. . .	13	18
Algebra II	. . .	. . .	. . .	27	31
Trigonometry	. . .	. . .	. . .	13	9
Precalculus	. . .	. . .	. . .	24	21
Calculus	. . .	. . .	. . .	22	20
ACT composite score	20	19		19	20
SAT combined score	860	966		912	953

Source. National Center for Education Statistics, *National Postsecondary Student Aid Study NPSAS*, 1996, 2000, 2004, 2008, 2012.

Note. Sample includes all undergraduates receiving a Pell Grant in their first year of college, regardless of sector. Race/ethnicity variables listed as N/A did not appear in that year's data. AGI = adjusted gross income.

costs — costs that render even reasonably secure families uncertain about their finances and fearful for their futures.

Only half of today's Pell recipients live below the poverty line (see table 4). But this does not mean that the rest have enough money to pay for college themselves and don't need financial aid. Families living within 200 percent of the poverty line, which includes 85 percent of Pell recipients, and even many families with children who live slightly above it, have very little disposable income to use for education.[28] Data from the Consumer Expenditure Survey indicate that middle-class families earning $50,000–$70,000 per year are able to spend only about 1.3 percent of their income on education. This is very similar to the fraction spent by low-income families, but it is less than one-third what rich families (earning more than $150,000 per year) spend.[29] The families of Pell recipients are economically fragile, but they are rarely welfare recipients — just 3 percent receive welfare.

Given the demographic changes in the population that are taking place across the country, one might assume that the overwhelming majority of today's Pell recipients are people of color, but this is not accurate either. As table 4 shows, non-Hispanic white students like Chloe Johnson receive more Pell Grants than any other single group, comprising 47 percent of all Pell recipients. Less than one in four recipients is African American and just 19 percent are Hispanic. These distributions have shifted only slightly over the last twenty years. Immigration politics play a role here, too, since getting a Pell requires legal paperwork that a growing number of undergraduates do not possess.[30]

Despite the stereotypes, by and large Pell recipients are not from broken or dysfunctional homes of the sort that politicians associate with the "undeserving poor."[31] Forty-four percent of all Pell recipients come from homes headed by married parents. Most have not yet formed families themselves — just 15 percent are married — and instead are working to get an education before forming a union.[32] Moreover, a lack of quality, affordable, on-campus childcare prevents most low-income people with children from entering college, and so barely one in three Pell recipients is a parent. [33]

Even more surprising, it is simply not true that Pell recipients are substantially less prepared for college than they used to be. If they were, then it might mean that we shouldn't blame the financial aid system and should look instead for another explanation of their high dropout rate. Over the last twenty years, as the fraction of undergraduates receiving the Pell Grant grew, levels of academic ability, as measured by standardized test scores, remained about the same. And test scores have also remained steady despite the increase in the number people taking the tests and receiving Pell. The average ACT composite score remained steady at nineteen until rising a bit to nearly twenty in the last few years, and SAT scores have risen almost a hundred points. There is some evidence, however, that the high school math preparation of Pell recipients has diminished.

So overall, data indicate that the average Pell Grant recipient looks very much like a middle-class American. What is different is the jump in attendance among Pell recipients at for-profit institutions. A combination of declining capacity in public colleges and universities, growing interest among students in the flexibility offered by online, nonresidential education, intense marketing campaigns, and a willingness by the federal government to allow financial aid dollars to follow students wherever they attend has facilitated the growth of a robust sector of for-profit higher education. In 1996, just over 12 percent of Pell recipients were enrolled in that sector, but today it is more than 21 percent (see table 5). Much has been written about the costs and quality of for-profit colleges and universities, which enroll a far more demographically diverse group of Pell recipients than the rest of higher education.[34] These students face substantial risks, since they are less likely to realize a significant return on their degrees and are more likely to have a sizable amount of debt on graduation.

What Pell Recipients in Public Higher Education Pay for College

The biggest and most important change in the Pell program is not who the recipients are or where they go to school but rather the price they pay for college. Almost 70 percent of all Pell recipients are enrolled in the public sector, and over time what they must pay

Table 5. Trends in the institutions attended by Pell recipients: 1996–2012

	1996 (%)	2000 (%)	2004 (%)	2008 (%)	2012 (%)
Institutional sector:					
Public	70.2	70.5	67.3	62.9	67.3
Private	17.3	17.2	15.9	13.9	11.5
For profit	12.5	12.3	16.8	23.2	21.2
Institutional type:					
Four year	51.4	53.7	51.5	52.4	52.8
Two year	40.7	39.2	42.3	41.3	42.8
Less than two year	7.9	7.1	6.2	6.3	4.3

Source. National Center for Education Statistics, *National Postsecondary Student Aid Study NPSAS*, 1996, 2000, 2004, 2008, 2012.

Note. Sample includes all undergraduates receiving a Pell Grant in their first year of college, regardless of sector.

has increased dramatically. As table 6 illustrates, at both community colleges and public four-year colleges and universities, increases in college prices far outstripped increases in grant aid, at a time when real family income declined. This is especially true postrecession. In constant dollars, the annual cost of attendance at community colleges (see table 2) grew from about $8,500 in 1996 to almost $13,000 in 2012, while the expected family contribution for a Pell recipient remained around $500 and the fraction of students unable to make any contribution grew from 63 to 73 percent. The resulting net price for a Pell recipient is now nearly $8,000 a year—for a community college—which amounts to 42 percent of the average Pell recipient's adjusted gross income.

Trends at public four-year colleges and universities are similar. There, costs have risen from over $13,000 per year to over $19,000, while the average expected family contribution grew by about $200. The net price went up by about $3,000, but because of declines in family income, so did the fraction of income required to pay the net price, which grew from 29 to 43 percent. Again, this net price is not the final price students will pay for college (though some sources suggest that it is); it is the starting price—what a student faces for the first year.[35]

The Pell Grant clearly provides an incentive for students to attend college by discounting the price of attendance, but it comes nowhere

Table 6. Trends in expected family contribution, financial aid, and net price facing Pell recipients in the public sector, by college type: 1996–2012

	1996	2000	2004	2008	2012
Community colleges:					
Average expected family contribution ($)	509	777	885	782	591
Average expected family contribution excl. no EFC ($)	1,364	1,564	1,998	1,921	2,188
Zero EFC (%)	63	50	56	59	73
Percentage of COA covered by Pell	30	28	32	29	32
Percentage with state need-based grant	30	38	33	40	24
Average amount	$1,340	$1,404	$1,508	$1,680	$1,367
Percentage with institutional grants	20	21	20	22	20
Net price (COA—all grants)	$5,483	$6,481	$6,686	$7,358	$7,959
Net price as percentage of income	26	NA	25	31	42
Public four-year colleges and universities:					
Average expected family contribution ($)	790	1,027	1,268	1,014	923
Average expected family contribution excl. no EFC ($)	1,375	1,569	2,082	1,955	2,323
Zero EFC (%)	43	35	39	48	60
Percentage of COA covered by Pell	20	23	22	20	23
Percentage with state need-based grant	40	36	50	56	44
Average amount	$2,766	$2,513	$2,839	$3,338	$3,351
Percentage with institutional grants	31	29	42	40	36
Net price (COA – all grants)	$8,465	$8,472	$9,248	$9,361	$11,144
Net price as percentage of income	29	NA	28	32	43

Source. National Center for Education Statistics, *National Postsecondary Student Aid Study NPSAS*, 1996, 2000, 2004, 2008, 2012.

Note. Sample includes all undergraduates beginning full time at a two-year or four-year public college or university and receiving a Pell Grant in their first year of college. Figures are adjusted for inflation and expressed in constant 2012 dollars. Net price as percentage of income was not reported in the *NPSAS*, 2000.

close to making college affordable. There is a lot of discussion about rising tuition and fees in the public sector, but most of the growth has been in nontuition costs, which account for two-thirds or more of the total costs. These include books and supplies and living costs, which must be at least partially covered if a student is to focus on school instead of working full time.[36] The Pell Grant would have even less purchasing power today had Congress and President Obama not acted to increase the maximum grant in the wake of the recession.[37] Instead, it remained steady during this period, covering 20–30 percent of the costs for Pell recipients in the public sector. But, just as the size of the grant increased, the dollar amount of the uncovered 70–80 percent grew as well.

In order to cover the remaining costs, students and their families looked to their states and to the institutions. The fraction of students receiving a state need-based grant increased over time until the recession, at which point states cut support for aid programs substantially.[38] Though the economy has recovered somewhat, the aid still lags. Today, less than half of all Pell recipients at four-year colleges and universities, and barely one in four at community colleges, receive any need-based aid from their state, and for those that do, the average grant is much smaller than the Pell, amounting to $1,300–$3,300 per year (see table 6).

Where states have stepped out, colleges and universities have tried to step in. During and following the recession, four-year colleges and universities increased their need-based aid to Pell recipients, while community colleges were unable to do so. Just one in five Pell recipients at community colleges receive any institutional grant aid, compared to 36 percent of those at four-year colleges and universities.

Making Ends Meet: The National Picture

How do students and their families deal with the high price of college? Up to now, we've made guesses based on national administrative and survey data. But we need to better understand the complex strategies students use in order to make ends meet. Let's look at the national picture and how the use of various approaches has changed over time.

It is impossible to pay attention to the media today and miss the nation's growing dependence on student loans. Total annual borrowing grew from about $25 billion in the mid-1990s to over $70 billion in 2013–14. As astute analysts have been quick to point out, graduates of professional schools (e.g., law) and people who have completed bachelor's degrees hold most of that debt. For the most part, they are managing to pay it off without falling into delinquency or default (though, they often struggle to make payments). But other people went to college and left with debt and no degree. They did not accumulate a lot of debt because they did not spend much time in college—however their incomes were often lower than average to begin with and remained low as they entered the labor market with only high school degrees. These low-income individuals, especially those who attended for-profits colleges and universities and community colleges, are the people at the epicenter of the student debt crisis.[39] They are defaulting because they took loans as their only way to afford college. That is why rates of borrowing are so much higher for Pell recipients than for people who do not have Pell (88% vs. 53%)—the Pell recipients have little choice but to take loans to pay for college.[40]

This is a startling turn of events. One purpose of the Pell Grant is to protect students from low-income families, for whom college is a risky—yet powerful—investment, from having to take loans. When the odds of noncompletion are high, and economic returns are uncertain, it is reasonable for a person to hesitate to invest in college. Since society reaps substantial benefits when the poor complete college, it is a sound public policy decision to lower the price to reduce the risk. Again, an explicit goal of the Pell Grant Program was to meet the financial need of low-income people so that they did not have to borrow for college. But as figure 9 shows, that goal is far from met. More than 40 percent of Pell recipients in the public sector have at least one federally subsidized loan, and between 1996 and 2012, the fraction with an unsubsidized loan swelled—from 6 percent to more than 30 percent. But while the terms of unsubsidized federal loans are suboptimal (e.g., they cannot be discharged in bankruptcy), they are still far better than those of nonfederal loans, which contain few borrower protections and often have a variable interest rate as high as 13 percent.[41] Private loans are not eligible for deferment, income-based repayment, or loan forgiveness options that come with federal student loans. Yet some Pell recipients are accepting these too.

The size of the loans held by borrowers has also grown. In constant dollars during their first year of college, loans for Pell recipients

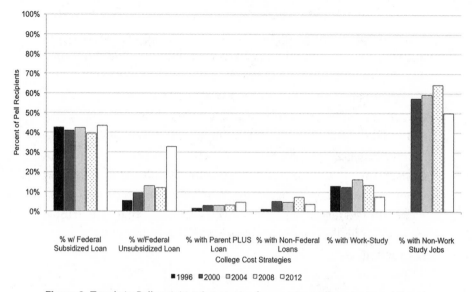

Figure 9. Trends in Pell recipients' strategies for covering college costs: public colleges and universities: 1996–2012. Sample includes all undergraduates beginning full time at a two-year or four-year public college or university and receiving a Pell Grant in their first year of college. Source: National Center for Education Statistics, *National Postsecondary Student Aid Study NPSAS*, 1996, 2000, 2004, 2008, 2012.

in the public sector increased on average from $4,300 to over $6,600. Most of that debt was contained in a federally subsidized loan, which offered the best terms but was capped at $3,500.

Attempts to avoid debt by working are common, and working one's way through college is an iconic American story repeated by politicians everywhere.[42] In a hearing on college affordability, U.S. Senator Lamar Alexander (R-Tennessee) noted, "My experience is probably like everybody else's: I had no money, so I had two scholarships and five jobs to try to make my way through."[43] Similarly, U.S. Representative Virginia Foxx (R-North Carolina) shared: "I went through school, I worked my way through, it took me seven years, I never borrowed a dime of money.... I have very little tolerance for people who tell me that they graduate with $200,000 of debt or even $80,000 of debt because there's no reason for that. We live in an opportunity society and people are forgetting that. I remind folks all the time that the Declaration of Independence says 'life, liberty, and the pursuit of happiness.' You don't have it dumped in your lap."[44]

Current Democratic presidential candidate and Secretary of State Hillary Clinton has a comparable story, which she has used to argue that students ought to work in exchange for a lower price of college: "Back when I went to college, my father told me, 'Here's the deal. Got enough money for your tuition and board, but anything beyond that, like buying books, you pay for yourself.' And I had worked summers and holidays since I was 13, so I was fine with that."[45]

But the ability of today's students to make ends meet through work alone has been compromised by at least two factors: underfunding of the federal work-study program, and a weak economy that offers few stable opportunities to part-time workers, which include most undergraduates. It is difficult to earn enough from work to avoid taking on debt. Consider that the federal loan maximum per year in 2008 was $5,500. A Wisconsin student working fifteen hours a week at minimum wage grossed $5,070 if they worked year-round, and they took home about $4,275 after taxes. Thus, a Pell recipient at a public university with a net price of $9,300 (the average at the time) could either take the maximum loans and work part time, or avoid loans and work nearly full time. If the net price of attendance was underestimated—as it commonly is—they would need to work even more.

One in two Pell recipients attending public colleges and universities work, for an average of twenty-five hours per week. The fraction working appears to have declined over time (though some of this change may be due to shifts in how federal data collection on work has changed). After employment rates among Pell recipients increased to a high of 64 percent in 2008, they fell to 50 percent in 2008. One likely reason, discussed in detail in chapter 4, is that the sorts of flexible part-time work sought by undergraduates for decades became harder to find and harder to keep following the recession.[46] Another reason is that fewer Pell recipients are offered work-study jobs. The funding formula for distributing federal work-study monies to institutions has not changed in many decades, and the current approach favors wealthier students at private schools.[47] Quite literally, the Federal Work-Study Program "rewards the most expensive institutions who have been in the program the longest."

The fraction of Pell recipients in the public sector in work-study positions fell from 13 percent in 1996 to 8 percent in 2012, even though the government spent $972 million on the program that year.[48] Work-study is a popular program with high levels of participant satisfaction and yet it does not pay well: for decades, students at public institutions have been unable to earn more than about $2,000 per year on average this way.[49]

Borrowing and working to pay for college sound like simple strategies in theory. After all, many Americans have financed college this way for decades. But the amount of debt and the difficulties finding and keeping a job have changed, as have the economic conditions facing lower-income families. The effort involved in paying for college has altered the college experience for lower-income students at a time when the conditions of college life have grown ever more comfortable for wealthy students. As the children of the well-off enjoy one-on-one chats with renowned faculty, experience outward-bound excursions with their classmates, become members of dining clubs, and exercise on climbing walls, Pell recipients are simply struggling to make ends meet.[50]

4

Making Ends Meet

Chloe Johnson filled out her FAFSA, and so did Ian Williams and Tyler Olson. Norbert Webster and Sophie Schmidt completed theirs nine months before they began college, and Nima Chaudhary's older brothers—both college students themselves—helped fill hers out correctly. As they awaited the federal computations, all six wondered, *How much money will I have to pay to make this work?*

With family incomes generally less than $30,000 per year, none of these students was able to pay more than $4,000 a year for college, according to federal calculations. But even after taking all types of grants and scholarships into account, everyone except Norbert was left with a substantial balance. In most cases, their net price (the difference between cost of attendance and all grants) amounted to 40 percent or more of their family's income for a year (see table 7). Indeed, for most of these students, their net prices were many times larger than their expected family contributions, the amount the federal government calculated they could afford to pay.

Take Ian, for example. The year before he started college, his family with five kids earned around $25,000. The public university nearest his home charged $7,300 for tuition and fees and estimated that the other costs (books, supplies, transportation, room and board) would amount to an additional $10,000. The federal Pell Grant provided Ian with $4,281 in support, and the state of Wisconsin added $2,768 (this was just for his first year of college; in his second year funding for the Wisconsin Higher Education Grant ran out and Ian did not receive it). But that was it—he was not eligible

Table 7. College costs and strategies for the first year of college: WSLS focal students

	Ian	Chloe	Norbert	Nima	Tyler	Sophie
Ability to pay:						
Adjusted gross income ($)	24,686	25,380	27,706	70,424	3,638	26,667
Expected family contribution ($)	425	2,520	2,315	3,800	1	3,939
Costs of attending college (COA)						
Total ($)	17,633	15,512	15,457	15,512	15,457	18,973
Tuition and fees ($)	7,305	3,196	6,037	3,196	6,037	7,564
Nontuition costs ($)	10,328	12,316	9,420	12,316	9,420	11,409
Grant and scholarships:						
Total grants from all sources ($)	7,049	2,958	15,363	3,292	8,961	3,251
Resulting price:						
Net price (COA – grants) ($)	10,584	12,554	94	12,220	6,496	15,722
Net price as percentage of income	43	49	0.30	17	179	59
Strategies to cover price:						
Total federal loans ($)	5,500	5,500	0	0	3,500	5,500
Work-study allocation ($)	0	0	0	0	0	2,400
Unmet need (COA – EFC – all aid) ($)	4,659	4,534	-2,221	9,132	2,996	3,883
Number of hours worked per week, first term of college	16	30	0	0	0	30
Total private loans ($)	0	0	0	0	0	7,876

Source. WSLS data.

for anything else. Ian had just enough in hand to cover tuition and was short the rest.

He was not alone: Chloe Johnson and Nima Chaudhary were in similar situations—even though they had enrolled in the same two-year technical college where tuition was lower than at Ian's university, they had higher expected family contributions and qualified for less grant aid. Chloe's family had about as much money as Ian's, and while Nima's mother earned more by working two jobs, her father was disabled and her two older brothers were also in college. Chloe and Nima each needed to come up with about $12,000 for their first year of school.

Sophie Schmidt was attending a more selective and expensive university than the others, but because her family was judged capable of contributing almost $4,000 per year to her education, she qualified for a much smaller Pell—just $890. A Wisconsin Higher Education Grant added another $1,011, and she was fortunate that her university also provided additional federal grant aid of $600.[1]

Like most students at her university she lived on campus, so she faced a net price of $15,722, equivalent to almost 60 percent of her family's income. To make matters worse, Sophie's family was not able to contribute the amount expected of them.

Tyler Olson was in slightly better shape. He attended a university that was a bit less expensive than Ian's but he qualified for more grants because he'd done pretty well academically in high school. He received a $1,400 grant from Wisconsin's Talent Incentive Program, and two years later as a college junior he got a $1,300 SMART grant from the federal government.[2] That combination meant that his net price was much lower than Sophie or Ian's, at about $5,600 per year. But his family earned less than $4,000 a year, and the federal computations assessed his expected family contribution at just one dollar. The $5,600 he needed was far out of reach.

Norbert Webster was the only student whose financial aid package matched his needs. His mom earned less than $28,000 during his senior year of high school and was judged capable of contributing about $2,300 toward the annual costs of attending university. She stretched to make it work, and federal grants plus a large scholarship from his tribe, the Oneida Nation of Wisconsin, took care of the rest.[3]

Given these prices, it is remarkable that the other five students were still enrolled in college when we met them for the first time in October 2008. But they were not unusual. As table 8 shows, our students had an average expected family contribution of about $1,400 and faced average costs for their first year of college of $14,850. Thirty-eight percent of students had no expected family contribution at all. Had the rules allowed, the information provided on their FAFSAs suggests that 16 percent of our students overall (and 24% of those at two-year colleges) would have had a negative expected family contribution averaging more than $10,600. In other words, for some students, not only could they not contribute to college costs but also, in order to ensure they had what they needed to succeed, payment would need to be provided to their families to offset lost income. Of course, this did not happen. Instead, they received $6,000 in grants on average, leaving them with a net price of almost $7,500.

Table 8. College costs facing students for the first year of college: WSLS full and subsamples (2008)

	Overall	Four-Year Starters	Two-Year Starters	Interview Sample
Ability to pay:				
Expected family contribution	$1,372	$1,631	$1,083	$1,629
Percentage zero EFC	38	31	46	35
Percentage negative EFC	16	8	24	14
Average EFC among those with negative	-$10,647	-$7,472	-$11,812	-$10,383
Costs of attending college:				
Official cost of attendance	$14,850	$15,528	$14,100	$15,839
Tuition and fees	$5,122	$6,568	$3,522	$5,998
Nontuition costs	$9,728	$8,960	$10,578	$9,841
Grant aid				
Total grants (not including WSG)	$6,144	$7,469	$4,278	$7,150
Pell amount	$3,020	$3,263	$2,679	$3,366
Percentage with state need-based grant	88	97	76	97
Average amount among recipients	$1,913	$2,203	$1,389	$2,114
Percentage with institutional grants	15	20	7	28
Average amount among recipients	$938	$934	$952	$694
Price students must pay:				
Net price (COA − grants not including WSG)	$8,706	$8,059	$9,822	$8,689
Net price as percentage of parent income	35	30	46	40

Sources. Author's calculations using WSLS data; and U.S. Department of Education, "Integrated Postsecondary Education Data System" (IPEDS).

Note. Cost of attendance for four-year students includes housing on campus, and for two-year students includes housing off campus not with family. Parent income and net price as percentage of parent income are reported at the median. "Ability to pay" and "Costs of attending college" include the entire sample. (Overall, n = 3,000; four-year starters, n = 1,500; two-year starters, n = 1,500; interview sample, n = 50.) "Grant aid" and "price students must pay" include subsample where financial aid is observed. (Overall, n = 1,438; four-year starters, n = 827; two-year starters, n = 611; interview sample, n = 44.)

These sizable net prices were partly bad luck and poor timing. The recession was just getting underway and federal adjustments to the financial aid formula to provide more assistance to families had not yet taken effect. Thanks to Congress and the president, had they enrolled in college a year later, students like Sophie, Ian, Chloe, and Norbert, whose families earned more than $23,000 but less than $32,000 per year, would have received more grant aid (a larger Pell and likely a larger Wisconsin Higher Education Grant) and would not have been asked to pay an expected family contribution. That is because the College Cost Reduction and Access Act of 2007 raised the income threshold for receiving an automatic zero expected family contribution from \$20,000 to \$30,000 beginning in 2009–10. It remained at or slightly above that level until budget cuts in 2012 reduced the threshold to \$23,000.[4] For the 2015–16 school year, it was \$24,000.

The additional support from grants might have made a difference for some students, allowing them to work less and study more. The evidence we obtained from an experiment with grant aid, described in chapter 9, suggests it could have been helpful. However, in an important sense these students were not in an uncommon situation. The history of federal student aid since its inception has been a series of ebbs and flows, periods of generosity and periods of cuts, all while college costs continued to rise. Support for helping economically vulnerable students like ours secure a better future through higher education has been inconsistent, leaving their opportunities subject to a volatile mix of politics and economics. In the midst of it all, students are simply trying to get ahead.

Getting Started

Embarking on the first year of college required that students come up with the funds to cover the net price. Websites and glossy brochures from colleges and universities often say that students use "a combination of loans, work, and other gifts" to accomplish this task.[5] That doesn't sound too bad. But what this task looks and feels like is something else entirely. The goal is straightforward: come up with enough money to pay tuition and fees, buy the necessary books, and supplies, and cover the bills associated with living a modest life. How did they do it?

Despite the intentions of the Pell program, which hoped to protect lower-income students from loans and work by providing grants, today's Pell recipients endure a process similar to most undergraduates. Their first challenge is to get their families to contribute the expected family contribution. Then, they need to decide whether to take federal loans. That decision is often closely intertwined with another key decision: whether and how much to work. As mentioned earlier, work-study is available to only a small number of students. So it is important to figure out where else to find work and how to make a schedule that fits with school. These challenges—borrowing and working—are the focus of this chapter. The next chapter describes what happened to our students who did not borrow or work very much. Some fell into great fortune, while others coped with scarcity.

Why Work When You Can Borrow?

Twenty years ago working part time while in school was a viable way to pay for college and avoid loans.[6] Today, students are much more likely to both borrow *and* work—and given the desires of students and their families to avoid taking out loans, it is clear that this behavior is not based on a change in preferences.[7] While much has been said about the growing problem of student debt and the controversial terms and rules associated with student loans, our data reveal that the need to borrow changes the way that students experience college. Debt has implications not only for financial capabilities postcollege but also for the odds of completing a degree in the first place.

Student loans are the most common form of financial aid in the United States. In fact, since the early 1980s (partly facilitated by the passage of the Middle Income Student Assistance Act of 1978), student loans have been the primary means by which American families have financed postsecondary education.[8] With the costs of attendance at an all-time high, and significant grant aid available to relatively small numbers of financially needy or exceptionally talented students, nearly two-thirds of all undergraduates receive at least some government-backed loans to cover those costs. This credit is comparatively accessible, requiring a lengthy application but no credit history for most loans. There is no underwriting done to assess ability to repay, with the exception of very limited underwriting for Parent PLUS loans. Students and families can borrow a sizable amount of money. In 2014, total student loan debt in the United States reached an all-time high of $1.1 trillion.[9] Fifteen million young adults under age thirty hold one-third of that debt, and much of the growth in borrowers occurred at for-profit colleges and universities and community colleges.[10]

Prior to the 1992 reauthorization of the Higher Education Act, federal loans consisted almost entirely of subsidized loans targeted to needy families. These loans are the "best" of the available federal loans since they do not accrue interest until a student leaves college and a grace period ends. Interest on unsubsidized loans begins accruing as soon as a student takes them.

Total federal loan volume was around $22 billion (in 2011) dollars in 1991–92. Over the course of the next year, with the introduction of unsubsidized loans, that number grew by almost 50 percent. Still, at the time, unsubsidized loans constituted 9 percent of all student loan dollars across all sources. Unsubsidized loans have grown dramatically since then. From about $10 billion (in 2011) dollars in 1995–96, the volume of unsubsidized loans doubled to more than $20 billion in 2005–6, and then doubled again to almost $50 billion in 2011–12. That increase happened at the same time families lost income during the recession and college costs soared. Subsidized loans grew much more slowly. One reason for this is that, even though millions of families lost income, many did not fall low enough to qualify for substantial subsidized loans under the means test.[11]

On a per-student basis, loan growth was also significant. Between 2001–2 and 2006–7, average total borrowing per full-time equivalent undergraduate student rose by 45 percent, from $3,677 (in 2011 dollars) to $5,335. By 2011–12, the average total had grown another 4 percent to $5,540.[12]

How much can undergraduate students like those in this study borrow? The answer, as table 9 reveals, is a lot. Between subsidized and unsubsidized Stafford Loans, students can borrow between $5,550 and $7,500 for each year of college, up to a lifetime maximum of $31,000. For low-income students, up to three-quarters of those loans can be subsidized.

Still, even these loan limits are not always enough for some students to cover the full price of going to college. This is especially true for African American students, whose families possess far fewer

Table 9. Federal Stafford Loan maximums for dependent students

	Maximum Subsidized Loan ($)	Total Possible Stafford Loan ($)
First year of college	3,500	5,500
Second year of college	4,500	6,500
Third, fourth and beyond (per year)	5,500	7,500
Lifetime limits	23,000	$31,000

Source. U.S. Department of Education, "How Much Can I Borrow?"

Note. A dependent student is under age twenty-four, unmarried, with no children or other dependents, not a ward of the court or homeless or serving in the military, and not a veteran.

assets and more debt. A disproportionate fraction of our African American students (38% as compared to 11% of white students) had a negative expected family contribution, signaling that their families had a great deal of financial need. In 2011–12, 52 percent of black undergraduates had a student loan compared to 42 percent of white students and 36 percent of Hispanic students.[13] In "The Color of Student Debt," researchers Robert Kelchen, Jason Houle, and I explored the reasons why African American students are more likely to borrow. Much of the difference has to do with racial disparities in wealth. The racial wealth gap is three times larger than the racial income gap and more unequal than ever before, and it exists among families of all income levels.[14] White families hold as much as twenty times the wealth of black families.[15] Between 1984 and 2009, the absolute racial gap in wealth increased by $151,000.[16] Moreover, during the recession, racial/ethnic minority families lost more wealth (in percentage terms) than their white counterparts.[17]

In other words, income translates into wealth differently for black and white families. Sociologist Thomas Shapiro and colleagues found that "each dollar increase in income translates into about five dollars of wealth for white families (at the median) and only about 70 cents for African Americans."[18] Wealth (both assets and debt) are largely neglected by the calculation of expected family contribution and thus students with similar financial aid packages may face very different capacities to avoid taking student loans. When this combination of greater need for loans is coupled with the increased likelihood of dropping out, the result is potent. As Mark Huelsman of the public policy organization Demos points out, indebted college dropouts are disproportionately low-income African Americans.[19] He writes,

> In an America where Black and Latino households have just a fraction of the wealth of white households, where communities of color have for decades been shut out of traditional ladders of economic opportunity, a system based entirely on acquiring debt to get ahead may have very different impacts on some communities over others. . . . Our debt-financed system not only results in higher loan balances for low-income, Black and Latino students, but also results in high numbers of low-income students and students of color dropping out without receiving a credential. In addition, our debt-based system may be fundamentally impacting the post-college lives of those who are forced to take on debt to attend and complete college.

Given that the Pell program was created to ensure that people from low-income families could afford to attend college without putting themselves and their loved ones into economic jeopardy, it is notable that more than half of our students took a loan for their first year of college. As table 10 shows, that included 77 percent of the students who began at a university, and even 25 percent of students who enrolled at America's main "low-cost" college option—the public two-year college. On average, students borrowed more than $4,000 for that first year alone.

Ian, Chloe, Tyler, and Sophie all accepted federal loans. Since they faced net prices around $10,000 or more, this was not surprising. Ian and Sophie signed their promissory notes at the start of the term, while Tyler hesitated for a bit, worried about putting his family—which earned practically nothing—into debt. Would he finish college and be able to repay those loans? He simply didn't know. While Ian and Chloe took the federal maximum ($5,500), Tyler accepted only the $3,500 subsidized loan. Chloe applied for her loan toward

Table 10. Strategies for covering college costs: WSLS full and subsamples

	Overall	Four-Year Starters	Two-Year Starters	Interview Sample
Loans in first year of college:				
Percentage with any loan	56	77	25	76
Average amount	$4,182	$4,477	$2,881	$4,935
Percentage with federal subsidized loan	61	76	40	72
Average amount	$3,212	$3,295	$2,990	$3,764
Percentage with federal unsubsidized loan	27	37	13	44
Average amount	$1,965	$2,000	$1,825	$2,033
Percentage with Parent PLUS loan	2	3	2	4
Percentage with nonfederal loans	3	2	0	7
Average amount	$4,066	$4,731	$3,410	$4,913
Employment:				
Percentage employed (any job)	62	51	76	50
Average hours worked per week	17.7	13.9	21.1	17.2
Percentage with work-study	12	15	7	11
Average amount	$1,157	$1,026	$1,568	$1,554
Second year of college:				
Percentage employed (any job)	66	63	73	63
Percentage with multiple jobs	20	17	25	22
Percentage working 8 A.M. to 6 P.M.	83	83	83	89
Percentage working 6 P.M. to 10 P.M.	61	62	59	54
Percentage working 10 P.M. to 2 A.M.	16	16	16	17
Percentage working 2 A.M. to 8 A.M.	11	10	14	7

Source. WSLS data.

Note. "Loans in first year of college" includes only the subsample where financial aid is observed (overall, n = 1,438; four-year starters, n = 827; two-year starters, n = 611; interview sample, n = 44). Questions under "Employment" were part of the fall 2008 survey (overall, n = 2,127; four-year starters, n = 1,146; two-year starters, n = 981, interview sample, n = 50). "Second year of college" questions were part of the fall 2009 survey (overall, n = 1,436; four-year starters, n = 912; two-year starters, n = 524; interview sample. n = 49).

the end of September, hoping to avoid borrowing by working, but did not receive the funds until early December.

Loan Trouble

Media reports often highlight former college students who owe federal student loans of $100,000 or more. A reasonable person might wonder how often this happens.[20] Overall, six figure loan totals are rare. A student cannot borrow $100,000 in federal loans unless they attend graduate school. Parents who take out PLUS loans can also occasionally borrow over $100,000, but in those cases the parents owns the debt, not the students. Most people with debt in the six figures have multiple degrees, and multiple degrees are strongly correlated with higher incomes.

An even more serious problem faces people who do not finish degrees and yet have debt. Every student, of course, accepts some risk by going to college, since they know that degrees are earned, not given. But students who get grants, work a job or two, and take out loans are not just risking their time should they fail to graduate. If they end up with debt and without a degree, they are at the greatest risk of defaulting on their loans or falling into delinquency.[21] This is why the amount of debt is inversely correlated with the likelihood of loan trouble—the less college you complete, the less debt you have, but the less likely you are to repay.[22] Without a college degree, and having forgone years of work experience and seniority to attend college, former undergraduates without degrees can find only low-paying jobs. Even paying off a modest amount of loans puts them in compromising positions. This is the real student debt crisis.

Private, nonfederal loans create more trouble. These loans come with few of the protections offered by federal loans, and they often carry variable interest rates. And, due to a provision slipped into bankruptcy legislation passed in 2005, they are virtually impossible to discharge in bankruptcy court. There is no cap on how much an undergraduate can borrow in private loans—just how much the bank is willing to lend.[23] Facing a net price of more than $15,000, Sophie turned to the private market, with her mother as cosigner, after maxing out her federal loans.[24] Discover Loans made Sophie a $7,800 loan for her first year, and she continued take a loan from them each year thereafter.

With declining family resources and rising net prices, we might expect more students to be utilizing loans. They are. The total number of federal Stafford Loan borrowers is growing quickly. In the decade from 2001–2 to 2011–12, the number of borrowers increased by a whopping 95 percent, from 5.4 million to 10.4 million.[25] As a share of all undergraduates, the percentage holding a loan grew from 23 percent to 35 percent. And the share of undergraduates borrowing both subsidized and unsubsidized federal loans grew from 9 percent to 25 percent. [26]

Students from lower-income families are *more* likely than those from other income groups to use loans. Of course, these students often receive Pell Grants, but as stated previously, those grants do not have nearly the purchasing power they once did. An analysis of bachelor's degree recipients graduating from public universities in 2007–8 found that 68 percent of students from families earning less than $30,000 per year had an average cumulative debt load of $16,500. That means that, if the family stopped all other spending— which is impossible since it would involve spending nothing on food, shelter, health care, etc.—it would still take all their income for more than six months to repay the loan.

The situation at the upper end of the income scale is completely different. Just 40 percent of students from families earning $120,000 or more annually hold any student debt at all. The average amount of debt is $14,500. The resulting disparity in the debt-to-income ratio is substantial: low-income families hold student debt amounting to about 70 percent of their income, while wealthier families have student debt amounting to around 10 percent of income (a rate deemed manageable by the financial industry).[27]

Evidence from several waves of the *National Postsecondary Student Aid Study* suggests that between 40 and 50 percent of students borrowing subsidized Stafford Loans took the maximum allowable amount over the past two decades, even after two increases in the maximum. These numbers indicate that students would probably take more if the maximum were higher. Indeed, more than one in four students who borrowed the maximum amount of federal loans in the 2007–8 academic year also took out a private loan or had a parent who took out a federal PLUS loan.[28] Thus, even in the face of growing concern about the overall amount of borrowing, there is reason to think that until prices are reduced students from low-income families might be more successful in college if they were willing or able to borrow more.

Most discussions about student loans focus on how people work to repay their debt after they leave college. But loans are important during college. On the positive side, credit allows students to finance expenses, which sometimes means that they don't have to work or that they can work fewer hours. Loan dollars can buy supplies, making the difference between buying books for class or going unprepared. But in our study, many students reported a downside: intense, daily worry about loans and debt. That stress can change what it means to be an undergraduate. Psychologically, the moment a student accepts a loan—an action that often does not feel like a choice—they begin paying a price.

Who Doesn't Borrow?

Whether to borrow money for college is a decision that students make and remake throughout their path to a degree. They often start thinking about the possibility of using loans to pay for college several years in advance—it is part of the calculus of whether to attend college at all and also of where to attend. A person from a low-income family who is unwilling to use loans to finance college is less likely to enroll in higher education at all. Since it is nearly impossible for a low-income or middle-income student to attend a for-profit college or university or a private nonprofit without borrowing, students who do not borrow enroll in those sectors at very low rates. They mainly go public.[29]

A lot of students follow this path. Even faced with sizable short-term financial constraints when it comes to paying for college, national estimates indicate that 45 percent of students from low-income families who are enrolled in college did not accept the federal loans offered to them. Rates of refusal are notably higher among low-income students. For example, an analysis of 2011–12 data indicates that among students who needed at least $2,000 to cover their college costs (student budget minus the expected family contribution and all grants), 54 percent of students from families earning less than $30,000 took no loans, compared to 41 percent of students from families earning $65,000 to $105,000.[30]

Our data suggest that many Pell recipients enter public colleges and universities not sure how they feel about loans and undecided about how they will use credit to finance their degree. Some appear "debt averse" when describing their opinions about loans on a survey, only to accept loans when they are actually offered. Others accept loans while also expressing a strong dislike for debt.

Regardless of whether their feelings or opinions change, the way many students use loans changes over their time in college. We found that one-third of students took on larger loans in their second year. This may be because as they are closer to completing a degree, they feel more confident that they will graduate and be able to repay their loans. But it's also possible that they are accepting more loan money because the price of a second year of college is often higher (sometimes substantially so) than the first year, and they can no longer avoid taking loans without dropping out.

Loan Averse in the Badger State

My colleague Robert Kelchen and I spent many hours poring over the confidential financial aid records of individuals in the Wisconsin Scholars Longitudinal Study, comparing them to their surveys and interviews. Despite their Pell Grants, these students needed to borrow—over 85 percent of them had unmet need exceeding $3,500 (the maximum subsidized Stafford Loan for first-year students), and 72 percent had unmet need of greater than the $5,500 that first-year students may borrow in subsidized and unsubsidized loans.

We tried to understand who was "loan averse," who wasn't, and why. First, we looked at which students were offered loans when they began college, how much subsidized and unsubsidized loan money was offered, and how much was accepted. We were fortunate to be able to obtain this information, since most analysts only have data on the loans accepted and cannot see when students decline loans. Students who declined all of the loans offered to them during their first semester of college, despite having demonstrated financial need, we termed "loan averse."[31] Nineteen percent of students met this criterion.

Next, we compared students' decisions to take or refuse loans with their answers to a series of financial questions on our survey. Inconsistencies appeared immediately. We looked at how our students answered one of our survey questions that same semester: "Suppose you could take out a loan up to $10,000 with a 7 percent interest rate. How much money would you take?"

Students could choose from the following five options: $0, $1,000, $2,500, $5,000, and $10,000. In fall 2008, the interest rate on subsidized student loans was 6.0 percent and for unsubsidized student loans was 6.8 percent.[32] We did not tell the students this information in the survey, and their overall responses and level of financial aid knowledge suggested by responses to other questions in the same survey gave us little reason to think that they were aware that the rates we asked about were similar to the actual prevailing rates.[33] We called students who said they would take *none* of the loans they were offered loan averse. Forty-one percent of students were loan averse according to this criterion.

On the survey, most students were not averse to all forms of debt. However, about 75 percent did not think that debt was a normal part of today's lifestyle or that taking out loans was a good thing to do.

We then compared the results from the financial aid records and the surveys. There were many differences between students' expressed preferences (on the survey) and their borrowing behaviors. The two rarely agreed. Only 52 percent of the time did students indicate on both measures that they were not opposed to taking loans. But only 12 percent agreed on both measures that they were loan averse. The correlation between the survey and administrative measures was not particularly strong ($r = .21$) and the measures aligned for only 64 percent of the sample. Twenty-nine percent of the sample was classified as loan averse using the survey measure, even though in reality they had accepted loans. On the other side of the spectrum, 7 percent of students who said they would borrow, according to the survey, did not accept loans according to the administrative data.

Critically, willingness to borrow seems to have nothing to do with a student's expectations for receiving a financial return on their college degree. The substantial earnings premium that students anticipated from finishing college (a median increase of $20,000) was not related to their stated preferences for borrowing (on the survey) or their actual borrowing behavior.

The differences between reported preferences and actual behavior could be due to other reasons we didn't ask about. For example, students might report not wanting to take loans but took them anyway because they had no other options. The apparent disconnect we uncovered illustrates the problem of sorting out who does, and who does not, want to take loans and why.

Nima Chaudhary is a good example. In general, she abhorred debt but her thinking about student loans was more complicated. On a survey, she agreed that "being in debt is part of today's lifestyle" but she also agreed "it is hard to get out of debt once you get in debt." Moreover, she somewhat agreed that "it is wrong to owe money." In interviews, she explained that her brothers took out sizable loans to attend the University of Wisconsin–Madison, but Nima was worried about putting her family even further into debt, and this concern was a key reason why she enrolled in a technical college instead. But her technical college was not inexpensive. Even living at home, Nima had trouble coming up with enough money for the art supplies she needed for classes. She did not have a computer of her own to do her schoolwork, and she could not afford to eat in the school cafeteria. Perhaps for these reasons, on that same initial survey, she indicated that if she were given the opportunity to take out a loan up to $10,000 at a 7 percent interest rate, she would accept the maximum. When the technical college offered Nima federal subsidized and unsubsidized loans during her first year of college, she initially accepted them—but then she did not complete the paperwork and counseling required for the school to disburse the funds. She said, "I don't need a lot of things in life, like fancy cell phones or whatever. I just don't want to worry about all the bills and the things that my parents have to go through."

At the same time, Nima desperately wanted to avoid the part-time work available to her, as an aide at a nursing home. Taking a loan might have helped her do this, providing her family with the money needed to replace her work earnings and freeing time for study, but she resisted. During interviews, she proudly reported that she still had no debt.

Loan aversion is far more complicated than it is often portrayed.

It is not a stable characteristic but rather an attitude, sometimes generalized and sometimes specific. It is malleable. Feelings of dislike toward loans evolve in context, and they change over time. Financial counseling, including loan counseling, may affect these choices— but a one-time meeting is unlikely to change someone's mind. Rather, ongoing (or at least repeated) financial counseling might help students think about their entire strategy for making ends meet and succeeding in college, rather than focusing exclusively on loans.

Stress

Loans come with stress created by both the amount of debt owed and a sense that repaying the debt will be difficult.[34] Data indicate that low-income people are the most likely to default on their loans. Those defaults often happen on what seem like, in an absolute sense, small loans. Yet those small loans are actually big relative to both debt holders' current income and their families' broader financial situations (which rarely include significant assets and instead are full of other forms of debt, including credit cards and payday loan debt).[35]

Is loan aversion irrational? Some argue that it is. Most policymakers and researchers think that because college offers the most promising pathway to socioeconomic mobility in the United States, it is reasonable to expect families to take out loans. After all, children almost always outearn their parents, and they are more likely to do so if they attend college.[36] Since risk of default is therefore minimal, they think that low-income students and their families should feel comfortable taking on the risk of a loan as an investment because of the greater earning power a degree will bring.[37] But the real issue is that these students are at great risk of default because their prospects for degree completion are low and because they disproportionately attend for-profit and community colleges where financial aid is scarce and the price of attendance is high.[38]

The assumption that gains in lifetime earnings justify broad utilization of loans overlooks the fact that college income gains are far from certain. While it is certainly true that college enhances mobility overall, low- and moderate-income people cannot be assured that it will lift them into middle class. For example, 38 percent of people from low-income families will remain in the bottom 40 percent of the income distribution even if they earn a college degree. And that is an important "if," given that only 11 percent of them are likely to complete degrees.[39] These realities help explain why students from low-income families are right to question whether borrowing is worthwhile.

Like many students in the study, Ian Williams accepted the loans he was offered, but his decision to take the loans weighed on him. If he had had more money, Ian said that he would have preferred to avoid taking loans:

> It's stressful to me, I just take every loan I can get and I know I have to pay it back, so I'm budgeting for the future. Like, ok, I'm going to have to pay this amount back every month if I take this. . . . So I'm skeptical in taking out loans—but then again I need it. . . . [If I had more grants] I'd be able to pay the bills and I wouldn't be focused more on my bills than my books. I'd be mainly focused on my education instead of my bills. It's scaring me—even though I'm doing my work and I'm getting good grades, I'm still worried about having to pay this money back.

We followed up, asking him "If you didn't get any financial aid, any loans, would you be in college?" Ian responded, "No, I know I wouldn't be in college."

Ian's situation illustrates a critical point. In today's high-price environment the new economics of college means that student loans preserve the ability of many students to attend college at all. They are unlike other financial products—because they are available even to the most economically insecure families without credit checks, and they therefore involve substantial risk for the lender. During the course of this study the U.S. government took over loan origination from banks. This allows funds that used to be spent paying banks to originate loans to go toward funding Pell Grants. But the change also put the federal government on the hot seat, as new questions arose about the terms of student loans and the heavy reliance on them. This debate placed the issue of student loan access for families like Ian's front and center.[40]

Some of our students began working to pay back their loans while they were in college, so they could stop worrying about it. Even though Norbert Webster received far more financial aid than other students in the study, thanks to the Oneida scholarship, and was able to avoid taking loans in college, he still worried about owing money:

> I haven't needed them [loans]. I think that's actually pretty cool for me because . . . my roommate does have to take out loans and he talks to me about that. Last year he had to take out a parent [PLUS] loan and then this year he took out one for himself, under his name. . . . He's so stressed about it, like what if he doesn't do well and has to drop out and pay it right away? And he's a little worried about that. But I don't think he's going to do badly because he is working a lot harder now and going to the library and stuff. It's a little weird because it's a situation I haven't been in myself to understand it, but to hear him talk about it is stressing for me. . . . It does kind of freak me out when he does talk about it because I'm thinking to myself, this could be what it's like when I do—if I do—have to [take out loans]. It does place a burden on me, getting stressed about it.

In his fourth year of college, Norbert said he wanted to study abroad but knew that his tribal scholarship did not cover those expenses. He thought about taking a small student loan to finance it but decided against it.

When I Was in College, I Worked—and So Should You

Many assume the alternative to borrowing is working. There is a common misperception that today's students are simply facing the same challenges as the students of yesteryear and should not be whining about needing to work to pay for college.

Lots of Americans feel strongly that working while in college is a positive American tradition.[41] It underscores the Protestant ethic and the American commitment to work. Thus, it is reassuring, in a way, to know that the majority of students and parents today share this belief.[42]

But the idea that, because a previous generation worked its way through college, this generation can, too, relies on crucial assumptions: that part-time jobs exist, that they pay decent wages, that those wages are enough to help students pay their bills and cover their needs, and that they are scheduled and located in ways that leave enough time left to study.

In the Wisconsin Scholars Longitudinal Study, work was a central strategy that students used in order to pay the bills. However, the character and availability of work for college students has changed, making this strategy much less reliable than it once was.

Working Today

Stacey, a young woman with brown hair falling into her eyes, sat in the second row of my Sociology of Education course at UW–Madison, watching as I delivered the term's fourth lecture. She took a few notes, nodding along, leaning forward at first, then back. As I talked and paced the room of forty-five undergraduates, it was easy to lose sight of her, as she blended in with the rest of the juniors and seniors—that is, until her head went down and she folded in a heap on her desk. Now she had my attention: she was asleep.

I was offended. Here I was, teaching at the state's flagship university, struggling to do research while teaching a full load, and this student had the nerve to nap in my class! I paced over to her and tapped her desk. She woke, and I glared at her. After class, I told her to come see me during office hours. I had no idea what I would say or what good it would do, but I did not want her to nap though my lecture again.

Three days later, Stacey came into my office and took a seat. I said hello and asked a simple question, "What is going on?" I awaited her answer, expecting a stuttered apology and little more. Maybe she thought I was boring. Maybe she and her friends had gone out too late the night before. Maybe she had been drunk. These were a few of my assumptions.

I was wrong. Copps, the grocery store located two miles from campus, pays a higher wage for employees who work the night shift. That was an offer that Stacey could not pass up. Several days a week, she left school and traveled to Copps to stock shelves from 11 P.M. until 6 A.M., before returning home to change her clothes, drink some coffee, and come to my class. She was motivated, the first in her family to attend college, and trying her best to make ends meet, but she was also exhausted. School and work were both required, but they were not coming together the way she had planned. As her professor, I knew none of this—until I asked.

Sixty-two percent of our students, who all began college with a full-time course load and a Pell Grant, worked during their first year of college (see table 10). Work was especially common among two-year college students: even though they were enrolled in college full time, 76 percent of them worked. Overall, the students in our survey averaged almost eighteen hours a week on the job, while those at two-year colleges averaged twenty-one. Most of their work (81%) took place off campus. Like Stacey, 23 percent of our students in their second year of college worked between the hours of 10 P.M. and 8 A.M. Some 20 percent of these Pell recipients worked more than twenty hours a week while taking at least twelve college credits per term.

Times have changed. In 1960, 25 percent of full-time college students between the ages of sixteen and twenty-four worked while enrolled.[43] Five decades later, national statistics show that over 70 percent of undergraduates are working (this is on average, not for Pell recipients only). Twenty percent of all undergraduate students are employed full time, year-round. Among those working part time (52% of all students), half work more than twenty hours a week (26% of all students).[44] Employment is not limited to older students—40 percent of people age sixteen to twenty-four who are enrolled in college full time are working, and 64 percent of them are clocking at least twenty hours a week.[45]

Considering the billions of dollars that the public, the students, and their families are spending on college, all this time working may be far from optimal. Too much work decreases the chances of graduating.[46] Working through college not only threatens degree completion but also crowds out social activities. Things like school-related events, organizations, clubs, or leisure time are important, yet long working hours limit a student's ability to participate, shutting out opportunities for social connections.[47] Economist Rajeev Darolia found that five or fewer hours of work per week was associated with a higher grade point average. More than fifteen hours a week had no impact on grades.[48] But sociologist Robert Bozick found that working more than twenty hours per week during the first year of college is associated with higher dropout rates.[49]

Indeed, work takes on a different meaning, and may have more negative consequences, when it is mandatory rather than optional and requires long hours. Many studies conducted over the last thirty years suggest that students who work more than twenty hours a week are less likely to graduate.[50]

Inequities in undergraduate employment mirror those in the broader population: people from families with less money work longer hours. In 2003, a study in the *Review of Higher Education* found that 52 percent of students from the bottom fifth of the family income distribution reported working extensively, compared to 37 percent of students from the highest fifth.[51] The college students working the most paid hours are the ones with the least time to spare. Students from lower-income families are more likely to struggle with academics in college so need more time to devote to classes and studying. Unlike their wealthier counterparts, Pell recipients often do not experience the type of rigorous college preparatory curricula in high school that can make much college course work a breeze. Pell recipients also tend to carry more familial obligations. The bottom line: time spent at work may reduce the odds of degree completion for Pell recipients even more than it does for wealthier students.

Typically, society pictures undergraduates working part-time jobs on weekends or full time during the summer. While some students do work these schedules, many work during class times or at night. Sometimes students work two or even three jobs at a time.

Of course, while there can be academic costs to working during college, there may be some benefits as well. Some studies indicate that working while in school teaches time management, instills students with a sense of responsibility, and builds a strong work ethic.[52] One reason for the popularity of work-study programs is that most Americans agree that some work while in school is a productive use of time and may even help keep students out of trouble and aid in their productivity. Many students we interviewed agreed, stating that working allowed them an opportunity to get their homework done. One student reflected on her job as a break from her hectic life and consequentially preferred longer shifts because, "it's better than studying at home because it's so noisy there and stuff like that." Another student said that even though juggling work and school could be a balancing act, she liked that she "could do her homework during that time, so that was really helpful." Yet other students found that work built camaraderie and social support between them and their coworkers, as in the case of a student who recounted, "I kick it with a lot of girls that I go to work with."

New to College but Experienced on the Job

Some students work in college is because they have always worked, or at least they worked during high school. Matt, a non-Hispanic white man, worked in a factory for seven months before he enrolled in a university. He explained: "I wanted a better job than working in a factory my whole life. That's why I came to college." During his first semester he took eighteen credits and expected to complete a bachelor's degree in four years. But his financial situation felt precarious, and he decided that he needed to work: "I've always had back-up money, money in my savings account that I could fall back on if I needed it, and it's kind of depleted now that I'm in college. Expenses arise, and I just feel kind of financially insecure."

After receiving nearly $10,000 in grants, Matt was still about $10,000 short of what he needed to pay for college—at least according to the official calculation, which we know often underestimates the price students really face. Matt told us that he thought every day "about every bad thing that could happen" and wondered how he would cope financially. So he accepted the maximum available student loans, $5,500, and began working forty hours per week as a certified nursing assistant at a nursing home.

In fall 2008, when our study began, the minimum wage in Wisconsin was $6.50 per hour. A year later it went up to $7.25 per hour where it remains today.[53] A student working twenty hours per week, fifty-two weeks a year at minimum wage in 2008 would gross $6,760. Many students work more than one job.

When we asked Matt if working improved his financial situation, he replied, "Not really, the bills . . . I don't know, they add up, and I wouldn't survive if I wasn't working as much."

Given his work schedule, Matt cut back on school, taking just enough credits to qualify as a full-time student: nine credits during the regular semester and a three-credit class during the winter interim period. At that point, he began to say that it might take longer than four years to finish school, depending on how much he worked. The next semester, Matt added a second job.

When asked later how long it would take for him to graduate, Matt laughed and said, "Never, at the rate I'm going." He explained that making progress toward his degree "seems like it's taking forever." Yet college still seemed worth it.

Many high school students are like Matt. In a longitudinal study that followed a group of ninth graders in Saint Paul, Minnesota, starting in 1987, sociologist Jeylan Mortimer found that working while in high school was common and seemed to positively predict college enrollment. She also found that while working in college was not positively correlated with graduating (the reverse is true)— compared to other students, those who worked on a steady basis throughout high school were much more likely to earn a bachelor's degree within seven years of high school graduation.[54]

Norbert Webster's mother encouraged him to work while in high school. She wanted him to save money so that he would not have to work during his early years of college. "Since my first year of high school [my mother] told me that we had to start saving up for school—she really did not want me to have a job while I'm here [in college] because she wanted me to focus on school. She told me to save my money for when I'm here . . . so I could get used to the environment and not worry about juggling school and work and focus." He did as he was told. In his first year of high school, Norbert took a job as a dishwasher at the hotel where his mother worked. He worked each night from 5 P.M. to 9 P.M. and then began working weekends as a housekeeper in the same hotel. During his last year of high school he worked sixteen hours a week. "I created a savings account and put $100 a week (half of my earnings) into that account from my paycheck." This enabled him to buy a used car and put the remainder toward college.

The work earnings (almost $8,000), coupled with an uncommonly generous scholarship from his tribe, made it possible for Norbert to focus on academics during the first year of college without needing to work or borrow. During the following summer, he worked ten hours a week in the accounting department at the Oneida Casino and worked weekends in housekeeping at a hotel, because he, like Matt, felt financially insecure without a cushion from some savings.

Studying While Underemployed

It was not always possible for students in our study who sought work to find jobs. Studies of undergraduate employment tend to simply measure whether students are working. But we found that among the 34 percent of our students who were not employed during their second year of college, more than half had looked for work in the last month but had been unable to find a job. According to the Bureau of Labor Statistics definitions, they were in the labor force—not out of it.[55] In 2008, the year the students in the study began college, the Wisconsin unemployment rate for eighteen- to twenty-four-year-olds with a high school diploma was 11.5 percent. A year later, the youth unemployment rate in Wisconsin jumped to almost 23 percent in 2009. It remained high during the period of this study—in 2010 it was 18 percent and in 2011 it was 24 percent. The lack of available jobs may have caused some students to focus on attaining college degrees, since they knew there were few options in the job market. At the same time, the economy made it difficult to find work needed to generate the funds to pay for school. Students who are not seeking work are not technically considered part of the workforce—while those who wish to work but cannot find it are unemployed, and those who want to work more hours but cannot get them are considered underemployed. Unemployment and underemployment experiences were common. One student felt that even though he kept applying for jobs, he was never applying at the right time. He said, "When I apply, they stop hiring and stuff or whatever, so I'm kinda always late, which kinda sucks." Underemployment, we found, was more common in Milwaukee, a problem discussed in chapter 8.

Real Work

Sometimes the work students did in college was physically demanding, reducing the energy they had available for school. Seeking to avoid loans, Nima Chaudhary worked as a certified nursing assistant at a nursing home in order to finance her degree in graphic design. She told us, "It's really hard because you have a lot of responsibility—all the people you have to care for are under your watch so you have to be really, really careful. I work the night shift from 10 P.M. until 6 A.M. And I don't really get to punch out at 6 A.M. because I still have to take out the garbage and I don't finish on time."

She wished for a different job that was "cleaner and had less back strain. I have to lift heavy people and turn them over." Before starting the second year of college, Nima left the job, explaining:

> It was so stressful. I can't take the risk of people falling. I was really scared—one time there was a resident and I was with him the whole time and he kind of slipped, and the nurse thought he fell. . . . Every time I go there I have so much nervousness and anxiety in my stomach. There are some residents who talk dirty to you. They're old and not thinking right. It wasn't worth it—it was twelve dollars an hour for the whole night shift on the weekends. My parents are disappointed because they want me to work hard so I won't have to ask them [for money] all the time. . . . I just need to get a job. I want to help my mom a lot, because I see that her hands, her wrinkled face, and feet all swollen.

Nima went to college in order to escape this sort of work. Her father was disabled, and Nima wanted to earn a college degree in order to help her family have a better life. But the family could not survive losing Nima's wages as she pursued school, and so she worked—and felt pressured to work in positions that left her too tired for school. She was facing impossible choices, and while describing them during interviews she often cried.

No Time to Spare, and No Money, Either

There is another major obstacle that undergraduates who work their way through college face. Part-time jobs involving relatively light tasks like clerking at a store or stocking grocery shelves may seem flexible, but flexibility comes with a cost—they are a form of very loose employment with no minimum weekly (or daily) hour guarantees. Researchers Charlotte Alexander and Anna Haley-Lock explain: "The reality faced by many low wage job holders ... is no longer one of *overwork*, but rather of *underwork*. As firms seek to align their labor expenditures closely with customer demand, they employ a variety of cost-cutting strategies, including replacing permanent jobs with temporary work, converting full-time to part-time employment, classifying workers as independent contractors instead of employees, and relying on 'just-in-time' scheduling to make finely tuned adjustments to workers' hours during the week, day, and evening shift."[56]

In underwork situations, the number of hours of work available changes from day to day and week to week. Workers—including student workers—may have their shifts canceled suddenly or be sent home early from a partial shift without first having earned the money they need to survive. They have to be "on call," without pay, ready to come to work at a moment's notice, and are also asked to stay late at the last minute. Workers who cannot fulfill these fast-shifting scheduling requirements may be terminated. This instability is the downside of flexibility.

While many low-income workers experience underwork and haphazard scheduling, students must grapple with the ways these phenomena interfere with school.[57] Caught in this dilemma, our students wondered if they made the right decisions. One woman asked: "Is it even worth it to work all these hours and go to school? You're supposed to be going to school to get a good job, not sitting here working all these small jobs to go to school. Do you know what I mean? That's what I never understood about college."

The combination of low, limited, and insecure hours and wages available for college students can create a substantial income problem and a simultaneous time bind, as students juggle the logistics of competing demands between work and school.[58] Class attendance is crucial for learning and for securing the grades required to make progress toward graduation, stay in college, and retain financial aid. When students miss class because of a schedule change, their professors don't simply overlook it. Attendance is expected, and absences can lead to lower grades, incompletes, or the denial of course credit. But if students instead choose school over work, they may lose the job that allows them to pay for college.

Real Lives

Student work is not merely "low wage," it is low paid. As Chloe Johnson learned, this makes it hard to make ends meet, and wreaks havoc on the pursuit of a degree.

When Chloe started college she tried to avoid going into debt by working not one but two jobs. She had already sold her horse to help cover her family's expected family contribution, and hard work was nothing new to her. "When I graduated from high school I had two jobs—PetSmart and the A&W Drive-In—and I picked up a third job at a bait shop during the summer. . . . My idea of a day off was working only one job. Otherwise, I was working every day."

As she began the first year of a vet technician program at a technical college, Chloe thought that her jobs would align with her class schedule because she usually worked evenings. PetSmart required her to do a variety of tasks that she felt competent doing, including cashiering, stocking, and grooming dogs and cats. Having worked for the company for two years, she felt like a senior employee plus she enjoyed the work since it gave her a chance to spend time with animals. But Chloe was unable to find a job in the franchise's location nearest to campus and instead had to commute to a store thirty miles away. Her commute home from work took fifty-five minutes. Chloe found a weekend job at Kohl's Department Stores, closer to her apartment. But the Kohl's job was not a replacement for PetSmart. Because each job paid just above minimum wage, Chloe needed them both.

From September until November, Chloe spent hours in the car, driving from home to school to work and back home again. She began her days with a half a pot of coffee. "I get down whatever I can before I have to leave. Some mornings I wake up and keep hitting the snooze button. All of a sudden, in ten minutes I am supposed to be out the door. I get up, get dressed, throw on whatever I can find, brush my teeth, and leave. I usually don't eat breakfast—I am just not hungry."

Here's what Chloe's schedule looked like. Each day she drove forty-five minutes to school. "On Tuesdays and Thursdays I start [classes] at 7:30 A.M. and go until 3:30 P.M., and on Mondays, Wednesdays, and Fridays I start at 9 A.M. and go until 12." She then drove thirty-five or forty minutes to work, where she remained until 10 or 10:30 P.M., before driving almost an hour home. On the weekends, she worked as well. Days off were rare.

Soon, juggling full-time work (forty hours a week), twelve hours a week of driving, and a full course load began to take its toll. There was left very little time for studying. "More than a couple of times I would fall asleep during my 7:30 A.M. class. I would get there and I am trying to stay awake and doing the 'head bob,' and before you know it my head is in my book. And every once in a while I woke up with a puddle of drool."

Chloe's grades began to suffer, and she worried about whether she was taking too many courses. She went ahead and applied for a loan, hoping it would help out. And then in mid-November, PetSmart cut her hours. "I have no idea why. I just wasn't scheduled, and that made me nervous," she reported. She used the loan that had just arrived to pay her bills and did not immediately seek another job. But it was too late in the semester to repair the damage done to her grades.

Chloe's approach felt necessary, but it was risky. Not only did her long work hours compromise her grades, but they also put her financial aid in jeopardy.

What about Work-Study?

The Federal Work-Study Program is intended to help students work to pay for college while providing only minimal distractions from school. An on-campus job is in many ways an ideal situation. Compared to an off-campus gig, the location reduces commuting time. Campus employers are often more able to offer students steady hours (at least during the term), and they are usually willing to align regular schedules with student course work. The wages earned in work-study are part of the student's financial aid package and do not count as part of the federal needs analysis in the next year's aid application. And in the best scenarios, on-campus jobs help students connect with faculty and staff in ways that enhance their academic programs.

While the premise of Federal Work-Study is simple and promising, securing a work-study job is difficult and the jobs do not always pay off as planned. This is especially true at community colleges, where the number of eligible students and their total financial need simply dwarf total work-study funds. The federal formula that determines institutional allocations has not been revised in many decades.[59] Inequities have emerged. Today, far more resources flow to private colleges and universities.[60] Thus, while some Ivy League schools have sufficient resources for work-study and employ Pell recipients to clean bathrooms and residence halls using those resources (rather than hiring unionized staff),[61] the University of Wisconsin–Milwaukee is able to provide only about one in ten eligible students with a work-study position. Of the six students profiled in this book—all of whom had significant financial need—only Sophie was offered work-study funds from the financial aid office. Just 12 percent of our students received that support, including just 2 percent of students who, like Ian, went to college in Milwaukee. Sophie's institution, which has far fewer Pell recipients compared to other schools, has the largest work-study budget on a per-student basis.

Even after taking loans, Sophie needed to work (since her family had financial challenges not included in the federal needs analysis) and she was fortunate that her university had sufficient work-study funds available to help her.

Many students rightly call work-study "potential" money. It is allocated in the financial aid package. But just because a student has work-study funds in their financial aid package does not mean that she will be able to use those funds to cover her expenses. Getting a check from work-study funds first requires that the student identify and secure a work-study job. If she does not do this by midyear, institutions typically rescind the offer and reallocate the funds to other students. Since the clock is ticking, getting a work-study job quickly is especially important, but the benefits of work-study are often unclear to students. The process of finding a work-study job can be confusing, too. Consider these two exchanges:

INTERVIEWER: Did you get work-study in your financial aid package?
STUDENT: Yes, I did. That's $2,400 they figure into my package. But I haven't gotten any of that because I'm not working.
INTERVIEWER: How did that happen?
STUDENT: They actually didn't offer me a job. I applied to some jobs to try and get one but I didn't end up receiving one.

The student above was expecting his university to provide information about available work-study positions and help him secure one. He is not alone. Another student explained why she did not have a work-study position: "I had work-study last year, and basically if you don't use it, it evaporates. You don't get it. I have work-study for this semester as well and for next semester. I'm kind of irritated with the concept because I'm kind of bitter about not being able to get a job through campus housing, and I can't use my work-study at Forever 21. I asked them, and they won't let me." We asked if she tried to use university information services to find a work-study job. She responded:

Well, there is a website that posts university jobs, nonuniversity jobs and it indicates if work-study is required. I looked at all of them. There was a couple that I was going to apply to. I got lazy and I never applied to them. [My job at] Forever 21 was a spur of the moment thing. I kind of just seized it. But by the time I was hired, and I asked them about work-study, they were like, "Yeah, it doesn't happen that way. We don't have work-study." So work-study to me—I don't know if I have the wrong concept of what exactly it is—but to me the only real perk that I saw out of it is that you don't have to pay taxes on it, which is great. That's huge, but besides that, I'm still going to get a job, and I'm still trying to get money whether or not it's work-study money or just a paycheck.

Work-study allocations are also limited on a per-student basis, which means that a work-study student is a good deal for a university employer until the funds run out.[62] Since the work-study salary comes from a separate account than other departmental expenses, faculty and researchers like myself often hire work-study students. We pay little, and we are happy with the arrangement—until the funds expire. At that point, the employer often ends the position without warning. The student, who does not know how the funding works (and frequently does not know about the employer subsidy), often doesn't know what happened. The job simply ends.

The Upside Downside

Despite an American cultural commitment to hard work and a popular sense that working during college is expected, earning too much can result in students losing eligibility for federal financial aid. For students, the loss of aid can feel sudden and unexpected. Their ability to finish school may be jeopardized.

Sophie learned this the hard way. Her mom was unemployed when she began college, so even though the federal government estimated that her family could contribute $3,939 to the cost of her college, they could not. Sophie had to cover it. Given her financial needs, she took federal and private loans, worked on campus at a work-study job, and also found a job at the local mall for thirty hours a week. The job frustrated Sophie because the shift schedule was rarely announced even a week in advance. Her hours fluctuated, making it hard to plan for school, hard to participate in on-campus activities, and especially hard to pay the rent. The more she worked, the less involved she could be in campus clubs, but when there were fewer shifts available at work she did not have enough money to get by. She and her boyfriend decided to live together and share resources to try to help each other out, but he was laid off twice from part-time jobs.

Sophie got a little relief midway through her first year of college, when the Fund for Wisconsin Scholars selected her to receive its $3,500 grant. She noted that this private philanthropy was paying for about half of her grant aid. "They're giving me this—I should be grateful, and I am."

But then Sophie got caught in the downside of income gains. During the year, her mom finally secured a good job that paid $35,401 a year, causing an increase in her expected family contribution to $6,323. But that was just the beginning of a cascade of changes. The financial aid letter for the second year of college told the tale. Her mom's income made Sophie ineligible for the Pell Grant and the Wisconsin Higher Education Grant. Moreover, since the Fund for Wisconsin Scholars Grant required Pell eligibility, she lost that grant as well. To top it off, the grant she got for good grades in high school was for the first year of college only. The nearly $7,000 in grants she'd received the prior year were no longer part of her aid package. So, for her second year of college, Sophie's own share of the bill (even now that her mother could cover the expected family contribution) had increased by about $3,000. She didn't know what to do: "I don't look at the numbers; I just hide the numbers under my pillow. . . . The way that it [the financial aid] changed so much from last year to this year, I honestly don't even know what to expect for next year. I guess I'll just wait and be surprised because I just . . . I honestly . . . I don't even know how to begin to predict what they . . . how it's going to change."

Sophie had reached high for college—she was attending arguably one of the best schools in the state—but the promises of financial aid did not match the reality.

When you're in high school you just think you'll get financial aid in college. Well, yeah, you can get financial aid, but there's still a lot more that aid does not cover that you have to come up with. I think it's a little "catch"—[it seems like] all financial aid will take care of you and it doesn't. There are a lot of things that you don't really realize, like book expenses and food expenses and all this stuff. You don't really necessarily think about until you have to pay for it, and then all of a sudden you're like "whoa, whoa, whoa."

The federal government is not out to get students like Sophie. The requirement that students refile the FAFSA for each year of college, even when they remain enrolled at the same institution, is part of an effort to ensure that students with need—and only students with need—receive federal grant aid. An annual look at families' finances allows financial aid officers to identify students who need more help and to remove aid from those who seem like they need less help. But students like Sophie can be caught off guard. Without grants, they and their parents can only turn to loans and longer work hours.

"Being in school is just exhausting. Mentally and physically, it's just exhausting," Sophie reported midway through her second year. But she felt she had to persist: "As far as I'm concerned, I don't have a choice [about continuing in school] because I am on a lot of loans to be here, and, if I don't finish, those loans become due immediately. That's a lot of money that I don't have. [. . .] And there's only one college graduate in my entire family on both sides, which is a lot of people. We have over a hundred people, and there's only one college graduate, so I'm going to make it two."

That semester, Sophie's income fell several hundred dollars short of her expenses each month. Her mom tried to help by paying for her daughter's health insurance and the cell phone bill, and Sophie looked for another job. "There's only so much she [my mother] can do," she said. Meanwhile, financial pressures were always front and center. "I've become this money freak," Sophie sighed. "I'm always worried about money."

When Sophie's mom tried to get a better job, she most likely did not know that the financial aid system exacts an implicit tax on parental income.[63] It is easy to assume that the more money parents earn, the less expensive college is for their children. But this is not what happened to Sophie. When parents' salaries increase while students are enrolled in college, students are financially harmed unless their parents are able to make up for lost financial aid with an equal contribution to college expenses. More specifically, parents need to cover both the expected family contribution (which rises along with income) and the lost financial aid in order to hold the student harmless. In other words, since an extra dollar of parental income reduces the child's college grants by at least twenty-two cents, then the students' costs will rise if the parent does not spend at least twenty-two cents of the new dollar of income on college. Many parents, especially those who have accrued debt while unemployed, cannot or do not do this.[64] In those cases, when parental income increases, the net price the student must pay also increases.[65]

When a Pell recipient's expected family contribution rises during college, it may be a sign of trouble. Forty percent of our students who attended a public university saw their expected family contribution increase between their first and second year of college. The median increase was $1,215. Between their second and third years, 36 percent of those who remained enrolled saw an increase with a median of $1,312. Twenty to thirty percent of those students experiencing increases in their expected family contribution each year lost their Pell Grant and all other aid conditional on Pell eligibility.[66] Unless their families were willing and able to pay both the increased expected family contribution and covered the lost grant aid, those students' net price for college grew more expensive. The perverse result is that children whose parents are unemployed worry about losing aid if their families' income increases.[67]

The federal needs analysis pays no attention to family debt. Maybe this is because parents might go into debt to help their children qualify for more financial aid, or perhaps debt is omitted because federal aid formulas were originally determined in the years before the recent explosion in personal debt. At the same time, the federal needs analysis uses just a single prior year of income from tax returns, failing to make the sorts of distinctions that social scientists have repeatedly found matter to children's educational opportunities. Families living with persistently low incomes for decades experience very different circumstances than those who suffer a temporary loss of income. Lower middle-class families with steady incomes provide different opportunities than families with spottier employment records who circulate in and out of needing the social safety net for support.[68]

The blunt and clumsy manner in which the financial aid system fails to take into account these nuanced issues can create stress for families. One woman sat down for an interview with us and made an announcement: "A month ago my dad got a job! It was just like *ta- da!*" The interviewer congratulated her and then asked, 'How do you think that is going to change things?' 'It's really helped him . . . he feels like a new person. And my mom has been working less because of it, which is fantastic!" She explained how her mother now had time to spend with her sister, which was important for the family. But in the next breath, her tone changed and she began to cry: "But as far as what else has changed, there is kind of like this fear now. My dad's worried because all that money I got from financial aid was because he was unemployed, and now he's scared because he is employed I'm not going to get that again. But just because he's employed doesn't mean they have any money. They can't pay for my college. . . . So it's like a bittersweet thing, really completely reversed." Today's financial aid system leads undergraduates to worry about the adverse side effects of their parents' good fortunes.

After parsing the complex systems students must navigate to pay for college, let's look at the students themselves. Are they to blame, as many policymakers allege? Are they making poor personal, academic, and financial choices?

5

On Their Own

What kind of decisions do students make when the grants, loans, and money they earn from employment aren't enough?

Our students tried lots of things. Many tried to cut costs, making changes to what they purchased and how they spent their time. Some tried to add more hours of work. Some were saved by unexpected interventions. And others seemed to get in their own way, making difficult situations worse.

With thousands of dollars in unmet need as they began school, financial challenges emerged for many students right away. Midway through the first semester, 78 percent of students we surveyed said that they were having at least a little difficulty paying their bills, with 25 percent having a lot of difficulty. Many were surprised. About one in three indicated that they were "having more problems affording college than I expected."

Most saw the writing on the wall. Almost 90 percent of students were at least a little upset or worried that they did not have enough money to pay for the things they needed in order to attend college. Forty percent were very or extremely upset. Just 9 percent of students felt confident that they could pay for college and resolve any financial challenges they would face without needing to drop out. Conversely, when we asked the students to rate their level of worry about not having enough money to pay for the things they needed in order to attend college on a 1–5 scale (with 5 being the most worried), 40 percent rated their level of worry at least a 4.

Table 11. Actions taken due to lack of funds in the first year of college: WSLS students

	Percentage
Did not buy all required books and supplies	14
Did without a computer	18
Reduced utility usage	21
Put off paying bills	22
Postponed medical or dental care	23
Increased amount of time spent working	38
Borrowed money; used credit cards more	39
Stopped or cut back on driving	49
Changed food shopping or eating habits	70
Cut back on social activities/entertainment	80

Source. WSLS data.

Note. Sample includes WSLS students who responded to the first-year survey questions on financial adjustments (n = 1,997).

Money troubles directly affect schoolwork when they lead students to forgo the books or supplies they need for class. During their first semester of college, 14 percent of students did not buy some required books or supplies because they could not afford them, and 18 percent did without a computer (see table 11).

For Pell recipients, making ends meet in college requires careful planning and work. Generally, students devoted a great deal of care and attention to stretching limited resources. One woman who received a maximum Pell Grant described how she spent the living expenses check she received after tuition and fees were paid:

> I don't spend it on luxury items, I don't buy stuff that I just want. I actually never really have, unless there's a need for it. Three weeks ago, I went and got some nice black pants, which you need for college business, for interviews, etc. It's my only pair of black pants and I got a nice button-up shirt because you need to look nice for interviews. Other than that it's just, you know, dues for the sorority or stuff if I need it for classes or for college. I try not to go out and buy food too much, I don't spend a lot on food, but I do try to buy like some applesauce and milk. Just breakfast items. I do have some snack items, hot chocolate, but other than that it's just . . . I can get by without buying luxury items.

Even a clear-headed, focused student like Norbert Webster who had almost all of his college costs covered found it hard to feel financially secure. By his second year of college, Norbert began working in order to have spending money and savings for emergencies. His search for a part-time job was extensive, since he wanted to work only on weekends because he did not want to disrupt his studies: "I'm a little nervous about how to work out the schedule since I have this routine and I don't want to affect it. Right now on the weekends all I do is read and hang out with a buddy in the dorm. So it's going to be a little different because on weekends I'm not going to be able to do as much schoolwork, so I'm going to have to get more of it done during the week. So I'm a little worried about it, but I hope it plays out well."

Norbert's concerns were justified. When he started working in the fall of his second year, he was scheduled for twenty-five hours a week, working weekends plus Tuesday and Thursday evenings. He reported that it was "too much." "I would need to study for class or do homework but I had to work until 9:30 P.M. and go to the library after that, studying for three or four hours." After several months, Norbert reduced his work hours to fifteen per week, cutting his weekly take-home pay from $150 to ninety dollars. He was lucky his employer allowed this, and even more fortunate he could make ends meet on the lower amount. "It was still fine because I was just saving for my 'consumer money' that I would spend on video games and chips and all of that fun college stuff." To save money, Norbert moved in with roommates off campus and learned to cook.

The majority of our students (60%) tried to make do without credit cards, even though at the time almost four in five Americans used at least one.[1] One in four students had one credit card, 9 percent had two or three, and just 6 percent had more than three cards. First-generation students were much more likely than continuing-generation students to have and use a credit card to cope with financial needs (43% of children of high school graduates vs. 30% of children with bachelor's degree–holding parents).

The number of credit cards a student held did not vary according to their expected family contribution, but the size of their balances did. Seventy-six percent of Pell recipients with a nonzero expected family contribution owed less than $100 on their cards, compared to 58 percent of students with a zero expected family contribution. The latter group was three times as likely to owe between $500 and $1,000. Clearly, students with fewer resources looked to credit when other options ran out.

Getting Lucky

Many of our students spent their first semester of college muddling through, doing the best they could. But midway through the term, 40 percent of them (twelve hundred students in all) got a surprise in the mail. A letter from the Fund for Wisconsin Scholars revealed that additional grant aid was on the way. None of the students knew why—they knew only what the letter told them.

The Wisconsin Scholars Grant provided welcome relief for those who received it. Sophie Schmidt's unmet need (since she had already accepted all federal loans) was (temporarily) cut to less than $400. The grant diminished Nima Chaudhary's unmet need by more than one-third, and reduced Ian Williams's by a little more than half. They were happy and surprised. Nima said that this was the second most important lottery she had ever won—the first was the visa lottery won by her mother that enabled them to leave Nepal for America.[2]

Good fortune continued to shape the course of Ian's college experience, making it increasingly possible for him to make it through college despite inadequate financial aid. A counselor at his school nominated him for a private scholarship aimed at encouraging men of color to go into business administration, and he won. As the years went by, college became easier and easier for him to afford.

Chloe Johnson was not so lucky. While she, too, had been selected for the Wisconsin Scholars Grant, she never opened the letter. It was probably lost in the shuffle as she ran from home to work to school. In any case, she was no longer enrolled by the time the funds arrived.

Text of Award Letter from the Fund for Wisconsin Scholars

October 22, 2008

Dear Student,

Congratulations! We are delighted that you were selected to receive a grant from the Fund for Wisconsin Scholars, Inc. (FFWS) for the 2008–2009 academic year. The FFWS was established by John P. and Tashia F. Morgridge to provide grants to graduates of Wisconsin public high schools to attend colleges and universities of the University of Wisconsin and Wisconsin Technical College Systems. You can view more information about the FFWS at www.ffws.org. The recipients of the FFWS grants were chosen from a group of eligible students through a random selection process completed at the office of the Wisconsin Higher Educational Aids Board (HEAB). The amount of your grant is $3500/year if you are a four year student and $1800/year if you are a two year student; you will receive half of the grant in the fall semester and half in the spring semester. The grant is available to you for up to ten semesters, if you continue to meet the eligibility criteria. We hope to maintain active communication with you throughout your college experience and beyond. Our dream for you is that you will successfully complete a degree and leave college with less debt than you might have otherwise had and with the skills, knowledge and willingness to contribute to our society.

There are a few steps that you need to take to accept and receive this grant.

1. verify your eligibility
2. acknowledge and accept the grant and
3. consent to the release of your high school and college academic and financial information to the FFWS from: your current school, the Department of Public Instruction (DPI) and the HEAB.
4. Return the completed Form in the envelope provided.

Once I receive your completed and signed document, I will send you instructions to enroll in our secure, recipient information system on the web. This will be the means by which I communicate with you most often and by which you can communicate with other recipients. It will also be the system where your academic and financial data will be stored. Once you are enrolled, your school will be notified of your receipt of the FFWS grant and the money will be sent to your school for distribution to you. We wish you the best in your college endeavors and look forward to meeting you.

Are the Wrong Students Going to College?

Of course, not all of our students made responsible financial decisions. As with many adolescents, they were sometimes not good money managers. Were it not for financial aid, college would have been entirely out of reach for Tyler Olson. He received the maximum Pell Grant ($4,731), the Wisconsin Higher Education Grant ($2,980), and $1,400 from the state's Talent Incentive Program. Still, Tyler had to come up with about $5,600 to cover the costs his university estimated he needed to get through his first year (and, as noted earlier, estimates of that sort are often low). He took out a federally subsidized loan of $3,500 and planned to work to come up with the rest.

It was not easy. During Tyler's first two years of college he put off paying bills and postponed the medical care associated with his blood disorder. He tried to lower his bills by reducing driving, cutting back on food shopping, and forgoing a laptop and books he needed for school. He turned to credit cards to finance what he could not afford; by the second year of college he carried a balance of $1,000. He worked an array of jobs, including a gig for Yahoo, a stint as a bouncer at a local bar, and a roofing job, but he never held one job for very long. Sometimes he donated plasma, for which he received twenty dollars per visit. Roofing and siding work was more lucrative, paying twenty-five dollars an hour and offering seven or eight hours of work a day, but it was hard, physical labor.

Stress took a toll on Tyler's health. He slept about four hours a night and sometimes had trouble staying awake during the day. He needed to nap almost every day and said that he sometimes didn't have enough energy to get things done. When he began college, he judged himself as extremely good at organizing his time and schedule, but a year later reported that he was performing those duties only "slightly well." "I planned it out where I had enough financial aid to budget $300 a month in a three-bedroom house to cover everything from heat, water, electricity, cable, Internet, and I'd still have about $400 or $500 a month to spend. So, about $150 each month was extra cash that I could just screw around with from the financial aid I got."

Clearly, budgeting was a challenge for Tyler, but it was a problem exacerbated by his lifestyle. He was a young man sorting out who he was and struggling to create an identity while grappling with the desire to have a good time. During the time we spent getting to know Tyler, he found himself in what he called "trouble" at least eight times. There was a disorderly conduct charge for a car accident during his first year of college. He spent several nights in the county jail for infractions, including fighting, deer hunting without a license, and a ticket following a night of drinking that same year, and a ticket for driving while intoxicated. In a way, Tyler was lucky—he was never severely punished by the criminal justice system or his university, and he escaped real tragedy. The story of his life as he told it was a series of near-fails. The researcher who interviewed him remarked, "You're always getting out of things—this happens, and that happens, and then something else happens." He replied, "Everybody who knows me says that, and they always say that someday it is going to run out."

Sometimes, especially when he was low on cash, Tyler lamented the choices he had made:

It seems like every time I get my financial aid money I always want to do something good, but I always have to pay off something I screwed up. My aid money is going towards paying for my rent and my car—and me being dumb. On a Friday night I'll have five to ten beers and then between five to ten shots before I leave to go out, and the same number wherever I end up at. But I don't really like going to bars, and I don't really like drinking. You're not going see me on a Thursday coming home from school or work, if I had a job, and sitting down to crack open a beer. I don't drink like that. I just drink at parties. . . . I've just got to stop screwing up because that's really taking a lot of my money away from me. It's my fault—if I wouldn't have gotten in trouble, I would have been fine.[3]

In order to pay the repair bills for his 1993 Audi and his mounting legal fees, during his second year of college Tyler took a private loan from Campus Door (offered by Lehman Brothers), put more charges on his credit card, and borrowed money from his father and grandparents. At the same time, he was proud of the fact that he regularly declined the federal unsubsidized loans offered to him and was pleased that his total federal borrowing was low, especially when compared to his brother's. His brother went to one of the state's private colleges, and Tyler often spoke of the difference between his debt (over $100,000) and Tyler's own (just over $10,000 by his third year of college). Of course, that $10,000 federal debt did not include the other sources of credit on which he leaned. Paradoxically, Tyler spoke repeatedly in interviews about his credit score, which was a 745 when he was twenty years old, something he was proud of and closely monitored.[4]

Students like Tyler make some people who work in the financial aid system wonder if the system is working. A seasoned financial aid officer with more than thirty years' experience told me what she had seen happen: "I'm sure we have made strides, but when you look at the big picture, I'm not sure if we've gone forward or backward. Tuition then was nowhere what it is today. Financial aid was really meant to cover tuition and fees and books. This whole thing about living expenses—it was there but that money was meant for direct educational expenses. With the expansion of the loan program the whole thing just mushroomed, where now I see students using financial aid as their income. I struggle with that, I do."

Is she right? Should students who need funds in order to make ends meet participate in college? Are they cut out for the college experience? This aid officer echoed concerns we heard repeatedly in interviews around the country:[5]

> I wonder if higher education isn't trying to be all things to all people. From where I sit I don't know that everyone is college material. I'm not saying that in a negative way—everyone has their gifts and their abilities. But sometimes we push people into avenues that aren't quite right for them.... There's a group of students that has such life issues that their concentration, their focus, isn't really on the academic experience. So they come and start classes, and borrow a lot of money.... They get stuck at a

certain point in time, they have to exit, and take care of whatever life things are going on for them . . . sometimes I feel like we have become a halfway house.

Another financial aid administrator that I spoke with expressed similar sentiments: "At eighteen, incoming freshman today are younger than they were ten or twenty years ago. They are coming to college and don't have the financial piece figured out. There are lots of ways to figure out how the bill is going to get paid, but there shouldn't be any students that don't know how to pay that bill as of September 1 and a lot of students don't know and don't pay." Some students, aid administrators report, are "grateful" while other students "think they are owed" financial aid and do not behave responsibly with it.

It is hard to say whether Tyler is exceptional. We met very few students like him in our study, but it is possible that people like him were less willing to volunteer for interviews. If these are exceptional cases, then one policy question is whether we ought to take actions to deal with rare "bad apples."[6] What we can say for sure is that we saw a wider array of situations where students were left with far too few resources to cover their living expenses, and this rarely seemed to be their fault.

Groceries or Graduation?

Nationally, about half of all Pell recipients at public colleges and universities are from families living below the poverty line, and many of these students come to college to escape the material hardships they have long lived with (see table 4). Forty percent of our students said that as children at least sometimes they had to "wear second-hand clothes," and one in four reported that at least sometimes there "wasn't enough to eat at home." Furthermore, 34 percent said that there was not always "someone available to care for and protect" them when they were young.

What these students often did not realize was that attending college without sufficient resources meant that they would continue to go without their basic needs met. For others, they would experience situational poverty for the first time. This is part of the new economics of college.

During his first three years of college, Ian Williams lived at home with his family, where no one had enough to eat. He rationalized this as a continuation of his childhood. "Sometimes we don't [have enough money to eat] but I just feel like I'm used to that. I'm used to not eating a lot so . . . another person might find it a problem but to me, it's not, because I'm used to it."

When asked about her main challenges on a daily basis, another undergraduate attending a public university told us, "Eating. That's my main issue . . . money, shelter, and clothing."

She was not alone. Twenty-four percent of our students indicated that in the past month they did not have enough money to buy food, ate less then they felt they should, or cut the size of their meals because there was not enough money (see table 12). When asked if they ever went without eating for an entire day because they lacked enough money for food, 6 percent of students said yes.[7] Of course, students need not be hungry all the time in order to be food insecure. When an individual has to make trade-offs between food and other essential living expenses, such as paying for housing or medical expenses, it is also a sign of food insecurity.

Ours is not the first study to identify food insecurity among undergraduates, but the topic has received scant attention from

Table 12. Rates of food insecurity since beginning college: WSLS students

	Percentage
Any food insecurity in fall 2009 (answered yes to any question below)	24
Did you not eat for a whole day because there wasn't enough money for food?	6
Did you cut the size of your meals or skip meals because there wasn't enough money for food?	19
Did you eat less than you felt you should because there wasn't enough money for food?	19

Source. WSLS data.

Note. Sample includes WSLS students who responded to the second-year survey questions on food insecurity, $n = 1,400$.

researchers and policymakers. After discovering food and housing insecurity in Wisconsin, my team of researchers set out to examine it further at community colleges around the country. We partnered with the Association of Community College Trustees, the nonprofit organization Single Stop, and the Healthy Minds Study at the University of Michigan and fielded a survey at ten community colleges in Louisiana, Pennsylvania, California, Wyoming, New Jersey, New York, and Wisconsin. We had a very limited budget and so conducted the survey online without using monetary incentives to help increase response rates. Of the forty-eight thousand students surveyed, 4,312 students responded—a 9 percent response rate. This was low, of course, but the characteristics of respondents looked very similar to community college students nationally, and if anything, it would seem likely that we would miss hungry and/or homeless students, who hardly have time to answer surveys. Nevertheless, the survey revealed that one in five students was hungry, and 13 percent were homeless.[8]

Indeed, studies at colleges around the United States and abroad suggest that college students experience food insecurity at a higher rate than the general public, but incidence rates vary by location.[9] At the University of Alabama, 14 percent of students alter their food intake due to resource limitations and an additional 20 percent are anxious about their food supply, and at the University of Hawaii, 21 percent of students reduce their food intake and an additional 24 percent are anxious about getting enough to eat.[10]

The incidence of food insecurity is unevenly distributed. Racial/ethnic minority students, those with low incomes, employed students, and parents are more likely to be food insecure than their more advantaged peers.[11] A 2011 survey conducted at the City University of New York (CUNY) by public health researchers Nicholas Freudenberg and his colleagues found that almost 40 percent of students in that urban system were suffering from food insecurity. They wrote: "Students reporting household incomes of less than $20,000 a year (about 26% of all CUNY undergraduates) were more than twice as likely to report food insecurity as those with household incomes of more than $50,000 a year. Students who support themselves financially were 1.6 times as likely to report food insecurity as those not supporting themselves. Students working more than twenty hours per week had a higher rate of food insecurity than those who did not work."[12]

Those who work directly with students, thankfully, notice these problems. My colleague Wick Sloane, professor of English at Bunker Hill Community College, sent me an update from Boston toward the end of 2013. At his campus, there is a food pantry, and a national organization called Single Stop helps student sign up for food stamps.

> Last Friday, a student who said he was homeless asked me how he could register for classes without an address. "Have you had anything to eat today?" I asked. This is a question many colleagues ask all the time. He had not. I gave him money to go to the cafeteria, and I told him to buy two sandwiches. I know students will often not take as much food as they need. This student brought me one of the two sandwiches. I gave that back to him. Another who had told me, "I guess you could tell that I haven't eaten since yesterday," took only some juice. With encouragement, she accepted a hot dog, which she ate, and three sandwiches that she said she would take home to her children.[13]

At New York University, professors are writing about the "big squeeze" placed on their students because of high college costs. A recent report quotes a third-year undergraduate: "I live on two dollars to five dollars a day. That means two meals a day, and incredibly unhealthy food. I'm hungry all the time. Being so hungry while you're trying to work two jobs to pay your rent and still keep up with your coursework is practically impossible—and more common than you would ever think at a university like this."[14] After years of watching students struggle on his campus, Sloane has written repeatedly to the U.S. Department of Education with this request: "One peanut butter sandwich per school day for each of the nine million students on a Pell Grant. How many of these are the same students who were eligible for free and reduced lunch in high school? No one knows and no one is counting. How many are from households on food stamps? No one's asking, either. Why not, then, 45 million peanut butter sandwiches at colleges each week? Until we come up with a better idea."[15]

Researcher Minhtuyen Mai analyzed the challenges facing our food insecure students and learned that the primary obstacles they encountered were a lack of time to get food they could afford (70%) and insufficient funds (58%). Just 14 percent of these students were receiving food stamps.[16]

The problem is that when a student is hungry, she has difficulty learning. Madeline Pumariega, now chancellor of the Florida College System, told me when she was president of Miami Dade College's Wolfson campus, "When a student is hungry, he does not feel safe, and it is hard to help him synthesize class material. We have to meet students' basic needs in order for them to fully concentrate on assimilating the information in a class in a way that they can apply it, learn, and take it forward."[17] She is right. Studies of elementary and secondary school students show an inverse relationship between food insecurity and academic achievement.[18] In higher education, just one study has examined the relationship between food insecurity and academic achievement, using data from two community colleges in Maryland. Fifty-six percent of students in the sample were food insecure, and food-insecure students were 22 percent less likely to report a 3.5–4.0 GPA rather than a 2.0–2.49 GPA.[19] One student told us that it was difficult to concentrate in class because of hunger pangs. Others described what it was like to watch students eat in the school cafeteria when they could not afford to dine there. Students who spent their childhoods worrying about food continued to have those worries during college. A key difference is that while the National School Lunch Program was available to them during high school, there was no such program for them in college.

Lack of food is more than a distraction. Hunger reduces the ability of some students to take advantage of the opportunity to attend college. For example, a woman said that if she had more money she "would not be looking at other peoples' faces when they're eating. . . . I can't focus, can't be myself . . . going to school is a waste of time for me." In some cases, students struggled with food insecurity after turning down loans.

Unfortunately, none of the colleges or universities our students attended had a food pantry while they were in school. Things have changed since then, as one by one University of Wisconsin campuses have begun offering this service. There is now a College and University Food Bank Alliance, with chapters all over the country, cofounded by student affairs professionals Clare Cady and Nate Smyth-Tyge.[20] The nationwide network of food banks, Feeding America, reports that one in ten of its 45.5 million clients are students.[21] Organizations such as Single Stop and the Working Families Success Network are helping community colleges develop these services, responding to calls for help like this one from CUNY chancellor Matthew Goldstein: "One of the saddest moments that I have experienced recently occurred at a Council of Presidents meeting when some presidents indicated to me and other members of the chancellery that more and more students appearing on their campuses are hungry. They have not had breakfast or may have missed a meal the night before. In light of the difficult economic times facing very low income students, I have asked the Office of Student Affairs to develop . . . programs to focus on issues of hunger, nutrition and homelessness."[22]

Indeed, nearly 20 percent of our students also experienced housing insecurity. The FAFSA recently began asking students if they were homeless—in order to say yes, students had to file paperwork to verify their claim—and in 2012–13, at least fifty-eight thousand students said yes.[23] We asked our students if they were ever unable to pay their rent or utilities during the past year. Sixteen percent of students indicated they were unable to pay their rent, and 17 percent were unable to pay their utilities at least once during the past year (see table 13). Students were also given a list of common housing problems (e.g., incidence of loud noises or pests; leaking roof; broken plumbing, heating, electrical system, or windows; and holes in

Table 13. Housing situation since beginning college: WSLS students

	Percentage
Was there ever a time in the past twelve months when you were unable to:	
Pay your rent or mortgage on time?	16
Pay the gas, oil, or electric bill on time?	17
Are there any of the following conditions present where you currently live?	
Regular loud noises from the neighbors or from outside	44
Problems with pests such as rats, mice, roaches, or other insects	7
A leaking roof or ceiling	3
Broken heating system	4
Broken window glass or windows that can't shut	5
Exposed electrical wires in the finished areas of your home	2
A toilet, hot water heater, or other plumbing that doesn't work	4
Holes in the walls or ceiling, or cracks wider than the edge of a dime	11
Holes in the floor big enough for someone to catch their foot on	1
How safe do you feel where you currently live?	
Extremely safe	26
Very safe	56
Somewhat safe	16
A little bit safe	2
Not at all safe	1

Source. WSLS data.

Note. Sample includes WSLS students who responded to the second-year survey questions on housing insecurity, *n* = 1,400.

the walls or floor) and asked to indicate if the condition was present where they currently live. The most common issue was regular loud noises (44% of students), followed by holes in the walls or ceiling, or cracks wider than the edge of a dime (11% of students) and problems with pests such as rats, mice, roaches, or other insects (7% of students).

We also asked students to report on their sleep. Nearly 30 percent of students reported having restless sleep for three or more days in the past week. Ten percent indicated that they took medicine to help them sleep at least once a week, and the same percentage had trouble staying awake every day or almost every day in the past week. Eighteen percent rated their sleep quality as fairly or very bad (see table 14).

The importance of sleep is underscored by a "preponderance of scientific evidence [showing] that human perception, cognition, and decision making suffer when people are sleep deprived."[24] Periods

Table 14. Sleep quality since beginning college: WSLS students

	Percentage
Restless sleep 3+ days in past week	29
Sleep quality is fairly or very bad	18
Take medicine to help sleep at least once a week	10
Had trouble staying awake during the day almost every day or every day in past week	10

Source. WSLS data.

Note. Sample includes WSLS students who responded to the second-year survey questions on sleep, *n* = 1,400.

of sleep longer or shorter than seven to eight hours per night have been shown to be associated with learning and memory problems, depression, obesity, and accidents.[25] These relationships have been identified not only in correlational studies but also in experimental studies where sleep deprivation is induced; such studies have found negative impacts of both acute and chronic sleep loss on cognitive performance.[26]

Experts state that, in order to be optimally alert, adolescents need 9.25 hours of sleep per night through their early twenties.[27] While studies of sleep among college students are uncommon,[28] a nationally representative study of adults found that 28 percent sleep less than seven hours per night, while 9 percent sleep nine hours or more.[29] Our students reported 7.8 hours of sleep per night on average, with 28 percent sleeping less than seven hours and 11 percent sleeping more than nine hours. This suggests that many in our sample of low-income students was not getting the sleep needed for high-quality cognitive functioning—and this likely is not uncommon among low-income college students, particularly since they are also known to keep erratic schedules.[30]

These challenges are the impetus behind efforts like Single Stop, Benefits Access for College Completion, and other programs that attempt to help undergraduates connect with benefits programs. The purpose is to provide a comprehensive approach to all the available on-campus and off-campus social services, to meet the needs of students who are often stymied by bureaucratic offices operating in silos. In the public sector, accessing benefits such as food stamps and Medicaid often requires long visits to a series of different offices. Many people are unaware that they are eligible for benefits, and others feel a sense of stigma that prevents them from applying. The investment of time required to obtain benefits can also be unmanageable for students struggling to keep up with schoolwork, juggling multiple jobs, and handling family responsibilities. Single Stop responds to this problem by uniting a suite of services under one roof, using a software program known as the Benefits Enrollment Network to synthesize thousands of pages of regulations and statutes into a single screening tool. After spending about fifteen minutes with a client, site staff can use this software to calculate a student's likely eligibility for multiple public benefits, helping to ensure that they only visit other offices if those visits are likely to pay dividends.

In a recent evaluation of Single Stop's implementation on a range of community college campuses across the nation, my team learned that college administrators and faculty often felt a strong desire to improve the degree prospects and life chances of their students and were visibly frustrated by their seeming inability to do this with limited resources. When we asked them how they responded to students before Single Stop came to campus, their responses sometimes became emotional. Asked what he could do for students before Single Stop came to campus, one administrator simply said, "I could pray for them." Another senior member of campus administration remarked that when faced with a student with severe needs before Single Stop arrived, she sometimes cried. She explained that, before Single Stop, "when students came into our office, we referred them, to the best of our ability, to the resources that were available. They were in academic distress and did not understand all of the rules and why they were having trouble. They said things like 'Ma'am, I'm living in my car.' We are the entrée to higher education for our community . . . and fundamentally all we could do was just close our doors and cry."[31] We do not know how the people serving our students at Wisconsin's public colleges and universities felt given these substantial needs, but we do know that they had limited resources with which to respond. The students told us that they often felt quite alone.

Scarcity

Food and housing insecurity and poor sleep—these topics rarely find their way into studies of financial aid, let alone research on college completion—and they are too important to overlook. Having too few resources can create barriers to achievement, finds Harvard economist Sendhil Mullinathian and his colleagues.[32] Scarcity imposes psychic costs, reducing mental bandwidth and distorting decision making in ways that make their situations worse, not better. Fearing that there is no way out of bad situations leads people to make especially poor choices. Some 17 percent of the students we surveyed said that they were "not at all confident" that if faced with financial problems they could get the help needed to avoid dropping out of college.

These and other stressors can lead to the kind of mental health challenges that were common among our students and are increasingly common among undergraduates nationwide. Since 2007, economist Daniel Eisenberg and his colleagues at the University of Michigan have led an effort called the Healthy Minds Study, an annual survey examining mental health and related issues (depression, anxiety, substance use) and service utilization among college students. With Eisenberg's assistance, I examined the results for public universities and colleges in Wisconsin and was disturbed to learn that 43 percent of students surveyed felt that they felt they could use support for their mental health. Thirty-seven percent had been diagnosed with a specific disorder such as depression or anxiety, but just 24 percent had received counseling or therapy in the last year. Notably, 12 percent of these Wisconsin undergraduates said that they had thought about suicide in the last twelve months.[33] Nationally, 10 percent of students report either seriously considering suicide or attempting suicide in the last year.[34]

Our students were similar. The first survey we administered included several assessments of mental health, and 17 percent of those surveyed assessed their mental health as fair or poor. Their coping abilities were not always strong. Nine percent said that they did not handle unforeseen situations well, and 10 percent said they could not be confronted with problems without giving up. But only 3.5 percent had sought support to address their mental health. This appears to be common. Eisenberg and his colleagues find that, among students with depression or anxiety, up to 84 percent do not receive services, "even in an environment with universal access to free short-term psychotherapy and basic health services." Students from lower socioeconomic backgrounds were especially unlikely to get care, he found.[35] This is unfortunate, since studies suggest that counseling is associated with improved academic performance and a greater likelihood of remaining in school. A recent report by researcher Erin Winterrowd for the University of Wisconsin System's Counseling Impact Assessment Project indicated that of the 22 percent of students seen by counseling centers who said that they were considering leaving college, 75 percent said that counseling helped them stay in school.[36] Of course, it is impossible to conclude from such reports that counseling is effective at increasing retention rates in college, but the high incidence of mental health problems and the existing availability of counseling resources points to the need for rigorous research examining that possibility.

Feeling Invisible

The experience of going to college, while often thought of as a time of great social interaction, can be a lonely one for students with financial challenges. Even students who know why they enrolled and have a strong sense of purpose may find that their sorts of struggles are not the kind people talk about on campus. While our students opened up during interviews, they often explained that they did not tell others about their troubles. Ian Williams never told his academic adviser what it meant to him to receive additional scholarship support—he never revealed that it meant he could finally eat every day. Tyler Olson did not reveal his struggles with alcohol to a counselor, partly because he was not sure they were struggles at all. Sophie Schmidt never cried in front of a professor when she was depressed; she was embarrassed to feel so desperate.

In written testimony to the National Commission on Hunger,

University of Wisconsin–Madison undergraduate Brooke A. Evans described what it felt like to be homeless while attempting to attend classes at the state's flagship university: "Without a home and without meals, I felt like an impostor amongst my brilliant peers. I was shamefully worrying about food, and shamefully staring at the clock to make it out of class in time to get in line for the local shelter when I should have been giving my undivided attention to the lecturer."[37]

Sometimes silent struggles, like those experienced by Brooke and her peers, resolve themselves. Once in a while a Good Samaritan like the Fund for Wisconsin Scholars steps in to make life easier. But more often than not, students suffer alone. The advising and counseling systems that serve them rely on students to come forward to reveal their needs—rarely do they reach out to students to ask how they are. That approach is termed "intrusive" and seems antithetical to the ethos in higher education that prides itself on treating students as "adults." This is a shame. Even adults need support. And sometimes, even adults are afraid to ask.

6

Family Matters

American families have changed in many ways since the financial aid system was created, but the assumptions that the system makes about families and the ways it interacts with families have changed very little. Many children are motivated to pursue college at least in part because it will please their parents, bring recognition to the family, or set a good example for younger siblings.

How students pay for higher education has a great deal to do with the changing nature of the American family. The reverse is also true: the increasing costs of higher education are creating changes in family life. At one extreme, some analysts link declines in average birth rates among U.S. women to the "soaring costs of ushering offspring to functional independence."[1] It costs the average middle-class family nearly $250,000 to raise a child to age eighteen—and that figure does not include a dime in savings for college.[2] The circumstances, constraints, and conditions of family life have shifted substantially while the higher education financing system has remained largely the same. This mismatch can result in demands on parents to make "expected" family contributions that are unrealistic. This is just one example of the ways in which the current system stands at odds with the realities of the lives of many—perhaps even most—families today.

Key Changes in Family Life

Ordinary American families look very different today than they did in the 1960s. Over the past five decades, the income gap between the wealthiest families and all other families has grown dramatically. The average wealth of the bottom 90 percent of families, according to data from tax returns, was equal to $80,000 in 2012—the same amount (adjusted for inflation) as in 1986. In contrast, the average wealth for the top 10 percent increased by about 84 percent (since 1966) while the average wealth for the top 1 percent more than tripled.[3] The top tenth of 1 percent has done even better.[4]

While the wealth of the bottom 90 percent has remained stagnant, costs have grown. Consumer debt levels have increased dramatically, particularly among working-class families.[5] Today, many families struggle to pay mortgages, credit card balances, and student loans.[6] Health care and childcare costs have risen, too, taking bigger and bigger bites out of family budgets.[7] Most families have actually stopped saving. On average, families in the top 10 percent now save 35 percent of their income. The average family in the other 90 percent saves nothing.[8]

The growing wealth disparity has been accompanied by related changes in family structure.[9] Less than half of all children under eighteen in the United States are growing up in families with two heterosexual parents in a first marriage, compared with more than 70 percent in the 1960s.[10] This change is primarily due to the increasing numbers of women who give birth outside of marriage. These women tend to be disadvantaged on almost every measure, including less education, lower income, and a higher likelihood of receiving government assistance.[11]

Low-income, single-parent households like these have a much harder time providing money for their children to attend school. Johns Hopkins University sociologist Kathryn Edin draws a key contrast: "In the middle class, the divorce rate has gone down, and family life is in many ways simpler than it used to be . . . there's far more complexity and churning of households among the poor, a turnover of partnerships, lots of half-siblings."[12]

That churn is related to educational attainment. As noted earlier, the income disparity between those with and without a college education has never been greater. College graduates outperform their high-school-only peers on nearly every measure of economic well-being.[13] Earnings of college graduates have risen since 1965, while workers with only a high school diploma have seen their earnings fall.

Many of these single mothers could benefit from college. While men still outearn women with the same level of education, women get a bigger boost in their wages from obtaining a college degree—a boost of 50 percent in earnings, as of 2013.[14] This is not to say that men do not benefit. The college earning premium for them was 48 percent in that same year. Indeed, men without a college degree are at a particular earnings disadvantage. Men between the ages of thirty to forty-five who lacked college educations made less in 2013 than they did in the 1990s.[15]

Economic changes have hit African American and Hispanic families particularly hard. Such families enjoy far less economic security and stability than non-Hispanic white families.[16] At the bottom end of the spectrum, nearly one in four Hispanic (24%) and African American (24%) households had no assets other than a vehicle, compared with just 6 percent of white households. This has a lot to do with the destruction of home equity during the Great Recession and the collapse of the housing market. Between 2005 and 2009, the median level of home equity held by Hispanic homeowners declined by half—from $99,983 to $49,145, while for African Americans it fell from $76,910 in 2005 to $59,000 in 2009. White families enjoyed far more housing wealth to begin with and took smaller losses, experiencing a decline from $115,364 in 2005 to $95,000 in 2009. The debt that families accrued during this time was unevenly distributed, too. For Hispanics, the median level of unsecured liabilities rose by 42 percent, compared to 32 percent for whites, and 27 percent for African Americans.[17]

Inequality grew during the economic recovery. The Pew Research Center found that while the wealth of non-Hispanic white families grew, it fell for African Americans and Hispanics. Over time, then, the ratio of white wealth to black wealth fell from 10:1 in 2007 to

8.3:1 in 2010, only to rise to almost 13:1 in 2013. The ratio for whites to Hispanics grew steadily, from 8.2 to 8.7:1 between 2007 and 2010, to 10.3:1 in 2013.[18]

These disparities—in income and wealth, family structure, and educational attainment—mean that the act of paying for college feels very different for lower-income and moderate-income families than it does for their wealthier counterparts. These measures are indicators of well-being—they mark the ability of families to pay for the things they need, rely on liquidity in times of stress, and enjoy a sense of economic power over their own lives.[19] This is one reason for class disparities in how people think college should be paid for. When you have money, you think about paying for your child's college differently than when you're poor. Just 9 percent of people in families earning $100,000 or more say that students should be primarily responsible for paying for college, compared to 31 percent in families earning less than $35,000 per year. In contrast, 48 percent of wealthy families think that parents should be primarily or solely responsible for paying for college, compared to just 18 percent of low-income families.[20] What households without financial assets have to give up in order to send a child to college is significant—and critical. For the American mobility narrative to function, for hard work to actually pay off, all families must be able to make college possible for their children.

Doing It for the Family

This commitment to doing better for one's family provides a powerful motivation for college attendance. The growing economic insecurity young people are experiencing, especially in homes led by single parents, contributes to a deep sense of gratitude among children when they finish high school and begin down the path to college. An eighteen-year-old woman we spoke with, who was raised by a single mom, explained her plan this way: "I decided that when I graduated [from high school] I was going to provide her everything. She helped me through, you know, so I'm going to try to make her life better than mine was. . . . I've seen her struggle her whole life.

And it's something that I didn't want to see. So if I can help her in any way, now that I have money, now that I have what I graduated for, I can give back . . . you know, to thank her for how much she did for me." This woman had completed high school, and college was just getting underway. There was a high price to pay to succeed at that next stage, but as she explained, she already felt both success and an obligation to say thanks. What money she now had came from her work earnings and her financial aid, but in absolute terms she did not have much.

Our students do not seem to be unusual. Other researchers have also found that students cite their parents and other family members as central to their decisions to pursue postsecondary education.[21] Pleasing and repaying a parent feels good and provides a positive source of motivation. Attempting to please a parent can also bring stress, but sometimes that stress is what endocrinologists call "eustress," the feeling you get when overcome with the excitement and anticipation of a desired outcome. A student felt this way when thinking about her family's high academic expectations for her. She said, "They all really expect me to succeed [because] I'm the first one and everyone is so proud of me, and I kind of feel like I have to do it in a way to, like, fulfill what they want. But I know it's good for me, too." As first-year students, 93 percent of our students reported that their families expected them to do well in college, and 92 percent said that their families encouraged them to stay in college.

Norbert Webster spent the early years of his life in a large Midwestern city, where both his mother and father had family. His father was seventeen and his mother sixteen when they had their first child, a son. Norbert was born a year later. When he was in kindergarten, his parents decided to move the family to Wisconsin, away from the poor, often violent neighborhood where they lived. As described earlier, the family's move to the Oneida reservation gave Norbert access to a community he came to care about and enjoy. But his father was often in and out of work, "having hard times," and had inconsistent contact with the family, beginning when Norbert was twelve, and his parents separated. They divorced when Norbert was sixteen. His mother then was earning about $29,000 a year.

When Norbert got ready for his first year of higher education, he had a brother in college, a younger sibling still in high school, and divorced parents, both of whom had inconsistent jobs. The FAFSA that Norbert submitted that year shows a student who could rely on very little financial help from his family. But these records, while illuminating, miss some of the most important parts of Norbert's life, and some of the critical, nonfinancial aspects of family support.

Norbert enjoyed a broad family network that included an uncle with a professional degree working in Chicago, an aunt with a bachelor's degree, and a mother firmly committed to her son's success. Few other students in the study spoke as frequently and fervently of unending, positive support from their parents. Norbert expressed a desire to spend more time with his mom and dad and other family members. College took him away and that made him uncomfortable, especially during the first year of school, when he often found himself homesick and driving more than an hour to get back home.

Each time I met with him, Norbert talked about his mother and the consistently positive encouragement she provided him. In his first year of college, he said, "She is really happy, very glad that I get to meet new people and stuff like that." He described his mother's education and his desire to help make his family more economically stable:

My mom never went to college. I see her income and how she has to live. I wanted to go to college and take that extra step and learn. We all work, and if my brother and I did not work we wouldn't have as many things in [the family home] as we should. Sometimes I see her struggling and it just kind of hurts me to see that. So I have always wanted to go to college and do better. Mom always talked to us and said that we'd better go to college, "I don't care what you do, just go. . . ." She sat me down and said, "Even if you have to take loans and stuff, it's fine. College is always a positive experience, you'll get something good out of it, and so if you have to, just take them out." She was a big motivation for me. I also have an aunt and uncle that went to college and I see how they live—they have a really nice house and a daughter.

Norbert's mother was so intent on her son attending college that when mail came from the U.S. military, she threw away the recruitment materials. During college, she kept track of his grades and let him know that she was proud of him. Whenever I asked him how it felt to do well in school, Norbert referred to his mother's encouragement.

Despite the unconditional support from his mother, attending college created some tensions in Norbert's relationships with his family. Norbert explained that he struggled to keep his status as college student from creating a social distance between himself and family and friends who never attended. "I'm super proud [to be in college] and it brings me joy. But there's another feeling since my mom and dad did not go to college. Sometimes I think that they think that I think I'm better than them. It's kind of like that with the people from home who didn't go to college. When I see them and tell them I'm going to school, they get the sense that I think I'm better than them."

Norbert said that in an effort to lessen that tension, he tried to avoid talking about college while he was at home. Instead, he focused on just hanging out with his friends. At the start of his second year of college, he described strategies he developed for dealing with what he often felt was an awkward situation. "I don't try to talk college up or anything, but for the ones [friends] that haven't been to college they kind of make me feel like I'm talking down to them. It's a weird situation. It makes me feel like I'm talking to them like I'm better than them and it makes me uncomfortable, because that's not what I'm trying to point out to them and that's not how I feel at all . . . I just try to change the subject to something else." As college progressed, Norbert grew more independent but remained close to his family. He chose to spend more time on campus and traveled home less frequently. Still, Norbert consistently spoke about family members as a source of encouragement and found their support to be a comfort. When he needed advice, he often turned to his older brother, who was also a college student.

If I ever need anyone to just sit down and talk to, I know I can always go to him or give him a call. . . . It's helpful [to talk to him] because we know what each other is going through. I call him and say, "Dude, I'm so stressed out, I have three papers due tomorrow and I just finished one and I don't know what I'm doing." And he gives me that motivation and says "You know you can do it, come on. . . . I'm writing five papers right now." So he knows where I'm at . . . sometimes when I call my mom and tell her stuff she's not really—she doesn't know the college life. But she does support me in everything. . . . She usually just tells me "You're in college now, you've got to get your work done." She tells me that college is my job so "Do good at it and it'll pay off." It's always nice to hear that. It's support to get you back up on your feet and think, maybe I *can* do this.

While Norbert was in college, his mother had a series of jobs. For a while she worked in housekeeping at a hotel, and from time to time she needed some financial support from Norbert. But eventually she moved into an accounting job, which also provided benefits, and she was better able to support herself. (In Norbert's second year of college, she earned $34,000, up from $29,000 the prior year.)

Even as Norbert settled into college life, he maintained responsibilities at home, particularly around mentoring and providing support to his younger brother. For example, when his brother struggled in math, Norbert spent time on the phone helping him talk through those challenges and tutoring him. "He's in a rebellious stage. He's at that age where he hates school. . . . I kind of like being a role model for him . . . me and my [older] brother are both in college and we are pushing him. I think he has this image that college is going to be the same as junior high where you're at school all day and don't have any free time. I'm like, do you realize that some days you only have one class a day? And he ponders and says, oh that's not so bad." Norbert was fortunate—and grateful—that his Oneida scholarship allowed him to spend time on these activities, rather than working long hours at a job.

As Norbert's story illustrates, even when there is little money to be had, low- and moderate-income families support their children in other ways not always recognized by the system. In response, students often spend time and even contribute money to help their families. The financial aid system—and college more generally— fails to recognize the complexity and interdependence of families.

Supporting Their Students

When college administrators speak about parents, they often refer to the buzzing of so-called helicopter parents, who zoom in to campus with ceaseless inquiries and demands about their child's education.[22] It is not clear exactly how much substance there is to these anecdotes (i.e., how many helicopter parents are truly landing on campuses), but it is clear that such parents are rarely, if ever, low income. In fact, the opposite is true. These are parents who tend to have financial resources, discretionary time, and social networks that help them exert influence. College administrators may find these parents irritating, but they are fundamentally respected as people with power.[23]

Low-income parents are, in contrast, framed quite differently. They are parents without: people who do not, cannot, or will not provide their children with what college requires.[24] Financial aid officers speak of these parents with some sympathy but also with frustration, first and foremost because they appear to stand between the students and their completed FAFSAs. Indeed, some students speak of their parents this way as well. One woman had to postpone college for a year because she could not obtain her parent's information and, without it, could not complete the FAFSA in time to qualify for the aid she needed. Even after she started college the following year, she continued to have trouble getting her mother's data. "I go to my mom and say, mom, I need your social security number," she told us. But her mom responded, "I don't give my stuff out to nobody."

Fifty-seven percent of our students said that when deciding on a school, it was at least somewhat important that the college they attended be located near their parents' home. Only 15 percent said the opposite, that it was important to attend school far from their parents' home.

Family members of our students provided many types of help. Most (56%) helped to buy groceries or other food, and 55 percent

Table 15. Family assistance parents provided to students: WSLS students

	Full Sample (%)	Zero Expected Family Contribution (%)	Positive Expected Family Contribution (%)
Paying for groceries or other food	56	53	58
Paying for cell phone bill	55	49	59
Paying for health insurance	58	39	67
Paying for car insurance	43	33	48
Paying for housing	28	23	31
Paying for other car-related costs	24	20	25
Paying for tuition	19	8	24
Providing a ride to school	14	18	12
Paying for credit card bill	5	5	5

Source. WSLS data.

Note. Sample includes WSLS students who responded to first-year survey questions on family assistance and consented to link with administrative data, n = 1,359.

also covered cell phone bills (see table 15). More than half of students had assistance with health insurance, but just four in ten received help with car insurance. Barely one-quarter of our students could depend on their parents for help with paying for housing or related expenses, and, as expected, few received help with tuition. The financial aid system anticipates this, of course, by determining that a family can make only a small contribution to college expenses, and thus providing the Pell Grant. But as shown earlier, even Pell recipients are left with sizable bills to pay, and while their parents sometimes help, that help is less common with big-ticket items. This is especially true for students whose families are estimated to be unable to pay anything for college. These families, national data indicate, are also far less likely to have a contingency plan for funding in case of financial emergencies.[25]

Getting and Giving

It is not surprising that families with few resources make limited financial contributions to their undergraduates. But what is not discussed, and is largely unknown, are the ways in which undergraduates contribute to their families while pursuing their studies.

Sharing is a skill that many parents struggle to teach their children. Relinquishing a piece of something you want or owe to another person can be decidedly difficult, even if you love them. Yet the experience of sharing can be different in very low-income families. Ian Williams, for example, learned how to share with his brothers and sisters in a way many of his college professors and administrators likely did not. He shared his food.

Growing up poor, the idea that family members would help each other out as needed was a given in Ian's home. "That's how my mother raised us," he explained in an interview, "If a piece of us falls, we all fall." The goal, he clarified, was for all family members to be OK. For some to succeed while others fell behind was unacceptable. He learned this lesson early, sharing a story he recalled from second grade:

> I remember it was Halloween and my father told me he was going to buy me a costume because there was supposed to be a party at my school. So I'm like, "good, I'm having a costume," and I was as happy as ever, [being] selfish. I wasn't thinking about my little brother who wanted one as well—he asked and my father said he was going to get one too. But instead of getting me the whole [costume] like he was telling me he would, my dad gave me part and gave my brother a part. I was so mad. He basically took my costume and divided it among us.

Our researcher asked him, "You would have gotten a full costume if your brother hadn't been asking for one?" To which Ian replied:

> Yes, and I was so frustrated. My father just went over it with me. You're always supposed to look out for your family, no matter how much money you've got. If you've got a dollar or something, if there are four quarters and four kids then you give them a quarter apiece. That's how we were raised and how ever since then I've been trying to do it. Whatever I come across, it doesn't have to be much, as long as I come across a certain amount of money that can benefit me and my family, I'm going to try and do that as much as possible.

For Ian's family, sharing resources was a matter of survival. When he became a college student, the practice continued. Ian shared the limited funds he had—obtained from grants, loans, and work—with his mother and brothers. "If I can do it then I can maybe take away some of the bills that mama's using to keep us up. That's why I've got to do something, I've got to help my mother out." Even though sharing money meant that Ian himself had fewer resources for college, he explained that he benefited emotionally from this exchange: "It's a lot of relief that comes off my chest. . . . It's an unexplainable feeling. I'm in the position to help my family out now. . . . I know the only reason I'm in the position that I'm in right now is because of my family. . . . [That's] why I always relate back to my history. The things they did for me and everything—that's what makes me want to do more for them. That's what pushes me through college so I can help them out a lot." Ian continued, articulating the ways in which his family made college possible for him and therefore why sharing resources with them while he pursued his degree made sense.

> My mama was my motivation, she kept me out of trouble and that type of environment, even though it was hard for her because she was going to work most of the time. . . . She [said] "I'm going to whup you if you don't come home, if you don't stop going on the corner and hanging with them [friends on the corner]." She motivated me a lot because she was a strong black woman taking care of five kids. . . . If it wasn't for [my family], I don't know what would be happening. They keep me focused, they wake me up for school, and they help me somewhat financially. You know my mama ain't got that much income coming in but the amount she gets, she helps me a lot.

Stretching dollars is easier when family members live together, so Ian lived at home while attending university. The family home hardly had the necessary resources for an undergraduate, however. It had neither Internet access nor laundry facilities. Even food was sometimes scarce, with so many children to feed. Ian spent twenty hours a week during his first year of college caring for his family and struggling to align the timing of his classes so he could meet responsibilities at home and at school. He also began paying for one of his older brothers to take a class at a local community college since that course could not be covered with financial aid. He was worried that this brother was about to return to the streets.

> I'm like, no, you aren't going out back on the streets—you're going back to school. That's why I paid his way. . . . He appreciated it a lot. He said, "thank you brother" because school was better than the crazy out on the street. In my family, we all like challenges . . . and just being on the street, that's not a challenge. You only survive, that's the only thing . . . to get money and stuff like that, and it's not really like a challenge. He likes challenges just like me, and that's why he went to school.

But the emotional investment Ian made to keep his brothers safe wore on him. He stayed up late at night waiting for them to come home, and he tried to catch up on that sleep during the day on weekends, before again waiting up for them on weekend nights.

> I try to study but my mind is on the streets. That is how it goes. It still creeps up on me, but that's why I like to study a lot and do a lot of work, and basically just keep busy . . . the streets are helping me out a little bit—if I were in a different type of neighborhood then I wouldn't mind going back to the house, and I'd be distracted if I did go back. But the only way to stay away from the streets is coming to the university and studying and keeping my mind off of it—so in a way, it's helping me out.

In his second year of college, Ian's mom lost her job, and there was a delay before she began to receive unemployment support. The need to help her became his main focus. By then, Ian was receiving the Wisconsin Scholars Grant and another scholarship, but even so he was struggling. He told us: "I'm having problems, like, I don't want to say 'providing' for my mom, but at times she needs help with all of her stuff, so I've been helping her with her bills. . . . Sometimes you don't really understand the position a person is in unless they tell you, and she was telling me she needed help." Ian understood that other students might react differently to a parent asking them for money: "Yeah, at times I probably feel like I don't want to pay for this. But at the same time, when I look back and I needed this when I was younger, she worked hard and [provided] everything for me. So why I can't I do that the same way? That's how I look at the situation." Ian sometimes described wanting to move away to attend a school in Atlanta, and occasionally spoke of how much easier life would be if he lived on campus, but ultimately felt that it was essential that he live at home. He did not move to an apartment of his own until he was twenty-two years old and about to graduate.

Ian surprised us with his openness about sharing money with his family as a college student, but he was not alone. About one in three students in our study reported that interdependence of resources was a facet of their lives. For them, family financial reciprocity was a way of life before, during, and likely after college. It shaped how they went to college and why they went, and it affected their chances of finishing school.

The students in this study are not unusual. Young adults are often critical sources of support to their families, especially low-income families, to which they frequently contribute money, time, or both.[26] These responsibilities are rooted in norms of interdependence, obligation, and reciprocity, and they help ensure the family's economic survival.

Urban anthropologist Carol Stack's seminal study in 1974 of a severely disadvantaged African American community was among the first to highlight the use of reciprocal patterns of giving among community members as a strategy to survive poverty. Stack found that community members ascribe to a "what goes around comes around" mentality, calling for people to help one another and expect the same in return. As one of her participants explained, reciprocal exchanges are essential for survival, given limited resources: "You have to have help from everybody and anybody, so don't turn no one down when they come round for help."[27] Reciprocity is a collective adaptation to poverty—in other words, the basic belief that "people should help one another" is not an *effect* of a culture of poverty but, rather, a characteristic, rational *response* to poverty. This finding is echoed in the work of economists, who have found similar patterns of intrafamily resource transfers, typically called remittances, moving into, between, and among poor communities around the world.[28]

One of our students continued to provide childcare for her kindergarten-age brother while her parents worked. She worried that, as a college student, life on campus would pull her away from those commitments and hurt her parents' ability to earn income the family depended on. She balanced her studies and her caregiving responsibilities for her brother with a waitressing job. While at her parent's home, she sometimes grabbed her mother's purse—not to borrow money but, rather, to stick a twenty-dollar bill inside.

Another student who immigrated to the United States from Thailand explained: "In my culture, we believe in family and helping out each other. . . . For example, [if] something crops up and it requires financial assistance, if I don't have it [money or another form of financial assistance], my sister will have it. [If] my sister doesn't have it, my brother will have it." Four of her siblings were also in college and, during her first semester, she gave money to one sister who needed a laptop, another sister who needed money for school, and an ex-boyfriend who lost his job and could not afford to pay some bills.

The federal needs analysis that determines financial aid eligibility assumes that for "dependent" students resources flow in one direction: from parent to student. By design, they should have always been helped by their parents (or at the very least held harmless) and never the other way around. Rarely do discussions about the challenges facing college students recognize the possibility that money might need to flow from the student to the parent or to other relatives—let alone the frequency with which this actually happens.[29]

So the financial situations of low-income students and their families are much more complicated and challenging than FAFSAs reveal. The level of material support children receive from parents during the transition to adulthood, including the college-going years, is strongly associated with family socioeconomic status. In economically advantaged and disadvantaged families alike, college attendance of a child leads to increased financial and housing support from their parents.[30] Although the proportion of household income spent supporting young adults is consistent across income brackets at around 10 percent, the actual amount of money working-class and poor college students are likely to receive from their families is, of course, far less than their more affluent peers due to their more modest resources.[31] Parents from the top 25 percent of the income spectrum provide over three times as much financial support, on average, to their children throughout young adulthood than parents from the bottom 25 percent.[32] There is some racial variation within income bands, however. In "Bootstraps Are for Black Kids," researchers Yunju Nam, Darrick Hamilton, William A. Darity Jr., and Anne E. Price, in an analysis of national data from the Panel Study of Income Dynamics, found:

> Black parents with more limited resources display a greater inclination to provide financial support for their children's education than their white counterparts. Median parental wealth was a mere $3,699 among black parents who did not provide any financial support for their children's higher education, but it was $73,878 among white parents who provided no support to their children. Median net worth was $24,887 and a markedly higher $167,935 for black and white parents who did provide support for their children's higher education respectively.... Our results are consistent with the exceptional black American commitment to education over the course of the long history of the United States.[33]

With less money from their parents coming in, it is no surprise that low-income college students take on far more debt than their more affluent peers. Nor, given the stories told here, should it be a surprise that low-income students often feel obligated to share some of the loan money they do get with their families to ensure the family's survival.[34]

More than one-third of our students somewhat or strongly agreed with the statement that while in college "I feel obligated to support my family financially." They spoke of a cycle: student helps family, family sometimes helps student, and even in the absence of that help, the student helps the family again. They draw on resources from work, from loans, and from grants to do whatever they can to assist. And they know this pattern is not unusual. In fact, across a wide range of studies, scholars have found that young adults from low-income families often express a strong sense of obligation to family and a desire to give back to parents and other family members.[35] This is part of a strategy of adaptation created by adolescents in families facing economic hardship who are often enlisted early to fill family roles and responsibilities typically reserved for adults—a phenomenon known as parentification or adultification.[36] Thus, for many such college students, providing support to their family is a continuation of roles they assumed earlier in life.

In many ways, this reciprocal giving is similar to what sociologist Linda Burton and Carol Stack call kinscripts, a framework that describes an "interplay of family ideology, norms, and behaviors over the life course."[37] Drawing on sociological theories of family life, their approach emphasizes the dynamic and temporal nature of life (there are different places and times associated with life events), as well as the interdependence of family members. University of California, Los Angeles, psychologist Andrew Fuligni and his colleagues have also written about this, describing "the extent to which family members feel a sense of duty to assist one another and to take into account the needs and wishes of the family when making decisions."[38] They find that a sense of family obligation is associated with more positive emotional well-being. Just as the flow of remittances among immigrant families has important consequences for both senders and receivers (and their nations), financial exchanges between college students and their families may have implications for the educational outcomes—and therefore prospects for social mobility—of the children.[39] For example, in a study of the relationship between family obligation and college enrollment, researchers found that young adults with a strong sense of family obligation often felt "torn" between doing what they want to do and doing something that will make enough money to help support their parents.[40]

These circumstances are often portrayed as affecting primarily community college students, but we observed them among students at public universities as well. Eleven percent of students at universities reported on surveys that they gave their families at least fifty dollars per month, and 14 percent also reported spending at least ten hours per week taking care of an older family member or a younger sibling. A Hmong student attending a university provided an estimated 75 percent of his work earnings to his family and also brought home food from work to serve for their dinner. His family regularly held meetings where they discussed finances and planned how bills would be paid: "We talk about finances . . . my dad, my mom, my older sister, my uncle, and me. But now my older sister's gone so my younger brother has to come up with, not his 'portion,' but he has to be there when we need help. For instance we have a lot of car insurance to pay. . . . And they'll be like, 'I'll pitch in this much, you pitch in that much, you pitch in that much.' So that my dad will have enough money to pay the mortgage and all that stuff."

Calling their actions merely "helping out" or "pitching in," our students commonly downplayed their roles in family finances. This may be because giving also came with some "feeling good," as Ian explained earlier. But there were downsides, too. In his dissertation, University of Wisconsin–Madison researcher Peter Kinsley examined how these obligations affected how our low-income students performed in college. He found that, even after taking into account demographics and other factors, providing regular cash transfers to parents more than doubled the odds that a student would also work more than twenty hours per week during the first year of college and reduced by 7 percent the odds that a student would reenroll for a second year of college.[41]

Life at Home

Financial aid administrators and policymakers often recommend that undergraduates live at home to save money, and more students are doing this.[42] A recent national survey by the Sallie Mae Corporation reports: "Families are adopting multiple strategies to reduce the cost burden of paying for college, such as opting for in-state tuition (69%), living closer to home (61%) or at home/with relatives (54%), filing for education tax credits (42%), getting a roommate (41%), accelerating the pace of coursework (28%), or not deferring payments on student loans (23%). . . . Most families, however, are likely to adopt a combination of cost-reduction approaches, such as opting to go to school in state and living at home or with relatives (43%)."[43]

But this advice should be qualified—there is evidence that living at home reduces the odds of becoming part of campus life, and it may even reduce the chances of graduation.[44] Students who live at home during college appear more likely to experience negative relationships with parents than those who live independently.[45] Not surprisingly, such students also experience greater pressure to fulfill family responsibilities.[46] A student we spoke with had obligations at home that limited the number of credits he could take each term, thereby prolonging the time it would take him to graduate. He explained: "You have to have thirty credits each year. But this year I only have fourteen, and the next one I can only fit in four classes because at night I have to come home before 1 P.M., because 1 P.M. is when my baby cousin comes over. I have to babysit him. And then [at] 2 or 2:30 I have to go pick up my sisters from high school— [actually] my sister, my younger brother, my youngest sister, and my other brother." Not only did this schedule make it difficult for him to pursue a faster-paced program at college with more courses, but his family responsibilities also made it hard for him to study. His father, he explained, "expects me not to have any [homework to do]."

The assumption that living at home is less expensive is so ingrained in our imaginations that many colleges and universities budget very little to support the living expenses of financial aid recipients living with their parents. At the Wisconsin colleges and universities where our students went to school, the typical financial aid budget for a student living at home was about $5,000 less than the budget for a student living off campus alone. We found that many students didn't know this, and if they did, would point out that this assumption was misplaced.

Consider Tyler Olson, whose father left high school before earning a diploma, and later went on to obtain a high school equivalency credential from a technical college and work at a local prison. His mom graduated from high school and then trained as a certified nursing assistant, though she never worked in the field. After transferring universities and losing his athletic scholarship, Tyler considered living at home in order to save money. But as he noted, his parents "don't really have any money" either and if he lived with either of them (they divorced while he was in high school), they "would have made me pay rent." He got very little financial help from his family, which is unsurprising given that they were persistently poor throughout his childhood. The whole family—including Tyler—continued to struggle with food insecurity. "I don't really go to my family with problems or for emotional support, but they say I'm doing good, that kind of thing. They can't really help me financially, so if I need money I go to my grandparents. And I always have to pay them back—I never get anything handed to me financially by family that's just a gift, unless it's Christmas. But I mean, if I really needed help with anything they would find a way to do it." That expectation went both ways. During the school year, Tyler spent between four and six hours a week helping his family. During the summer before his second year of college, Tyler's father was denied refinancing on his home and fell into financial difficulties. He came to Tyler, seeking $1,175. Tyler described the conversation: "He said, 'Trust me, I'm just borrowing it, just give it to me and I'll get it right back to you'—that kind of thing. Well, I never saw it again. I was planning to use that money to pay off my credit card bill. He thinks I'm a kid who doesn't know the way the world works, and he is being greedy. We stopped talking for a month. Now I only talk to him maybe once a week, and I used to talk to him five times a week or so." Since living at home was not going to save him money, Tyler moved to a house with three other friends. But these friends were not college students and, as he repeatedly noted, proved a great distraction from school. "My high school friends," he admits, "are just kind of shocked that I'm actually in college." He indicated that he did not feel very safe in this new living situation, which he also found noisy and bug infested.

And after a year with those roommates, they fought, and Tyler found himself living in his father's basement. "I hate it," he said at the time, "My bedroom is this space walled off with sheets."

Tyler was not alone in feeling frustrated by his father's inability to support him. Some might assume that only immigrant or racial/ethnic minority families need their children's income to survive, but this is not what we observed in Wisconsin where our sample was largely white. For nine of the fifty students we interviewed, no financial support was available because the children were estranged from family members with resources.

Families worry about college costs, and for good reason. A national survey conducted in 2014 indicates that 30 percent of parents of low-income college students are seriously concerned that grant aid will diminish as their student pursues college, 31 percent fear that tuition will be raised, 19 percent worry that loans will become less available, and 33 percent think that loan rates will increase.[47] These concerns are generally shared among people regardless of income, but the consequences of the concerns differ, as people from lower- and moderate-income backgrounds are more likely to turn away from college when faced with financial shortfalls.[48]

Students feel this insecurity. In general, in the second, third, and following years, not only does the price of college rise but also the support students get from their families falls. For example, 51 percent experienced a reduction in financial support from their parents in their second year of college. We assessed the level of financial support by comparing students' ratings of agreement with three survey measures:

- Your parents provide money for your education
- Your parents provide room and board while you obtain education
- Your parents provide significant financial assistance in times of need

In the second year, students often experienced a drop-off in nonfinancial forms of family support, too. We assessed the level of emotional support students received from their parents by asking them to rate their agreement with the following statements:

- Your parents make you feel worthwhile, special, and unique
- Your parents share a reliable relationship with you
- Your parents make you feel better when you are upset
- Your parents make you feel proud of yourself
- Your parents listen to you when you feel stressed

Forty-two percent of students felt that in their second year of college they received less emotional support from their families than they did during their first year. Our analyses indicate that the financial and emotional aspects of these interactions are related. The struggle to pay for college sometimes felt like a personal failing on the part of the family, and for the parents in particular. The resulting dynamic created tensions in families' relationships.

The money undergraduates provide to their parents helps buy more than food and shelter. One woman said that her family expected her to use her student loans to purchase clothing for her sister's children. As described earlier, Ian used his financial aid to help his brother pay for courses at a local technical college, in an effort to protect him from spending time "on the streets."

Our interviews gave little indication that parents explicitly required their children to pass money along. Rather, student contributions to their families seem rooted in implicit understandings. One undergraduate said that she has "started to listen for the things that my mom needs . . . and then I'll usually just go and get it for her." She is quick to clarify: "Not that I have money for it, but a part of me sometimes feels like I have more money than she does right now."

Among the world's large financial assistance programs, financial aid for higher education stands out for its explicit stance against remittances. In many other settings, policymakers allow impoverished people to share their money how they choose, with the understanding that they are best able to decide what will help their lives the most. If sharing helps them survive, they do it. If it does not, they do not. Some studies find that flexible financial assistance works better than programs with more restrictions.[49] Yet when it comes to financial aid for college, it is simply understood that the money is for the student, not the family. There is a specific term used by policymakers and financial aid officers—and even some advocates—when it comes to talking about money that is used elsewhere. It is spent on "noneducational expenses," they say, and this is considered misuse, even fraud.[50] This judgment is based on the admirable general objectives of college financial aid—but it gives short shrift to the real lives of low-income students and their families.[51]

As described in chapter 3, the claims of fraud among financial aid recipients have increased in recent years, corresponding to the rise in program costs. Since the Great Recession and the corresponding devastation of wealth (especially for African Americans and Hispanics), long-struggling families have had fewer assets to live on. For many, a tight credit market has made even small amounts of capital hard to come by. At the same time, more and more students from low-income families are choosing to go to college, where they are often offered a combination of grants and loans that give them access to money they may choose to spend elsewhere. These conditions practically drive aid recipients to draw on that aid to help their families—even though doing this means they are viewed as frauds and cheats who are undeserving of support.

Perhaps the advance of such claims could have helped Ian. If rules against transfers to others were enforced, Ian would have been able to spend more of his aid on college needs. The mental anguish Ian felt in deciding who to choose—himself or his family—might have been reduced. His life might be simpler, and his prospects for degree completion better. Maybe.

But it is also possible that such rules would have encouraged his family to be less invested in Ian's education—literally. His time away from home, spent in the classroom and the library, could have become more intolerable—and the pressure for him to do something that brought home cash could have been even stronger.

Nima Chaudhary understood this pressure. In exchange for living at home, she was expected to provide extensive care to her family. "My dad doesn't work because he is disabled. My mom is the only one working, sixteen hours a day since we got here from Nepal. Nobody else works because we are all full-time students. . . . She gets up at 5 A.M. and leaves at 6 because her job [in housekeeping at a hospital] starts at 7 A.M. and she works until 3 P.M., then comes home and has thirty minutes to eat and then leaves for the second job [as a janitor] until she comes [home] at 1:30 A.M."

To help out, Nima spent eight hours a week caring for her disabled father during her first year of college. "It's our culture. You live with your family. The parents raise you from baby to older and then your family grows and you take care of your parents because they are growing old. Kind of like a circle." Living with her family required personal sacrifices. She enjoyed very little freedom. Her brothers kept an eye on her time and her friends. "They drill me with questions. Where are you going? Who are you going with? How late are you going to be?"

Nima had to borrow money from her parents to participate in activities and buy books. Sometimes she also borrowed from her friends (including for books and food). As described previously, she also worked in places and in ways that made her very uncomfortable, and she endured near-constant criticism from her family.

A Financial Aid System That Does Not Understand Its Customers

Our evidence suggests that the financial aid eligibility and distribution system doesn't take into account the realities of many low-income families. The system fails to adequately recognize families' struggles with poverty or near-poverty status, income volatility, and the lack of available support from social programs. While financial aid demands an expected family contribution from all but the very poorest families, parents are frequently unable to make that contribution. This creates tension between children and parents that recurs throughout college, as aid reapplication occurs annually, creating friction every academic year. It also breeds resentment and mistrust of financial aid, a policy intended to help.

Students who are the first in their families to attend college make up a significant portion of low-income students. In our study of Pell recipients, first-generation college students made up 57 percent of the total. These students are often viewed as the most accomplished and successful family members, and so it should not be a surprise that they are often called on (directly and indirectly) to support their families with all available resources. Contributing time or money—or both—to their families may be done out of love, in response to pressure, or out of a sense of reciprocal obligation and may make students feel proud or resentful, appreciated or exploited. Regardless, these contributions can be counterproductive to their educational goals. Increasing college attainment for these individuals may require finding ways to resolve these challenges. Otherwise, for as long as low-income families continue to experience severe financial stress, we can expect their children to struggle with extra burdens as they attempt to succeed at college.

Parents and their students are willing to make sacrifices. National survey data indicate that 61 percent of people in families earning less than $35,000 a year strongly agree that they are "willing to stretch myself financially" to pay for college—compared to 52 percent of middle-income families, and 58 percent of wealthy families. Almost 60 percent of low-income families also say that they are willing to borrow for college rather than not go at all, and 70 percent say that a degree is more important now than ever. Willingness to make these sacrifices is again more prevalent among lower-income families. Perhaps most tellingly, 34 percent of these families say that attending college is worth it for the experience, despite uncertainty about future earnings. Just 19 percent of middle- and upper-income families say the same.[52]

7

Making the Grade

Over the last decade a series of research studies and news articles has painted a distinctly negative portrait of the American undergraduate. Students are portrayed as more interested in social activities—particularly drinking alcohol, doing drugs, and partying—than in academics. They're not interested in hard work and studying and they are lost and "academically adrift." Conversely, they are also obsessed with grades rather than with substantive learning.

This picture contains at least a grain of truth. *Academically Adrift*, an influential longitudinal study by sociologists Richard Arum and Josipa Roksa, suggests that a substantial number of students learn relatively little during college. A historical analysis by economists Philip Babcock and Mindy Marks finds that today's students spend far fewer hours studying than did undergraduates in years past.[1]

These characterizations of undergraduates make for good stories. According to influential education analyst Kevin Carey, *Academically Adrift* was "the rare piece of serious academic scholarship that jumps the fence and roams free into the larger culture."[2] Peter Lindsay, associate professor of political science and philosophy at Georgia State University, wrote in a 2015 column in the *Chronicle of Higher Education* that "at large urban institutions like mine, where many students live off campus and cannot merely roll out of bed, don some approximation of near-appropriate dress, and drag themselves 100 yards to an adjoining classroom building, arrival at any point during a 75-minute period is often presented as a feat of epic proportions."[3]

While this picture is compelling, the data on which it is based

include few public institutions. These concerns matter little to writers like Thomas Lindsay of the Center for Higher Education at the
Texas Public Policy Foundation, who simply agree: "Having taught
undergraduates at several institutions, public and private, over the
past 20 years, I needed no corroboration. From my experience, I have
long suspected what [Academically] Adrift and the Wabash Study
[of Liberal Arts Education] confirm. It's hard for me to believe that
my fellow academics don't also know this in their bones."[4] The vision
of students drifting aimlessly through higher education is, in other
words, so pervasive that we should simply accept it and move on.[5]

But the reality is more complicated. The studies that paint the picture of lazy students don't look at family economic status at all. Indeed, they are not studies of financial aid recipients. As we've learned
from our study in Wisconsin, money makes a huge difference across
many measures of college success. We simply can't accept simplistic
explanations of complex problems. We don't know what we don't
ask about.

In higher education, academics and economics are often thought
of as separate and distinct. Elite institutions boast about their "no
loans" policies that purport to eliminate financial worries.[6] When
charging different amounts of money for different college majors
or hiking tuition, universities claim to use aid in order to "hold
harmless" students with few financial resources.[7] But in fact, the
new economics of college are tightly intertwined with the academic
experiences of undergraduates.

We found that academics were a central focus of students' time in
college. They cared a great deal about learning the material needed
to earn degrees and win jobs that would improve their economic
standing and those of their families. But how they went about pursuing that learning was shaped by the economic circumstances of
their existence.

Do Students Care about School?

In a *New York Times* article titled "Your So-Called Education," Richard Arum and Josipa Roksa write that "the funds from Pell Grants
and subsidized loans . . . have empowered students for good but

also for ill."[8] This statement follows on the heels of their critique of student behavior: "Many look for ways to attain an educational credential effortlessly and comfortably. And they are catered to accordingly. The customer is always right." The implication is clear: students, including Pell recipients, are not learning as much as they should be—and it is because they are not focused on school.

Economist Richard Vedder agrees with Arum and Roksa. He blames the financial aid system. "Lazy or mediocre students can get greater subsidies than hard-working and industrious ones," he writes. "Take Pell Grants. A student who works extra hard and graduates with top grades after three years will receive only half as much money as a student who flunks several courses and takes six years to finish or doesn't obtain a degree at all. In other words, for recipients of federal aid there are disincentives to excel."[9] Reihan Salam, writing in the *National Review*, concurs with Vedder in a blog titled, "If You're Going to Accept Direct Loans and Pell Grants, You Should Tell Us If Students Are Actually Learning Something."[10]

Clearly these writers and researchers haven't talked to the students in our study who struggled each and every semester to make ends meet. They have no empirical data with which to differentiate the behavior of Pell recipients from those of other students. In fact, the authors of *Academically Adrift* did not collect any information on students' family income or their financial aid, so they did not know who was receiving financial aid and who wasn't.[11] For policymakers considering the future of higher education, this should be a red flag.

The Wisconsin Scholars Longitudinal Study was designed to look at the relationship between money and college success. In an analysis that University of Wisconsin–Madison researcher Peter Kinsley and I conducted, we examined information collected on student surveys to see what we could learn about students' motivations.[12]

For students from low-income families, getting ahead in life is a main reason for attending college. Nearly 70 percent of our students cited a love of learning as a "very" or "extremely" important factor in their decision to pursue postsecondary education. Ninety-four percent believed that education would pay off in the future, and 88 percent felt that how they did in college would affect their success over time. These highly motivated students were also ambitious. Not only did they want to earn an undergraduate degree but 67 percent wanted to then go on to pursue a graduate degree.

Critically, while learning for its own sake was important to students in this sample, they also felt that they were good at school. Seventy percent believed that they were just as smart as their classmates, and 60 percent felt that they were able to get good grades. As first-year students, 50 percent said that they were effective at managing their time and schedule well enough to focus on school, and that grew to 56 percent in the second year of college.

Performing well academically and maintaining a strong GPA were central concerns for these students. A first-generation college student pursuing a business degree reflected on her academic performance: "I feel really pretty good. I mean looking back there's times when I wish I had studied harder for this test, or I wish I had worked harder in this class. [But] I think I'm sitting at a pretty solid GPA. I'm at a 3.47 and I really want to be at a 3.5 or a little bit above because then that's honors."

A woman pursuing a degree in elementary education highlighted the importance of pacing and psychological rewards to successful studying: "[I used to] try to do all my homework [at once] by going from one thing to the next thing to the next thing. I've learned that I kind of need at least a little break between each [assignment]. So I'll set a goal to finish a certain assignment, and then when I finish that I'll give myself like thirty minutes of TV watching or something. Then after that I'll do another assignment and then once I finish that assignment I'll give myself another little reward."

Of course, a desire to learn does not by itself guarantee that school will always be stimulating. In the first year of college, a time dominated by introductory classes and required course work, just 40 percent of students said that they found their classes interesting. An even smaller percentage (34%) found classes challenging during the first year, though by year two that number increased to 51 percent. The vast majority of the students (86%) felt that they were getting as much academic support as they had expected from their institution. To what extent that number reflected true satisfaction with the levels of support provided by the institutions, or simply low expectations of support on the part of the students, is not entirely clear.

The Most Serious Students on Campus

How do students spend their time? Many studies have asked how much time college students spend on campus. In our study, we wanted a more detailed picture, so we asked students how they allocated their time. First, some context. Higher education analyst Thomas Mortenson used data from the American Time Use Survey (2003–9), administered by the Bureau of Labor Statistics, to look at what undergraduates do each weekday. His sample was similar to the one in this study. It included people between the ages eighteen and twenty-four who were enrolled full time in college. He found that undergraduates devote about 14 percent of their time to school, including attending class and studying.[13] Focusing on weeks instead of days, Philip Babcock and Mindy Marks examined changes in student time allocation choices as measured by several distinct surveys of undergraduates attending four-year colleges and universities.[14] Both studies concluded that students don't seem to spend much time on school, and certainly not as much as they used to. And both claim that rather than focusing on school, many students appeared to be devoting themselves to leisure.[15]

Are financial aid recipients different? The Arum and Roksa and the Babcock and Marks studies don't look at whether students' time use varies by family income (although they do look at whether time use varies by parental education). Mortenson does examine this issue, and finds some evidence that low-income students (from families earning less than $25,000 a year) spend a bit more time on educational activities. But again: *none* of these studies explicitly examines the behavior of financial aid recipients, even though their results have been used to characterize that group.[16]

We looked at time use among Pell recipients attending both two-year and four-year institutions. We asked students to report on time spent caring for family (either older relatives or younger siblings)—something not included in any of the other studies. The

Table 16. Comparison of undergraduate time use: American Time Use Survey vs. Wisconsin Scholars Longitudinal Study

	Percentage of Time Devoted to Activity in 24-Hour Period		
	ATUS		
Activity	All Students	Low-Income Students	WSLS
Sleeping	38	37	32
Educational activities (class and study time)	14	15	28
Working and related activities	10	10	6
Family time	N/A	N/A	6
All other activities: travel, eating/drinking, grooming, exercise, and leisure	38	38	28

Sources: American Time Use Survey (ATUS), as reported in Mortenson, "Time Use of Full-Time College Students Ages 18 to 24 Years, 2003 to 2009"; and WSLS data.

Note. "Low-income" means an annual income of less than $25,000 per year. "N/A" indicates that the ATUS did not ask about family time. WSLS sample includes students who responded to the first-year survey questions on time use (*n* = 2,045).

results suggest that Pell recipients may be more focused on their academics and spend more time on educational activities than the average undergraduate portrayed in these other studies. As table 16 shows, our students devoted over one-fourth of their time to school. In addition, they devoted time to family, an activity that may be incorrectly folded into leisure activities in most time use research. These findings suggest that financial aid effectively reduces the time that students might otherwise spend on work (a possibility we will explore in more detail later in this chapter). It also suggests that financial aid may be well targeted to students who are indeed devoted to their schooling.

A serious challenge to students' abilities to spend even more time on school is their work schedules. Students usually attend classes between 8 A.M. and 4 P.M.[17] But these are the same hours that people usually work. Many colleges offer limited undergraduate classes outside of the 8 A.M.–4 P.M. span, and while some companies offer early or late shifts—or flexible schedules—many do not. Combining work and school can be difficult. Fifty-one percent of working students in the second year reported working between 8 A.M. and 12 P.M., and 73 percent reported working between 12 P.M. and 6 P.M.

But there are trade-offs even for students who worked other hours. Sizable fractions of students worked outside of standard workday hours. Sixty-one percent worked between 6 P.M. and 10 P.M., when they could be studying or in evening classes, while 23 percent worked between 10 P.M. and 8 A.M., time that could interfere with sleep.

Sophie Schmidt was a strong student in high school who appeared quite capable of college-level work. But as she put it, "Everyone I know who is getting straight As in college does not have a job! There's a lot of stress and a lot of drama. And you add that to school and it's a little overwhelming, and you have to prioritize; and sometimes, you know, studying gets pushed to the bottom of the list. And that's just the way it goes."

Sophie's thirty-hour-a-week work schedule affected her grades. Since she did not know her work schedule far enough in advance she was unsure how many credits she could take each term. Her work schedule often changed midsemester. She found herself adding and dropping classes, sometimes losing tuition she had paid as a result. She always aimed to "go for fifteen"—that is, to take fifteen credits per term—per the recommendations of her school, but it was hard to juggle classes and work while achieving a B average.[18] Her grades were Bs and Cs, sometimes putting her at risk for violating the satisfactory academic progress standard required for continued receipt of financial aid.

Sophie's case is not unusual. Peter Kinsley and I found that many of our students were concerned about maintaining a good GPA and selected a class load accordingly. Even so, 24 percent had a GPA below 2.0 (a C average) for their first year of college, including 19 percent of university students and 28 percent of two-year college students. Celina, a Latina who aimed to become a pharmacist, described her efforts to get good grades:

INTERVIEWER: How many credits are you taking this term?
CELINA: This term, fourteen.
INTERVIEWER: So is that the same for last term as well?
CELINA: I think last one I had twelve. Because my main focus was to

bring everything up, like my GPA, straight up. It was like a booster, because I took three science classes.

INTERVIEWER: You decided to take twelve because you thought that would help boost your GPA?

CELINA: Yeah, and it did—I took three classes so it was good. I could dedicate much more time to what I needed to do.

Only after first securing her GPA did Celina feel that she could take more credits. She had a lot on the line. At one point, her GPA was around 2.42, putting her at risk of not meeting the satisfactory academic progress requirement. Had that happened, she would have lost her $3,100 Pell Grant. However, by the next term she had pulled her GPA up to a 2.57, further above the standard.

Slow and Steady?

Do the GPA requirements associated with financial aid really encourage students to move through school at a slower pace? An experimental analysis Peter Kinsley and I conducted suggests that this is indeed possible.[19] We used transcript data to examine the grades that our students received in their first term of college and compared those grades to the number of credits they attempted to take in the second term. In the first term, all the students were receiving the Pell Grant and thus were subject to satisfactory academic progress standards requiring at least a C average—that is, a GPA of 2.0. In addition to Pell a random subsample of students was also offered the Wisconsin Scholars Grant, worth an additional $3,500 per year. For those students, the stakes associated with keeping their Pell Grant were especially high—keeping the Wisconsin Scholars Grant depended on it.

Our theory was that weaker students at risk of not making satisfactory academic progress and losing their financial aid would be more likely to take fewer credits. To reduce the risk to their aid, we hypothesized (based on data from interviews with students) they would opt for a slower pace to degree completion. We tested this by comparing the Wisconsin Scholars Grant measure (zero if they were

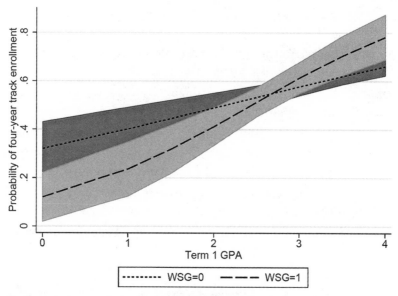

Figure 10. Predicted probability of four-year track enrollment (enrolling in 15 or more credits) in second term of college, by first-term GPA and offer of the Wisconsin Scholars Grant. WSG = 0 represents the control group, who did not receive the grant. WSG = 1 represents the treatment group, who received the grant. The solid lines above and below the WSG = 0 and WSG = 1 lines represent 95 percent confidence intervals. Sample includes Wisconsin Scholars Longitudinal Study participants who started at a four-year college, who consented to use of their college administrative records, and who were enrolled in classes during the first two weeks of their second term during their first year (n = 779). Source: Wisconsin Scholars Longitudinal Study data.

offered the grant, one if they were not) with the student's first-term GPA and modeling behavior for the second term. Figure 10 displays the results.

For students with first-semester GPAs below 2.0, there was a large and statistically significant reduction in the likelihood of taking fifteen or more credits in the second semester of the first year of college if they were offered the Wisconsin Scholars Grant. For students who were not at risk of failing to make satisfactory academic progress, there was no such impact.[20] In other words, it seems that raising the financial stakes on low-income students may cause some of them to proceed more slowly through college, potentially lengthening their time to degree (and raising their total costs) over time.

Heroic Focus

Sometimes the way in which students put together their schedules in college reflects an array of influences of which their professors and advisers are unaware. For low-income students in particular, efforts to prioritize school and learning may require spending time doing a variety of nonacademic activities to make college possible in the first place.

Ian Williams graduated from a small high school in Milwaukee, the same school that both his parents attended. He was not exposed to a rigorous college preparatory curriculum and received an eighteen on the ACT. Ian knew that he would need to spend a substantial amount of time studying in college, so he took a year off before beginning higher education: "I was trying to build up a work history because I knew that when I went to college it was going to be hard for me to work and get my education at the same time. So I dedicated one of my years to working and after that I said, it's time to go back to school."

Ian earned a 3.9 GPA in his first year. How he did it is instructive. During the summer before entering university and during his first semester, Ian participated in a "summer bridge" program, an introduction to college that provided tutoring and advising.[21] Ian credits the program with helping him feel more prepared academically and helping him establish friendships. Yet when he enrolled at the university, he was placed in remedial courses in both math and writing. Ian was frustrated, believing that the year he took off between high school and college, a year he hoped would prevent him from having to work during school, caused a learning loss that led him to need remediation. Since those remedial courses did not count toward his degree, the total time he would need to remain in college was extended.

Ian was focused. During his first interview, we asked him, "What kinds of things do you do when you're not in class? " Ian replied immediately: "Study. They told us every class is three hours [of studying] so I just study."

Ian enjoyed being in college. "I feel older now, like I'm doing something. When I was in high school I felt like I wasn't really impressing my family or anything, but since I came to college I feel like I'm really impressive." His commitment to studying continued. The fourth time we met with him, in the spring of his second year, he reported that with three academic classes on his schedule he was studying at least nine hours a week. He provided an example of his daily schedule: "Today, for instance, my class started at 9 A.M. and I have another class at 12 P.M. So I study between classes, and then after the second class, I study for three more hours until 5 P.M." Because Ian's family home did not have Internet access, he studied at the library.[22] When he felt he needed additional help, he sought tutoring. His goal was to gain entrance to the business school at his university, which required a GPA of at least 2.5, and he exceeded that. In his third year of school, his cumulative GPA was a 3.65.

But Ian had to contend with significant distractions. He avoided parties and alcohol because he knew that they often led to fighting and other trouble. And he tried to stay away from girls, since as he put it, "I'm not trying to have a relationship get between me and my schoolwork." He felt a strong pull from the neighborhood where he and his family lived and tried to spend as little time as possible on the streets around his home.

> I didn't want to go that negative route, I already knew it was a negative route, so I was more focused on the positive route. . . . [I told myself,] "If I go back in the streets it's going to be boring, real boring. There isn't anything to do in the streets, just sit around and think about where you're going to get your next month. I feel like being in school and studying makes time go by fast, way faster than being in the streets. . . ." That's why I'm always on campus or studying, and at night I just go home and sleep. I have morning classes every day because I know in the morning, that's when everyone will come to your house saying "drive me there, drive me there, come on and kick it, and all that stuff." So they go to my house now, and I'm in class. I just try to dodge it as much as I can. I feel like every day I'm in class something is probably happening at the house.

In other words, Ian built his life at school to counteract what could have been his life on the street. Sometimes he struggled to maintain a focus on school. "Every day I feel like bad stuff happens, but I still try to concentrate on my work as much as possible. . . . When you're at school, don't think about what's happening at home. Keep that on the outside. When you come to school, think about studying. . . . But since I'm in that type of environment at home, I can't really do that. I've got to think about what's happening at the house otherwise it can be a surprise to me if I went to the house and something happened." While Ian wanted to spend as much time and mental energy on school as he could, ignoring what was going on at home didn't always work. Once, he didn't answer a call from his sister because he was in class. She was calling him because his brother had just been in a fight. "My brother doesn't have morning classes like I do. He has afternoon classes, and when I'm in class I'm like 'Oh, don't let them after my brother. . . .' That's why I go home sometimes to see if he has school. And when he does, I feel relief because I really want him to get his education like I am." If Ian could not keep his family safe, he might not stay in school.

The grants and scholarships Ian had unexpectedly received eased his financial situation considerably, and given his academic talents and commitment, he had no trouble meeting the scholarship's requirements of a 3.0 GPA. The more he studied and tried to push the calls from home to the side, the more money he had for college. His grants and scholarship grew and his net price shrank, falling from almost $11,000 in his freshman year to about $5,000 by his junior year. This made it possible for him to work just twelve hours a week and focus on school. He was going to make it.

What Money Can Buy

It is clear that financial pressures can reduce the amount of time students spend on school. So if we give students more money, will they study more? The answer is not straightforward. Funds can release students from time they would otherwise spend working, making it possible for them to allocate more time to school. But the newly available time might go elsewhere, either because it is needed (in the case of childcare) or because of students' preferences. Struggling students who feel they are unable to afford important things or who are concerned they are taking out too many loans may opt to use additional grant money to buy those things or to take out less in loans rather than reducing work hours.[23] Also, students often can't easily adjust their work hours.[24] Employers hire people to work a certain number of hours, and students may not be able to reduce their hours without quitting their job altogether. And, unlike regular wages, grant money comes with rules and restrictions that limit how it can be used.

In a quasi-experimental analysis of the effects of financial aid on time use, researcher Stephen DesJardins and his colleagues found that a merit-based scholarship reduced the time undergraduates spent working and increased time spent on cultural activities and community service but had no effect on the amount of time students spent studying, relaxing, or doing other extracurricular activities.[25] Most experimental studies of performance-based scholarships, however, report that additional aid has no impact on students' employment.[26]

Sociologists Katharine Broton, James Benson, and I examined whether the Wisconsin Scholars Grant effectively reduced the time students spent working. Our experimental analysis indicated that the grant modestly reduced long working hours, but it was not a dollar-for-dollar displacement. An additional $1,000 of annual grant aid reduced the number of hours that students worked, on average, by only thirty-five minutes a week.[27]

Still, offering students additional grant aid can reduce their need to work very long hours, and we found that it also helps them avoid working at night, which may be a particularly important objective for policymakers. The Wisconsin Scholars Grant cut the fraction of students working extensively—twenty or more hours a week— from 30 to 25 percent, and reduced the fraction of students working between 2 A.M. and 8 A.M. from 14 to 8 percent.

Notably, the impacts on extensive and off-campus work accrued entirely to Pell recipients who were first-generation college students (more precisely, neither parent has a college degree). There was a ten-percentage-point gap in the probability of extensive work among students who did not receive the Wisconsin Scholars Grant—35 percent of first-generation students worked twenty or more hours a week, compared to 25 percent of second-generation students. But the Wisconsin Scholars Grant eliminated that gap entirely. Among first-generation students who got the grant, just 24 percent worked extensively.

The Price of Underpreparation

Most students who begin college without strong high school academic preparation are not as fortunate as Ian Williams. They don't have the benefit of summer bridge programs, nor do unexpected scholarships appear out of the blue. They have to work, and for these students, it is especially difficult to get good grades, since they often need additional time—time they don't have—for studying, meeting with professors, and tutoring. Without these supports, their grades suffer. But most students don't understand this relationship between having a job and grades. They've never felt particularly successful in school, and they are accustomed to working, so they focus on earning enough to pay for college rather than studying.

That is the situation that Chloe Johnson faced. Her standard Wisconsin high school diploma did not prepare her for the rigorous science required for the veterinary technician program she chose. For starters, she needed another chemistry course, which she took at the technical college nearest her home before moving away to attend the technical college where she would pursue her degree. When she enrolled, she started working at PetSmart and Kohl's, as described in chapter 4, and tried to do her best in her five courses. She was caught in a double bind. She started school poorly prepared to succeed academically, then her work hours meant she had less time to study, and lack of money kept her from benefiting from extracurricular opportunities offered by her professors that might have helped her grades. She reported: "They [the program] are planning this [class] trip, and you have to pay for it. One of the instructors planning it feels that it's a really good experience for everyone who goes—she highly recommended it. But I can't go. So I'm missing out on this experience because I don't have the money to go." When Chloe realized she wasn't doing well in school, she dropped one course to focus on the other four. But she faced unexpected consequences: "I was looking into dropping one of my classes, maybe putting it off until next semester. [The financial aid officer] talked me out of it—she's like, well, you could quit now and lose out on the money [tuition] because you waited too long [past the add/drop period]. Or I could stick it out and just do my best."

The Price of Part-Time Enrollment

Losing tuition money that had already been spent did not seem wise to Chloe, so she kept all five classes. She thought about switching to part-time enrollment during the next term so that she could more easily make her schedule work and do better in her classes. But she didn't know how this would affect her finances. Students who attend college part time receive a partial Pell Grant that is exactly half the amount received by full-time students, based on the assumption that there is a linear relationship between college costs and number of hours enrolled. But in practice, the costs of attending college are not split in half when a student takes two courses (six credits) instead of four (twelve credits). While tuition varies linearly by the credit hour, other college costs do not. For example, while students taking fewer courses may not need to buy as many books, the books they do need are not necessarily less expensive. Moreover, living costs must still be covered, and students taking even a few courses often have to work only part time rather than full time, which, as discussed in chapter 4, does not pay as much on an hourly basis and rarely comes with benefits.

Chloe was frustrated by the trade-offs involved in attending college full time simply to get enough financial aid. "It's going to take me three years to finish (rather than two). Financial aid requires twelve credits a semester to be a full-time student. So I have to take an extra class next semester that's not in the program. And in the third and fourth semesters I have to take an extra class not in the program just so I can get financial aid. So it's like you take an extra class to get the financial aid but you're still going backwards because you're spending more money." Finally, during the exam period of her first term of college, Chloe dropped a class. "I talked to my instructor and told her what was going on, and she said I should probably withdraw from the class I am doing the worst in and try and concentrate on my other classes. My grades improved a little bit but not enough to put me over the top. I mean, the stuff wasn't hard for me at all, it was just that I was so exhausted."

Some researchers and policy analysts have recommended changing federal policy to increase the financial aid penalty for attending college part time. Some even suggest upping the Pell definition of full-time status to fifteen credits from the current twelve.[28] Proposals like these would further reduce the size of the Pell Grant received by students like Chloe, who struggle to balance school with work.

Clearly, school was not going well for Chloe, yet she tried to remain optimistic. When I asked her in December of her first semester, "How sure are you that you're going to be here next semester?" she responded: "I'm pretty sure. I'm pretty dead set on this and I'm pretty determined to do it." At the same time, she admitted that, "by the looks of it, it would take a miracle to pull off passing one of my classes because I've just fallen so far behind."

Chloe did not realize it, but she was in danger of failing to meet her college's satisfactory academic progress requirements: a C average and completion of 67 percent or more of cumulative attempted credits. But Chloe was cornered. Dropping a class would lower the ratio of courses that Chloe had completed, and getting a bad grade in that class would lower her GPA. In other words, at that point in the semester Chloe was about to face academic and therefore financial consequences for having attempted college without sufficient funds. But she didn't understand exactly what was happening. She simply knew that she was exhausted from working long hours trying to pay for college and not doing nearly as well as she had hoped. But it was not until the semester was over and she was preparing for the second term, having just taken out a loan to pay for tuition, that she learned the truth.

It was the Saturday right before school started again [for the term] that I found out. I got a letter in the mail that just said that I was dismissed. It pretty much said "You're kicked out because you failed too many of your classes." Or as they put it, I was "dismissed" from the program, because my grades weren't up to par. This was hard because I was sleeping in a lot of my classes to try and catch up with sleep. It was a combination of just stress and driving and trying to hold two jobs just so that I could afford everything on a day-to-day basis.

Chloe was stunned, in tears, and unsure what to do next. The online description of her program offers the following warning to students considering employment during school: "Whether or not you hold a part-time job should at least be partially dependent on your scholastic ability and how well you do in your college courses. About 90 percent of [our] students have some part-time employment while attending school. However, working too many hours at outside employment has been demonstrated to seriously impair student success in the Veterinary Technician Program."

But apparently no one had shown this information to Chloe or explained the implications. Critically, she did not know what she could have done differently, given the high price of college and the limited financial aid she received.

I was like, ok, I'm dismissed from this program, and I thought it was something I really wanted to do, and it just hit me hard. I was just crushed. I had my hopes set real high . . . it was kind of a relief, but then again it was pretty stressful. . . . It was like, "You know, I went through all of this work and I accomplished nothing. I failed." It was kind of a little bit of both and it actually hit me pretty hard because I was just crushed. I was like, "Wow, I'm never going to get anywhere." I've got, you know, pretty much no hope for the future.

Chloe panicked, and made a sudden move. "I called my dad . . . he lives in Florida . . . and I told him what was going on. I ended up getting on a plane the next day at 6 A.M. I was like, I've gotta start over.

The only way I thought about starting over was, you know, picking up my stuff and moving." Chloe and I were sitting in a Tampa-area coffee shop when she told me this story.

> I had a return flight, but I never took it. . . . I was registered for classes but after I got the letter I pulled out of all of my classes and I took my parking sticker back so that I wouldn't be charged for it. . . . I kept checking on my account to make sure I didn't owe any money and was out of my classes. They awarded me financial aid for the spring and I didn't know what to do with it. You know, I was sitting there with this check—I was like, what do I do with it? I didn't know if I should send it back or what. And then I ended up getting a letter from [the loan servicer] saying that because I was no longer enrolled I needed to pay the amount in full from first and second semesters. But all the money from first semester was pretty much all gone from trying to pay bills and everything. So I'm like, uh oh, what do I do? About two weeks ago I finally got everything figured out . . . my loans defaulted. But I got it figured out and now I'm in an automatic payment plan where they automatically take money out of my checking account the same day every month.

Chloe began waiting tables at the restaurant her father managed while she hunted for another job. In some ways, life as a so-called college dropout suited her better than the life she had experienced while in school. "I definitely feel less stressed out. I mean, when I was going to school I got really sick. . . . I ended up having to get muscle relaxants because I was grinding my teeth at night and I was getting horrible migraines from all the stress. . . . It makes you drool a lot when you sleep and gives you bad cottonmouth. I had to watch when I took them so that I wouldn't take them and then fall asleep on the way to school or on the way home from work or anything."

She now ate regularly, and, to my eyes, looked healthier. Her late nights now occurred a few times a week, rather than almost every day—and those nights were now spent socializing, instead of working the late shift. Chloe was unsure about her next steps. While she thought that she might eventually return to college, she was sure she would never return to Wisconsin. Her stepsister was enrolled at a for-profit university, and Chloe began to consider that possibility. One year after beginning college, Chloe started an entirely new life in a state a thousand miles away. Her attempt to gain a degree had yielded Chloe little more than bad memories and monthly automatic loan payments.

The Element of Surprise

Many of the students in our study were surprised by the amount of work their college courses required. Forty-three percent of our students reported that their first-semester college classes were more difficult than they had expected, and 40 percent of all students said that their grades were lower than anticipated. In their first year, 72 percent of them sought academic guidance, and among those who sought it, the vast majority received help and found it useful. Yet 15 percent of students indicated that they were getting less academic help from their college than they had expected.

Some students clearly misunderstood what was required to succeed in college-level courses. Mai, an immigrant from Thailand, reported:

> My first semester I didn't do so well. I thought that the grading scale was if you are in class and you participate and you do your assignments and stuff, you'll have a decent grade. But . . . it doesn't matter if you come to class or not. If you do well on your exams and your final, then you'll get a good grade based on your exam and finals. And even though I was there every day, I did the work and I read, I have test anxiety, so I kind of bombed my tests and I didn't receive the grade I thought I would receive.

To cope, Mai started meeting an adviser once or twice a week, a practice she continued for several subsequent semesters. She told us that she was very motivated to do well because getting a good education was a way to make her parents proud, secure a good job, and be able to provide for herself, her younger siblings, and her parents.

In subsequent semesters, Mai changed her major several times. She switched from biology to business to accounting before finally settling on communications. Dogged by stress about both grades and finances, Mai offered the following analogy: "Every time I look up, there's like a knife just dangling [above me], and, if I do something wrong, I could totally destroy everything I have going for me." To Mai, these "knives" were grades and financial problems, and she emphasized how stressed she felt that she was not making enough to cover her expenses. She said her biggest goal was helping her family. In her words: "If I'm not able to help my siblings when they need financial help, am I really a good sibling to them?"

Toward the end of her third year of college, both of Mai's parents lost their jobs, and Mai transferred to a for-profit college campus near her home. She made this decision even though she knew the for-profit college would accept only two-thirds of her previous credits, meaning it would take an extra year to graduate. Mai explained: "I was thinking . . . I can stay one year [at the university] and I guess my parents will suffer through one year, or I could come back home and be able to help them but also continue my education. . . . I know that the little things I do back at home will help them out a lot. So I kind of . . . weigh my options and weigh the benefits. So, when I did that, my best choice is for home."

Choices and Doubts

Nima Chaudhary took school very seriously. During her first year of college she took ten courses, six in the first term, and four in the second. She attended school four days a week from 8 A.M. until 8 P.M., except for Wednesdays when she got home at 4 P.M. She never skipped class and disapproved of her friends who did: "My friends skip class and it kind of makes me angry because you're paying for it. I don't know why people skip, it's your money that you're losing." But being present was not enough, and Nima found that sometimes she did not do well enough in a course, often because of the speaking requirements (English was not her first language) and would end up dropping it. She did this during her second year of college, switching from four courses to three. She tried to find a replacement course to remain full time but couldn't. She lost the Wisconsin Scholars Grant, which required full-time enrollment, and her Pell was reduced. "I got tired of trying to get financial aid because it is so hard, and they are always saying, 'You're missing this and that,' and so I just paid the whole thing with my own money and closed out my bank account."

Her mother was a nurse who worked very long hours, and Nima felt that her mom's job was grueling and that her mother looked older than her years. She was determined to make different choices. At the same time, she appreciated her parents, and wanted to do her duty at home. "I feel so bad for my parents. Their whole life has been so bad. My mom has had to work since she was a kid—my grandma sold my mom to her relatives or somebody to make money, because they were really poor." Nima's love, affection, and gratitude toward her father came through as Nima described how he cooked and cleaned for his children even while struggling with chronic pulmonary disease. As she pursued her degree, she spent time each week at home caring for him.

The family was close, but Nima's choice of program—graphic design—was a constant source of tension at home. "I'm so into art, and they [my family] just don't get it. They told me to go into nursing because at the end you have a job right away. But I don't know about nursing. . . . I have to go into nursing so that I can help my mom. . . . They say, art isn't going to feed you, and I mean I see their point but at the same time it's what I really want to do."

Money mattered to Nima and her family. The lack of available jobs in her city was one of the most important reasons why she attended college. She thought that college would help her get a good job. Her oldest brother pursued a degree in engineering, and the other brother a degree in nursing. "My brother says, we have to get a job, we just have to—he wants to graduate really fast so he can get a job and make her [their mom] cut down her hours."

In every interview Nima spoke about her family members, often at length. Her brothers excelled at the University of Wisconsin–Madison but also incurred debt and, after graduating had a tough time finding jobs. When they eventually succeeded, they lifted up the family (one even bought a house and moved everyone into it), but when they struggled, Nima watched carefully, and took away the lesson that she needed to be especially cautious with her choices. A year after we first met, Nima reported: "My parents still don't like that I'm in graphic design. I feel like they don't really support me. I think they want me to do good but they don't really see me getting a job at the end of it. . . . I understand that part but I just want to make some art . . . they joke about it, they call it Garbage Design when they're mad at me." This lack of support affected how Nima saw herself and her work. She noted that being entrepreneurial was important to her success as an artist but found that her insecurities and anxieties kept her from showing her work to others. "I don't feel like I'm talented. I just feel like I'm doing what my brother said, a hobby. He told me to go into nursing and then take art as a hobby. But I'm being selfish in a way because I'm not doing anything to help my parents' situation." Nima struggled with anxiety and depression that went untreated throughout college. "I always have self-doubt, I can't help it," she said. Strong feeling of deprivation from her childhood lingered, leaving her feeling unsure of herself and her relationships with others, and she often wondered whether she was valued. These feelings were made more complicated by her status as a Nepalese woman; she perceived that Nepalese culture held certain expectations. She was supposed to be obedient, submissive, and quiet and remain home with her family. She was not taught to drive, was asked to account for her time outside the home, and was derided for her choices when it came to schooling, friends, and hobbies. But Nima wanted to be expressive, creative, and independent. This showed in her artwork (which often included portraits of people with eyes full of passion and hope), her interest in makeup and hair design, and her persistent focus on graphic design despite family pressure for nursing.

Bad Information, Bad Choices

Students can enter college with great expectations that are sometimes unrealistic. Ideally, colleges would help students realize their ambitions, while also helping them understand reality—including the specific requirements needed for graduation and the postcollege implications of their choices. That does not always happen.

Tyler Olson, the former football player, started college with big plans—plans he would later scale back. At first, Tyler wanted to go into business administration. In that field, Tyler expected he would be able to make $100,000 a year once he had a bachelor's degree, and he wanted to focus on classes that counted toward a business management degree with a minor in German.[29] While his grades in high school were not strong, he had taken rigorous course work, and received a $1,400 Talent Incentive scholarship from the state as a reward. With a year at another university already under his belt, he reported: "I don't understand why people say college is so hard. I find college a helluva lot easier than I found high school. College isn't challenging to me whatsoever in any way." He responded to surveys indicating that he found college life "extremely" fun and interesting, he liked the freedom of being in college, and he enjoyed the people he went to school with.

Even though Tyler found his courses easy, he soon discovered that completing his degree on time was not straightforward. Many of the courses he was taking did not count toward his major, an error he attributed to inadequate advising. While he saw his adviser each term, he felt that she did not listen to him. Instead of putting him on a track for a major in marketing information systems, she directed him to courses required for computer information systems majors. Once he figured this out, he dropped several nonrequired courses, including a math class that he was failing. "Because of my adviser, I now have three years of school left instead of two. Awesome. I'm sitting here thinking, wow, I'll be twenty-four years old when I graduate!" His efforts to take the classes he needed when he needed them were further hampered by his struggles to pay for books. He started each term by registering for at least sixteen credits and then dropping classes after he figured out how much the books cost.

Over time, Tyler began to question why he was bothering with college. Two years after we first met him, we asked him to look back and reflect on his experiences in college thus far. He replied:

> That's something I've thought a lot about, and it kind of sucks but I really don't know why I'm going to school anymore. . . . There's

not even one thing I'm looking forward to [this semester]. . . . I don't know what I'm going to do with what I'm majoring in. I mean, I know what I can do, but it sucks thinking about a 9 A.M. to 5 P.M. everyday job, and how hard it is going to be to get a job right now. Don't let anyone tell you different—it's just going to get worse, this economy, and it's going to make finding a job even harder. I'm going to keep going to school because there's no way to stop, I'm already three years into it, but the only thing that is keeping me going is thinking that someday I can work for myself. All it will take is me putting in the time and effort.

Around that time, Tyler stopped talking about business administration and a possible future in graduate school and started to consider enrolling in the army.

Making Learning Possible

With an exceptionally generous tribal scholarship in hand, and fairly strong high school preparation, Norbert Webster was in many ways destined to succeed in college from the moment he began. He did not need to work and/or take out loans, and he was able to live like students with far more resources—on campus, closely connected to other students, organizations, and faculty. Norbert appreciated this and, anticipating the hard work involved in college academics, had prepared himself. During his last year of high school he enrolled at the College of the Menominee Nation to take a math class and a course to prepare him for college-level reading. Those courses, paid for by his school district, allowed Norbert to start off prepared and with some college-level credits completed. It wasn't long before he saw the benefits. "I was always pretty good at math, so I thought I would take a math class there to get started before college. My roommate [in college] has had to take two remedial math classes before even getting into a regular math class, so I'm kind of glad I did that."

Norbert was the rare student who could afford to live on campus. Just 13 percent of undergraduates nationwide do this, as did 45 percent of our students.[30] Norbert made the most of this opportunity.

For his first year, he opted to live in a residence hall for international students. He wanted to meet different kinds of people and felt that this was an important piece of the college experience, a piece that really engaged him. Referring to his high school, he said, "It is so small that you don't get to meet different people, especially since everyone is Native American. But here there are so many different types of people! Since I live in the international dorm where people from all different countries live, I can just sit down in one of their rooms for an hour and talk about where they are from and what they believe and such." These early college experiences became even more important to Norbert when, as a business major, he had to learn about different cultural expectations. His living experiences connected to his academic experiences. He felt like his schooling was paying off—it was teaching him something useful. The ability to live on campus made other types of connections possible for him as well. For example, he chose a roommate who was also Oneida, and who shared Norbert's commitment to academics. "It's really motivating for me because he [the roommate] says, 'I'm going to the library for an hour,' and then I'm like, 'Well, you know what, I'll go there for an hour, too,' and I will knock an hour out reading or studying my notes." His roommate also helped him keep the costs of attending college down by joining him for evenings playing Xbox in their room rather than going out to parties or bowling, since these things would cost additional money. More than once a week, Norbert decided against going out with friends in order to save money. When he did go out, it was a conscious decision: "Yesterday when we went bowling, my roommate and I had a big debate about whether we wanted to go because he doesn't have that much money either, so we were both just kind of sitting there and I was like, 'Well, let's just go, it's Friday night and we don't want to just sit here and study all night, so let's go bowling.' And that's what we did. It's about having this debate, like, do I want to spend this money [his savings for college] on this, knowing that it's probably not going to be replenished?" Norbert's desire to remain connected to and supported by his tribe was enhanced by a special adviser who supported Native American students. The presence of such an adviser on campus was one reason he chose that particular university. He also joined the campus's intertribal student organization.

He attended class regularly and went to office hours, too, building strong relationships with his college professors. He was among a small handful of students we interviewed who described in detail how professors interacted with them (he especially loved that they knew him by name).

Academics were important to Norbert. When frustrated with noise in his dorm, he found a quiet study room. In his first year of college, Norbert's attendance in class and his diligence resulted in a 3.27 GPA. His standards were high: each year he focused on keeping a B average or better. This was a benchmark he set for himself, since both his Pell Grant and the Oneida scholarship only required a C average.

> You have to submit your grades to [the tribe] every semester and tell them what classes you are taking. At the end of every semester, you need a C average to continue funding and if you get below that they will put you on academic probation. They'll pay for the next semester while you are on probation, and if you again fail to meet the C average they will cut off funding until you take twelve credits and receive a C average. . . . I think about that a lot. But even without that requirement, for me to get into the business major, I need a 2.2. That's kind of a double motivator for me because I need to keep it up to get from Oneida and I need to keep it up to get into business. It helps out a little bit to know that as long as I'm doing and studying, getting my stuff done, I will be receiving some money. . . . I've always tried to get at least Cs on everything—no matter what—I usually get higher.

His commitment to getting good grades lasted, and he maintained a GPA of about 3.3 over time.

Norbert also made use of the interim periods offered at his university during the winter and summer terms to earn more credits, usually adding three credits (at no additional cost) during that time. He reported enjoying interim courses because he could focus on them with fewer distractions.

In his second year of college, Norbert learned that he could get a certified public accounting license if he stayed for a fifth year of college and, after assessing the available financial aid, decided to do that. Three semesters into college, he talked about also pursuing a master's degree in entrepreneurship and starting his own accounting firm in the Green Bay area. His Oneida Scholarship allowed five years of support, as well as funding for graduate school, and Norbert recognized the benefit of more time in school. By his fifth year, he was what he called a "super senior" with enough credits to earn both a bachelor's degree and an accounting license.

Norbert attributed his success to his hard work, a message he wanted others from his community to understand.

> A lot of the kids from my [high] school say I'm smart, but a lot of the time I just work hard and stuff with my studying. I study a lot and do my work. When people say, "Oh you're smart and you're going to college," I tell them that it's not about being smart, it's about how much you put into it. I am not the smartest . . . I just pay attention and get my work done. . . . It's about paying attention in class, not falling asleep and dozing off, taking good notes—I know the material a little better because I studied it, and that's how I see it. . . . They don't realize that if they did the same thing, if they studied and got their stuff done, it's not that far of a stretch to be considered smart.

Norbert was among the fortunate one-third of students in the study who were not surprised at how difficult it was to afford college. "[Financial aid has] been pretty beneficial to me. I don't have to go to work, and it helps me have more time for studying and getting my schoolwork done, as opposed to working on weekends."

The freedom created by a stable financial situation enabled Norbert to devote himself to college life in ways that we rarely observed in other students. Sophie Schmidt, for example, was also well prepared for college in the academic sense, and she went to a university filled with opportunities. But the difficulties Sophie faced paying for school overshadowed each day, as she spent time worrying, stressed, and often in tears. Ian Williams focused on school but was unable to live on campus or participate in extracurricular activities the way that Norbert could, since he had to work and help his family. Chloe Johnson was just as eager as the others to learn the skills needed for the job she wanted, but she could not stay awake in class after working too late the day before. Norbert was unusual not because he cared about classes or studies but because he didn't have to worry about having enough money to pay for school.

8
City of Broken Dreams

For most students, going to college in America doesn't mean venturing far from home. More than three in four students attend colleges within fifty miles of their homes, continuing their relationships with families, neighbors, and nearby institutions as they pursue degrees.[1] Proximity to home is an especially important factor in the college decisions of low-income and race/ethnic minority students.[2] The college opportunities presented in a given home city or town, therefore, help to determine what the college experience looks like. It also largely determines the price that students pay.

While there is a great deal of attention devoted to how much states contribute overall to their public colleges and universities, there is much less discussion about how funds are distributed among those institutions. The robust conversation about funding equity and adequacy in K–12 education has not yet taken place in higher education. Some colleges and universities are better positioned than others to draw on resources from diverse sources, including endowments and private funds, while others depend heavily on the state. When those resources are not forthcoming, students and families pay the price.[3]

In Wisconsin, the importance of location, community, and funding equity is nowhere more evident than in the city of Milwaukee. In 1936, Milwaukee was crowned "the best governed city in the U.S." Home to strong social services including excellent public parks, libraries and civic centers, and a notable work relief system, Wisconsin's major metropolitan city was in many respects a wonderful place to live and learn.[4] Consistent with the meaning of its Algonquian name, it was a beautiful and pleasant land.

Today Milwaukee is one of the poorest and most segregated cities in America. One-quarter of families live below the federal poverty level, nearly 27 percent of households are on food stamps, and over 36 percent of households take in $25,000 or less in annual income.[5] The level of black-white segregation in Milwaukee is the second highest in the nation. Some consider the city one of the worst places in the country to live for African Americans.[6] Its stock of college graduates lags behind nearly every other major central city in the country.[7]

Even though it is Wisconsin's largest and most diverse city—and only a ninety-minute drive from the state capitol in Madison—Milwaukee is often treated as an afterthought when it comes to state politics and policy. Reforms and budget cuts to social welfare programs like BadgerCare and changes to public education, including the expansion of private school vouchers at public expense, and increased spending on corrections, disproportionally impact Milwaukee residents. Meanwhile, at the K–12 level, Wisconsin has the largest educational disparities between African American and white students in the country, and its schools suspend African American students at the highest rate in the country.[8]

Poverty and race are intertwined in cities across the United States, and the same is true in Milwaukee. While 13 percent of white households fall below the poverty line in Milwaukee, the rate is 30 percent for Latinos and 39 percent of African Americans. That is to say, while only one in eight white residents live below the poverty line, three in ten Latinos and about two in five African Americans do.[9] The city isn't home to the widest racial disparities in poverty—Dane County, the home of Madison, holds that distinction—but the scope and scale of the challenge is far greater in Milwaukee.[10]

The concentration of poverty, coupled with what sociologist William Julius Wilson terms the "disappearance of work," has created extraordinarily difficult living conditions, creating challenges for pursuing educational opportunities.[11] It is hard to imagine how the city will ever get ahead when its residents are constrained in this way. As Mark Bittman, writing in the *New York Times*, noted: "When people are undereducated, impoverished, malnourished, un- or under-employed, or underpaid and working three jobs, their lives are diminished, as are their opportunities. As are the opportunities of their children."[12] With barely three in ten white Milwaukee residents over the age of twenty-five, and just one in ten African American residents, holding bachelor's degrees, the future of the city is in jeopardy.[13] Thirteen percent of African American men in Milwaukee are currently in prison, and half of all African American men in their thirties have been in prison, whereas just 9 percent hold bachelor's degrees.[14]

Political leaders at the state, county, and municipal levels are all trying to increase the percentage of college graduates among their constituents because people with higher education bring social and economic benefits. Graduates make higher wages and can spend more money. They contribute more to local tax bases, attract business investment, and are more likely to start their own enterprises. And they are less likely to need government public assistance services.[15] Falling behind in the competition to have a more educated workforce has dramatic consequences. One study estimated that if Wisconsin's educational attainment and incomes were equal to Minnesota's, Wisconsin residents would bring home $26 billion more every year.[16]

Milwaukee needs a college-educated workforce more than anywhere else in the state. Like other large, diverse cities in America, Milwaukee needs the educational and research enterprises of its higher education institutions to spur personal, community, and economic development. When higher education fails, Milwaukee loses out to other cities that offer expanding economic improvements and chances for equitable, inclusive futures. Some people and businesses have left Milwaukee, while others are choosing not to move there. As the old manufacturing base of the industrial Midwest continues to decline, those left behind have fewer and fewer opportunities.

Many of our students who were attending college in Milwaukee grew up under tougher circumstances than students from other parts of the state. They were more likely to come from single-parent families, and their parents earned less money. Life in the city often brought additional perils. Ian Williams wasn't the only man we met who worried about the influence of "the streets" on his family members. While Milwaukee students were not the only ones to voice concern about neighborhood violence, they did so more frequently than students from anywhere else.

The financial wager involved in attending college has higher stakes in Milwaukee, with some of Wisconsin's highest net prices and lowest graduation rates. Many students in this study attended the University of Wisconsin–Milwaukee (UW–Milwaukee), an institution that shares a research mission with UW–Madison but receives far less state support and has a much smaller endowment (Milwaukee's is just over $10 million while Madison's is close to $2.2 billion).[17] So even though many of the study's Pell recipients in Milwaukee needed a great deal of support to graduate, they were much less likely to find what they needed than students elsewhere in the state.

The Grinder

Alicia, an African American woman born in Milwaukee, graduated from a public high school and entered college with big ideas. She intended to earn a master's degree and become either a teacher or a social worker. Either of those careers, she thought, would pay about $30,000 a year. She felt that it was very important to get more education and a better job than her parents had—neither of them had finished college and both were struggling to hold onto their jobs. Alicia understood college was an important step toward her specific career goals and felt optimistic that education would pay off. Her daughter, two years old and born during her junior year of high school, was a strong source of motivation.

> I don't want to see myself where my mom is. I don't want to ever have to depend on a guy to take care of my daughter and me. It's all about us—everything I do is about us. . . . I look at people who don't go to college and I know I've got to do something. Without a college education you can't get a decent job anywhere. . . . I don't want to have to live paycheck to paycheck, struggling like

I am now. I just want me and my daughter to be happy and not worrying about anything. I've got to do it for us.

Alicia was determined. On her initial survey during the first few months of college, she said that there was no way she would drop out of college.

During that first semester, Alicia spent about 7.5 hours a day in class and studying and about four hours a day caring for her child. She was happy to have found affordable daycare at a program in the basement of her grandmother's church. Since she had no expected family contribution, she received the maximum Pell Grant and was chosen to get the Wisconsin Scholars Grant, too. But she still needed to pay more than $10,000 a year. "If you don't have the money, you have to find a way to get it or you can't go. They're not just going to let you in because, oh you have nice eyes, and you can go to college."

To pay the bills, Alicia took out a subsidized loan and worked thirty hours a week. She worked both a work-study job and another job off campus, earning a total of $840 per month (about seven dollars per hour). She also used a credit card, carrying a balance between $500 and $1,000 per month. She slept about five hours a night.

Even though she had a busy schedule, she did not feel overwhelmed. When asked during our survey to rate her level of agreement with the statements "I'm having more problems affording college than I expected," and "I'm not as happy in college as I'd expected," Alicia strongly disagreed. She really liked the freedom of college life and found the classes interesting but difficult. She was only minimally concerned about money and paying for college. She wished, however, that she had the resources to concentrate her energy where it was most needed: "If I had more money, I wouldn't have to work as much, and I could spend more time with my daughter. That's one of my downfalls now—I'm so focused with school and work and then, I mean I do see her, but by the time we make it home it's like, 'Okay: eat dinner, bath, bed.'"

During that first semester, Alicia was only somewhat confident that if she faced financial problems, she could resolve them without dropping out of college. Like many other students who grew up in a persistently poor home, she was not sure she could get financial support from her family if she needed it, and she didn't feel strongly that they encouraged her to stay in college. But they did help her with childcare. Sometimes her father got off working the third shift and came right over in the morning to help Alicia get ready for school. This was important, because the childcare program at her university was greatly oversubscribed, as are the majority of such programs across the country.[18] In exchange for this help, she provided regular financial support to her family, especially to her mother who was unemployed.

Toward the end of that first year, however, things began to fall apart. Her daughter's daycare situation had grown unstable, her mother had begun staying with friends out of state because she could not pay rent, and she was no longer communicating with Alicia. Alicia managed to enroll for a second year of college but was able to spend very little time at school. Instead she spent most of her time taking care of her baby and working at a coffee shop off campus for thirty-nine hours per week at $8.25 an hour. Some days she worked from 8 A.M. to 6 P.M., other days, she worked 2 A.M. to 8 A.M. She slept just four hours a night, and she got up at 5:45 A.M. each day. She had to take sleeping pills at least three times a week and sometimes had trouble staying awake during the day. "School is a struggle," she said. "When I get stressed out my body just wants to shut down, but I can't let it because I have things to do."

Even with extensive work hours, Alicia had trouble regularly paying her rent and utilities and was very worried about having enough money to pay for things she needed. Her sister moved in with her but was not employed and received only a small amount of cash assistance from the state. They fought often.

At that point, Alicia was taking twelve credits and had a C average. She was spending less time on school than she would have liked and was not doing as well as she wanted to despite trying hard. She met with professors during office hours and visited her adviser. She studied alone. She felt overwhelmed; she was not academically prepared for college work, she was exhausted, and she was now afraid of failing. Between work, her responsibilities to her daughter, and the demands of other family members, there was too much going on for her to focus on school. She wished she could simplify the situation and have more time for class. She still wanted that master's degree and now hoped that if she got it she would earn $55,000 a year. "Oh, I'm going to graduate—I don't have a choice. There ain't no stopping me," she told us.

Six months later, Alicia was still enrolled in college but had moved in with a man after her apartment was broken into while she was in class. She was now twenty years old. She still had difficulties with her mom, who came to visit from time to time and created "drama." Her boyfriend made her feel safe and helped take care of her daughter, and she felt better equipped to focus on school. She had less financial aid than in the past, likely because of her work earnings, but she felt it was easier to make ends meet with a partner.

That was the last time we saw Alicia. At the end of her sophomore year, she dropped out of touch. She was no longer enrolled in college and did not return phone calls. We were able to confirm through administrative records that though she spent eight semesters in school, by 2014 she had not earned a degree.

Big City, Big U

Improving educational attainment and economic conditions has been the driving force in public higher education in Milwaukee since its inception. The University of Wisconsin–Milwaukee began in 1956 when the Milwaukee State Teachers College was combined with a UW–Madison-run extension center in Milwaukee. This move redefined the scope and purpose of higher education for the region. Like many public urban universities, UW–Milwaukee affords much greater access to four-year higher education for working-class students throughout southeastern Wisconsin than would otherwise exist.[19] At the same time, it is a research university classified as having "high research activity," with thirty-two doctoral programs. Faculty and administrators often feel these dual missions are at cross-purposes. Students, however, speak only of the university's perceived "open door" policy—they know they can get in and re-search is not something they talk much about.

The major public two-year college in the city is Milwaukee Area Technical College (MATC), which began as a continuation school in 1912. Today it is one of the largest technical colleges in the Midwest, serving about 40,000 students with 170 degree, diploma, certificate, and apprentice programs. It has long focused on job training, but as the only two-year college in the area (the UW System does not have a two-year branch campus in the city), it is also tasked with provid-ing open access for those who plan to transfer to the university to complete a four-year degree. Whether a transfer mission belongs in a technical college is an open question. Certainly, few students trans-fer out of MATC, especially when compared with the UW Colleges.

Most students of color who attend public higher education in Wisconsin are enrolled at either UW–Milwaukee or MATC, the former of which enrolls almost 40 percent of all students of color in the entire UW System. In 2014–15 this meant it educated 2,176 African Americans (8% of its total enrollment). In contrast, its sis-ter research institution, UW–Madison, enrolled just 961 African American students that year—just 2 percent of total enrollment.[20] Students of color represent a little over 18 percent of all enrollment in the Wisconsin Technical Colleges statewide,[21] but at MATC, stu-dents of color make up 56 percent of the student body.[22]

The Milwaukee Public Schools (the city's K–12 public school sys-tem), which are the primary feeder for both UW–Milwaukee and MATC, like many urban school systems, are marked by low per-formance. The four-year high school graduation rate in Milwaukee Public Schools is 61 percent, compared to the statewide average of 88 percent. The graduation rate for black students in Milwaukee Public Schools is 58 percent and 57 percent for Hispanic students.[23]

Aspirations for college have increased among Milwaukee Public School students over time, such that by 2011, over three-fourths of Milwaukee Public School seniors said they planned to attend college. But far fewer than three-fourths seemed ready for higher education, given that the mean ACT composite score of the school system's seniors was just under seventeen and that only two-thirds

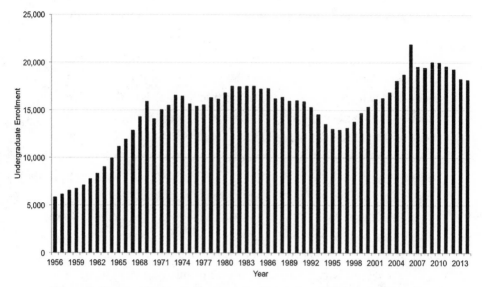

Figure 11. Undergraduate enrollment at the University of Wisconsin–Milwaukee: 1956-2014. Source: University of Wisconsin–Milwaukee Office of Assessment and Institutional Research, *Fact Book 2013-14*.

of seniors planning to attend college completed the Free Application for Federal Student Aid (FAFSA). These seniors did not fare well: only 35 percent of high school graduates enrolled in college within a year and fewer than 13 percent received a postsecondary degree of any kind after six years. [24]

Over time, just as in the rest of the state, a growing number of Milwaukee students like Alicia have finished high school and enrolled in college. Moreover, faced with weak employment prospects, many adults across Milwaukee have returned to school. Over the past fifty years, enrollment in Milwaukee's public colleges and universities has grown substantially. Figure 11 shows this increase in enrollment at UW–Milwaukee. Between 1995 and 2010, the headcount expanded at a rate of several thousand students every five years. By contrast, UW–Madison enrollment grew at less than half that rate. [25]

Milwaukee Area Technical College is even larger than UW–Milwaukee, with a total headcount over just over 40,000 students. Full-time equivalent enrollment grew more slowly at MATC and has leveled off since about 2004. [26] Many MATC students are part

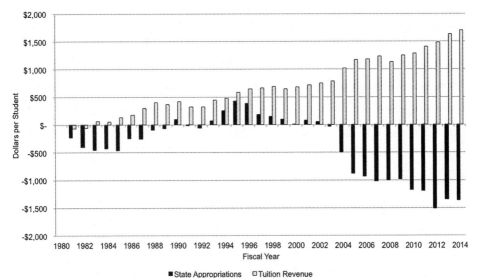

Figure 12. Trends in state appropriations and tuition revenue per student at the University of Wisconsin–Milwaukee: 1980–2014. All figures are constant 1980 dollars. Sources: Wisconsin State Appropriations and Tuition, Redbook Budget—Exhibit II and University of Wisconsin System, "Fact Book 13–14."

time (the full-time equivalency is about 13,000 students), but each and every student requires support services, regardless of how many courses she takes.[27]

Funding for public higher education in Milwaukee has not kept pace with enrollment growth. As state support has declined, tuition has grown, practically in lock step (see fig. 12). As a result, the share of undergraduate education funded by the state has dropped substantially on a per-student basis, to the point that tuition now constitutes the major source of funding.

Figure 13 shows that, at UW–Milwaukee, tuition passed state support to become the largest source of university funding around the time that this study began. In 1990, when students like Alicia and Ian Williams were born, the state of Wisconsin covered almost 70 percent of the costs of instruction for undergraduates at UW–Milwaukee, passing just 30 percent on in the form of tuition. But by the time our study students went to college in 2008, they paid about 60 percent of the costs via tuition.[28] In other words, the public

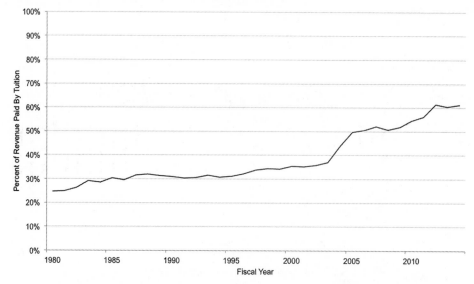

Figure 13. Trends in percent of per-student revenue paid by tuition at University of Wisconsin–Milwaukee: 1980–2014. Sources: University of Wisconsin System, "Wisconsin State Appropriations and Tuition, Redbook Budget—Exhibit II," and University of Wisconsin System, *Fact Book 13-14*.

and private roles reversed, a trend reflected across the nation. Once, going to UW–Milwaukee cost relatively little because of the large state subsidy. Today, students and the families must use their incomes and savings—if they have any—along with grants and loans to pay the tuition bills that provide the lion's share of the school's budget, which receives only a modest contribution from the state.

This funding switch flies in the face of what we know about expected payoffs. The individual returns on higher education are more uncertain than ever because students are far from assured that they will complete a degree and are more likely to accumulate debt in the attempt. At the same time, we are more certain of the general benefits to the public of increasing the number of college graduates. The city of Milwaukee is struggling with economic growth partly because of inadequate human capital resources.

Similar trends in state support have occurred across Wisconsin public higher education but cuts to state support have not fallen equally on all institutions. As figure 14 shows, costs have been shifted

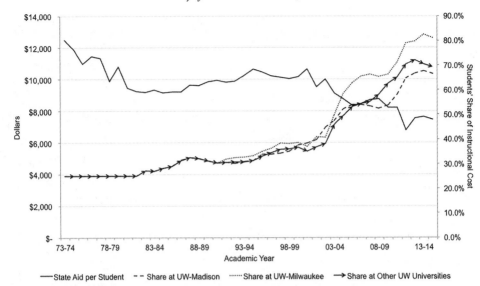

Figure 14. Trends in Wisconsin state appropriations per student and student's share of instructional costs at UW–Milwaukee, UW–Madison, and the UW System comprehensive universities: 1973–2014. Instructional cost is simply the sum of state appropriations and tuition. This is a common practice throughout higher education—it is not the true cost of instruction. All figures are in constant 2014 dollars. Source: Wisconsin Legislative Fiscal Bureau, "University of Wisconsin Sysem Overview: [2015]."

far more quickly to students at UW–Milwaukee than to students attending the other universities throughout the state. Whereas in 1990 there was essentially parity among UW–Milwaukee, UW–Madison, and the rest of the eleven universities in UW System, there are now clear disparities. Today, students at UW–Madison cover about 65 percent of their costs of instruction, while students at UW–Milwaukee shoulder more than 80 percent. Yet they are, on average, much less well off financially.

One in five applicants for financial aid in the UW System attend UW–Milwaukee. One in four applicants for financial aid in the Wisconsin Technical College System attend MATC. Together, the two institutions process about 45,000 FAFSAs annually. A huge concentration of the state's moderate and low-income students attend these two schools. Out of the forty-two public colleges and universities around the state, MATC and UW–Milwaukee together are home to 21 percent of all financial aid recipients. The result is de facto economic segregation in higher education.

Many familiar with Wisconsin higher education readily acknowledge that UW–Milwaukee has long been treated as a stepchild in the UW System.[29] In fact, administrators at UW–Madison and the board of regents fought against the creation of a four-year institution in Milwaukee, believing it would undermine UW–Madison's prestige and compete for resources.[30] Today, the two research institutions are part of the same system but they are vastly different. Not only does the state appropriate more than twice as much per full-time equivalent student for UW–Madison than it does for UW–Milwaukee, but the institutions serve divergent populations. Ninety percent of UW–Milwaukee undergraduates come from Wisconsin, and 39 percent of them are first-generation students. At UW–Madison, just under 63 percent of undergraduates come from Wisconsin (and the school just eliminated any cap on out-of-state enrollment), and less than 20 percent are first-generation.[31] More than 33 percent of new freshman at UW–Milwaukee are students of color, while at UW–Madison, this figure is less than 10 percent.[32] At UW–Milwaukee, around 1,800 first-year students need math remediation each year, compared to fewer than fifty at UW–Madison.[33] Higher education scholar Estela Bensimon and her colleagues describe the UW–Milwaukee situation perfectly as "diversity without equity."[34]

The risk of dropping out for all students, including Pell recipients, is very high in Milwaukee. At UW–Milwaukee, about three in ten students do not return for a second year of college,[35] while only about 14 percent of entering students complete a bachelor's degree within four years. By six years, that rate rises to 43 percent. But these averages conceal sizable disparities. In fall 2012, 1,279 Pell recipients enrolled at UW–Milwaukee for the first time. One year later, 440 of them were no longer enrolled.[36] In contrast, all but forty-seven of 833 Pell recipients who enrolled at UW–Madison at the same time returned for a second year. While 44 percent of students who did not receive a Pell Grant at UW–Milwaukee graduated within six years, just 33 percent of Pell recipients did so. Pell recipients were more than twice as likely to earn a bachelor's degree at UW–Madison, where their graduation rate lagged behind that of other students, but was still 73 percent.

In fall 2012, 251 African American students enrolled at UW–Milwaukee for the first time. One year later, a hundred of them were no longer enrolled. By comparison, that same year UW–Milwaukee enrolled 2,403 white students and retained 1,723 for a second year of college (a retention rate of 72%, compared to 60% for African Americans).[37] Similarly, barely half of students who enter MATC for the first time and enroll full time return to the institution for a second year of schooling, and just 15 percent complete an associate degree within three years.[38]

The Milwaukee Price

The price of attending public higher education in Milwaukee is higher than it is elsewhere in Wisconsin in both absolute and relative terms (see table 17). Our students in Milwaukee had an average expected family contribution of $1,370, almost identical to the $1,372 average expected family contribution of students living in other parts of the state. Yet, the sticker price of attending college was about $2,300 more in Milwaukee, and the net price was about $1,600 more. There are two major reasons for this. First, the Milwaukee students faced higher tuition and fees, largely due to the lower levels of state subsidies offered to UW–Milwaukee. Second, while students in Milwaukee were more likely to receive state grant aid (96% vs. 88% elsewhere), they were less likely to receive institutional aid (7% vs. 16%).

In 2012–13, Milwaukee Area Technical College awarded about $375,000 in institutional grants and emergency aid to a total of about 475 students. That was a substantial increase from 2008–9, the year our students began college, when just $100,000 of institutional grant support was distributed to about two hundred students.[39] Over at UW–Milwaukee, in 2012–13, just 217 first-year students received institutional support, totaling about $630,000.[40]

Thus, in 2008, Milwaukee students faced a net price about 19 percent higher than that of students enrolled elsewhere. That net

Table 17. College costs facing WSLS students for the first year of college, by location

	Milwaukee	All Other Locations
Ability to pay:		
Expected family contribution	$1,370	$1,372
Percentage zero EFC	41	38
Percentage negative EFC	15	16
Average EFC among those with negative	-$7,986	-$11,005
Costs of attending college:		
Official cost of attendance	$16,901	$14,551
Tuition and fees	$6,411	$4,934
Nontuition costs	$10,490	$9,617
Grant aid:		
Total grants (not including WSG)	$6,810	$6,048
Pell amount	$3,390	$2,967
Percentage with state need-based grant	96	87
Average amount among recipients	$2,003	$1,899
Percentage with institutional grants	7	16
Average amount among recipients	$2,192	$862
Price students must pay:		
Net price (COA - grants)	$10,091	$8,503
Net price as percentage of parent income	42	34

Source. WSLS data.

Note. Cost of attendance for four-year students includes housing on campus, and for two-year students it includes housing off campus not with family. Parent income and net price as percentage of parent income are reported at the median. All differences between columns are significant at $p < .05$, other than EFC differences, and state need-based grant "average amount among recipients." "Ability to pay" and "costs of attending college" include the entire sample. (Milwaukee, $n = 541$; other, $n = 2,459$.) "Grant aid" and "price students must pay" include subsample where financial aid is observed (Milwaukee, $n = 253$; other, $n = 1,185$.)

price was 42 percent of family income in Milwaukee, compared to 34 percent elsewhere.

In order to cover the remaining price, students in Milwaukee were more likely than those in the rest of Wisconsin to take loans (see table 18). Seventy-four percent of students attending college in Milwaukee took loans for their first year of college, compared to 53 percent of students attending college elsewhere in Wisconsin. Among those who borrowed, students from Milwaukee took about $1,200 more than other Wisconsin students. Most importantly, not only were students in Milwaukee more likely to accept federal loans, but they were also much more likely to take out private loans—15 percent of

Table 18. Strategies for covering college costs for the first year of college, by location

	Milwaukee	All Other Locations
Percentage with any loan	74	53
Average amount	$5,224	$3,973
Percentage with federal subsidized loan	63	62
Percentage with federal unsubsidized loan	46	25
Average amount	$2,363	$1,859
Percentage with nonfederal loans	15	1
Percentage employed (any job)	55	63
Percentage with work-study	2	13

Source. WSLS data.

Note. All differences between columns, except for subsidized loans, are significant at $p < .05$. Sample includes the subsample where financial aid is observed (Milwaukee, $n = 253$; other, $n = 1,185$). "Percentage employed" includes students who responded to first-year survey questions on employment (Milwaukee, $n = 376$; other, $n = 1,751$).

Milwaukee students made use of a private loan compared to just 1 percent of students outside of Milwaukee. In some cases, students in Milwaukee accepted private loans without first using federal loans. Nationally, about half of all private loan borrowers have not first taken all available federal loans, according to the Institute for College Access and Success.[41] Thirteen percent of students who enter loan repayment after leaving MATC default on their federal loan within two years, and 4 percent of students from UW–Milwaukee do as well.[42]

Students in Milwaukee were about eight percentage points less likely to have a job, compared with other students in our study. There appear to be several explanations. First, rates of underemployment are higher for undergraduates in Milwaukee. In 2008, the unemployment rate of sixteen to nineteen year olds in the metropolitan area was 13 percent, and a year later it climbed to 24 percent. It remained there until 2013, when it dropped to 15 percent. This especially affected African Americans, whose unemployment rates were three times those of whites during that period.[43] In 2009, when we asked students who were not working if they had been searching for a job during the last four weeks, 60 percent of Milwaukee students said yes, compared to 55 percent of students living elsewhere.[44]

Milwaukee students were also much less likely to have work-study funds: just 1 percent of Milwaukee students had this form of financial aid, compared to almost 13 percent of students elsewhere in the state. At MATC, there are about 12,500 Pell recipients (about 58% of total enrollment), but just 220 students receive support from the work-study program. (Things aren't much better at UW–Milwaukee, where just about five hundred students out of the more than nine thousand Pell recipients have work-study funding.) Since Milwaukee students, on average, had fewer financial resources, it seems unlikely that these differences were due to less need for aid. Rather, the differences are likely attributable to the disparities in work-study allocations from the federal government, discussed in chapter 4. For example, UW–Milwaukee receives just over $1 million in work-study funds, while UW–Madison (with a much smaller and more economically advantaged population of Pell recipients) receives $4.2 million. Even Marquette University, a private institution across town from UW–Milwaukee, receives more work-study funds ($1.46 million vs. $1.32 million at UW–Milwaukee), even though only 17 percent of its students receive Pell (vs. 38% at UW–Milwaukee) and it enrolls far fewer students.[45]

The Slow Road to Success

José went to college to pursue a degree in criminal justice and dreamed of joining the Milwaukee Police Department. He was a new father: his girlfriend had given birth to a baby girl shortly after he graduated from high school. He did not file as an independent student, which would have helped him qualify for about $2,500 more in grant aid, because he didn't know he could. (He did not learn about this important option until midway through his second year of college.) His father, the family's breadwinner, earned $45,000 during José's senior year of high school, and the family's expected contribution was $3,000 a year. After putting together his partial Pell Grant, state grants, a $3,500 subsidized loan, and the payment his father made, José still needed to come up with over $8,000. He worked to cover this amount and also tried to earn a bit more to save for his daughter's future. But it was not easy to secure steady employment. The first semester of college he worked at Sears, in a job he'd begun during the summer after high school. A few months later he reported, "Now they're giving me like twenty, twenty-five hours so as time goes on they are increasing. But they are also hiring other people—it's like, okay, you're barely starting to give me more hours and you're hiring more people now?" Within six months, he had to pick up a second job cleaning an office building because Sears was only offering him five hours a week. "I have a little girl," he said, "Five hours a week isn't going to help me at all."

José tried to balance out his uneven earnings by scrimping and saving his financial aid. Whenever he received a check for living expenses, he put most of it aside for a rainy day. He described in detail how he put together a budget and stuck to it, distinguishing between what was "a need situation versus just a want situation." José even opened a second savings account for his financial aid check, referring to it as separate from "my money," by which he meant his earnings from work.

He was grateful for the grants he received, which he said made college possible for him. He also explained how useful the financial aid administrators were in interpreting the aid rules and regulations. "They are really helpful. . . . They get everything straightened out. They tell you what exactly you need, what you need to do, or they tell you: 'Go do it online, go to the library and just come back and see me.' So every time I've gone there it's been, 'Do this, this, and this. Ok you're done. Just wait two or three weeks until you get your refund check, you can check it on the computer.' It's been real easy with financial aid to go through the process of it."

Midway through his third semester of college José dropped the second job, in part because the commuting time it required did not feel worthwhile, especially in the winter. Then a new challenge arrived: his father lost his job, a casualty of the recession. "He was earning $500 per week," José explained, "But with unemployment the most he can get is $360, and that's just barely putting us through with the bills. I try to help out whatever I can . . . there is only so much you can do, you know, and I have my little daughter, too. It's like you're just sitting here feeling hopeless and saying, I wish I had a better job, or I wish I took a year off of school and worked at a real job."

Given that his parents no longer had any earnings, his family was no longer expected to contribute to college, and his grant aid increased by about $4,000. This helped, but the financial demands on José increased as well. His family needed his help to stay afloat more than ever. José responded by working more: during his first year of college he earned $9,500, and during his second, he earned more than $14,000. This meant he worked nearly full time, about thirty-five hours a week.

"Money has a lot to do with stress," he said, "You're worried about it—that's a lot of money, I don't know if I can pay for this. People obviously start thinking, should I just stop going to school? This is a lot of money I'm paying for classes, I shouldn't be here, and I'm going to go to work somewhere to make money."

The irregular hours of his job continued to frustrate him, especially when he needed more hours than his employer offered. He explained: "Right now, I would say anywhere from fifteen to twenty-five per week. Every week it's different. One week I might have ten and one week I have twenty-five, eighteen, twenty —they are pretty different. Before that I was getting twenty-five or thirty hours."

Despite this instability, José persisted in school because he was confident that over the long-term joining the police department would help his family. "If I can get ahead, I can help them out. That's one of a lot of things I think about. If I hit the lottery the first thing I would do is help my parents out, pay for whatever they have to pay. . . . They've helped me out so much, they support me going to school, they just keep pushing me and pushing me." He understood that his prospects for providing this support were slim if he did not finish his degree, and spoke of wanting to ensure that other people in his community knew that too. "High school is almost nothing nowadays. You *have* to get a degree. . . . There's a few people with college degrees and they have bigger and better jobs. . . . [Employers] see them as smarter people—they actually did their work, did their time in school and things like that." Even as he pursued his studies, José understood that not everyone had the opportunity to obtain a college degree. "There are people who just can't afford it. They can't go to school and do those things that people like me can do—for them it's really unfair." Drawing distinctions between his family (which at the time had no income other than unemployment benefits and his meager paycheck) and the families of his high school classmates, José noted that when college was not possible, most people went to a different institution, "the house of corrections." He aimed to join the police force in part because he wanted to address gang violence in the city, explaining, "I used to be with them . . . but there's no sense to it. . . . I used to be scared, wondering, 'Oh what if this happens?' . . . I know the streets, and I know where this stuff happens. Not many cops know that, and I do." After six semesters of attending school full time, José finally completed an associate degree. "It seems like it's been forever—a two-year degree is supposed to take two years," he noted. But he was "relieved, happy, and proud of myself" that he was finally done. He planned on going back to school to pursue a bachelor's degree if he didn't find a steady job within two years. He would need to finish that degree in no more than six semesters, since he was already half way to using up his lifetime Pell Grant allotment.[46]

The sheer will exhibited by students like José, who grow up and attend college in Milwaukee, is amazing given the obstacles they face. Writing in the *Washington Monthly,* journalist Jamaal Abdul-alim described what he learned from reporting on the situation facing African American students at UW–Milwaukee: "With remarkable consistency, the students I met . . . who were struggling or failing to graduate blamed themselves almost entirely for their fate. That willingness to take personal responsibility is admirable, and very American, and something to be encouraged, not undermined. But the truth is that the fault isn't all with them."[47] Abdul-alim described in detail the need that many Milwaukee students have for intensive advising to help them navigate their colleges and universities. Our data complement his and suggest that the advising needs to go further, to help students seeking degrees as they also traverse the many broken institutions in the city. Too often, researchers trying to understand problems in higher education fail to recognize that challenges created by the health and human services systems and the criminal justice system also affect college graduation rates. While researchers focus on what is happening inside school, critical parts of the undergraduate experience—parts that determine the success or failure of many students—occur outside.

No Full-Time Students Here

Anne went to college seeking the skills to find a good job and a better life for herself and her mom. She grew up in public housing, as her mom cycled on and off of assistance from the state, struggling to hold a job while coping with lupus (a chronic inflammatory disease characterized by fatigue and fever, joint pain, a rash, and shortness of breath). Anne attended one of the city's better high schools where she completed an International Baccalaureate program. During high school she was focused and maintained good grades. When she finished, she chose the university closest to her: "I only had to catch one or two buses there and we were able to afford it," she said during our first interview with her, four months after she'd begun school.

What felt affordable to Anne? In her first year of college she received a Pell of almost $4,000 and a state grant of nearly $2,900. But that was the extent of the grants offered, so her net price was over $9,000—despite an expected family contribution of just $250. How would Anne and her family pay a price thirty-six times higher than what the federal needs analysis determined they could afford?

This price was only manageable for Anne because she lived at home, she and her mother did not pay for housing, and she received food stamps as well as support from the local energy company to cover the electric bill. She was very careful with her financial aid dollars, which she saved. "I put it up, in an envelope in a little area in my room where I know that it is," she said. With those supports in place, she was able to focus on school.

She had a strong, positive relationship with her mother and felt that she received a great deal of emotional support from her. During her first semester, she attended full time, taking math, English, German, and an economics of business class for a total of sixteen credits. She estimated that she spent six hours a day in class and two hours a day studying. The classes were interesting and she was making friends—life seemed to be going smoothly, and for this, she was grateful. But in contrast to many of her peers, she had some doubt that she would achieve her goals, estimating on a survey that it was only "somewhat likely" she would complete a bachelor's degree.

One day in November, there was a knock at her door. The manager of the apartment building where she lived informed her that by enrolling in college full time, she had violated the terms of the family's subsidized housing. "The management says that if you're living at home and you're in college, you're not allowed to enroll full time. So I had to switch [to part time]."

Anne did not know what policy dictated this situation, but thought it might have to do with perceptions of undergraduate behavior. "I guess they're saying that they think if you're in college you might try and turn it into a dormitory, throwing parties or getting out of control. I don't really understand it. But if I didn't agree to go part time we would have to move. So I really didn't have a choice, we couldn't just up and move like that."

Anne had run up against her local public housing authority's definition of eligibility, which deprioritized full-time students. If the idea of this policy was to prevent people from taking advantage of public housing, it made little sense in Anne's case. She was not a student seeking a new, inexpensive place to live for a few years but, rather, a long-term resident who had lived in the building for years and who had very few assets of her own—and little ability to make significant money without a college degree. Public housing policies regarding college enrollment run the gamut. Ironically, had Anne's housing been funded by Section 8, she would have been pushed to remain enrolled full time—if she dropped to part time, she would no longer have been considered her mother's dependent and would not have been allowed to remain in the unit.[48]

Anne could see no recourse, so she switched to taking classes part time. Her adviser typed up a letter she gave her landlord to prove that she had done this. It seems that no one at Anne's school, including her academic adviser and financial aid counselor, called the housing authority in an effort to clarify the situation or intervene. But as a part-time student, Anne received much less grant aid. She was also concerned that by going part time and taking just three classes at a time, it would take longer to complete her degree. "I think it was going to take me five years anyway, and now maybe six." She spoke with her adviser about her concerns on several occasions but did not know whom else to turn to.

It became increasingly difficult for Anne and her mom to make ends meet. She had been helping to pay for household expenses with her financial aid, contributing half the grocery costs not covered by food stamps. Anne had few options. If she worked, her income could disqualify them from receiving the housing subsidy. She did not want to take student loans. They were not truly a form of financial aid, she said, and they felt risky. She did not have a credit card and said, "I'm not really sure if I want one." She did not feel that debt was an acceptable way to get funds or that it was appropriate to take out a loan to enjoy a better life. She also worried that it would be hard to get out of debt.

At the same time, she knew college was worth the investment. By the time she was thirty, Anne planned to have a master's degree and work in accounting or finance. She thought that this path would mean she would earn about $50,000 a year. "I really like working with numbers and math," she said, "This will mean I am able to support myself and my mom." In contrast, if she left school without a degree, she estimated that she would earn just $20,000 a year.

She continued to try to focus on school: "I'm just keep trying to bring my GPA up higher each semester and stay focused, working harder." But then midway through her second year of college her mom grew very ill and went into the hospital. "It was all at once, everything was coming at me, and I didn't know what to do," she said.

> I mean, it's one thing when you're prepared for a situation but when it comes out of nowhere as far as the bills and food and then still going to school, well, I just didn't know what to do. When she got out of the hospital she needed someone with her twenty-four hours a day. I was like, what am I gonna do for school? Because

I didn't want to miss something. I would rather miss school than miss being at home, but what was I going to do at home all day? My aunts and uncles would help out, too, but they needed to take care of their families too. I was just like, what am I gonna do, with everything coming at me at once?

After a few weeks of supporting her mom, the stress took its toll. "I get a lot of headaches," she said, also noting that though she felt hungry she was too sick to eat. On a survey she indicated that she often felt blue and bothered by things that didn't used to bother her. She was depressed and lonely. Yet she was trying to make things work at school. In the midst of these difficulties, she reassessed the likelihood that she would complete the bachelor's degree and decided that it was now "extremely likely."

Low-income families face a different situation than middle- and upper-income families when a family member becomes sick, because the family can't pay someone to help out. Hiring a home health aide is not affordable.

Anne's teachers seem to have had little indication that she was facing troubles at home, and she was having difficulty telling them about it. "I don't really have time to go and see them because I have to go home. . . . They [professors that she needed to talk to] have office hours from 3 to 5 P.M. on Tuesdays but I have to go home every day. I've been wanting to go but every time I plan on going, I have to go talk with a doctor about what's wrong with my mom. So I'm never able to go."

While her mom was in the hospital Anne took an exam she had not studied for, having been with her mom all night before. "I wanted to tell him [the professor] but I just didn't. I didn't want people to keep feeling sorry for me. It was a thing for myself—to not really want to put it out there. . . . So I just took the exam and went back to the hospital and that was it."

As her mom began to feel better, Anne focused again on school. She began doing her homework long before it was due and got tutoring for her accounting and statistics courses. Her grades began to improve. The apartment manager had returned to tell her that she could now enroll full time, but Anne did not trust this information. It seemed to her like some kind of "loophole," and she did not want to go through the paperwork and hassle to switch again. "I'll just stay part time and go from there, because I have a feeling that if I do go back to full time she will come with something else where I have to go back down again. She's like that—she will just find something else to bother you with. I will just keep everything calm and stay part time and I can deal with it."

Anne's feelings of confusion and distrust were neither uncommon nor unusual, but they had significant implications. For each additional semester she stayed in school, the costs mounted and the odds of completing a degree diminished. Many researchers have found that low-income people are subject to rules that are not explained to them and that are often inconsistent.[49]

The last time we saw Anne was at the start of her third year of college. She'd taken a job working at a local retailer called the Boston Store, completed her midterm exams, and said that her mom was feeling better. She was trying to work a little, but not too much, since she needed money to pay the bills but did not want to make too much and be disqualified from her housing. Half of her earnings went to help her mom with the bills and half went into savings, which she now kept in a bank rather than in an envelope. She seemed on track with school, and administrative records indicate that she remained continuously enrolled until spring 2014. But then she left, without a degree in hand. After six years of attending college we don't know why she gave up.

No End in Sight

The low degree-completion rates of our students in Milwaukee stand in stark contrast to the rest of the students in this study (more on that in the next chapter), but they are generally consistent with the pattern observed for Milwaukee college students overall, and students of color in particular. Six years after beginning college, just 41 percent of Milwaukee students in our study had completed a cre-

Table 19. Degree attainment rates for WSLS students, by location

	Milwaukee	All Other Locations	Difference Test
Completed any certificate or degree within six years	41%	52%	***
Completed certificate or associate degree:			
Within 2 years	2%	11%	
Within 3 years	4%	17%	***
Within 6 years	7%	24%	***
Completed bachelor's degree			
Within 4 years	11%	15%	
Within 5 years	33%	41%	***
Within 6 years	44%	50%	
No degree, still enrolled in 2014	18%	11%	***
Number of terms enrolled over six years	10	9	***
No degree, not enrolled	41%	37%	
Percentage who borrowed during first year of college	66%	47%	**
Amount borrowed among borrowers' first year of college	$5,123	$3,762	***

Source. WSLS data.

Note. Numbers are weighted averages and may not sum to 100 percent. Associate degrees and certificates are combined because National Student Clearinghouse data doesn't make it possible to distinguish between the two. Completion and enrollment include the entire sample (Milwaukee, n = 541; other, n = 2,459). "Percentage who took loans during the first year" and "average amount borrowed" use the subsample where financial aid is observed (Milwaukee, n = 253; other, n = 1,185).

**p < .05

***p < .01

dential of any kind, compared to 52 percent of students in the rest of the state (table 19). They were far less likely to have completed an associate degree, whether in two years (2% in Milwaukee vs. almost 11% elsewhere) or six years (7% in Milwaukee vs. almost 24% elsewhere). Bachelor's degree completion rates in Milwaukee lagged as well, though not by nearly as much. Students in Milwaukee were more likely to still be enrolled in college but not yet have a degree as of spring 2014. But most importantly, students in Milwaukee who left college without a credential were much more likely to be in debt (66% vs. 47% elsewhere) and held on average $1,500 more debt (from the first year of college) than their peers in the rest of the state. They carried these incomplete college experiences and compromised financial circumstances back into a community already full of financial hardship.

9
Getting to Graduation

Norbert Webster came from a very modest background but had lots of positive family input. With several family members who had gone to college and a hardworking and supportive mom, Norbert knew what he wanted—and he got it. Five years after he began college, he completed his bachelor's degree, received a certified public accountant license, and went to work as an accountant. He had accumulated no debt at all.

Norbert attributed his relatively smooth path through school to his mom and to his tribe. The Oneida Nation of Wisconsin had given him substantial grant support and conveyed clear expectations for his success. Norbert knew that grants made it possible for him to avoid working long hours, live on campus in a residence hall, and participate in activities that helped him practice cultural and social skills he would deploy in the workforce. Some opportunities were still not open to him (he was sorry that he couldn't afford to study abroad) but generally he'd felt a part of university life.

Norbert was lucky. He was born two years after the Oneida began Wisconsin's first lottery program. Starting with a pair of bingo parlors, the tribe had built an enormously successful set of gaming ventures that had transformed their economic circumstances.[1] When Norbert was young, the Oneida were deeply impoverished, but as he grew older the revenue from gaming gave the tribe the means to provide health care and educational support to all Oneida. The Oneida's new social supports included the development of per capita payments and college scholarships, which have helped in turn to build the community's wealth. The jobs that Norbert's family held in the tribe's casinos, and the job he holds in the casino today as an accountant, were not available to prior generations. Given how much more generous Norbert's financial aid package was than that of our other students, how frequently he spoke of the tribe's support, and how critical his family's economic well-being was to his ability to stay in college, it seems safe to say that Norbert's odds of completing a degree would have been much slimmer without the tribe's backing. But very few Native Americans benefit from scholarships like the Oneida's—the vast majority of tribes lack the resources. Today, the Oneida Nation is a major employer and source of support for its young people—and Norbert's college degree will help the tribe grow stronger in the future. In Norbert's case, to borrow a phrase, it took a village. And the village will benefit.[2]

Half Measures, Half Results

Six years after beginning college, just one in two of the students in the Wisconsin Scholars Longitudinal Study had graduated with a credential of any kind (table 20).[3] Graduation rates were higher for students who began at a university compared to those who began at a two-year college (58% vs. 42%). This difference is consistent with trends nationally and is only partly due to differences in academic preparation. Fifteen percent of students in the study (including 30% of those at two-year colleges) completed a sub-baccalaureate credential such as a certificate or an associate degree within three years, and another 6 percent (including an additional 9% of those at two-year schools) did so within six years. Not everyone who earned a certificate or associate degree started at a two-year college; 6 percent of four-year starters reverse transferred to a two-year college to do this.

The Fortunate Few

Like Norbert, Ian Williams came from a family with very few economic resources, but unlike Norbert, he entered college with very little grant aid. The university he attended had few scholarships to

Table 20. Degree attainment rates for WSLS students, by sample

	Overall	Four-Year Starters	Two-Year Starters	Interview Sample
Completed any credential within six years	50%	58%	42%	73%
Completed certificate or associates:				
Within 2 years	9%	1%	19%	2%
Within 3 years	15%	2%	30%	7%
Within 6 years	21%	6%	39%	9%
Completed bachelor's degree:				
Within 4 years	14%	16%	5%	25%
Within 5 years	39%	44%	16%	56%
Within 6 years	49%	54%	25%	83%
No credential, still enrolled in 2014	12%	13%	11%	7%
Average total number of enrolled terms	9	10	8	11
Percentage who took loans during first year	66%	84%	41%	76%
Average amount borrowed	$4,055	$4,391	$3,148	$3,626
No credential, not enrolled in 2014	38%	29%	47%	20%
Total number of enrolled terms	4	5	4	5
Percentage who took loans during first year	55%	72%	36%	84%
Average amount borrowed	$3,934	$4,369	$3,105	$4,195

Source. WSLS data.

Note. Completion and enrollment include the entire sample (Overall, n = 3,000; four-year starters, n = 1,500; two-year starters, n = 1,500; interview sample. n = 50). "Percentage who took loans during the first year" and "average amount borrowed" use just the subsample where financial aid is observed (Overall, n = 1,438; four-year starters, n = 827; two-year starters, n = 611; interview sample, n = 44). Numbers are weighted averages and may not sum to 100 percent. Associate degrees and certificates are combined because National Student Clearinghouse data doesn't make it possible to distinguish between the two. Bachelor's degree completion data among two-year starters are available for students at UW Colleges only—this information is unavailable for Wisconsin Technical College System students. Percentage of those who completed a bachelor's degree and percentage of those who completed an associate's degree do not add to percentage of those who completed any credential because some students earned both degrees.

offer and following a long period of declining resources from the state, the price of attendance was very high. To make ends meet, Ian borrowed the maximum federal loans available ($5,500) for his first year, lived at home, worked, and sometimes made do without enough to eat. While his community was unable to offer him scholarships, it did provide him with a strong motivation to push forward and succeed at school. The university complemented and built on his motivation with academic support programs, and his response—a strong focus on school—eventually paid off. Private philanthropy stepped in and gave him grants beginning in his second year.

Ian was one of just a handful of students we came across who had to pay less, rather than more, the further he went in school. He remained continuously enrolled and unlike many of his counterparts, his need to work did not interfere with his ability to attend college. That said, he was far less able than Norbert to participate in the nonclassroom aspects of college life that expand social networks and help drive the economic returns to college degrees. He had faced family obligations and distractions. For all five and half years of his college education, Ian lived at home.

Still, those eleven semesters paid off. Ian graduated with a bachelor's degree in business administration. He then went on to complete a master's degree in the same field and is now gainfully employed in the Milwaukee area. He estimates that he owes about $30,000 in student debt from his undergraduate years, and a great deal more from his graduate work. But he is finally able to live in his own apartment and speaks with great pride about his accomplishments.

He should be proud. He is among the very few African American students in our study who completed college. Of the 216 who began college full time in 2008, less than one in three earned any credential by 2014. Twenty-four percent finished a bachelor's degree during that time. Twenty-six percent were still enrolled, working on their degrees. Forty-two percent had no degree or certificate, were no longer enrolled, and were in debt.

White students fared far better. Of course, these students had somewhat more financial resources to begin with: the average expected family contribution for white students in our study was just over $1,600; for African American students it was $571. Whites were less than half as likely to have no expected family contribution (30% compared to 71% for African Americans). Whites were far less likely to borrow student loans but equally likely to work while in school. However, while white and African American students were about equally likely to have work-study employment (just one in ten did), white students were allotted more work-study funds compared to African Americans ($1,229 vs. $703). They were also less likely to report on surveys that they were having trouble paying the bills or were worried about money. Almost 60 percent of white students completed a credential, nearly all of those earned bachelor's degrees, and 34 percent left college in debt and without a degree.

That's not to say that their road to graduation was easy. Would-be motivational speaker Sophie Schmidt finished college in four years at one of the state's best public universities. That fact alone would mark her in most studies as an unquestionable success. But her undergraduate experience left scars. She agonized over money daily and she ended up disconnected from, and angry with, her family. Of all of the students we interviewed, Sophie incurred the most debt, borrowing more than $13,000 for the first year of college alone.[4]

Many students contend that the "four-year college" and the "two-year college" are poorly named since associate degrees are rarely finished in two years, or bachelor's degrees in four. This held true in our study as well. Just 19 percent of students who started at a two-year college finished a degree or certificate within two years, and just 16 percent of students who started at a four-year university finished a bachelor's degree within four years. Nima Chaudhary was among the students who took longer than anticipated to finish her degree. In May 2011, three years after entering technical college, Nima graduated with a degree in graphic design. On the same day, her brother graduated from a different university with a degree in nursing. She and her family attended his ceremony rather than hers. Despite her accomplishments, her family's need for money hung over her college choices:

> I feel like my dad is waiting for me to fail. . . . He thinks graphic design is not worth it. He says, "As a girl you should go into nursing, it's much safer and there's always a job," and I say, "You know all Asians are nurses or doctors, I just don't have the passion for it." I became a certified nursing assistant and I hated it and I didn't want to be in a hospital setting and I like art so I went into it. . . . I really can't believe I did it. . . . I'm really proud of my degree and I don't care what they say—I'll find a job soon and I'm looking everywhere.

Two years passed, and Nima was working in a hospital cafeteria, having been employed at six different part-time jobs since college, none in art. She maintained a website and a Facebook page for her art and continued to actively seek employment.

One in four of our students completed a bachelor's degree in five years, and one in ten took six years. It took longer to get degrees for students who started at two-year colleges, where the need to transfer to complete a bachelor's degree mean a longer time in school. Five percent of students who entered UW colleges (the two-year branch campus of UW's universities) did manage to transfer and complete a bachelor's degree in a total of four years, but most of the 25 percent who did so took five or six years.

The Slow Road

When we last checked in on them in spring 2014, some students—including Tyler Olson—were still enrolled. These students (12% of the entire sample) had not yet finished a degree but were taking classes six years after they first began college. However, the overwhelming majority had not gone to college continuously. On average, they had only attended school for nine semesters. In other words, they had taken off the equivalent of a year-and-a-half, interrupting their college education before returning. More than three in five had student debt from their first year of college, and this was especially true for students who had initially enrolled at a university and who were still enrolled in the spring of 2014—82 percent had taken a loan. Those still-enrolled borrowers owed on average $4,470, based on the amount they took during that first year.

By May 2014, Tyler had been enrolled in college for six straight years but still had not finished his degree. He'd hit his lifetime Pell Grant limit, a limit set by a law passed by President Obama three years after Tyler had first started school. We repeatedly attempted to contact him to find out more, but his phone was disconnected.

This was unusual. The students we interviewed, while representing a wide array of students in the broader study, were very responsive throughout the six-year study period and in many ways represent best-case scenarios. By 2014, four in five of them had either completed college or were still enrolled—just one in five had left college without a degree. This is somewhat surprising. While many researchers recruit students for interviews in ways that produce a more advantaged sample (e.g., by relying on people to take multiple actions to volunteer, producing samples of especially motivated people seeking help), we had attempted to do the opposite. We asked students if they were willing to participate in interviews on a survey, and almost half of all students volunteered. We knew this question of interest might introduce a form of selection bias, so we then sorted all the students who had volunteered into groups based on where they were enrolled, and sampled among those volunteers at each institution based on their gender and race/ethnicity. Whenever there was more than one volunteer available, we chose at random. We are therefore able to compare the graduation rates of students we interviewed with very comparable students whom we did not interview, and even that analysis suggests higher graduation rates. Does this mean that the students we interviewed had preexisting advantages that escaped our initial efforts at randomization? Perhaps. But it is also possible that simply sitting down with someone for an interview for an hour or two a few times a year was an intervention that increased their chances of completing a degree. The possibility is certainly intriguing, and we are trying to learn more. At minimum, it means that if those stories represent the more positive range of events then life was likely even more challenging for the other 2,950 students in the study.

Students like Chloe Johnson who left college without a credential represented 38 percent of our students overall, and 47 percent of those who began at a two-year college. They had completed on average two years of schooling, and almost half had taken loans during their first year of college. Six years after first completing the FAFSA and enrolling in college full time, they were in debt without degrees in hand.

Very few people who study or work with college students have the opportunity to get to know them after they leave college, especially if they leave without a degree. We wonder what happened, why they departed, and what they are doing now. Without this information, their stories are incomplete and often misunderstood. This is why it was so important that we followed these young adults wherever they went, continuing to learn from them whether or not they stayed in school.

A year after I met with her in a Florida coffee shop, Chloe and I reconnected, this time via Skype. Two years after our first encounter in a Wisconsin cafeteria, Chloe was living in San Diego, in training in the navy. She had not been able to find steady employment in Tampa. Her father had sold his restaurant, and she applied at "numerous places" for jobs including "Hard Rock casino, five different vet clinics, four different stores in the mall, various Starbucks locations, bookstores, McDonald's, Bed Bath and Beyond, the list goes on and on. . . . I got discouraged after three months of this." Referring to that period of her life, Chloe looked grim as she told me:

> I'd pretty much hit rock bottom, and there was nowhere to go but up. The bottom is scary and you just don't feel like you're really worth anything, and you're trying to get back on your feet. You just beat yourself up. I went to interviews and kept getting shot down and shot down and shot down, and I just kept taking it personally. It kinda makes you feel like you're not good enough. And that's pretty much when I just said, you know, I should probably join the military. I'm going to have job security and worse case, if I hate it, I can get out in four years and have money for college. . . . For once in my life I had something planned out and nothing could really go wrong with it.

After considering advice from her father, uncle, and grandfather—all of whom had been in the military—Chloe enlisted in the navy with plans of serving as a sonar technician. She found life there suited her, especially the structure: "I'm really looking forward to everything. I'm getting enough sleep and eating more of what I should, and not just what's fast and easy. I know when I go to boot camp they give you eight hours of sleep every night and three square meals a day. . . . You're guaranteed to have time to eat your meals and do everything you need to get done and you're still going to get eight hours of sleep and have time to shower." This structure was nothing like Chloe's experience in technical college, where she hardly found time for a cup of coffee and grabbed her meals while commuting between work and school. When comparing life in the navy to life in college, Chloe expressed a strong preference for the organization of navy life:

> It's kinda nice because you don't really have to worry about managing your time too much because you've got someone else doing that for you. And you get in such a habit, a routine, that it kind of carries over. When you're in college, that's not really the case. Some things could run longer, or shorter. . . . I like structure, I like to know what I'm going to be doing that day and knowing I'm going to get it done at this time. In college it just all depends on when your classes start, you know one day you could be getting up at 4:30 A.M. and the next day your classes don't start until 10 A.M., it's such inconsistency.

Surprised to hear Chloe decry the flexibility of college life that she had initially prized when college began, I asked her "What does that inconsistency feel like to you?" She replied,

> It feels like chaos, in all honesty, and I think that's what really got to me. If I'd had put more thought into it, planned something out . . . if I would have put it [college] off for a year and spent some time saving up money so that I would have extra money to fall back on when my hours get cut at work. . . . Because I meant it, it really doesn't matter how many hours I work now [in the navy]. I'm always going to have the same paycheck every month, I can count on that paycheck to be there.

Chloe was exercising and eating regularly, and continued to see college in her future: "The navy pays for college and you can take courses while serving your time, and seeing places I don't think I would otherwise. I'll have job security for the next four years, and as long as I'm in the navy I will never have to pay rent, electric bills, etc. I'll only have to pay for my cell phone, car, and student loan, and I can have my loan and car paid off easily in my first eight months of service." She talked about taking psychology classes online and planned to get a laptop so she could take online courses while enlisted.

One year after enlisting, Chloe told me that she felt like a success in her new life. "I haven't felt bad or regretted any decision I've made. It's always been one more step towards getting out of debt, creating a future for myself." She was still paying off her student loans. But the University of Phoenix had contacted her, so she was also thinking about returning to school.

Sometimes, More Grant Aid Helps

While the graduation rates of our students were not high, they were higher than they might have been had the Fund for Wisconsin Scholars not existed. Beginning in fall 2008, the fund began distributing grants to twelve hundred of the three thousand students we studied: six hundred at universities and six hundred at two-year colleges. My research team was eager to find out how these grants would affect graduation rates. Since the fund used a lottery to select its grantees among eligible students, all of whom had financial need and received the Pell Grant, we were able to track them along with a group matched for comparison purposes. By comparing their outcomes, we could know with a great deal of certainty what impact the fund's grant had on academic outcomes and student debt.

Financial aid administrators, using the standard processes described in previous chapters, handled the grant distributed by the Fund for Wisconsin Scholars. Since the money came from a private source, there was also some additional paperwork involved—at the beginning of the process, students were informed that they had received a grant from the Fund for Wisconsin Scholars. It was not, therefore, as if students simply got extra cash deposited in their hands.

The Wisconsin Scholars Grant offered students at universities $3,500 per year, while those attending two-year colleges were offered $1,800 per year. Students who remained eligible could renew the grant for up to ten semesters (i.e., $17,500 for university students).

Two-year students who transferred to a university could receive increased support, but few did.

The grants had different levels of purchasing power. At the universities, the WSG cut the students' net price (cost of attendance minus all grants/scholarship) for a year of college substantially, reducing it from just over $8,000 to just over $4,500. However, the grant did not become available to students until the end of the first semester, by which point almost four in five students had already accepted loans, averaging about $4,400. In many cases, this meant that, when added to the financial aid package, the new grant simply displaced some or all of a student's loans, rather than making more money available for immediate use.[5] For example, among students who had less than $3,500 of remaining unmet need when the WSG was awarded (which generally meant that they had accepted loans, while others had unusual amounts of grant aid), 69 percent saw their loans reduced as the result of the award, with an average reduction of $2,612. Just 38 percent of those students received at least $1,000 in additional funds they could spend to help pay for college in the short term. In contrast, among students who had unmet need of $3,500 or more when the WSG was awarded, 89 percent received at least $1,000 they could put to immediate use. It is hard to find a clearer example of how grants distributed via the financial aid system differ from cash or its equivalent. Some students never received more cash in hand at all.

Many students had difficulty keeping the grant. Nearly half of the students offered five years of support from the Fund for Wisconsin Scholars stopped receiving the grant before three years had passed. Some students lost eligibility because they switched to part-time enrollment. Others failed to make satisfactory academic progress (required for all federal financial aid as well as for the WSG). Another group experienced an increase in family income that caused loss of Pell eligibility, another requirement for the WSG. Some of those students may have been receiving small Pell Grants, and a modest rise in family income slid them over the "Pell cliff," which meant all their Pell-contingent aid disappeared.

Over at the two-year colleges, the net price of college was lower, but the grant amount was smaller, too. The WSG cut the net price (for a student living off campus, not with family) from around $9,800 to $8,000 for students who received it, a reduction of 18 percent. Far fewer students—just 25 percent—at the two-year colleges had accepted loans by the time the WSG arrived and they tended to take only subsidized loans. As a result, there was typically more room for the $1,800 WSG to translate into cash instead of loan reduction. But the criteria for keeping the WSG were the same as those at the universities (continued full-time enrollment, Pell eligibility, satisfactory academic progress) and students at the two-year colleges had a great deal of trouble with these, so they rarely held onto it for long. One year after the WSG was initially offered, barely one-third of students at two-year colleges were still receiving it.

We tracked how the WSG affected students' financial aid packages, asked them how well they understood the grant, and traced their academic progress over time. We did the same for the matched comparison group. Then, we compared the outcomes and estimated the impact of the grant. Researchers Robert Kelchen, Douglas N. Harris, and James Benson joined me in evaluating impacts for university students, while Drew M. Anderson led the analysis for two-year students. A summary of our analyses follows.[6]

For students beginning at universities, the WSG did not immediately change their academic trajectories. Eighty-one percent of the comparison group enrolled for a second year of college, as did just over 83 percent of the WSG group. Those small differences could be due to chance. Students who were offered the grant did spend a bit less time trying to earn money in the second year of college, but over three years they did not complete more credits. However, as figure 15 shows, the WSG increased the on-time bachelor's degree completion rate by 28 percent, pushing it from about 16 percent to 21 percent. Moreover, the WSG also reduced students' debt by just under $3,200 for their first three years of college.

Furthermore, it made a difference if the offer of an additional $3,500 in grant aid actually translated into funds that could be used to reduce work hours or help with other college costs, as opposed to simply reducing debt for loans already received. Second-year

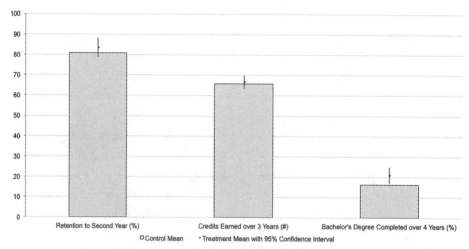

Figure 15. Impact of offering the Wisconsin Scholars Grant to university starters in the Wisconsin Scholars Longitudinal Study on academic outcomes. *n* = 1,500. Source: Wisconsin Scholars Longitudinal Study data.

college attendance was substantially enhanced when the WSG put money into students' hands, as opposed to reducing their debt. Among students who faced at least $3,500 in unmet need before the WSG was allocated (usually because they did not take loans), the grant boosted retention rates by an additional 11.5 percentage points, for a total impact of 14.7 percentage points. Would larger grants—grants big enough to actually improve the current cash position of students—have had more of impact on students with greater need? We don't know, but the question deserves further research.

The WSG was less effective at promoting retention and degree completion for the two-year college students (fig. 16). The modest reduction in their net price created by the grant did not result in any statistically significant changes in either credit completion or degree completion. The only statistically significant impacts were a $578 reduction in students' two-year aggregate debt and a reduction in the probability of transferring to a different college or university.

This study was an effort to understand whether increasing the amount of grant aid students received after they'd already begun to attend college would boost their rates of degree completion. Results were mixed. On the one hand, it helped some students complete

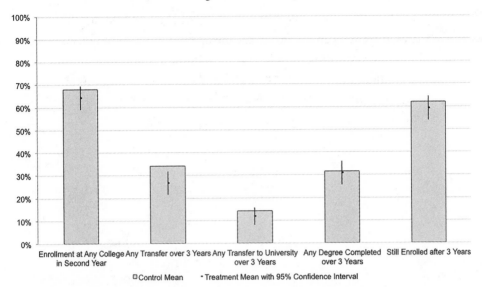

Figure 16. Impact of offering the Wisconsin Scholars Grant to two-year college students in the Wisconsin Scholars Longitudinal Study on academic outcomes. Source: Wisconsin Scholars Longitudinal Study data.

their bachelor's degrees on time, likely reducing their debt even beyond what we have data to examine here and accelerating their entry into the labor market. The effects for university students were sizable, at least as large as those detected in the few prior studies of grant aid. The results for the two-year students—who received a smaller investment, continued to face a very substantial price (almost $8,000 per year), and had more difficulty retaining the grant—were less promising. While all of the data described in earlier chapters clearly indicate that students at two-year colleges faced a great deal of financial need and uncertainty, delivering this amount of funding in this way may not be a cost-effective approach to making college more affordable and promoting degree completion. For students like Chloe Johnson, it was too late—and for others, perhaps too little.

The most important lesson this experiment taught us is that financial aid is not money. Money clearly matters a great deal to how students experience college and whether they complete degrees. The Fund for Wisconsin Scholars was smart to focus its resources on students like those in this book. They do need more resources, and when students receive them, they are helped. But, unlike cash gifts or wages, the grants and loans that make up financial aid include complex rules, procedures, and requirements. If we want to lower the price to help people focus on school and complete their degrees on time, then financial aid as it is now designed may not be the best approach.

10

Making College Affordable

Despite its good intentions, our current financial aid system is failing today's students. For fifteen years, I have listened to financial aid administrators, deans of students, student affairs practitioners, and college presidents describe the problems of undergraduates on their campuses. They talk about their personal experiences of college and those of their friends to craft a picture of struggle met with fortitude, success gained through hard work, and the achievement of what looked impossible. In their day, college looked affordable—and in their eyes, it can look affordable still.

The people who tell me these stories have genuine empathy for students. When they talk to me they look worried, sometimes pained, always concerned. Their eyes convey a sense of wishing for better behavior, sensible decision making, and an easier process that wasn't always so complicated. But fundamentally, at some basic level, they tend to agree that the system itself is fine—it can work, if only students work it. If today's students only had a certain moral fiber, like the students of yesteryear, they would be fine.

Other people I encounter, whether at community meetings, on airplanes, or the staff of state and federal legislators from both sides of the aisle, are frustrated. When I mention my research on financial aid, many parents say, "We save, work hard, and pay a lot of money to attend college and still we can't cover the bills—and the school takes our hard-earned dollars and gives it to someone else. It's unfair." The redistribution of funds from the rich to the poor in order to finance

234 * CHAPTER 10

programs is a common approach, and at least in theory, sometimes these individuals support it. But the kind of anger expressed in the above quote comes from the sense that when it comes to affording college they aren't "rich" but rather middle class. And it's hard to watch your daughter's college roommate receive a Pell Grant while your child is offered only loans.

We have to learn from the experiences of both Pell recipients and the middle-class families left out of that program. Today's undergraduates are experiencing college very differently than those in previous decades. It is no longer the case that, if students from low-income families work hard, college will be affordable (recall that the average net price for a year at community college equals 40% of their annual family income). At the same time, it is out of reach for middle-class families as well (for whom a year at a public institution ranges from 16% to 25% of their annual family income).[1] When nearly 75 percent of American families find college unaffordable, and the means-tested financial aid system fails to do its job even for the poorest, it is time for a change.

Not everyone agrees. "Two years of college for a low-income student is already free, or nearly free," and paying for college is easier than most people think, says Senator Lamar Alexander, the Tennessee Republican who until recently chaired the Senate education committee.[2]

It is a "myth" that "college is unaffordable for all but the very rich," wrote higher education analyst Sandy Baum in a blog for the American Council on Education.[3]

"Getting more low-income students into college isn't about the money, it's about the curriculum," opines the headline over a column by former Under Secretary of Education, Sara Martinez Tucker.[4]

I have made the case, in this book, that these assumptions don't hold. Why, then, do so many people believe our current system of financial aid is working well for those with the most need?

The first reason stems from a popular liberal myth: by targeting a social program to the poor, you will ensure they get the resources they need. This is a vastly oversimplified approach. True, among the financial aid distributed using the federal needs analysis, the majority of dollars flow to the bottom of the income distribution not the top. But that is not enough. Directing dollars one way does not ensure their purchasing power if it does not also control costs and ensure that other subsidies remain. It also does not mean that the system is reliable, trustworthy, accessible, or even remotely transparent. The Pell Grant is targeted but it can't promise that enough state appropriations will go to the institutions serving low-income students and it does nothing to keep college costs in check. Grant aid simply doesn't go as far as it used to, especially at institutions like UW–Milwaukee, where a disproportionate number of Pell recipients attend college. The result is that even after taking all grants into account, Pell recipients face a net price of more than $8,000 per year—at the nation's least expensive option, the public community college.

The second reason that some people believe that college— especially community college—is already free has to do with the technical jargon used in the financial aid system today. Tuition and fees are called "direct educational expenses" while everything else, including food, rent, gas money, and books, is called "indirect" or "noneducational." Language is powerful, and it has had consequences: it is easy to dismiss things that are "indirect" as optional. Yet covering those expenses is essential for full participation in college. Paying tuition allows students to go to class, but they will fail if they have no books, no pencils, no gas money to get school, and no food in their stomachs.

Full-time enrollment promotes degree completion not only because of the pace of progress it allows but also because of the academic focus it facilitates. It is very hard for students like Chloe Johnson to learn the material they need for their careers when they are running between PetSmart and Kohl's and college. Covering living costs, at least enough to ensure that their basic needs are met, is a productive investment of resources as long as it increases the odds that students finish degrees. In fact, by helping people from low-income families move up the economic ladder via college attainment, we greatly reduce the likelihood they will need social welfare programs in the future.

Reiterating the myth that college is affordable perpetuates inequality. Relying on standard aid numbers, which frequently overestimate a family's ability to pay and underestimate the true cost of attendance, provides a false sense of assurance that a full aid package (such as that offered by well-endowed private schools) truly takes money off the table for some students. It also encourages educators and policymakers to think that students' financial situations are not affecting their academic performance. If graduation rates are too low, the problem must lie with students themselves or with their colleges. If there is a crisis in America's college system, it must be, we are told, all about the students and the youth culture, the teaching and the advising, the remediation and the standards. Because, in effect, we believe what financial models seem to tell us: even when we provide Pell Grants that are supposed to cover college costs, low-income students still do not finish college.

This leads to the final reason why so many insist that college is affordable, despite abundant evidence to the contrary: it is politically useful. Decades ago, sociologists Frances Fox Piven and Richard Cloward noted that welfare benefits provided just enough assistance to gain the acquiescence of the poor even though it failed to afford them a decent life.[5] Today, the financial aid system serves the same function. It allows liberals to feel good and the poor to feel indebted, while at the same time providing a scapegoat for conservatives to blame. The problems facing public higher education, we learn, are not a function of too few resources but, rather, the fault of those who use the resources.

We are not asking the right questions, so it's no wonder that many think that college prices are a secondary issue when it comes to success or failure in higher education. They are not. As any student and parent outside of the top 5 percent income class who pays for college can tell you, the need for money comes first. You must, quite literally, pay to play.

How Did We Get Here?

The promises of federal student aid are ambitious, and its policies have been formulated over time by well-meaning people who themselves attended college and wish more Americans could do so as well. The basic premise is simple: lack of income should not keep you from attending college, so simply demonstrate financial need and financial aid will take care of the rest. With grants like the Pell, and some institutional funds for strong academic performance, buttressed by several flavors of student loans and a federal work-study program, the portfolio of options can seem robust. A student's financial aid package could include layer on layer of funds and requirements described by labels and acronyms—the ACG (Academic Competitiveness Grant), SEOG (Supplemental Educational Opportunity Grant), subsidized Stafford and Perkins, the Pell and the PLUS, the work-study allotment, and the private loan—and yet ultimately, vast numbers of students face a single, simple truth: financial aid pales in comparison to the real costs of attending college. Today, nine of every ten students that Senator Pell's program supports graduate from college with debt, with an average of over $30,000 per student.[6]

The price of college attendance is not merely a financial fact. It is a political fact reflecting policy choices and values. Compare the way students must pay for higher education to the way every child has access to free public K–12 education, or the way Americans access public roads, or the benefits of the fire department, which never asks you to describe your financial situation or contribute a means-tested check before putting out a blaze. College has a price and is not free today for a reason: because higher education in the United States is broadly considered a privilege and not a right.

Let's be honest. Not everyone thinks that college should be accessible. Political scientists Benjamin Page, Larry Bartels, and Jason Seawright find that while 78 percent of the general public agree that "the federal government should make sure that everyone who wants to go to college can do so," only 28 percent of the richest Americans agree.[7] And Kay Scholzman, Sid Verba, and Henry Brady find that wealthier Americans have more influence than average citizens at almost every stage of the public policy process.[8] So the privileged class is largely determining the policies concerning college access.

But college is now essential, and unfortunately there are no alternatives. If you cannot buy a home, you rent. If you cannot buy a car, you ride a bike or walk. But if you cannot attend college, you're lost. You are systematically locked out of nearly every decent-paying job opportunity, every safe neighborhood, and every opportunity to create safe futures for your children. We, as a society, recognize that a person without a high school degree can hardly survive in the United States, so we do not attach a price to public high school (and don't forget that public schools also house a massive federal free-and-discounted lunch program, which recognizes free access to classes alone will not do the job). Yet when it comes to college, we charge even the very poorest among us as much as $15,000 a year.

Today's system—let's call it Financial Aid 1.0—was created as a higher-education policy that involved a deal between two parties: the federal government and low-income students. The federal government would provide money to students, who would then use the funds to buy college. But the parties setting the price—state governments, colleges, universities, and a host of others—were not at the table. States have their own interests. So do colleges and universities, both public and private. Not to mention all of the undergraduates and their families who do not qualify for financial aid, and the businesses that benefit from a supply of undereducated, low-skill workers they can hire for minimal wages. All these parties have a stake, a reason, to believe that the price of college should not be zero—it should be higher. When college costs a lot, the public perceives it as more valuable, more exclusive, and it signals privilege.[9]

It is not that America lacks the resources or know-how to make college universally affordable—it is that we have strong incentives to maintain the status quo. What if all children were able to go to college simply by filling out an application and walking in the door? What would be left to distinguish the elite?

Graduate school is one new marker of success for upwardly mobile middle-class families. Sociologists have shown that those at the top will find ways to differentiate themselves and hoard opportunities to keep themselves and their children ahead of everyone else.[10] We should not fool ourselves—making college affordable won't end inequality in America. But it will increase the odds that people will finish the college degrees they start and eliminate the debt that they carry forward. It will not end inequality, but it will reduce poverty, and increase the ability of poor young adults to do better than their parents. These things matter.

The Risk of Inaction

Education has benefits that go far beyond economics. They are not as easy to measure as wage returns, so it can be easy to dismiss these public benefits. But they exist.[11]

Price, not intellect or effort, is the primary sorting mechanism in today's colleges and universities. As students move from one year of college to the next, class materials should get harder and students should need to study more. In a system like that, a degree would say something about ability. But that is not what's happening today. Time after time, the failure to complete college does not reflect intellectual inability but, rather, an inability to pay. We have no idea what Chloe Johnson's abilities are when it comes to veterinary medicine—we never had a chance to find out. Her love of horses and the knowledge she gained growing up around them were unimportant because her entire life became about paying the price of enrolling in college. What we learned is that at age eighteen she could not hack a schedule that included two jobs and five classes, no sleep, and too little food. We have no idea what Chloe could have become if only she could have focused on school.

This is an American tragedy. Sending a child to college is a proud moment for all parents, and it is especially so for parents who themselves never had that opportunity. But too often that moment of celebration turns into a period of intense stress and conflict over how to pay the price of attendance. Nima Chaudhary's relationship with her family was forever changed by the need to pay for school. Rather than feeling pride in her artistic talents and her ambitions to express herself through graphic design, her family wondered if her time in school was taking too much of their income. Because of Financial Aid 1.0's unwillingness to recognize that contributions often flow from child to parent, not merely parent to child, Nima's financial aid could not help offset their need for her to work. Had the system given her a stipend to buy her out of those family obligations,

Nima would have been better able to focus on school. She could have taken internships in graphic design instead of working nights at a nursing home. Perhaps her family would have come to her college graduation.

When college does not work out because the money isn't there, families and communities view the results as a powerful warning sign about the broken promises of public education in this country. The palpable sense of risk involved in student loans has generated a backlash against government and schools that frame student loans as aid. Some describe loans as "financial band-aids over a bullet hole" and say that calling them financial aid is "deceptive" and part of those "lies we tell ourselves."[12] As more students and families experience the failure of the financial aid system to support their college aspirations, trust in the system is likely to decline further. As tomorrow's qualified low- and moderate-income students become aware of those struggling in college and left with debts today, many may choose not to apply to college at all.

Even as financial aid fails the very students it is meant to serve, those students have become the target of animosity. At the start of the Great Recession, spending on the Pell Grant grew by over $10 billion a year, mainly due to three factors: policy changes that expanded program eligibility, growth in college enrollment, and economic conditions that raised unemployment and reduced family financial strength. But rather than viewing this increased spending as a positive step toward maintaining support for college access during a time of national economic distress, many in Washington, DC, began to question whether grants were an effective way to boost college attainment. Legislators, policy analysts, and newspaper articles began to brand Pell recipients as unmotivated, undeserving, and fraudulent, even though there was little evidence that widespread abuse existed.[13]

This shoddy treatment of a public program that is designed to help poor people is not uncommon.[14] Such targeted programs only appear to garner political support when they are seen as rewarding hard work or promoting opportunity, and critics of the Pell frequently question both.[15]

Financial Aid 1.0 today is a pale shadow of what its creators intended. Rather than supporting the hopes and dreams of people who seek to study and get ahead through higher education, it is punitive. It acts as an enticement to try college but then sets up students to face prices they cannot afford to meet year after year. It pits students against parents, financial aid administrators, and each other. It makes those who end up short of funds feel as if they've done something wrong. It is an invitation to debt.

What about Debt?

Student debt should not be at the center of this debate. Debt is the symptom, not the disease—the real problem is that college is unaffordable. Financial Aid 1.0 doesn't make college affordable but it is not a waste of money. It is simply an approach that is broken.

The lesson from today's debt crisis is that we have to do better for tomorrow. It is fine to improve the situation for current borrowers by lowering the interest rates, installing bankruptcy protections, or providing loan forgiveness. But these shifts will only help today's students and will do little to keep tomorrow's students from finding themselves in the exact same position. Instead, energy from concern about debt should be channeled toward creating sustainable shifts in college financing. Privatizing the federal student loan program, returning lending to the banks, or ending loan programs like Parent PLUS *before making college affordable* is not the answer, since without federal loans, broadly accessible to everyone, many Americans could not afford to enroll at all. The attack on loans is fundamentally an attack on the accessibility of today's system and must be understood as such.[16]

There are things we can do today to shore up Financial Aid 1.0, and there are other steps we can take to reduce college costs. But ultimately, we have to build a new system—a Financial Aid 2.0 that is based on accessible and affordable high-quality public higher education. Rather than offering more financial aid to keep up with rising prices, this future system should start by making the first few years of college or the initial degree free to all, as a public good.

Better Definitions

Let's begin with simple things—changing the words we use. Cost of attendance is misleading, since what students face is a price, not a cost. Increases in cost of attendance may stem from actual increases in costs but are more often caused by declines in operating subsidies from government or the institution's endowment. People need to know the difference, so it should be called the *price* of attendance.

Similarly, expected family contribution overstates what families can really afford. It should be called the *estimated* financial contribution. It is, after all, just an estimate of the students' ability to pay—and that money might come from the student or her family. Moreover, if a parent subsidizes the student's living expenses by allowing her to live at home, that should count toward the estimated family contribution rather than contributing to a reduction in the price of attendance.

Truth In Advertising

We also need to help students understand where their grants and loans come from. Taxpayers pay for Pell Grants and the subsidy attached to federal loans. In fact, the federal government bears a great deal of risk in originating student loans. All financial aid packages should clearly list the name of the financial aid given along with the source of that aid (federal, state, institutional, philanthropic). Simply beginning the title of a grant with "Federal Pell Grant," as in the current Financial Aid Shopping Sheet distributed by the U.S. Department of Education, is not enough. There should be a separate column that explains the source of funds, and government dollars should say "taxpayer-supported federal grant."[17]

In addition, the specific requirements associated with each type of aid should be clearly stated. If the Pell Grant requires students to maintain a 2.0 GPA, then it must say so, right next to the dollar amount. Students need to know. The conflicts and complexity created by attaching different requirements to different forms of aid must be made clearer to students, their academic advisers, and their financial aid administrators.

If a struggling student is attending college full time to meet the terms of a private scholarship of $3,500, what will happen if she reduces her course load to meet the GPA requirements associated with a $3,000 Pell Grant? If she keeps her full-time load and her GPA drops to a 1.8, she will lose her Pell. We might not know the right advice to give this student, but we can be certain she deserves to know exactly what's at stake.

No Surprises

We should be giving students more information earlier. Recently, President Obama made it possible for students to learn about financial aid almost a year in advance of college enrollment, rather than just a few months before.[18] That is a step in the right direction. Education scholar Robert Kelchen and I have also outlined the benefits and costs of telling students about Pell eligibility far earlier, when they are in middle school.[19] Early notification that aid is available may help some young people begin to think about college in concrete terms and take steps to prepare academically.

Surprises derail students. Universities often include an asterisk or some fine print somewhere in their voluminous literature they send to prospective and incoming students to note that prices may change. But, in general, students are led to believe that the price they pay for the first year of college will be the price they face in later years. Colleges, universities, and states benefit from understating the likelihood and magnitude of future price increases, but doing so reduces the odds of degree completion and harms all the institutions involved (not to mention that this practice is also unfair to millions of students and their families).

There has been some discussion about "tuition guarantees" that lock in the rate for students for the duration of their degree, or at least for four years, but these, too, have problems. First and most importantly, tuition is just a fraction of what it costs to attend college today. Flatlining tuition does not prevent the total price from rising, but it does give a false impression that it won't. Also, tuition guarantees obscure an important piece of information students need to know: financial aid—especially aid from grants—often declines as students' progress through college. If aid fails to keep up with growing nontuition costs, if aid switches from grants to loans, or if aid declines overall, students will still have difficulty paying the prices they will face after their first year.[20]

States should work with public colleges and universities to develop budgets that allow an entering student to have a road map of what the real price of attendance will be over the next four years. Projected tuition increases and nontuition increases should be included, and the methodology for these estimates should be clearly explained. Building on an idea first offered by Michael Dannenberg, U.S. Representative Patrick Murphy introduced legislation in 2010 called the Truth in Tuition Act. It would have required all colleges and universities to provide a multiyear estimate of actual and net costs for students at their school. This effort should be revisited.[21]

Public institutions should be accountable for maintaining any institutional grant support they provide throughout the course of a student's degree. The emphasis should be on stability and growth, and reductions in grant support for reasons other than noncompliance should not be allowed. Colleges and universities also need to take more responsibility for whether their students are able to meet the academic requirements associated with financial aid. If a college has a satisfactory academic progress standard that large numbers students do not meet, thus losing their aid, then at minimum incoming students need to know that. The fraction of students who meet satisfactory academic progress standards should be published, and this information should be provided in the aid package distributed to students, along with clear explanations of the consequences of falling short.

Along the same lines, families with incomes between $20,000 and $30,000 a year, many of whom are living on the knife's edge of poverty, deserve better than the current system provides. The threshold for an automatic-zero expected family contribution should be placed at $30,000 or above and remain there.[22] This might have helped students like Chloe Johnson whose family was judged capable of contributing $2,500 to her schooling in one year, but in the next year, their contribution was zero. Such shifts hardly breed faith in the system.

Separate Grants from Everything Else—and List *Everything* Else

Information about the price of attending college and the grants available to offset that price should be clearly separated from information about how students might cover the remaining price. This is partly to avoid information overload, but it also recognizes that taking loans and working jobs are not forms of financial aid in the same way that grants are. Some loans and work-study are subsidized by the government and should be acknowledged as such, but they are materially different from grants. Paying for college is not easy, and college should help students understand all their options. Beyond the current list of loans and work-study and educational tax credits, students should be told about other social benefits programs that students and their families may qualify for. These programs include food assistance, like the Supplemental Nutrition Assistance Program (SNAP, better known as food stamps) and Special Supplemental Nutrition Program for Women, Infants, and Children (called WIC). There are also important noneducational tax credits, such as the Earned Income Tax Credit (EITC).

As a recent report by sociologist Derek Price and his colleagues noted, "The issues and needs that public benefits aim to address do not occur in isolation, and individuals may require several types of non-academic supports to help them stay in college and earn a credential." The same is true for financial aid.[23] Making efficient use of resources requires retraining financial aid officers and student services personnel and equipping retooled financial aid offices with the resources required to provide integrated access to financial aid and all other social benefits programs that can help students pay for college. Single Stop provides one model of this approach and adds some useful additional services: tax preparation, legal counseling, financial counseling, and case management. My team led an implementation evaluation of this national program and found that all of the services were heavily utilized.[24] Had they existed in Wisconsin's colleges and universities when Anne was in school, she might have managed to remain enrolled full time and complete her degree without losing her housing.

Immediate Patches

Students clearly need better information to help them make more informed decisions and identify existing resources. This is important, but it is far from enough to render college affordable to all. Too many students are dropping out of college because they cannot cover their rent, utilities, childcare, gas, or other critical basic needs.

Emergency aid programs are an especially promising approach for retaining more students in higher education. These programs make money available for students' immediate needs far more flexibly than the financial aid system can. There are more than a hundred such programs operating nationwide, some homegrown by colleges and universities and others operated as part of the Dreamkeepers program run by Scholarship America. The Angel Fund used to serve students at tribal colleges and universities until it ran out of financial support.[25] We need many more such efforts. Student services personnel can work alongside financial aid administrators to structure a flexible, responsive program that takes seriously the idea that students need cash so they can focus on school. Administrative systems must move quickly to identify and meet needs, balancing efficiency and responsible stewardship. It is possible, we know, because it is being done now. Rigorous evaluations of these efforts and properly implemented efforts to scale them are needed.[26]

The American social safety net remains a critical source of support for many students from low-income families. The current disconnect between higher education policy and social policies aimed at helping poor, working, and middle-class families harms students. These policies must be aligned and coordinated. For example, when the reauthorization of the Temporary Aid to Needy Families law next occurs, education and training at the postsecondary level should be allowed without arbitrary time limits.[27] Parents with small children should be encouraged to get more education, not less, so that they can become stable sources of support for those young people moving forward. Funding for on-campus childcare must increase in order to make this possible, and "two-generation" models that help both parent and child obtain an education together should be explored and evaluated.[28]

Hunger is real problem for too many college students.[29] College enrollment should count toward the work requirement associated with the Supplemental Nutrition Assistance Program. Just counting work-study is not enough since only a small percentage of students receive this benefit. Requiring undergraduates to work twenty hours a week in order to receive food stamps works against the broader policy goal of encouraging college completion and may even be reducing the effectiveness of the federal Pell Grant Program. In the meantime, all colleges and universities should familiarize themselves with the benefits and eligibility rules for SNAP and provide students and their families with information that may help them meet their basic needs.

Colleges recognize that hunger is an issue for their students. Campus food banks and pantries have sprung up around the country to help undergraduates get the food they need, and the College and University Food Bank Alliance, cofounded by Clare Cady and Nate Smith-Tyge, provides a critical source of support in that regard. Its members run the gamut from the University of Arkansas, University of Michigan, and Stony Brook University to Simmons College and Vanderbilt University.[30]

The National School Lunch Program was introduced to K–12 education in 1946 because policymakers were concerned that students who were hungry could not learn.[31] The students who benefit from access to meals when in high school move onto college and find themselves stuck. The students who were hungry in high school are hungry in college. We need to start a serious policy discussion about extending that program to public colleges and universities.[32]

Eyes on the Prize

The rules and regulations associated with financial aid need to be adjusted to promote degree completion rather than encouraging students to ration money. Today, unfortunately, rationing access to education is the rule.[33] Again and again, federal, state, and institutional policies make it likely that students will receive less financial aid than they need (even when more money is available). Rationing is a hedging strategy, encouraging consumers to adopt scrimping and saving tactics to preserve a limited resource. This has to stop—even when more money isn't available, students need to know the extent to which their resources fall short. We know education is an investment that pays tremendous dividends for government. We also know that situations of financial scarcity and pressure reduce the likelihood of graduation.

The calculation of living costs for students living off campus should be removed from institutional responsibilities. Inaccurate estimates do real harm, and financial aid offices are already strapped for time. Standardizing living costs calculations will help students and families make better college decisions and ease colleges' reporting obligations. Congress should amend U.S. Code § 1087(II) "Cost of attendance" in the upcoming reauthorization of the Higher Education Opportunity Act to give families accurate price information and guarantee that eligible students receive the financial aid necessary for postsecondary success. This amendment should task the U.S. Department of Education with providing living cost calculations for all colleges and universities using existing federal data; currently it is expressly prohibited from doing so by law. In the meantime, the department should develop a clear method for colleges to calculate living costs so that allowances are comparable for institutions in close proximity to each other. Either of these changes would substantially improve both the accuracy and transparency of college living cost allowances while reducing workloads for colleges and universities already strained by reporting obligations.[34]

We need to make it possible for students to work their way through college. The implicit tax on students' earnings penalizes student employment. In 2014, U.S. senator Tammy Baldwin introduced the Working Student Act (S.2796) in an effort to enact an across-the-board, 35 percent increase in the income protection allowance for students. This was a good start. It should be higher, to allow students to keep more of their money, work less, and finish school.[35]

The Federal Work-Study Program is in desperate need of an overhaul. Economist Judith Scott-Clayton finds that just 23 percent of current work-study students come from families earning less than $30,000, while 20 percent come from families earning more than

$100,000.[36] The current formula rewards older and more expensive institutions and should be revised to focus on serving Pell recipients at public institutions, where it seems to be more effective.[37] Work-study is, in the words of Lumina Foundation president Jamie Merisotis, a "jobs and education program" and it could be a much better one. States should develop their own programs to complement the federal effort.

Helping States Step Up

It is time to rethink how states support higher education. There are many plans for bringing states back to the table, and the best ones recognize and attempt to mitigate the inclinations of states to prioritize wealthy citizens (who have the most political clout) over regular people.[38] According to a recent study, fully 40 percent of all high school graduates who do not attend college live in the South.[39] While there are many reasons for lower college participation rates in the South, one reason is financial. A critical key difference between states in the Deep South and other regions is the historically low levels of state-funded, need-based, student financial aid. "The Impact of the New Pell Grant Restrictions on Community Colleges: A Three-State Study of Alabama, Arkansas, and Mississippi," a report from the Education Policy Center, found that the Pell Grant provided $1.3 billion in need-based financial aid in 2010–11 in just those three Deep South states alone. Alabama's need-based state student aid program, the Alabama Student Assistance Program, provided just $16.8 million that year. Similar programs in Arkansas were budgeted at $12.4 million and in Mississippi at $3.2 million.[40] Nineteen studies of student aid policies by the Education Policy Center (located at the University of Alabama) over the past five years found that for many rural states, including the Deep South, the Pell Grant is, for all intents and purposes, the de facto state student aid program.[41]

One way the federal government might be able to help is by establishing a maintenance-of-effort requirement. This would allow federal funds to be used only to supplement state funding rather than supplanting existing state monies. Such a requirement would mean that states have to maintain spending above a certain thresh-old in order to receive federal funding tied to specific programs.[42] Bringing states back to the table when it comes to making college affordable will not be easy.

But it is also important to move beyond considering how much states spend on higher education as a whole and examine how they allocate those dollars. While state support flows to all public colleges and universities, some institutions depend on it far more than others.[43] Research universities can look to endowment funds, gifts, auxiliary enterprises, and federal funds for revenue when state funds decline, and their students are often more able to bear increases in tuition. But at community colleges and comprehensive public universities, state appropriations are the dominant source of funding, and when they decline, tuition must go up.

The issue of how funds are distributed among institutions is a common topic in K–12 education finance, but is often neglected in higher education. As chapter 8's discussion of higher education in Milwaukee illustrates, it matters. In 2012–13, the state of Wisconsin gave the University of Wisconsin–Madison approximately $12,410 per full-time-equivalent student (FTE), but only $5,157 per FTE to the University of Wisconsin–Milwaukee and just $3,211 per FTE to the two-year University of Wisconsin Colleges. The latter serve more first-generation students, more part-time students, and more adult undergraduates than any other institutions in the UW System. Is this enough financial support to provide academically vulnerable, economically insecure students, working parents, and nontraditional learners with a quality postsecondary education that will prepare them for the workforce and beyond? It seems unlikely.

Are UW–Madison students truly more expensive to educate, and if so, why? Why do students at UW Colleges receive a lower level of investment? Improving the sufficiency and fairness of state allocations for higher education will mean shedding more light on within-state funding distributions. It will also demand a more careful accounting of the resource costs—not just how much is spent—associated with educating different groups of students at the postsecondary level. Such data are currently nearly impossible to come by, but they must be collected. Absent an unexpected influx of new funds, the future of college affordability will depend on how state monies are spent. We need to start paying attention.[44]

Focusing Our Efforts

If the goal of financial aid policy is to break the link between family income and college attainment, several areas of current spending should be revisited.

The first is "non-need-based grant aid" or so-called merit aid. According to the National Association of State Student Grant and Aid Programs, in 2012–13, states distributed $2.3 billion in non-need-based grants—one-fourth of all grant aid distributed. Growth in spending has slowed in the last two years, and yet in many states (including Florida, Georgia, Louisiana, New Mexico, Tennessee, and Virginia), more than half of all state aid dollars are distributed without regard to need.[45] Moreover, a recent policy scan conducted by the Education Commission of the States revealed that many of the hundred largest state financial aid programs restrict eligibility to only students who enroll full time or conservatively cap the number of years they can receive support.[46]

Each year institutions of higher education distribute $9 billion in grants from their own coffers—about as much as the states manage to do.[47] But colleges and universities continue to allocate more than half of what they often claim to be "scarce" resources based on not the financial need of their students but rather specific "talents."[48] New America Foundation analyst Stephen Burd points out that about one-third of students receiving "merit" aid had less than a B average in high school and mediocre SAT scores.[49] These days, seven out of ten public universities (among 424 that Burd examined) provide non-need-based aid to at least 5 percent of their first-year class each year—while leaving students like those in this study with unmet financial need.[50] Donald Heller, dean of the School of Education at Michigan State University, finds that public universities are more likely to do this than private universities.[51]

Spending on non-need-based aid perpetuates inequality. Twenty-eight percent of all state aid and 31 percent of all institutional aid distributed in this manner flows to students from families in the top 25 percent of the income distribution. Students from well-off families not only have no unmet need but their needs are overmet—while those of middle- and working-class families go wanting.[52]

Further, these dollars often do not increase college attendance or completion among wealthy students, indeed several studies indicate that they incentivize detrimental academic behavior in college.[53] The most famous "merit" program—the Georgia HOPE scholarship—was mainly good at one thing: increasing sales at car dealerships.[54] When the children from families with resources get these scholarships, parents buy them cars. But when the children of poor families get financial aid, they eat.

First Degree for Free

Education pays substantial dividends, both for individuals and families, as well as for communities. There is a reason why every one of our students, from Ian Williams and his four siblings to Norbert Webster and Chloe Johnson tried so hard to obtain college degrees despite the price it required of them. The Oneida Nation also understands the benefits of making college truly affordable, as it continues to make a large and consistent commitment to ensuring that all tribal members can make it to the finish line. Higher education is valuable because it improves the social fabric in literally immeasurable ways.

The effects of higher education accrue across generations, not merely within cohorts. We have long understood this, building national prosperity in the twentieth century by making high school free. Yes, individuals reap economic benefits from attending high school, and wealthy kids attending good public schools reap many more benefits than low-income kids attending crummy ones. But we don't insist that individuals pay their way for high school because we recognize how important it is that everyone has an opportunity to finish high school. We do our best to ensure that money does not get in the way.

Decades ago, many Americans got a pretty good deal. With family support, some work, and perhaps a modest Pell Grant, college prices were such that those who did go could usually make ends meet. And they entered a labor market where a college degree conferred a bonus but was not required. There were a fairly large number of good-paying jobs available to people who were not college graduates.

That world is gone. Young people from all families and older workers in need of new skills want to attend college, and they plan on enrolling, even if it means ending up with debt and no degree, at risk of defaulting on loans.[55] Lower-income individuals, people of color, and women know that there's no economic security in their futures without at least some sort of college credential. Research confirms this: Ron Haskins has called a college education a "powerful" intervention like no other.[56]

In the 1970s, targeting financial aid to only the poorest individuals made sense—after all, most people didn't want to attend college, it wasn't required, and college prices were low enough that the Pell Grant largely covered the bills.[57] Today, that same model fails: the vast majority of the populace wants access to affordable, high-quality public higher education, it is required, and costs are so high that grants and scholarships provide only a meager discount restricted to only a fraction of students with financial need.[58] Means-tested financial aid, administered via a massive bureaucracy, leaves out the very poorest—who cannot navigate the system—and squeezes the middle class, who are offered only loans.[59]

America can't afford to ignore the calls for a broad, inclusive system of public higher education that helps families obtain economic security.[60] Of course, a universal, free system will have progressive effects—tearing down the price and bureaucratic barriers will matter most to the poorest people, who have made very little progress accessing college under the current system. But the benefits will be broadly shared. Completion rates for working- and middle-class students will rise as their costs of college are more fully covered.[61] Accreditation reform and greater accountability will accompany this shift to ensure quality and a high return on public investment. Everyone will benefit from a better-educated, more productive American workforce.

What about downsides? For example, will the movement of more students into higher education diminish the quality of undergraduates or the returns to their degrees? It is very unlikely. In a recent study that examines change in student quality over the last thirty years, economist Robert Archibald and his colleagues conclude: "Existing federal policies that have reduced the financial obstacles to college attendance have not caused lower completion rates. Reforms that stimulate further increases in college attendance, either by improving information about the net cost of attendance or by reducing the net cost, are not necessarily self-defeating given the remaining potential to move high-quality students into 4-year programs. In addition, state policies that reduce the net cost of attendance for students who have achieved some performance thresholds could complement federal assistance."[62]

When the movement for free public high school began in the 1800s, many opposed it, calling it "a contrivance of the rich to rob the poor."[63] They were wrong—when high school became free, families from all walks of life came to get educated.[64] Some argue that the United States can't afford to make college free. The truth is, we can't afford not to.

We should follow an incremental approach that begins by making the associate degree free to all students who pursue it.[65] This is the initial entry point to college, and all public institutions should award it. Many students start at four-year institutions, last four semesters, and leave with nothing in hand. It is important that these institutions reward that effort with an associate degree and that we establish that degree as the new "first degree." We should begin, as Federal Reserve Board chairman Ben Bernanke said, with the community colleges: "We must move beyond the view that education is something that takes place only in K-through-12 schools and four-year colleges, as important as those are. Education and skills must be provided flexibly and to people of any age."[66]

Then we can work on making the first degree free at any public college or university.[67] We need to work toward the time when "public colleges and universities" have the same meaning as public K–12 schools, or public parks, or public roads: goods paid for by all, intended for universal free use by all who wish to use them for their intended purposes. Students like those in this book would be greatly helped by a complete overhaul of the financing system for public colleges and universities. As many have said, "Programs for poor people make for poor programs."[68] A more inclusive financing system will also likely be a more sustainable one.

But money should not come without assurances. We can do much more to support the public sector so that its quality is high and its costs are reasonable. Neither do we have the same relationship with nor should we intrude on private colleges and universities. We have provided trillions of dollars in resources to both private nonprofit and private for-profit colleges and universities for decades and still can't guarantee that they are either accessible or affordable. But when it comes to working with public colleges and universities to update their approaches to student services, identifying effective practices to teaching and learning, and finding ways to increase capacity, we have plenty of experience and road maps to guide us.[69]

While there is a long way to go in public higher education, there has been progress. Governors and legislatures have gained control over tuition increases at their state's colleges and universities time and again.[70] Some have allocated additional appropriations to prevent increases, and this works to ensure that the institutions do not raise tuition while also ensuring they have the resources needed to support students. Community colleges across the country have shown a willingness to engage their states in thoughtful discussions about how best to fund their work and, in exchange, have received increases in state support.[71] In fact, today most states are *not* cutting public higher education.[72] They are reinvesting.

That is because there is a substantial public benefit to high rates of college attendance. It is far more difficult to quantify than the returns to individuals (expressed in terms of boosted wages) but that does not mean that it is smaller.[73] Listen to economist Walter McMahon, author of *Higher Learning, Greater Good*: "The private non-market benefits are estimated more comprehensively . . . their value is about $9,883 per year after graduation for each year of college degree. This turns out to be approximately equal to the benefits from each year of college to annual earnings ($9,967). This alone means that half of the private benefits of college to students and their families are being overlooked."[74] Twelve years of education does not go as far as it once did, and after a century of technological advancements and upskilling, it is reasonable to expect that some post–high school education is beneficial. States know that they cannot attract employers or grow their economies without an educated workforce.

But their efforts to do this are being undermined by the clear and growing risk that too many people encounter when pursuing that first degree. A year or two of college credits without a degree means not only wasted time but also significant debt. Those who are being left behind today are the people who decide that risk is too great.

The main barrier to college entry is price. By eliminating the price of admission, we can send a powerful message: there is no harm in trying. And for people who do try, like Chloe Johnson, by eliminating their need to work while in college, we improve their chances of success. If they don't make it, very little harm to students will be done—they can look back and assess what happened, but they will not be doing it while paying monthly bills to a debt collection agency for that failure.

In 2014, Republican governor Bill Haslam began to restore hope in Tennessee by offering tuition-free community college. To create this program, called Tennessee Promise, Haslam drew on the example of Knox Achieves, which helps young people who would have otherwise never experienced even a thirteenth year of education to earn college credits. [75] Using lottery funds, Tennessee is providing a "last-dollar scholarship" that fills in the gap between tuition and fees and existing grant dollars. While this means that students with less need (as assessed by the fallible expected family contribution calculation) get more dollars from this program, it also means that all students benefit from the clear, concise message that college is tuition free. That is the main goal—to overcome the barriers created by a confusing, untrustworthy system and send a resounding message directly from the governor: "My message to high school seniors is: this is your Tennessee Promise. This is an opportunity for you to fulfill your potential, and you have an opportunity to change the future for yourself and for our state."[76] According to the Tennessee Student Assistance Corporation, 15,830 students from the graduating high school class of 2015 were using Tennessee Promise benefits in fall 2015, the first year of implementation. The number of students attending community college right after high school jumped 14 percent in a single year, and Tennessee led the nation in the rate of FAFSA completion.[77]

This approach seems to be contagious. In summer 2015, Oregon governor Kate Brown signed into law the Oregon Promise, which will waive community college tuition for six thousand Oregonians beginning in fall 2016. The legislature allocated $10 million in support for the effort, which was spearheaded by Senator Mark Hass, who called it a "bold and visionary" idea deserving of implementation and rigorous study.[78] He is not alone. As of the time of this writing, dozens of states and localities across the nation are weighing the possibility of offering at least some version of a free college program. The list includes New York, Minnesota, Milwaukee, Chicago, California, Tulsa, and Arizona.[79]

Their efforts will be more robust and effective if they can move beyond simply covering tuition and fees and instead begin to address the opportunity costs of college attendance. Paying for room and board, transportation, books, and supplies is often what students struggle most with. In January 2015, President Barack Obama introduced America's College Promise, which would eliminate tuition and fees at community colleges, thus allowing existing need-based financial aid to be applied to cover opportunity costs.[80] Senator Tammy Baldwin of Wisconsin and Representative Bobby Scott of Virginia advanced the legislation for Congressional consideration. They added support for historically black colleges and universities, Hispanic-serving institutions, Asian American and Native American Pacific Islander–serving institutions, and other minority-serving institutions, wisely recognizing that some public colleges still do not fully address the needs of students of color.[81]

These initiatives were preceded by another smart initiative that began long ago in New York. In 1969, large numbers of African Americans and Puerto Ricans demanded that the City University of New York become a place that they could enter to pursue better lives.[82] University administrators responded by instituting an open admissions policy to complement a very low price. An evaluation conducted over the next thirty years revealed that while the new policy did not wipe out disadvantages due to race or class (or high school academic record), it more than doubled the proportion of black women who attained degrees.[83] That finding is consistent with more recent studies that raise sharp questions about the contention that "college isn't for everyone."[84]

National leaders need to provide hope to people everywhere. Simply providing financial aid isn't getting the job done.[85] Efforts to expand the maximum Pell Grant have never met with much success, and that laudable program continues to exclude (for lack of funds and because of administrative bureaucracy) many who face sizable price barriers. Simplifying the FAFSA is a technocratic fix, not a transformative one—it won't bring new money to the table. That is why it is time for a national conversation about what it means to provide high-quality thirteenth and fourteenth years of public education to everyone and how we are going pay for it. New taxes are an option—but we can also simply stop spending on investments that aren't paying off. Estimates vary, but many indicate that the costs are no more than $70–$100 billion—we could go a long way toward covering these costs by ending subsidies to for-profit universities and tax credits that are demonstrably ineffective.[86]

No Choice but Hope

For Ian Williams, what could feel more impossible than growing up on the streets of Milwaukee, being educated in a broken public school system, and trying to build a future at a public university where a year of college costs $25,000 a year? Yet, somehow, Ian sees possibilities. Indeed, he believes that optimism is his only option:

> I turned negativity to positivity throughout my whole college life. I use my past experience to get where I need to be going. I don't want to go back there, to basically not having much food,

living in poverty where people are robbing and stealing and all
that stuff. I don't want to go back there or turn to that. So I use that
as motivation. . . . I don't want to have a low-paying job and live
in poverty, not ever having food to eat. And I just picture myself,
knowing that when I get out of college that's going to help me out.
Hopefully I can try to help people who live back there, too, they
use me like an image. . . . When they look up to me, I'm going to
turn it around and show them which way they should really go.

Sixty percent of Americans aged twenty-five to sixty-four do
not hold a college credential. But 22 percent of them—32.6 million
Americans—have tried to get one.[87] They left college frustrated,
often saying it had something to do with money.[88] The ladder people
must climb to get to graduation has eroded, and a critical rung—
affordability—is almost completely broken. We have to repair it.
Doing nothing will be far more expensive than making an upfront
investment now.

The first step in addressing the college affordability crisis is taking
the problem seriously. Money matters. Lack of financial resources
is keeping students from succeeding. Suggesting that low-income
students merely need to learn how to live more frugally is usually a
misplaced recommendation—and an offensive one, to boot. As Os-
car Wilde wrote, "To recommend thrift to the poor is both grotesque
and insulting. It is like advising a man who is starving to eat less."[89]

Researchers need to do their part to help illuminate how and why
price is a barrier to education. As these new models of financing
emerge, they need to be evaluated not only for the impacts they
achieve but also for how they affect the college experiences and
lives of individual students. To help ensure that this work gets done,
I recently founded the Wisconsin HOPE Lab, an applied research
shop staffed by talented researchers committed to rigorous studies
that can be directly translated into action. This sort of research,
conducted in communities across the nation, must inform public
policies if we are to find better ways forward.

Forty-five million young people will turn eighteen in America
in the next ten years. Will the children of the wealthy leave college

with elite networks, the sons and daughters of the middle class with degrees they can use, and the next generation of low-income Americans with mainly debt and despair?

The new economics of college is undermining the fundamental connection between education and democracy that has helped our nation thrive. More than a century ago, American policymakers realized that the wealth of your family or the resources of your community should not determine access to K–12 schooling.[90] In time, every state, and the nation as a whole, shouldered the responsibility of educating all children through high school. In 1973, U.S. senator Claiborne Pell and his generation made noble strides to expand college access, helping America build the largest middle class the world has ever known. With economic inequality on the rise, and low-income and middle-class Americans under pressure, this generation must meet the challenge of making one of the best ways out of poverty and into the middle class—a college education—affordable for all.

Acknowledgments

The story of this book began almost eight years ago, with one of my exciting and always ambitious plans. At the time, my son, Conor, was just one year old, and I was years away from earning tenure. I didn't have a staff of researchers and hadn't yet partnered with any colleagues at the University of Wisconsin–Madison to conduct studies. But I was excited—thrilled to have the opportunity to get an up-close-and-personal look at the implementation of an innovative financial aid program I really hoped would improve young peoples' lives.

My former husband Liam Goldrick made possible what happened next. Partnering with me to ensure that I could commit the time and energy to what became the Wisconsin Scholars Longitudinal Study (WSLS), while also being a committed mom to Conor and eventually to Annie, who arrived a few years later—he epitomized the supportive spouse. He did the usual cooking, cleaning, and laundry but also provided me with the space I needed to build and lead a very large research team, something that stretched me in every way possible. I was not easy to live with, but he endured to allow me opportunity after opportunity. The WSLS became a temporary third child, in many ways, but Annie and Conor are forever my guiding lights.

They say it takes a village to raise a child—well, in the case of the WSLS it took quite a crowd. Alison Bowman emerged as its spiritual leader, managing the entire project with a warm-hearted smile that kept us together and on track. Two of my graduate students blossomed during data collection and developed as key investigators in this work. It's been a tremendous pleasure to collaborate with Robert Kelchen and Peter Kinsley over so many years.

Thanks to the influence of the greatest writer in my life, my maternal grandmother Geraldine Youcha, I took a very long time to put this story down on paper. The craft of writing is, for me, a collaborative one, and I owe Avi Green, Tammy Kolbe, and especially my mom Victoria Youcha an enormous debt of gratitude for making this book as accessible and readable as possible.

It is easy to lose touch with friends and even family during journeys like this study. As I finished this book, I lost someone who taught me to manage my energy instead of my time—I miss my aunt Sharon Youcha every single day. I am deeply grateful to my sister Lisa Rab, my grandfather Isaac Youcha, and my dearest friends who hugged me, laughed with me, and pushed me to keep going: Nancy Kendall, Lorie Wesolek, Tammy Kolbe, Katherine Sydor, and Elizabeth Vaquera. My love of studying public higher education comes from Kate Shaw, who along with Kathryn Edin and Christopher Mazzeo taught me how to conduct mixed-methods studies and policy implementation research that matters.

For challenging me to think through all sides, mean what I say and say what I mean, and cheering me on even when they did not agree with me, I thank Estela Bensimon, Michael Dannenberg, Amy Ellen Duke-Benfield, Mimi Bloch, Nate Falkner, David Figlio, Barbara Gault, Chad Goldberg, Pamela Herd, Jee Hang Lee, Anthony Hernandez, Andy Howe, Andrew Kelly, Katherine Magnuson, Minh Mai, Elisabeth Mason, Eliza Moeller, Thomas Mortenson, David Mundel, Jenny Nagaoka, Melissa Roderick, Mike Rose, Carlo Salerno, Kevin Stange, Scott Thomas, and Brent Wesolek. I'm also indebted to my friends and colleagues on Facebook and Twitter, who quite unexpectedly added both substance and motivation to this project.

For caring for my children and allowing me to work on this book while feeling confident that they were happy, I thank Emi Coffin, Patrice Coffin, Lydia, Anna, and Natalie Gruben, Sharon Hays, Julia Lampe, Jennifer Muchka, and Stephanie Proulx. For massages that kept me calm enough to keep writing, I thank Belinda Schaffitzel.

The University of Wisconsin–Madison created the chance for me to meet John and Tashia Morgridge and Mary Gulbrandsen, and the Wisconsin Center for the Advancement of Postsecondary Education along with its director, Noel Radomski, facilitated the creation of the WSLS. The Wisconsin Center for Education Research, led by Adam Gamoran, became its home. The Department of Educational Policy Studies, where I first met Douglas N. Harris—who became the co-principal investigator of the WSLS—gave me access to thoughtful colleagues and students and, fortunately, had the stomach to tenure me.

A multimethod book like this one is a beast to assemble, and I benefited from expert help and commentary provided by Drew M. Anderson, Alison Bowman, Katharine M. Broton, Emily Brunjes, Ellen Bruno, Karole Dacholet, Michael Dannenberg, Ben Emmel, Derek Fields, Anna Haley-Lock, Drew Hanson, Norbert Hill, Derek Houston, Dylan Jambrek, Mark Kantrowitz, Robert Kelchen, Peter Kinsley, Jason Lee, Minh Mai, Ben Miller, and Nick Strohl. Jed Richardson, as always the consummate manager, guided the manuscript through the final edits. Four of the smartest people I know, Leslie Bartlett, Debbie Cochrane, Katherine Sydor, and Scott Thomas, gave generously of their time to read drafts and ensure the technicalities were correct. My editor at the University of Chicago Press, Elizabeth Branch Dyson, was patient, kind, and unfailingly generous with her time and support. Thanks also to Yvonne Zipter, who improved the manusript with a careful edit, and Jan Williams, who constructed the index.

I have benefited from audiences all over the country who have listened and responded to this work in progress. Since this includes more than four dozen talks, I cannot name every one of them here, but special thanks go to Greg Duncan, Daniel Eisenberg, Howard Bloom, Brian Jacob, Jeffrey Smith, and Viviana Zelizer.

It should be clear by now that this study was only possible because of supportive funders. I thank the Bill and Melinda Gates Foundation (especially Ann Person), the William T. Grant Foundation (especially Bob Granger), the Spencer Foundation (especially Michael McPherson), the Great Lakes Higher Education Guaranty Corporation (especially Richard George and Amy Kerwin), the Lumina

Foundation (especially Zakiya Smith), the Institute for Research on Poverty, the Wisconsin Center for the Advancement of Postsecondary Education, and the Smith Richardson Foundation (especially Mark Steinmeyer). The William T. Grant Foundation's extraordinary Faculty Scholars Program provided me with a five-year-long fellowship with which to focus on this work. It also gave me access to tremendous mentors in the form of Eli Lieber, Rebecca Maynard, Thomas Weisner, Lindsay Chase-Lansdale, Steve DesJardins, and most of all, David Figlio. The discussions at our annual retreats and mixed-methods meetings, especially with Stefanie DeLuca, Carola Suarez-Orozco, Steve Raudenbush, and Phil Goff, made me so much smarter and wiser.

The work goes on. We are not done. My staff has blossomed into its current configuration as the Wisconsin HOPE (Harvesting Opportunities for Postsecondary Education) Lab, working together to build the nation's first translational research laboratory focused on making college affordable. Learn more about us at www.wihopelab .com. Creating the HOPE Lab was my way of thanking the three thousand participants of the Wisconsin Scholars Longitudinal Study *and* all of the researchers who took part in it, as we continue to sift and winnow our way toward a better system of college financing for all families. As Angela Davis said, "I am no longer accepting the things I cannot change but, rather, changing the things I cannot accept"—and it is an honor and a blessing to do so, every single day.

Wisconsin Scholars Longitudinal Study: Methodology

PETER KINSLEY AND SARA GOLDRICK-RAB

This book describes results from the Wisconsin Scholars Longitudinal Study (WSLS) examining the impact of a private need-based financial grant on the college outcomes of traditional eighteen- to twenty-one-year -old federal Pell Grant recipients. This appendix describes its methodological details. The WSLS is a mixed-methods study launched in 2008 by a team of researchers (see the list at the conclusion of this appendix). The research design and all methods described were approved and conducted under the supervision of the University of Wisconsin–Madison's Institutional Review Board, protocol #2008-0365.

Sample

The sample is composed of a stratified random selection of three thousand college students enrolled in all public two-year and four-year colleges and universities in the state of Wisconsin (for more information on these, see app. 2). We chose participants at random from among students who were eligible for the Fund for Wisconsin Scholars Grant program, described in chapters 1 and 9. Therefore, every student met the fund's eligibility criteria—every student was a Wisconsin public high school graduate who first enrolled full time in a Wisconsin public college in fall 2008, received the federal Pell Grant, and still had at least one dollar of remaining unmet need.

More precisely, the WSLS sample includes all twelve hundred

students who were selected to receive an offer of the Wisconsin Scholars Grant (WSG) and an additional stratified random sample of eighteen hundred students who were not selected. In an effort to increase the representation of students of color in the sample, and given the constraint that the administrative records used for sampling did not include race/ethnicity, we chose to draw a disproportionately large sample for the control group from students attending institutions with higher than average enrollment of students of color. All analyses therefore employ post-stratification inverse probability weights to accommodate the resulting unequal sampling probabilities among students across schools.

Among students in the full sample, the average adjusted gross income of their parents in the year before they started college (2007) was just under $25,000, and the mean age was between eighteen and nineteen years old (see table 21). The average expected family contribution (for a definition see chap. 2) was $1,370. Fifty-eight percent of the sample was female and 81 percent of the students did not have a parent with a bachelor's degree. The sample is representative of the more than six thousand undergraduates across the state meeting the Wisconsin Scholars Grant eligibility criteria. And with the exception of racial/ethnic composition, the sample is also generally representative of the national population of first-time, full-time Pell Grant recipients attending public institutions.

We interviewed a subsample of fifty students using methods described below. A comparison with the full WSLS sample reveals that the two groups were similar in terms of gender, age, and first-generation status. The financial profile of the interviewees was also quite similar to the full sample, though the interviewed students did tend to come from slightly more advantaged economic backgrounds. Nevertheless, the average adjusted gross income of their parents was still very low at just under $26,000. Where the two groups differed was in their racial composition and rates of two-year college attendance, and this was an intentional part of the sampling design. As we sought to examine racial/ethnic differences in how students experienced paying for college (and found relatively few— though important differences are described in the book), students in the interview sample were far more likely to be students of color.

Table 21. WSLS sample characteristics

	Full Sample	Interview Sample	National
Began at a two-year college	50%	26%	...
Began at a Milwaukee college or university	18%	24%	...
Female	58%	54%	62%
Race/ethnicity:			
White	70%	39%	44%
Hispanic	7%	22%	21%
African American	10%	16%	25%
Asian	8%	16%	5%
Other	4%	6%	2%
Age	19.5	18.5	20.2
First generation college student (no BA)	81%	88%	76%
Married	3%	2%	7%
Dependent children	10%	6%	21%
Expected family contribution ($K)	1.37	1.63	...
Zero expected family contribution	38%	35%	...
Parents' adjusted gross income ($K)	24.7	25.9	21.92
Parents' total cash/checking/savings ($K)	2.12	2.03	...

Sources. WSLS data; and National Center for Education Statistics, *National Postsecondary Student Aid Study NPSAS*, 2008.

Note. Includes entire sample (full sample, *n* = 3,000; interview sample, *n* = 50.) All figures reported at the mean. National figures are for first-time, full-time students enrolling in a public college or university and receiving a Pell Grant in their first year of college.

As we focused the interviews at four universities and two technical colleges, interviewed students were also less likely to have started college at a two-year institution.

Data Sources

We collected extensive survey, financial aid, and academic record data on study participants over a six-year period from 2008 to 2014 and interviewed fifty participants as many as eight times during that period regardless of whether they were still enrolled in college.

ADMINISTRATIVE DATA

We measured students' academic progress, including enrollment status, credits, and GPA, using their institutional administrative records. The University of Wisconsin System (UWS) provided record enrollments at the thirteen universities and thirteen two-year branch campuses in that system, while the Wisconsin Technical College System (WTCS) provided enrollment and degree completion information at the sixteen two-year technical colleges across the state. Student credit and grade data were obtained directly from University of Wisconsin System and Wisconsin Technical College System.[1]

Administrative data can only be linked to survey responses if students gave consent (48 percent of the sample). The main analysis of the impacts of the Wisconsin Scholars Grant on four-year students used both survey and administrative data, and the paper describing that analysis shows how four-year consenting students in the linked subsample differed from the full sample.[2]

In addition, we obtained information from the National Student Clearinghouse, a national centralized reporting system that collects publicly available directory information obtained from the colleges and universities attended by 92 percent of American undergraduates.[3] All public universities in Wisconsin participate in the National Student Clearinghouse.[4] By combining data from the clearinghouse as well as from institutional records, enrollment and year-to-year degree completion information was available for all students in the study, regardless of where they attended college.

Information about the student's annual financial aid package came directly from the institutional financial aid records. However, financial aid package information by year was only obtained for the consenting group of students described above. For those who started at a University of Wisconsin System institution, data came from the system's central database. However, for Wisconsin Technical College System students, financial aid package information came directly from the financial aid office at the student's college. Generally, financial aid reported in the book—including figures for individual grants and loans—represents the final amount of aid the student accepted in a given academic year. However, for the analysis of loan-taking behavior in chapter 4, information about the aid offered (obtained via screenshots provided by financial aid officer) was also employed.

Each year, college students are required to apply for financial aid by completing a Free Application for Federal Student Aid (FAFSA). The FAFSA collects a variety of demographic and financial information on the student and the student's family in order to determine aid eligibility. Information from the student's FAFSA, as well as the student's calculated expected family contribution, were obtained for the entire sample from the Wisconsin Higher Educational Aids Board, a state agency responsible for the management and oversight of the state's student financial aid system.

Cost-of-attendance information for individual institutions attended by students in the sample came from the federal Integrated Postsecondary Education Data System. For students starting at a four-year college or university, cost-of-attendance figures reflect estimates for students living on campus. For students starting at a two-year college, cost-of-attendance figures reflect estimates for students living independently off campus in a house or apartment.

SURVEYS

Many measures reported in this book, including those on time use, stress, financial knowledge, and family relationships came from a series of three self-administered surveys sent out to WSLS participants over a period of three years between fall 2008 and spring 2011. In each of those surveys, students received a comprehensive questionnaire covering a range of topics related to personal background, goals, and college experiences. During that three-year period, participants were also sent three shorter "check-in" questionnaires meant to refresh the student's contact information and to maintain engagement with the study in order to encourage high response rates on the longer surveys. All of the surveys were designed by our research team, extensively pretested with small samples of low-income college students, and administered on behalf of the WSLS by the University of Wisconsin Survey Center. Working with the survey center gave us access to their considerable expertise in survey methodology and management and also allowed student contact information to be kept confidential from WSLS research staff.

All participants received their first survey near the end of their first term in college during fall 2008. The year-one survey consisted of a twenty-eight-page self-administered questionnaire with a total of eighty-three questions. The major topic areas covered by that survey included high school experiences, college experiences, time use, earning money, financial aid, income and expenses, relationships, future plans, and personal background. A paper version of the survey was initially mailed to the sample in November 2008 and included a $5 cash preincentive. This mailing was followed by a series of prompter phone calls to nonrespondents, and finally e-mail invitations were sent, inviting them to complete a web version of the survey. The final contact e-mail was sent out in February 2009, and the survey was closed in March 2009. All respondents who completed the questionnaire received a $25 postincentive in the form of a check sent to their address. The final response rate for the year-one survey was 72 percent.

A second survey was sent to a subset of 1,879 WSLS participants the following year, during the fall of 2009.[5] Like the first year, the second survey was a twenty-eight-page self-administered questionnaire, but with a total of 104 questions, many of which were repeated from the prior year. New topics on the year-two survey that were not included in year one included living arrangements, health, diet, sleep, and college academic and social engagement. The mode of administration was the same as year one, with a paper survey and $5 preincentive sent out first, followed by prompter calls and an e-mailed web version to nonresponders. The final e-mail invitation was sent out at the end of the December 2009, and the survey closed in January 2010. As before, all respondents who completed the questionnaire received a $25 postincentive. The overall response rate for the year-two survey was 77 percent.

A final substantive questionnaire was sent out during the third year of the study to 2,992 WSLS participants.[6] This twelve-page, fifty-five-question, year-three survey continued to ask many of the same questions as the first two surveys but differed by adding an additional series of questions about their financial aid knowledge, community participation behaviors, and political engagement. Survey administration also differed from previous years by starting with mailed and e-mailed invitations to complete the survey on the web, followed by a mailed paper questionnaire to nonrespondents. The first invitation letter was mailed in May 2011, and the final paper questionnaire was sent out in late July 2011. Everyone in the sample was mailed a $5 cash preincentive with their initial invitation letter.

In collaboration with the WSLS research team, the UW Survey Center conducted an experiment on the effectiveness of different postincentives in the year-three survey. The sample was split into four treatment groups stratified by type of school originally attended and previous completion status: (1) a control group consisting of participants who did not receive a postincentive ($n = 746$); (2) participants who received a $10 cash postincentive ($n = 750$); (3) participants entered into a random drawing to receive a $50 check ($n = 748$); and (4) participants entered into a random drawing for an iPad2 on completion of the survey ($n = 748$). The overall response rate for the survey was 42 percent, with the $10 cash postincentive group responding at a significantly higher rate than the other three experimental groups at 49 percent.[7]

STUDENT INTERVIEWS

The book draws on interviews conducted with a subsample of fifty WSLS participants enrolled at six two-year and four-year colleges in southeastern Wisconsin who were selected for semistructured interviews using a stratified random sampling approach. Students in the larger WSLS sample were asked to participate in interviews, and from the pool of 1,130 who consented, our team drew a stratified random sample based on the college they attended, whether they had been awarded the Wisconsin Scholars Grant, race/ethnicity, and gender. That stratification resulted in the creation of a "cell" structure classifying the students at six colleges (four public Wisconsin universities and two public Wisconsin technical colleges), and a random sample was then drawn from within cells.[8] We then invited seventy-three students to participate in interviews, and fifty agreed, resulting in a response rate of 68.5 percent.

Between fall 2008 and 2014, Sara joined four graduate students in conducting in-depth, in-person interviews with each student, with interviews spaced at intervals of approximately six months.[9] For each interview, the team followed protocols containing questions on a broad range of topics, including college, family, work, time use, and finances. Although topics of conversation were guided by predetermined questions, interviewers purposefully engaged the participants in semistructured interviews; in other words, they used open-ended questions whenever possible, and when appropriate they followed the participants' lead in terms of the direction of the conversation. They paid particular attention to the affective nature of the interview, rather than strictly to the subject content. This approach allowed for themes to emerge organically from the conversation rather than limiting the interviews solely to our prescribed topics of inquiry. The interviews lasted an average of ninety minutes and were conducted in public spaces. Each participant received $20 in compensation and was treated to a beverage and a snack or meal each time an interview took place.

FINANCIAL AID ADMINISTRATOR INTERVIEWS

During the course of this study, we became increasingly interested in how the financial aid administrators working in the state and around the country viewed the challenges we were uncovering. Sara therefore conducted exploratory semistructured interviews with five financial aid officers among the thirteen working at universities in the University of Wisconsin System and complemented these with additional interviews with aid officers as part of an evaluation of Single Stop.[10] Topics in these interviews, which were tape-recorded and transcribed, included professional background and experience, philosophies and practices of financial aid packaging, assessments of the students with whom they interacted, and recommendations for improving the system.

Analysis

The analyses in this book draw on the rich tradition of mixed-methods research. Researchers have long recognized that both qualitative and quantitative methods have strengths and weaknesses.[11]

Qualitative research is well suited to provide nuanced insight into dynamic social processes and to understand the meaning attributed by social actors to those processes. However, qualitative research is less well-equipped to establish and confirm causal relationships or to examine whether a finding can be generalized to larger populations. Quantitative methods, in contrast, are much stronger in this regard and are therefore generally more appropriate when research is concerned with broader patterns present in social life. When research questions address both the lived experience of research participants and the effects of those experiences on particular outcomes, as they do in this study, a mixed-methods design can often leverage the strengths of both qualitative and quantitative data to provide a more comprehensive account of the area of inquiry.[12] Additionally, a mixed-methods design enables researchers to triangulate findings in order to enhance validity via corroboration or to reveal areas requiring further exploration via mismatch.

The specific approaches to mixed-methods analyses in this study varied by chapter and topic. But overall, our process followed a convergent parallel design.[13] This meant that we analyzed quantitative data and qualitative data concurrently and then merged the two sets of results into an overall interpretation.[14] This happened in real time as we conducted interviews and learned from those conducted by each other, while also creating and administering surveys and analyzing responses. The analysis process was iterative, flowing as new information was gained, but for each topic we considered, we focused on points of convergence and divergence. This helped us to gain a better overall understanding of the processes students were going through in order to pay for college, illuminating actions and decisions that we might have otherwise misinterpreted had we been limited to administrative data or interviews alone.

Interviews were transcribed verbatim and were entered into Dedoose—a web-based software program specifically designed for mixed-methods research. We used a hybrid approach to interview coding. First, we did an initial coding of interviews using a blend of a priori "parent" codes based on preestablished topics. Then we engaged in a cyclical process of data reduction, data display, and conclusion drawing.[15]

Throughout the analytic process, we strove to give qualitative and quantitative data equal standing. Our team thinks about methods as tools with which to address research questions and reject common epistemological and ontological assumptions about which methods are "better" or "worse." We simply seek to better understand the students and get closer to their lives. In some cases, the administrative and survey data helped us to ask additional questions of the interview data, not because we thought that administrative and survey data was more likely to be "accurate" but mainly because it provided a point of contrast and raised new questions. Other times, what we thought we understood from the administrative and survey data was called into question when we examined interview responses, prompting us to dig deeper to try to make sense of the differences.

Wisconsin Scholars Longitudinal Study Research Team (2008-2015)

A longitudinal, complex study like this cannot be executed alone. It has taken seven years, about $2.5 million in support, and the work of at least two hundred people—in addition to the three thousand study participants. All of the following individuals and organizations deserve substantial credit for this work.

CORE LEADERSHIP

Drew M. Anderson, James Benson, Alison Bowman, Katharine Broton, Derria Byrd, Douglas N. Harris, Robert Kelchen, Peter Kinsley, Courtney Luedke, Julie Minikel-Lacocque

FINANCIAL SUPPORT

Bill and Melinda Gates Foundation; Great Lakes Higher Education Guaranty Corporation and Affiliates; Institute for Research on Poverty; Smith Richardson Foundation; Spencer Foundation; William T. Grant Foundation; Wisconsin Center for the Advancement of Postsecondary Education

FUND FOR WISCONSIN SCHOLARS

Mary Gulbrandsen, John Morgridge, Tashia Morgridge, . . . and the entire board of directors

ADMINISTRATIVE DATA ACCESS

Gail Bergman, Michael Carney, Ray Cross, Jing Chen, Daniel Clancey, Morna Foy, Kelly Gallagher, Brandon Graf, Connie Hutchinson, Bob Jokisch, Heather Kim, Greg Lampe, Rebecca Martin, Barb Moermond, Sherrie Nelson, Gregg Nettesheim, Mark Nook, Kevin Reilly, John Reinemann, Jason Ring, Larry Rubin, Jessica Tormey, Vicki Washington, Kevin Welch, . . . and all financial aid administrators and registrars at the forty-two public colleges and universities of Wisconsin

DATA COLLECTION AND/OR ANALYSIS

Ryan Adserias, Nana Asante, Maha Baalbaki, Justin Bloesch, Emily Brunjes, Ellen Bruno, Cheng Cheng, Aaronson Chew, Smita Chopade, Michael Clifton, Kristen Cyffka, Jennifer Dykema, Belinda Falk, Derek Field, Maria Regina Figueiredo-Brown, Katy France, Victoria Frank, Eugene Fujimoto, Alexandra Gardner, Christin Gates, Lauren Gatti, Amanda Gaulke, Marci Glaus, Julia Goodwin, Frank Honts, Derek Houston, Sarah Hurley, Dakota Kaiser, Hyun Sik Kim, Kyong Kang, Annemarie Ketterhagen, Lisa Klein, Saili Kulkarni, Minhtuyen Mai, Craig McClain, Hannah Miller, Zitsi Mirakhur, Woodie Mogaka, Alex Mok, Carmen Montopoli, Casey Morin, Alicia Neweil, Amanda Oleson, Jason Orne, Cody Ostenson, Kathleen Paff, Nicolette Pawlowski, Tara Piche, James Pustejovsky, Shenita Ray, Kaja Rebane, Jesús Renteria, Kelly Rifelj, Brianna Salinas, Laura Saltzman, Anna Schenk, Lauren Schudde, Petrolina Sims, Tim St. Louis, Kyle Steele, John Stevenson, Tezeta Stewartz, Ricardo Torres, Jessa Valentine, Wendell Venerable, Kathy Villalon, Pa Tou Vue, Martha Walter, Shoua Xiong, Sun Young Yoon, Syed Tayyab Zaidi, Xin Zou

ADVISING

Paul Attewell, Aaron Brower, Lindsay Chase-Lansdale, David Figlio, Alberta Gloria, Robert Granger, Donald Heller, Eli Lieber, Adriana Lleras-Muney, Bridget Terry Long, Rebecca Maynard, David Mundel, Noel Radomski, Kevin Stange, Christopher Taber, Thomas Weisner

ADMINISTRATION

Russell Dimond, Allison Edl, Carl Frederick, Dolores Fries, Adam Gamoran, Brian Ganje, Robert Glover, Carrie Goetsch, Gwen Goplin, Mary Hegge, Josh Kandiko, Lillian Larson, Cathy Loeb, Jennifer Madigan, Teresa Mason, Jessica Miller, Jeff Nytes, Dung Pham, Jed Richardson, Suzanne Ripple Welke, Michael Scalia, Jeanne Schneider, Kay Schultz, Larry Schultz, Alexia Spry, Kathy Thomas, Chris Thorn, Janet Trembley, Leah Ujda, Julie Underwood

Appendix 2

Overview of Wisconsin Higher Education

DREW M. ANDERSON AND SARA GOLDRICK-RAB

In the spring of 2008, seventy thousand students graduated from high schools around the state of Wisconsin and faced an array of college choices.[1]

Wisconsin statutes establish two systems of public higher education: the University of Wisconsin System (UW System) and the Wisconsin Technical College System (WTCS). The University of Wisconsin dates back to 1848, the year Wisconsin attained statehood, but the UW System was created in 1974 by merging two public university systems under a single governing board.[2] The UW System now includes thirteen comprehensive four-year universities and one two-year college, with thirteen branch campuses. Wisconsin was the first state to establish a system of state support for vocational, technical, and adult education in 1911.[3] The WTCS now includes sixteen colleges, with a total of forty-nine branch campuses.

Students also have a variety of choices outside those two systems. There are thirty private, nonprofit institutions in Wisconsin. Of these, twenty-four are members of the Wisconsin Association of Independent Colleges and Universities, the statutory official representative organization of institutions in this sector. Members of this association are four-year institutions, including universities, liberal arts colleges, and special focus institutions, such as engineering, nursing, and art schools. Many are religiously affiliated. The private sector also includes for-profit or proprietary schools. There are around sixty for-profit institutions whose students receive federal financial aid, as identified by Integrated Postsecondary Education Data System. Finally, there are two tribal colleges in Wisconsin.

Colleges and universities are spread across the state. These institutions cover all types of degrees. The comprehensive UW universities all grant bachelor's degrees, eleven of thirteen also grant master's degrees, and UW–Madison and UW–Milwaukee grant doctoral and professional degrees and include large research enterprises. The primary mission of the UW Colleges is to provide a liberal arts education that prepares students for transfer to the four-year universities. Colleges in the UW System grant associate degrees. The primary mission of WTCS is to prepare students for jobs in industry. The WTCS grants a variety of technical and career certificates, as well as associate degrees. Five of the WTCS colleges also offer liberal arts programs to prepare students for transfer to four-year institutions. The private sector offers a variety of degree and career pathways as well, and both tribal colleges grant associate and technical degrees, with one also granting bachelor's degrees.

One important factor in a student's college choice is the price. Tuition varies across institutions, but the net price that students face also varies across students within an institution. For reasons explained in chapter 2, this study focuses on the net price. The net price is calculated by subtracting all grants and scholarships from the full cost of attendance.

The full cost of attendance (COA) to college includes more than tuition and required fees. It also includes books and supplies, room and board, and other expenses. Each college sets an official COA for each student in each year. The tuition part can vary by full-time or part-time status, and the room and board part can vary by whether a student lives on campus, off campus with family, or off campus not with family. Net price statistics are typically calculated using the COA for two full-time semesters.

The net price is what students must cover through loans and paying out of pocket from savings, work, and family help. Many factors go into the net price, but it serves as a good summary of what it actually costs students to attend college. The net price is generally lower for students from lower-income families and higher for other students.

For the UW System in the 2008–9 school year, the average net price paid by grant aid recipients, taking into account each student's housing choice, was $9,800 at the universities and $6,700 at UW Colleges. At WTCS, the average net price was $7,300. Grant aid recipients paid an average net price of $20,000 to attend the average Wisconsin Association of Independent Colleges and Universities institution in 2008–9. The net price in the for-profit sector for 2008–9 averaged $22,700.[4]

Sources of financial support are mainly need-based in Wisconsin. Considering grant aid as well as loan aid, federal need-based aid makes up the vast majority of need-based aid. Private and institutional aid represents a very small fraction at both UW System and WTCS institutions. State need-based aid makes up 17 percent of all need-based aid received at the UW System and 11 percent at WTCS.[5]

The Wisconsin Higher Education Grant is the state's oldest and largest financial aid program. Established in 1965, it offers grants to undergraduate students from low-income families. The Wisconsin Higher Education Grant is available to students attending institutions in all sectors except for the for-profit sector. It provides grants of varying sizes based on financial need and the sector of the college a student attends. The grants average between $800 (for a year at WTCS) to $2,500 (for a year at a private nonprofit college).[6]

Given the array of institutions, degree programs, and their prices, about one-half of Wisconsin's high school graduates end up immediately enrolling in a Wisconsin institution. Half of those enroll in four-year public universities. Counting enrollment at institutions outside the state, 60 percent of high school graduates immediately enrolled.[7]

Joining students just out of high school, adults and continuing students from in and out of state complete the 2008–9 undergraduate student body at each Wisconsin college or university. Statistics from state reports and the Integrated Postsecondary Education Data System give a sense of the size and characteristics of these student populations at each type of institution.

The size of the student body varies widely within the UW System and within the WTCS. The largest UW campus is UW–Madison, which enrolls about 30,000 undergraduates The average four-year UW college/university enrolls about 10,500 undergraduates. The UW Colleges, across all thirteen branch campuses, enrolls 13,000 total students.[8] Enrollments with the WTCS range across colleges from 1,000 to 13,000 (by full-time equivalent or FTE). The average WTCS college enrolls 4,500 FTE students. In total, the UW System enrolls 151,000 students by head count, over twice as many as the FTE count at WTCS, which is nearly 73,000. By head count, WTCS actually enrolls 375,000. This illustrates that many WTCS students attend part time.[9]

The undergraduate populations at these institutions differ in age, race/ethnicity, and socioeconomic status. Over 90 percent of UW System undergraduates are under twenty-five years old. Students at WTCS institutions are far more likely to be over twenty-five than at UW System schools, but a majority of undergraduates is nevertheless under twenty-five (70 percent). At both systems, around 85 percent of students are white. Just over half of students at UW System are women, while just under half of students at WTCS are women.[10]

The percentage of the undergraduate population that receives a Pell Grant is a common measure of the socioeconomic status of the student body. To receive a Pell Grant in 2008–9, a student must have had a family income below roughly $50,000 in 2007 and must have filed a Free Application for Federal Student Aid (FAFSA). At the average institution in the UW System in 2008–9, 20 percent of the first-time, full-time, degree-seeking cohort received Pell Grants. The percentage varied across the UW System. At UW–Madison, just 10 percent received Pell Grants. At UW Colleges the percentage receiving Pell Grants was 25 percent. Within the WTCS, the overall average was 32 percent Pell recipients.[11]

Member institutions in the Wisconsin Association of Independent Colleges and Universities enroll nearly sixty thousand students, about two-thirds of whom are from Wisconsin.[12] Less than a third qualify for the Pell Grant. The for-profit sector enrolls around fifteen thousand students statewide, with a 60 percent rate of Pell Grant receipt. The tribal college enrollments are relatively small, totaling around a thousand students between them. The majority of their students are enrolled members of tribes or descendants of American Indian tribes.[13] Over 60 percent of these students qualified for Pell Grants.[14]

Once enrolled, students had varying rates of retention and completion at their initial institutions. Across the four-year UWs, an average of 77 percent of students that first enrolled in fall 2008 also enrolled at the same institution in fall 2009. Retention was lower at WTCS, with 62 percent on average, and at UW Colleges with 58 percent. Of the same entering cohort in fall 2008, 36 percent of WTCS and 21 percent of UW College students had completed a degree at the same institution within the first three years (150 percent of normal time to degree). Using the fall 2007 entering cohort at UW universities, 54 percent had completed a degree at the same institution within six years (150 percent time). Across the board, these rates are close to national averages.[15]

Colleges are not required to report disaggregated college outcomes for Pell recipients to the federal government. However, the UW System does report this information to the public. On average, 76 percent of Pell recipients who entered universities and 60 percent of those who entered UW Colleges in fall 2008 persisted to fall 2009 at the same institution. Rates for nonrecipients were 81 and 58 percent, respectively.[16] Forty-eight percent of Pell Grant recipients who enrolled in a university in the fall 2007 semester graduated within six years, compared to 62 percent of nonrecipients.[17]

Including all sectors and institutions, Wisconsin adults today have rates of college completion near national averages: 38 percent with some college degree (national average also 38 percent) and 28 percent with a bachelor's degree or higher (national average 30 percent).[18]

Between 2008 and today, a lot has changed. Average in-state tuition rose by 25 percent at UW System schools and by 17 percent at WTCS institutions. Cost of living has also increased.[19] Availability of aid has not kept pace.

The Wisconsin Higher Education Grant has maintained and

slightly increased funding and the number of awards in recent years but not enough to meet growing demand. The program distributed over $105 million to over sixty-five thousand students each of the last two school years.[20] However, the funding is limited well below the amount that it would take to provide for every eligible applicant. Only about 60 percent of eligible students receive Wisconsin Higher Education Grant awards, which are given on a first-come, first-served basis according to the date they filed a FAFSA.[21] The allocation of funding is decided each year by the legislature. Except for the tribal college portion, the allocation comes from general program revenue, the same source that provides state aid directly to the public institutions.

The UW System's three largest sources of revenue in 2008–9 were state appropriations (25.1 percent), tuition (20.7 percent), and federal grants (20.6 percent).[22] In contrast, WTCS received 48.1 percent of its revenues from local property taxes and just 13.7 and 9.6 percent from tuition and state aid, respectively.[23] Since 2008, state aid has declined to 19.3 percent of UW System revenues and 6.7 percent of WTCS revenues.[24] These declines are representative of a long-term trend that is occurring in many states.

Figure 17 shows the trend in state fiscal support for higher education, per $1,000 of personal income, for Wisconsin and for the average across all states. From a peak in the 1970s of $14.73 (peak of $10.40 nationally), Wisconsin has steadily declined to $4.81, now below the fifty-state average of $5.74.

The job market also changed greatly during this period. Wisconsin lost 155,200 jobs from 2007 to 2010. Yet in 2010, residents with a bachelor's degree had an unemployment rate about half those with some college, and 40 percent of those with only a high school degree.[25] Students leaving college with different degrees earned different wages. Having attended some college provided no wage gain over only having attended high school, but an associate degree provided a 27 percent increase in wages over only high school. The value of an associate degree is higher in Wisconsin than the national average. Still, a bachelor's degree or higher led to a much greater—67 percent—wage advantage over only high school.[26] Wis-

Figure 17. State fiscal support for higher education per $1,000 of personal income: 1961–2015. Source: adapted from Mortenson, "State, Local and Federal Fiscal Support for Higher Education per $1000 of State Personal Income, FY1961 to FY2014." Original data compiled from the Center for Higher Education and Educational Finance at Illinois State University and the Bureau of Economic Analysis.

consin regained 24,800 jobs between 2010 and 2014 but still lagged behind the national job growth rate.[27]

Of students leaving Wisconsin colleges and universities with a degree in 2013, 70 percent had student loan debt. These borrowers owed an average of $28,000.[28] These amounts have risen from 64 percent and $21,400 among the class of 2008.[29]

Enrollment has seen less change in numbers but has grown as a percentage of high school graduates. Considering FTE enrollments in 2013–14, relative to the 2008–9 school year, enrollment at the UW System increased by 2.5 percent.[30] Within the WTCS it declined slightly overall, with ups and downs in between.[31] Enrollment in the WTCS swelled in the two school years following the Great Recession, then fell for three straight years. These small changes in college enrollment came alongside a sharp drop in number of high school graduates, to 59,000 in 2014 from a peak of 71,000 in 2009.[32]

Looking to the future, Wisconsin is projected to see slight increases in the number of high school graduates.[33] Job growth lags national averages, but educated workers can still expect a large payoff in terms of employment and wages.[34] The state legislature faces decisions about how much to support public institutions and students through financial aid. Institutions face decisions about how to serve students within funding constraints. Students graduating today will continue to navigate the complexity of this process as we look for ways to simplify and support their pathways through college.

Notes

Introduction

1. Baum and Ma, *Trends in College Pricing, 2014*, fig. 22A and fig. 2; Mitchell, Palacios, and Leachman, "States Are Still Funding Higher Education below Pre-Recession Levels"; Kelly and Goldrick-Rab, *Reinventing Financial Aid*, 4–7.
2. These figures understate the true costs of attendance because they only include tuition, other fees, and room and board and omit the costs of books and supplies as well as transportation and personal expenses. These omitted costs are part of the official federal definition of cost of attendance but are not included in the data source for fig. 1 here, which was assembled by the College Board. For more information, see chap. 2.
3. These figures are adjusted for inflation.
4. Baum, Elliott, and Ma, *Trends in Student Aid, 2014*, table 1A.
5. These figures are averages for full-time attendance and are for dependent students. They come from 2011–12, the most recent year currently available using the *National Postsecondary Student Aid Study*. See Goldrick-Rab and Kendall, *F2CO Redefining College Affordability*, 7. These figures differ somewhat from fig. 1 because (*a*) fig. 1 reflects only some of the costs of attendance while these figures includes all of the costs, and (*b*) fig. 1 is not discounted for financial aid. The data source for fig. 1 allows for a look at change over a longer period of time, while the data source for these figures allows for a more complete accounting of costs and price. For more information on college costs, please see chap. 2.
6. Cohen, "Middle Class, but Feeling Economically Insecure"; *Inside Higher Ed*, "Parents Are Saving Less for College."
7. Goldrick-Rab and Kendall, *F2CO Redefining College Affordability*, 7.
8. For point of comparison, consider that the U.S. Department of Health and Human Services' official affordability threshold for childcare is 10 percent of a

family's income. Gould and Cooke, "High Quality Child Care Is Out of Reach for Working Families," 2; Council of Economic Advisers, *The Economics of Early Childhood Investments*, 13–14.

9. Huelsman, "The Affordable College Compact."

10. Based on calculations from Wine, Janson, and Wheeless, *2004/09 Beginning Postsecondary Students Survey* .

11. Ibid.

12. Petrilli, "Pell Grants Shouldn't Pay for Remedial College."

13. Preston, "The Most 'Representative' State: Wisconsin."

14. Dresser, Rogers, and Navot, "The State of Working Wisconsin," 39.

15. Wisconsin's unemployment rate rose by 4.2 percent between 2006 and 2012, a change that was not as sharp as California's (7.4%) or Illinois's (6.4%) but was nonetheless higher than those of its Midwestern peers, Minnesota (3.7%) and Iowa (2.6%). During the same period, state appropriations for higher education on a per-student basis declined by just over $1,000 and tuition rose by $1,669 at public universities and $442 at public two-year colleges. The state did not increase its investment in grants to students during that period. Johnson, "College Costs, Prices and the Great Recession," 5 (unemployment figures), 18 (appropriations and costs).

16. In a paper written in 2008 and published in 2009, Douglas N. Harris and I described a set of hypotheses derived from prior theory and research that guided the study. See Goldrick-Rab, Harris, and Trostel, "Why Financial Aid Matters (or Does Not) for College Success," 1–45.

17. The expected family contribution is a measure of family financial strength based on information the student provides on his or her FAFSA, including family income, assets, benefits, family size, and the number of family members enrolled in college.

18. Mortenson, "State Investment and Disinvestment in Higher Education, 1969–2015," 20.

19. University of Wisconsin System, "Minutes of the Regular Meeting of the Board of Regents of the University of Wisconsin System," 33: "Financial Aid: 2015–17 WHEG-UW Funding Recommendation, Resolution 10363."

20. Numbers for UW–Milwaukee are expressed in 1990 dollars, adjusted for inflation. The cost of attendance in 1990 was $7,700 and in 2008 was $17,600. The average grant aid in 1990 was about $3,200 (assuming Pell Grant and Wisconsin Higher Education Grant maximums; the Integrated Postsecondary Education Data System—the core postsecondary education data collection program for the National Center for Education Statistics—did not report financial aid data then), and in 2008 was about $5,451 (according to the Integrated Postsecondary Education Data System). The federal loan limit for a dependent first-year student in 1990 was $4,625 (including both subsidized and unsubsidized Stafford Loans),

and in 2008 it was $5,500. These figures do not match those in table 17 because they are averages and not for the Wisconsin Scholars Longitudinal Study sample specifically.

21. Goldrick-Rab et al., "Reducing Income Inequality."
22. Wu-Tang Clan, "C.R.E.A.M.," Wikipedia, https://en.wikipedia.org/wiki/C.R.E.A.M.
23. Loss, *Between Citizens and the State*, 4–5.

Chapter 1

1. Mitchell, "Panel Calls for Overhauling Student Grants"; Robinson and Cheston, "Pell Grants: Where Does All the Money Go?"; and Petrilli, "Pell Grants Shouldn't Pay for Remedial College."
2. Graham, *The Uncertain Triumph*, 53–83.
3. Gilbert and Heller, "The Truman Commission and Its Impact on Federal Higher Education Policy," 2. For more information on the Truman Commission, see Hutcheson, "The 1947 President's Commission," "Setting the Nation's Agenda for Higher Education," and "Goals for United States Higher Education."
4. Lambert, *Privatization and the Public Good*, 46.
5. Goldrick-Rab, Schudde, and Stampen, "Creating Cultures of Affordability," 198; and Thelin, *A History of American Higher Education*, 324–26.
6. Goldrick-Rab, Schudde, and Stampen, "Creating Cultures of Affordability"; and Hearn and Holdsworth, "Federal Student Aid."
7. For more on California's public research universities, see Douglass, *The Conditions for Admission*; Geiger, "Postmortem for the Current Era", 4; and for more on the G.I. Bill, see Mettler, *Soldiers to Citizens*.
8. Geiger, "Postmortem for the Current Era," 3.
9. Goldin and Katz, *The Race between Education and Technology*.
10. President's Commission on Higher Education, *Higher Education for American Democracy*, 27.
11. Lauff and Christopher, *Education Longitudinal Study of 2002*, 8; and Bowen, Chingos, and McPherson, *Crossing the Finish Line*, 23.
12. For further reading, see Newfield, *Unmaking the Public University*; and Douglass, *The Conditions for Admission*.
13. Mortenson, "State Investment and Disinvestment," 1.
14. For further reading, see Bady and Konczal, "From Master Plan to No Plan"; Newfield, *Unmaking the Public University*; and Loss, *Between Citizens and the State*.
15. Gilbert and Heller, "The Truman Commission," 9.
16. Mortenson, "State Investment and Disinvestment," 1.
17. Ibid., 4.

18. For further reading, see Orszag and Kane, "Higher Education Spending"; *eCampus News*, "Will Further State Higher-Ed Funding Cuts Hinder Economic Innovation?"

19. Hiltonsmith and Draut, "The Great Cost Shift Continues"; Mitchell, Palacios, and Leachman, "States Are Still Funding Higher Education," 9–10; and Baylor, "State Disinvestment in Higher Education Has Led to an Explosion of Student Debt."

20. U.S. Government Accountability Office, *Higher Education*, 1–39; and Kelly and Goldrick-Rab, *Reinventing Financial Aid*, 4–7.

21. Mortenson, "State Investment and Disinvestment," 1.

22. Burd, "Undermining Pell," 3.

23. Deming, Goldin, and Katz, "For-Profit Colleges," 137–63; Darolia et al., "Do Employers Prefer Workers Who Attend For-Profit Colleges?" 881–903; and Deming et al., "The Value of Postsecondary Credentials in the Labor Market."

24. Stratford, "GOP Would Freeze Pell."

25. Selingo, "The Rich Get Richer in Higher Ed."

26. Jiang, Ekono, and Skinner, "Basic Facts about Low-Income Children," 1.

27. Porter, "The Measure of Our Poverty"; and O'Brien and Pedulla, "Beyond the Poverty Line," 30–35.

28. For further reading, see Shaw et al., *Putting Poor People to Work*; Soss, Fording, and Schram, *Disciplining the Poor*; Katz, *The Undeserving Poor*.

29. For further reading, see Alexander, Entwistle, and Olson, *The Long Shadow*; Levy, Mishel, and Berstein, *Running in Place*; and Ydstie, "Why Some Men Earn Less Than They Did 40 Years Ago."

30. Alon, "The Evolution of Class Inequality in Higher Education," 731–55; and Mettler, *Soldiers to Citizens*, 163–76.

31. Bailey and Dynarski, "Inequality in Postsecondary Education."

32. Bastedo and Jaquette, "Running in Place," 318–39.

33. Kahn, "The Long-Term Labor Market Consequences of Graduating from College in a Bad Economy," 303–16; Oreopoulos, Von Wachter, and Heisz, "The Short- and Long-Term Career Effects of Graduating in a Recession," 1–29; and Benson, Esteva, and Levy, "Dropouts, Taxes and Risk," 1–34.

34. Chetty et al., "Where Is the Land of Opportunity?" 1553–1623.

35. Gould, "High-Scoring, Low-Income Students No More Likely to Complete College Than Low-Scoring, Rich Students"; and Bowen, Chingos, and McPherson, *Crossing the Finish Line*, 20.

36. U.S. Department of Education, "Access Matters," 3-B.

37. Bound, Lovenheim, and Turner, "Increasing Time to Baccalaureate Degree in the United States," 375–424.

38. President's Commission on Higher Education, *Higher Education for American Democracy*, 2:23.

39. For further reading, see Piketty, *Capital in the Twenty-First Century*.

40. This figure is for a family of four. Dresser, Rogers, and Navot, "The State of Working Wisconsin," 1.

41. Center for Economic Development, University of Wisconsin–Milwaukee, *The Economic State of Milwaukee, 1990–2008*, 49.

42. Pew Research Center for the People and the Press, "January 2014 Political Survey."

43. Dresser, Rogers, and Navot, "The State of Working Wisconsin," 24.

44. While I identify the names of the colleges and universities in Wisconsin that our students attended and considered attending, I do not link specific students to specific institutions where they enrolled, in order to protect their confidentiality. All names used for students are pseudonyms.

45. Brown, Scholz, and Seshadri, "A New Test of Borrowing Constraints for Education," 511–38.

46. *Milwaukee Business Journals*, "Domtar to Close Wisconsin Mill, Cut 500 State Jobs."

47. For further reading, see Astin, *What Matters in College?* Lohfink and Paulsen, "Comparing the Determinants of Persistence for First-Generation and Continuing-Generation Students"; Pascarella and Terenzini, *How College Affects Students*, vol. 2; Pike and Kuh, "First- and Second-Generation College Students"; and Tinto, *Leaving College*.

48. Attewell, Heil, and Reisel, "What Is Academic Momentum?" 27–44; Kuh et al., "Unmasking the Effects of Student Engagement on First-Year College Grades and Persistence," 540–63; and Tinto, "Research and Practice of Student Retention," 1–19.

49. Arum and Roksa, *Academically Adrift*.

50. For further reading, see Armstrong and Hamilton, *Paying for the Party*; Muthén and Muthén, *Mplus: Statistical Analysis with Latent Variables*; Stuber, *Inside the College Gates*; and Stevens, Armstrong, and Arum, "Sieve, Incubator, Temple, Hub."

51. *Philanthropy News Digest*, "Fund for Wisconsin Scholars Establishes $175 Million Endowment for Scholarships."

Chapter 2

1. Hiltonsmith, "Pulling Up the Higher Ed Ladder."

2. There is a debate about whether the actual costs of providing a college education are rising unreasonably due to factors such as "administrative bloat" or even because of government subsidies, including financial aid. The research provides little clarity and focuses entirely on institutional expenditures rather than the actual resource costs involved in providing higher education. But overall, there

is little evidence that inflated costs are the source of the affordability problem at public colleges and universities—though there is some indication this may be an issue at public flagship universities, in particular, as well as at private institutions. A thorough treatment of the causes of college costs is beyond the scope of this book, and instead I recommend the following resources: Baum and Ma, *Trends in College Pricing: 2014*; Nelson, "Our Greedy Colleges"; and Archibald and Feldman, *Why Does College Cost So Much?*

3. The law is, however, silent on the subject of how much of the actual costs of college must be covered by the state and how much an institution can pass on to its students.

4. See n. 2 above, introduction, for an explanation of why these numbers do not align with those in fig. 1, which include only some components of the cost of attendance and are thus an underestimate. These more complete figures come from the *National Postsecondary Student Aid Study*, which has been conducted for a limited amount of time and thus does not facilitate the longitudinal picture displayed in fig. 1.

5. While England is ending maintenance grants in 2016, it is, however, replacing them with loans.

6. Mettler, *Soldiers to Citizens*, 61.

7. A recent national survey found that three in four financial aid officers felt that their students' financial literacy was "limited." National Association of Student Financial Aid Administrators, *2015 Administrative Burden Survey*, 9. Notably, surveys like these focus on the capabilities of students receiving financial aid— the knowledge held by other students (including those spending their parents' money) goes unquestioned.

8. U.S. Senate Committee on Health, Education, Labor and Pensions, "Alexander: If Colleges Share in the Risk of Student Loan Defaults"; Kelchen, "Is 'Overborrowing' for College an Epidemic?"; Institute for College Access and Success, "Data Show No Evidence of 'Over-borrowing' at Community Colleges"; National Association of Student Financial Aid Administrators, "Debt Load and Overborrowing"; and Deverey, "Promoting College Affordability and Limiting Over-Borrowing."

9. Kelchen, Hosch, and Goldrick-Rab, "The Costs of College Attendance," 3.

10. Of course, it is one thing to provide a bigger estimate of the living costs and another to provide the financial aid funds to cover it. The first helps to the extent that students benefit from having accurate information, but the latter is essential if they are to make ends meet.

11. Goldrick-Rab and Kendall, "The Real Price of College."

12. National Association of Student Financial Aid Administrators, "Monograph 24," 61.

13. Kelchen, Hosch, and Goldrick-Rab, "The Costs of College Attendance."

14. Kinsley, "The Pull of Home," 51. For further reading on the hidden costs of college, see Goldrick-Rab and Kendall, "The Real Price of College"; and Wisconsin HOPE Lab, "What We're Learning: Student Financial Contributions to Families."

15. Lewin, "Most College Students Don't Earn a Degree in 4 Years, Study Finds."

16. Goldrick-Rab, "Following Their Every Move," 61–79; Goldrick-Rab and Pfeffer, "Beyond Access," 101–25; Hicks, "Inequality, Nonlinearity, and the College Experience," 62–77; and Miller and Goldrick-Rab, "Making Sense of Transitions," 1–51.

17. For further reading on time to degree, see Bound, Lovenheim, and Turner, "Increasing Time to Baccalaureate Degree"; and Complete College America, *Three Policies to Reduce Time to Degree.*

18. Kelchen, "A Longitudinal Analysis of Student Fees," 19.

19. Parents are expected to contribute any income available after specific allowances, as well as 12 percent of their discretionary assets to their child's college education, with an equal share of the contribution going to each child enrolled in college. Students are expected to contribute all income above a certain threshold as well as 20 percent of their assets annually. Parent and student expected contributions are summed up to calculate the total expected family contribution.

20. Marcus, "Confusing Financial Aid Letters Leave Students, Parents Adrift."

21. Filing for aid as an independent student means that parental income does not count toward the expected family contribution calculation. This may or may not lead students to get more financial aid. Relative to their income, independent students actually pay a higher price, on average, than dependent students do. But most students do not know this. See Goldrick-Rab and Kendall, "F2Co Redefining College Affordability," 7.

22. Bergeron and Flores, "College for All."

23. U.S. Department of Education, "Completing the FAFSA."

24. Dynarski and Scott-Clayton, "There Is a Simpler Way for Students to Apply for Financial Aid"; and Bettinger et al., "The Role of Application Assistance and Information in College Decisions," 1.

25. "um i have a question. . . . .why is the financial aid process harder than college itself?" (rat mic [loopzoop], Twitter post, July 24, 2015, 9:50 A.M., https://twitter.com/loopzoop/status/624620282485981185).

26. Fortelny and Parkinson, "FAFSA and Application Processing System Update," 35; U.S. Department of Education, "Completing the FAFSA." As of May 1, 2015, the U.S. Department of Education estimated that once a student logged into the online application, it took about thirty minutes to complete (a claim that had disappeared from their site by January 11, 2016).

27. One challenging part of the FAFSA is that it requires tax information. Until

2016–17, that tax information had to be for the immediately prior year, so it was impossible to file until taxes were completed. This led students to miss some state and institutional deadlines associated with grant aid and meant that they sometimes had to make decisions about college without full information in hand. However, in fall 2015, President Barack Obama took executive action to allow the use of prior-prior year tax information on the FAFSA so that the process of applying for financial aid could begin in the fall, well in advance of deadlines.

28. Wisconsin HOPE Lab, "What We're Learning: FAFSA," 3.

29. Bird and Castleman, "Here Today, Gone Tomorrow?" 21.

30. Baum, Ma, Pender, and Bell, *Trends in Student Aid 2015*, fig. 24.

31. The Wisconsin Higher Education Grant was recently renamed the Wisconsin Grant but here I use the name applied when this study was conducted.

32. Anderson and Goldrick-Rab, "The Wisconsin Grant," 5.

33. Higher Educational Aids Board, *Report of the Commission on Financial Aid Consolidation and Modernization*, 42.

34. National Scholarship Providers Association, "Impact of Award Displacement on Students and Their Families," 3–4.

35. About 104,000 Pell recipients (1.2% of the total population) received professional judgments in 2013–14. U.S. Department of Education, "2013–2014 Federal Pell Grant Program End-of-Year," table 14.

36. The loan that costs the government more (because of the interest subsidy) is removed first.

37. Shapiro et al., "Transfer and Mobility," sec. 1.

38. Wisconsin HOPE Lab, "What We're Learning: Satisfactory Academic Progress," 2.

39. Schudde and Scott-Clayton, "Pell Grants as Performance-Based Aid?" 2.

40. The fund's executive director reported that very few students did so.

41. Executive director of the Fund for Wisconsin Scholars, personal communication to Sara Goldrick-Rab, n.d.

42. The Academic Competitiveness Grant was a federal grant program for low-income students with strong high school preparation. It provided up to $750 for the first year of college, and up to $1,300 for the second if students earned a B average. The program ended in 2011–12.

43. In order to receive the Supplemental Nutrition Assistance Program (SNAP) while enrolled in college students must meet at least one of a range of criteria. Most often, they need to receive work-study funds or be employed for at least twenty hours per week. Lower-Basch and Lee, "College Student Eligibility," 1–3.

44. For further reading, see Zelizer, *The Social Meaning of Money*.

45. For further reading, see Weatherly, Derenne, and Terrell, "College Students Discount Money 'Won' More than Money 'Owed'"; Thaler and Johnson, "Gambling

with the House Money and Trying to Break Even"; and Ackert et al., "An Experimental Examination of the House Money Effect in a Multi-Period Setting."

46. National Association of Student Financial Aid Administrators, *2015 Administrative Burden Survey*, 8.

47. Ibid., 11.

48. Bettinger, "How Financial Aid Affects Persistence," 207–38; and Castleman and Long, "Looking beyond Enrollment," 1–37.

49. For reviews of the evidence on the impacts of financial aid, see Goldrick-Rab, Harris, and Trostel, "Why Financial Aid Matters," 1–45; and Dynarski and Deming, "Into College, Out of Poverty?" 1–28.

50. For further reading, see Castleman, Schwartz, and Baum, *Decision Making for Student Success*; and Dynarski and Wiederspan, "Student Aid Simplification."

Chapter 3

1. U.S. Department of Education, "Federal Pell Grant Program End-of-Year Report," table 1.

2. Stratford, "Higher Ed Cuts in GOP Budget."

3. Smith, "$2.2 Million in Grants Awarded to Area College Students Who Quit or Failed"; and Tighe, "Student Aid Fraud."

4. Gehl, "Pell Grant Abuse Widespread."

5. Luzer, "The Lie about Pell Grants, the 'Welfare of the 21st Century.'"

6. Terkel, "Rep. Denny Rehberg."

7. Friend, "Death Knell for Pell."

8. Noah, "Everyone's a Queen."

9. Thelin, *A History of American Higher Education*, 350.

10. College Board Advocacy and Policy Center, *Rethinking Pell Grants*; and Nelson, "Two Pell Grants?"

   The College Board report shows growth in the fraction of Pell recipients who are classified as independent for tax purposes rather than dependent, emphasizes the lower completion rates of those students, and states that "it is time to rethink the Pell Grant program so that it continues to emphasize the provision of funds to those for whom access to postsecondary education requires public subsidy" (7). The authors go on to argue that independent students should be served under a revised and more limited version of the Pell program because "the Pell Grant program is not and cannot plausibly be generous enough to replace the wages of adults who are temporarily out of the labor force" (29). The authors call for other programs, part of the "social safety net," to step up to serve these students. These remarks stand in contrast to the provisions of the GI Bill, which is aimed at a similar population (people over age twenty-four, often with families), which does contend that replacing wages for adults is necessary and must be done by the program providing the funding for college. It is worth noting that while non-Hispanic whites are evenly distributed among dependent and independent students, fully two-thirds of all African American undergraduates are independents and would be greatly affected by the proposed changes (based on analysis of 2012 data from National Center for Education Statistics, *National Postsecondary Student Aid Study NPSAS*).

11. Sawhill, "Target Aid to Students Most Likely to Succeed," and "Make Pell Grants Conditional on College Readiness."

12. For further reading, see Haney-Lopez, *Dog Whistle Politics*.

13. Field, "Education Department Chases 'Pell Runners' Who Threaten Aid Program."

14. Cheston, "Pell Running"; and Field, "Education Department Chases 'Pell Runners.'"

15. Field, "Education Department Chases 'Pell Runners.'"

16. U.S. Department of Education, Office of the Inspector General, *Semiannual Report to Congress*, 9.

17. Payment Accuracy, "High-Error Programs."

18. Green and Densley, "Pell Grant Fraud Awareness."

19. Ware, Weissman and McDermott, "Aid Like a Paycheck"; and Patel et al., "Performance-Based Scholarships."

20. An actual refund happens when a student withdraws from an institution before the end of a term of enrollment and receives back some percentage of funds that have been paid for tuition and fees.

21. This approach is a hallmark of contemporary social policy in the United States, which focuses on "poverty governance" in order to bring discipline to the lives of the poor. For a thorough treatment of this approach, see Soss, Fording, and Schram, *Disciplining the Poor*.

22. Cramer, *The Politics of Resentment*; Folbre, "The Retirement Zone."

23. For further reading on how attitudes affect social programs, see Abramovitz, *Regulating the Lives of Women*; Gilens, *Why Americans Hate Welfare*; Katz, *The Undeserving Poor*; Piven and Cloward, *Regulating the Poor*; and Soss, Fording, and Schram, *Disciplining the Poor*.

24. Among people born between 1979 and 1982, 29 percent of people in the bottom 25 percent of the income distribution entered college, compared to 80 percent of those from the top 25 percent. Bailey and Dynarski, "Inequality in Postsecondary Education," 120.

25. Low-income fifteen- to twenty-four-year-olds are five times more likely to have dropped out of high school than their high-income peers. U.S. Department of Education, "Trends in High School Dropout and Completion Rates in the United States," 34.

26. This is the bottom 20 percent of the income distribution of all families—using

data from the Current Population Survey (http://www.census.gov/programs
-surveys/cps.html). See U.S. Department of Education, National Center for
Education Statistics, "Digest of Education Statistics," table 302.30: Percentage
of Recent High School Completers Enrolled in 2-Year and 4-Year Colleges, by
Income Level: 1975 through 2012."

27. The changes to Pell eligibility were included in the College Cost Reduction
and Access Act of 2007 and the Higher Education Opportunity Act of 2008,
and these acts increased the amount and types of income excluded from the
Pell Grant eligibility formula and increased the income level under which an
applicant automatically qualified for a maximum grant.

28. Johnson, Smeeding, and Torrey, "Economic Inequality through the Prisms of
Income and Consumption," 16–18.

29. Goldstein, "How the Poor, the Middle Class and the Rich Spend Their Money."

30. U.S. Department of Education. "Questions and Answers," 1–3.

31. For further reading, see Katz, *The Undeserving Poor*.

32. For more on the relationship between marriage and education, see Edin and
Kefalas, *Promises I Can Keep*.

33. Goldrick-Rab and Sorenson, "Unmarried Parents in College," 195; Gault, Reichlin, and Roman "College Affordability for Low Income Adults," 14–15; and
Fastweb, "Profile of Pell Recipients," 2.

34. For further reading, see Cottom, *Lower Ed*; Deming, Goldin, and Katz, "The
For-Profit Postsecondary School Sector"; Deming et al., *The Value of Postsecondary Credentials in the Labor Market*; and Mettler, *Degrees of Inequality*.

35. On net price versus final price, see Byndloss et al., "In Search of a Match," 27–28.

36. For more information on non-tuition costs, see Kelchen, Hosch, and Goldrick-
Rab, "The Costs of College Attendance."

37. New America Foundation, "Pell Grant Program Overview."

38. Mitchell, Palacios, and Leachman, "States Are Still Funding Higher Education
below Pre-Recession Levels," 1–11.

39. Baum and Johnson, "Student Debt," 1–15; and Looney and Yannelis, "A Crisis in
Student Loans?" 1–77.

40. Institute for College Access and Success, "Quick Facts about Student Debt."

41. Institute for College Access and Success, "Private Loans," 1–2.

42. *New York Times*, "Students Who Fight Their Way through College."

43. U.S. Senate Committee on Health, Education, Labor and Pensions, "Alexander:
'College More Affordable than Most Students Think.'"

44. Keyes, "Rep. Virginia Foxx on People with Student Loans."

45. Clinton, "Remarks on Student Activism at Wellesley College".

46. Lambert, Haley-Lock, and Henly, "Schedule Flexibility in Hourly Jobs," 293–315.

47. For example, a report by the Young Invincibles (a national organization that
works to engage young adults on such issues as higher education, health care,

and jobs) states that, "during 2011–2012, only 16.4 percent of dependent students whose families make less than $20,000 received FWS aid, while 8.2 percent of dependent students with family incomes over $100,000 received FWS aid." Setzer and O'Sullivan, "A Federal Work Study Reform Agenda to Better Serve Low-Income Students," 2.

48. Ibid., 2.

49. It is therefore unsurprising that extant program evaluations identify few positive impacts of work-study. The students who would likely benefit from work-study the most are the least likely to receive support from the program, and those who do receive support get only a small amount of funding relative to college costs. For further reading on the impacts of work study, see Scott-Clayton and Minaya, "Should Student Employment Be Subsidized?"

50. For further reading, see Armstrong and Hamilton, *Paying for the Party*; Jacob, McCall, and Strange, "College as Country Club"; and Jack, "Same Folks Different Strokes."

Chapter 4

1. The Supplemental Educational Opportunity Grant is a federal program that provides $700 million a year to students, buttressed by an additional 25 percent match from institutions. Allocations from this grant are unevenly distributed across institutions, so students with similar financial needs have different opportunities to access these funds, depending on which college or university they attend. See Kelchen, "Exploring Trends and Alternative Allocation Strategies for Campus-Based Financial Aid Programs."

2. The National Science and Mathematics Access to Retain Talent (SMART) grant program, now defunct, provided funds for students pursuing college majors in high-demand fields. A program evaluation suggested that it was ineffective at encouraging students to choose science majors or helping them persist in a science, technology, engineering, or math field. See Evans, "SMART Money."

3. Norbert's mom didn't actually have to pay the full expected family contribution since his scholarship largely covered it.

4. Kelchen, "Financial Need and Aid Volatility among Students with Zero Expected Family Contribution," 181.

5. University of Maryland University College, *10 Great Ways to Pay for Your Education*.

6. Perna, "Understanding the Working College Student."

7. For more on student debt aversion, see Burdman, "The Student Debt Dilemma."

8. The National Center for Public Policy and Higher Education, "Five National Trends."

9. Looney and Yannelis, "A Crisis in Student Loans?" 2.

10. Brown, et al., "Grading Student Loans," and "Measuring Student Debt and its Performance"; and Looney and Yannelis, "A Crisis in Student Loans?" 14.

11. Baum and Payea, *Trends in Student Aid: 2012,* 17.

12. Ibid., 21.

13. Goldrick-Rab, Kelchen, and Houle, "The Color of Student Debt," 12.

14. McKernan et al., "Less Than Equal," 1.

15. Taylor et al., "Wealth Gaps Rise to Record Highs between Whites, Blacks and Hispanics," 1.

16. Shapiro, Maschede, and Osoro, "The Widening Racial Wealth Gap," 104.

17. Pfeffer, Danziger, and Schoeni, "Wealth Disparities Before and After the Great Recession," 98.

18. Shapiro, Maschede, and Osoro, "The Widening Racial Wealth Gap," 107.

19. Huelsman, "The Debt Divide," 1.

20. For further reading, see McDonald and Brady, "The Plural of Anecdote Is Data."

21. Dynarski, "Why Students with Smallest Debts Have the Larger Problem."

22. Brown et al., "Looking at Student Loan Defaults through a Larger Window."

23. U.S. Department of Education, "Federal versus Private Loans."

24. This was a bit uncommon. While 15 percent of students in Milwaukee took private loans, barely 1 percent of students like Sophie and Tyler Olson, who went to college elsewhere in the state, used this form of credit.

25. Baum and Payea, *Trends in Student Aid: 2012,* 18.

26. Ibid., 19

27. While some argue that the relevant ratio is debt to postgraduation individual income, it is important to recognize that among low-income families money is often shared and that children continue to contribute to their families postgraduation. Low-income students also more often reside in areas with fewer employment opportunities and lower wages. Baum and Payea, *Trends in Student Aid: 2012,* fig. 2010_9.

28. Wei and Skomsvold, "Borrowing at the Maximum," 11.

29. Cunningham and Santiago, "Student Aversion to Borrowing," 15–17.

30. Wine and Riccobono, *National Postsecondary Student Aid Study.*

31. We also considered defining a student as loan averse if she or he declined at least half of all of the loans offered. The correlation between the two measures was weaker ($r = 0.16$), which is unsurprising since the survey measure required rejection of all loans offered. We also considered categorizing a student as loan averse if she or he declined all unsubsidized loans, since the interest rate in the survey question was more consistent with these. The correlation between the survey and administrative measured this way was $r = 0.28$, suggesting that at least some students thought of the survey question as regarding that type of loans.

32. Interest rates on unsubsidized Stafford Loans have been fixed at 6.8 percent from 2006–7 to 2012–13. The interest rate on subsidized Stafford Loans declined

from 6.8 percent to 6.0 percent for loans issued in 2008–9, 5.6 percent in 2009–10, 4.5 percent in 2010–11, and 3.4 percent in 2011–12 and 2012–13. It remained 3.4 percent for the 2012–13 academic year. Since July 1, 2013, all interest rates have been tied to the ten-year Treasury note.

33. Subsidized and unsubsidized Stafford Loans carry different repayment protections. Today, under income-based repayment, the government will pay the interest for up to three years for borrowers whose incomes are too low to cover interest payments on their subsidized loans, but this is not the case for unsubsidized Stafford Loans.

34. Kutz et al., "Meet Us in the Middle," 107.

35. Campbell and Hillman, "A Closer Look at the Trillion," 21–22.

36. Pew Charitable Trusts, "Pursuing the American Dream," 2–3.

37. For examples, see Baum and Schwartz, "How Much Debt Is Too Much?"; and Dynarski, "An Economist's Perspective on Student Loans in the United States."

38. Looney and Yannelis, "A Crisis in Student Loans?" 2–3.

39. Haskins, Holzer, and Lerman, *Promoting Economic Mobility*, 10.

40. For further reading, see U.S. Congress, Joint Economic Committee, *The Economic Exposure of Federal Credit Program*, testimony of Jason Delisle, and *Financing Higher Education*, testimony of Andrew P. Kelly; Dynarski, "An Economist's Perspective"; and Hunt, "How to Fix the Student Loan Mess."

41. Mills, "Study Finds Working and Paying for College Nearly Impossible."

42. Sallie Mae Corporation, *How America Pays for College*, 11.

43. Stern and Nakata, "Paid Employment among U.S. College Students," 27–28.

44. Davis, *School Enrollment and Work Status*, 1.

45. U.S. Department of Education, "Digest of Education Statistics," 730; and Turner, "Going to College and Finishing College," 35.

46. For further reading, see Dadgar, "The Academic Consequences of Unemployment for Students Enrolled in Community College"; DeSimone, "The Impact of Employment during School on College Student Academic Performance"; Kalenkoski and Pabilonia, "Parental Transfers, Student Achievement, and the Labor Supply of College Students"; Scott-Clayton, "The Causal Effect of Federal Work-Study Participation"; Stinebrickner and Stinebrickner, "Working during School and Academic Performance"; Van Dyke, Little, and Callender, "Survey of Higher Education Students' Attitudes to Debt and Term-Time Working and Their Impact on Attainment"; Bozick, "Making It through the First Year of College"; Ehrenberg and Sherman, "Employment While in College"; Horn and Malizio, *Undergraduates Who Work*; and Orszag, Orszag, and Whitmore, "Learning and Earning."

47. Darolia, "Working (and Studying) Day and Night," 38.

48. Ibid., 44.

49. Bozick, "Making It through the First Year of College," 261–85.

50. See Ehrenberg and Sherman, "Employment While in College." This research does not, however, demonstrate a causal impact of work hours nor does it tell us with certainty that twenty hours is the critical tipping point. Few studies ask students to report on the number of hours they work with an open-ended question rather than simply checking ranges of hours worked, and none come close to randomly assigning students to different numbers of hours to examine the independent impact of work on degree completion. However, there is a preponderance of evidence indicating that work is, at the very least, not boosting degree completion rates.

51. Walpole, "Socioeconomic Status and College," 55.

52. Light, "Estimating Returns to Schooling," 31–45; and Stinebrickner and Stinebrickner, "Working during School and Academic Performance," 473–91.

53. U.S. Department of Labor, "Changes in Basic Minimum Wages in Non-Farm Employment under State Law."

54. Mortimer, *Working and Growing Up in America*, 186–91.

55. U.S. Department of Labor, Bureau of Labor Statistics, "Labor Force Statistics from the Current Population Survey."

56. Alexander and Haley-Lock, "Underwork, Work Hour Insecurity and a New Approach to Wage and Hour Regulation," 696.

57. Ibid.; Haley-Lock, "The Structural Contexts of Low-Wage Work"; and Lambert, Haley-Lock, and Henly, "Schedule Flexibility in Hourly Jobs."

58. The tipped minimum wage has fallen in value by nearly 60 percent over the past forty years—waiting tables during college pays far less than it once did. Allegretto and Filion, "Waiting for Change," 3.

59. Marcus, "Taxpayer-Funded Aid Program Benefits Richer Students."

60. Huff, "Research Corner," 35–42.

61. Harvard Energy and Facilities, "Dorm Crew."

62. Federal work-study funds contribute up to 75 percent of a student's wages. Scott-Clayton and Minaya, "Should Student Employment be Subsidized?" 1.

63. For each additional dollar of net income to a Pell recipient's parents, the expected family contribution grows from twenty-two to forty-seven cents (depending on the level of income and assuming no dependent siblings in college). Pell Grant eligibility falls at the same rate. Pell Grants are usually not replaced by other aid unless the student has all costs covered by scholarships and grants. In a family that shares resources, losing forty-seven cents of the child's Pell Grant for each dollar of additional parental income is like only taking home fifty-three cents of each dollar earned. For students who are considered dependent but do not share resources with their parents, the child's Pell Grant is still reduced.

64. Dick and Edlin, "The Implicit Taxes from College Financial Aid," 295–322; Wightman, Schoeni, and Robinson, "Familial Financial Assistance to Young Adults," 6–14; Brown, Scholz, and Seshadri, "A New Test of Borrowing Con-

straints for Education," 1–28; Ensign, "How Not to Blow It with Financial Aid"; and Novack and Fitch, "When Work Doesn't Pay for the Middle Class."

65. Students reported on a five-point scale the amount of financial help they received from parents for education, room and board, and in general. According to this measure, 35 percent of students in this study did not receive any financial assistance from their parents in either of their first two years of college.

66. Other students, however, experienced a *decrease* in expected family contribution during college. Thirty-five percent of students saw their expected family contribution decline between their first and second years, and 35 percent saw a decrease between their second and third years. Since there is movement in both directions, the function of the annual FAFSA check is especially unclear.

67. Nationally, about one in five students with no expected family contribution sees their expected family contribution rise during college. Kelchen, "Financial Need and Aid Volatility," 193.

68. For further reading, see Brooks-Gunn and Duncan, "The Effects of Poverty on Children"; Corcoran and Chaudry, "The Dynamics of Childhood Poverty"; Duncan, Magnuson, and Votruba-Drzal, "Boosting Family Income to Promote Child Development"; and Raver, Roy, and Pressler, "Struggling to Stay Afloat."

Chapter 5

1. Swift, "Americans Rely Less on Credit Cards than in Previous Years."

2. The Diversity Visa Program is offered by the U.S. State Department in countries with low rates of immigration to the United States (including Nepal). Eligible individuals have at least a high school education or two years of work experience. Winners, chosen through a random computer-generated lottery, are given permanent resident visas to live, work, and study in the United States.

3. About 56 percent of students in this study indicated that they consumed alcohol, a rate lower than the national average. See Substance Abuse and Mental Health Services Administration, "Results from the 2013 National Survey on Drug Use and Health." Interviews revealed that many students avoiding drinking because of the cost of alcohol. Only 39 percent indicated spending any money at all on alcohol during the last month. Among those who did drink, they reported consuming four drinks per occasion and experiencing 1.5 episodes of binge drinking (four or more drinks for a woman, and five or more drinks for a man) in the last month.

4. Credit scores range from 300 to 850. A score of 745 puts Tyler in the top 40 percent of the general population. Equifax, "Different Credit Scores."

5. For further reading on students struggling with living costs, see Broton, Frank, and Goldrick-Rab, "Safety, Security, and College Attainment."

6. For further readings on how social programs attempt to eliminate "bad apples," see Schuck and Zeckhauser, *Targeting in Social Programs.*

7. Broton, Frank, and Goldrick-Rab, "Safety, Security and College Attainment," 19–20.

8. Goldrick-Rab, Broton, and Eisenberg, "Hungry to Learn"; Goldrick-Rab and Broton, "Hungry, Homeless and in College."

9. In 2013, 14 percent of households in the United States were food insecure, with "food security" being defined as "access by all people at all times to enough food for an active, healthy life." Coleman-Jensen, Gregory, and Singh, *Household Food Security in the United States in 2013,* 6. For further reading regarding food insecurity, see Cady, "Food Insecurity as a Student Issue"; Freudenberg et al., "Food Insecurity at CUNY"; Hughes et al., "Student Food Insecurity"; Lindsley and King, "Food Insecurity of Campus-Residing Alaskan College Students"; Maroto, Snelling, and Linck, "Food Insecurity among Community College Students"; and Patton-López et al., "Prevalence and Correlates of Food Insecurity among Students Attending a Midsize Rural University in Oregon."

10. Gaines et al., "Examining the Role of Financial Factors, Resources and Skills in Predicting Food Security Status among College Students," 378; and Chaparro et al., "Food Insecurity Prevalence among College Students at the University of Hawai'i at Manoa," 2099.

11. Cady, "Food Insecurity as a Student Issue," 265–71.

12. Freudenberg et al., "Food Insecurity at CUNY," 3.

13. Wick Sloane, e-mail to Sara Goldrick-Rab, June 10, 2010.

14. New York University Faculty against the Sexton Plan, *The Art of the Gouge,* 1.

15. Sloane, "Lunch for 9 Million?"

16. Mai, "Hunger in Higher Education," 16–17.

17. Goldrick-Rab, Broton, and Gates, "Clearing the Path to a Brighter Future," 2.

18. See, e.g., Cady, "Food Insecurity as a Student Issue"; Ashiabi, "Household Food Insecurity and Children's School Engagement"; Jyoti et al., "Food Insecurity Affects School Children's Academic Performance, Weight Gain, and Social Skills"; and Murphy et al., "Relationship between Hunger and Psychological Functioning in Low-Income American Children."

19. Maroto, Snelling, and Linck, "Food Insecurity among Community College Students," 515–26.

20. Resnikoff, "The Hunger Crisis in America's Universities."

21. Ibid.

22. Freudenberg et al., "Food Insecurity at CUNY," 1.

My team conducted an implementation evaluation of Single Stop. See Goldrick-Rab, Broton, and Frank, "Single Stop USA's Community College Initiative."

23. National Association of Student Financial Aid Administrators, *Financial Aid for Unaccompanied Homeless Youth*, 5.

24. Miller and Shattuck, "Sleep Patterns of Young Men and Women Enrolled at the United States Military Academy," 837.

25. Krueger and Friedman, "Sleep Duration in the United States," 1052.

26. Belenky et al., "Patterns of Performance Degradation and Restoration during Sleep Restriction and Subsequent Recovery," 1–12; and Van Dongen et al., "The Cumulative Cost of Additional Wakefulness," 117–26.

27. Carskadon, *Inside the Teenage Brain*; Carpenter, "Sleep Deprivation May Be Undermining Teen Health"; and Grace, "Help for Sleep-Deprived Students."

28. For exceptions, see Acebo et al., "Undergraduate Sleep Patterns"; Bigler and Carskadon, "The Sleep/Wake Patterns of College Students across a Semester"; and Carskadon and Davis, "Sleep-Wake Patterns in the High-School-to-College Transition."

29. Krueger and Friedman, "Sleep Duration in the United States," 1054.

30. Carskadon, *Adolescent Sleep Patterns*, 149.

31. Goldrick-Rab, Broton, and Frank, "Single Stop USA's Community College Initiative," 8.

32. See Mullainathan and Shafir, *Scarcity*.

33. Arria et al., "Connections between Mental Health and Academic Outcomes."

34. American College Health Association, *American College Health Association-National College Health Assessment II*, 14.

35. Eisenberg, Golberstein, and Gollust, "Help-Seeking and Access to Mental Health Care in a University Student Population," 594.

36. Winterrowd, "University of Wisconsin System Counseling Impact Assessment," 6.

37. Evans, "Public Testimony on Hunger in Higher Education," 3.

Chapter 6

1. Angier, "The Changing American Family."

2. Lino, *Expenditures on Children by Families, 2013*, 23.

3. Top 10 percent data are from Johnston, "Income Inequality"; and Saez and Zucman, "Exploding Wealth Inequality in the United States," 1.

4. Saez and Zucman, "Wealth Inequality in the United States since 1913," 1.

5. Foster, "The Household Debt Bubble."

6. Saez and Zucman, "Exploding Wealth Inequality," table 2.

7. Erickson, "The Middle Class Squeeze."

8. Saez and Zucman, "Exploding Wealth Inequality."

9. DeParle, "Two Classes, Divided by 'I Do.'"

10. Livingston, "Fewer Than Half of U.S. Kids Today Live in a 'Traditional' Family."

11. Child Trends Data Bank, "Births to Unmarried Women," 2.
12. Angier, "The Changing American Family."
13. Pew Research Center, *The Rising Cost of* Not *Going to College,* 3.
14. Economic Policy Institute, "College Wage Premium, by Gender, 1973–2013."
15. Kearney, Hershbein, and Jacome, "Profiles of Change," fig. 1.
16. Many Hispanics consider themselves white, so the technical phrase used by the census for white people who do not consider themselves Latino or Hispanic is "non-Hispanic white."
17. Taylor et al., "Wealth Gaps Rise to Record Highs between Whites, Blacks and Hispanics," 18–20.
18. Kochhar and Fry, "Wealth Inequality Has Widened along Racial, Ethnic Lines since End of Great Recession."
19. For further reading, see Wolff, "Recent Trends in Household Wealth in the United States."
20. Sallie Mae Corporation, *How America Pays for College,* 9.
21. Bryan and Simmons, "Family Involvement," 399–400; Fuligni and Pedersen, "Family Obligation and the Transition to Young Adulthood," 861–62; and Fuligni, Tseng, and Lam, "Attitudes toward Family Obligations among American Adolescents with Asian, Latin American, and European Backgrounds," 1033–35.
22. For further reading, see Joyce, "How Helicopter Parents Are Ruining College Students"; and Donatante, "Why Millennials Can't Grow Up."
23. For more on helicopter parenting, see Lythcott-Haims, *How to Raise an Adult.*
24. Annette Lareau describes a similar dynamic in K–12 education in her book *Unequal Childhoods.*
25. Sallie Mae Corporation, *How America Pays for College,* 49.
26. Fuligni and Pedersen, "Family Obligation in the Transition to Young Adulthood," 856–68; Rosas and Hamrick, "Postsecondary Enrollment and Academic Decision-Making," 63–64; and Stack and Burton, "Kinscripts," 157–70.
27. Stack, *All Our Kin,* 32.
28. Goldring, "Family and Collective Remittances to Mexico," 79–84; and Yang, "Migrant Remittances," 129–52.
29. There are a few exceptions, as this flow is inherent in research on why students choose to live in or near home during college, or why being the first to attend college can create family disputes.
30. Swartz et al., "Safety Nets and Scaffolds," 414.
31. Wightman, Schoeni, and Robinson, "Familial Financial Assistance to Young Adults," 7.
32. Schoeni and Ross, "Material Assistance from Families during the Transition to Adulthood," 414–15.
33. Nam et al., "Bootstraps Are for Black Kids," 5–10.
34. For examples, see Sanchez, "Makin' It in College"; Waterman, "Home-Going

as a Strategy for Success among Haudenosaunee College and University Students"; Goldrick-Rab, Minikel-Lacocque, and Kinsley, "Managing to Make It"; and Gilford and Reynolds, "My Mother's Keeper."

35. For further reading, see Newman, *The Accordion Family*; Grigsby, *College Life through the Eyes of Students*; Desmond and Turley, "The Role of Familism in Explaining the Hispanic-White College Application Gap"; Clydesdale, *The First Year Out*; Stuber, *Inside the College Gates*; and Fuligni and Pedersen, "Family Obligation and the Transition to Young Adulthood."

36. For further reading, see Burton, "Childhood Adultification in Economically Disadvantaged Families."

37. Stack and Burton, "Kinscripts," 157.

38. Fuligni and Pedersen, "Family Obligation and the Transition to Young Adulthood," 856.

39. Family obligation among poor adolescents is also highlighted in the work of Carola Suárez-Orozco and Marcelo Suárez-Orozco, who found that low-income Latino and Latina adolescents feel a duty to support their families. Their findings also show that, while family obligation is related to increased academic motivation, the responsibilities associated with family obligation can have negative consequences for school performance. Suárez-Orozco and Suárez-Orozco, *Transformations*.

40. For further reading, see Fuligni, Rivera, and Leininger, "Family Identity and the Educational Progress of Adolescents from Asian and Latin American Backgrounds."

41. Kinsley, "The Pull of Home," 121.

42. Sallie Mae Corporation, *How America Pays for College*, 18.

43. Ibid., 18.

44. Tinto, *Leaving College*, 62–65; and Bozick, "Making It through the First Year of College," 261–84.

45. Dubas and Petersen, "Geographical Distance from Parents and Adjustment during Adolescence and Young Adulthood," 3–19; and Flanagan, Fuligni, and Schulenberg, "Residential Setting and Parent-Adolescent Relationships during the College Years," 171–89.

46. Turley and Wodtke, "College Residence and Academic Performance," 506–32.

47. Sallie Mae Corporation, *How America Pays for College*, 28.

48. Goldrick-Rab and Kendall, *F2CO Redefining College Affordability*, 5–14.

49. Baird et al., "Relative Effectiveness of Conditional and Unconditional Cash Transfers for Schooling Outcomes in Developing Countries," 1–124; Haushofer and Shapiro, "Household Response to Income Changes," 1–57; and Chaluda, "Do Cash Transfers Increase the Wellbeing of Children?" 1–27.

50. Mitchell, "Student-Aid Scams Targeted by Schools, Government," and "Student

Loans Entice Borrowers More for Cash Than a Degree"; and Redden, "Many Community Colleges Opt Out of Loan Program."

51. Institute for College Access and Success, "Data Show No Evidence of 'Over-Borrowing' at Community Colleges," 1–2.

52. Sallie Mae Corporation, *How America Pays for College*, 47.

Chapter 7

1. Arum and Roksa, *Academically Adrift*; and Babcock and Marks, "The Falling Time Cost of College," 468–78.

2. Carey, "Academically Adrift."

3. Lindsay, "Attending to Attendance."

4. For further reading, see Lindsay, "Two Years after College, Too Many Grads Are Still 'Adrift'"; and Pascarella and Blaich, "Lessons from the Wabash National Study of Liberal Arts Education."

5. The notion that students are adrift, that they are to blame for their failure to take full advantage of college, and that they do not measure up to the students of yesteryear is also, in a way, comforting to many. For starters, it sets up students and former students (and parents and "culture") to take a large share of blame for the rising numbers of those who do not graduate and carry debt and also for the unemployment and underemployment crises that face many young Americans. It also implies a set of solutions that can loosely be encompassed under the category of tough love. While some of these solutions may be useful and others may not, these policy changes have precious little to do with the specific needs of low-income students, as we will see.

6. Bidwell, "Can Ending Student Loans Improve Outcomes?"

7. Finkelmeyer, "Is College Still Worth It?"; and Stange, "Differential Pricing in Undergraduate Education," 107–35.

8. Arum and Roksa, "Your So-Called Education."

9. Vedder, "Federal Student Aid, and Unintended Consequences."

10. Salam, "If You're Going to Accept Direct Loans and Pell Grants."

11. Josipa Roksa , personal communication, May 15, 2015.

12. Kinsley and Goldrick-Rab, "Making the Grade," 21–22.

13. Mortenson, "Time Use of Full-Time College Students," 1–16.

14. Babcock and Marks, "The Falling Time Cost of College," 468–78.

15. However, more recent data from the Higher Education Research Institute, whose surveys were used in the Babcock and Marks analysis, suggest the opposite. See Eagen et al., "The American Freshman," 11.

16. Williams, "Too Much College"; and Vedder, "Federal Student Aid, and Unintended Consequences."

17. Mortenson, "Time Use of Full-Time College Students," 3.

18. An influential national organization, Complete College America, also pushes schools and students to take fifteen credits in an initiative called "15 to Finish."

19. Kinsley and Goldrick-Rab, "Making the Grade," 33–35.

20. We considered alternative explanations, including the possibility that additional grant aid made lower-performing students lazier. Analyses of changes in time use, and in particular, allocation of time to leisure activities, suggest no support for this alternative hypothesis.

21. For a description of summer bridge programs and an evaluation of their impacts on college outcomes, see Barnett et al., "Bridging the Gap."

22. Ian's family is not alone in lacking Internet access. The U.S. Census Bureau reports that, as of 2013, one in four households still did not have Internet. In African American households like Ian's, that figure climbs to almost 40 percent. See File and Ryan, *Computer and Internet Use in the United States: 2013*, 3.

23. Binder et al., "Providing Incentives for Timely Progress toward Earning a College Degree," 19–23; Cha and Patel, "Rewarding Progress, Reducing Debt," 23–27; Mayer, Patel, and Gutierrez, "Four Year Effects on Degree Receipt," 9–10; Miller et al., *Staying on Track*, 21–24; and Patel and Valenzuela, *Moving Forward*, 46–49.

24. Lambert, Fugiel, and Henly, "Precarious Work Schedules among Early-Career Employees in the U.S.," 13–14

25. DesJardins et al., "A Quasi-Experimental Investigation," 456–75.

26. Barrow and Rouse, "Financial Incentives and Educational Investment," 42; Richburg-Hayes et al., "Rewarding Persistence," 69–70; Leuven, Oosterbeek, and van der Klaauw, "The Effect of Financial Rewards on Students' Achievement," 1259; MacDonald et al., *FINAL Impacts Report*, 48–49; and Mayer, Patel, and Gutierrez, "Four Year Effects on Degree Receipt," 17–18.

Performance-based scholarships typically offered students $1,000 or less per semester and payment is contingent on meeting certain course credit and GPA requirements (e.g., fifteen credits and 2.0 GPA).

There are two exceptions: Binder et al., "Providing Incentives for Timely Progress toward Earning a College Degree," finds that students offered $1,000 in additional performance-based aid per semester were induced to work 3.3 *more* hours per week than similar peers who typically work 9.4 hours. Also, Richburg-Hayes et al., "Providing More Cash for College," reports that students offered $1,000–$2,000 in performance-based aid were 4.7 percentage points less likely to work anytime during their first year of college (52.1% treatment vs. 56.8% control) and held statistically fewer jobs in year one. There were no treatment impacts on the proportion of students currently working, the number of current jobs, or the number of hours students worked in the past week.

27. Broton, Goldrick-Rab, and Benson, "Working for College."

28. Complete College America, "The Power of 15 Credits," and "State Financial Aid Programs and Full-Time Attendance," 1–3; and Dynarski and Scott-Clayton, "Financial Aid Policy," 67–91.

29. In contrast, Tyler thought that without the bachelor's degree, he would earn $60,000 a year. But when we interviewed him a year later, he had lowered his expectations, and he now only expected to earn $50,000 with a degree in hand—he was no longer confident that his degree would pay off.

30. The national statistic comes from the 2011–12 *National Postsecondary Student Aid Study* (National Center for Education Statistics).

Chapter 8

1. Author's calculations using the National Center for Education Statistics' *National Postsecondary Student Aid Study* of 2011–12, excluding students in solely online courses.

2. Turley, "College Proximity," 140; and Hillman, "Differential Impacts of College Ratings," 12–13.

3. Goldrick-Rab and Kolbe, "Rethinking State Support for Higher Ed."

4. Gurda, *The Making of Milwaukee*, 301–2 and 250–74.

5. Author's calculations using U.S. Census Bureau, "American Community Survey."

6. Logan and Stults, "The Persistence of Segregation in the Metropolis," 6.

7. Milwaukee Department of City Development, *2000 City of Milwaukee Urban Atlas*, 54–55.

8. Annie E. Casey Foundation, *Race for Results*, 13; and Richards, "Wisconsin Black Suspension Rate Highest in U.S. for High Schools."

9. Author's calculations using U.S. Census Bureau, "2009–2013 5-Year American Community Survey."

10. In Dane County, the white poverty rate is 9 percent, while the black poverty rate is 54 percent. Wisconsin Council on Children and Families, *Race to Equity Report*, 12.

11. For more on the economic state of Milwaukee, see Center for Economic Development, University of Wisconsin–Milwaukee, *The Economic State of Milwaukee*; and Wilson, *When Work Disappears*.

12. Bittman, "No Justice, No . . . Anything."

13. Author's calculations using U.S. Census Bureau, "American Community Survey."

14. Pawasarat and Quinn, "Wisconsin's Mass Incarceration of African American Males."

15. For more on the benefits of a college degree, see Oreopoulos and Petronijevic, "Making College Worth It"; and Hout, "Social and Economic Returns to College Education in the United States."

16. Martin, "UW System's Growth Agenda for Wisconsin," 2.

17. The UWM Foundation, Inc., and Affiliates, *Consolidated Financial Statements and Supplementary Information*, 3; University of Wisconsin Foundation, "*Connecting People, Inspiring Ideas*," 26.

18. Gault et al., "Campus Child Care Declining Even as Growing Numbers of Parents Attend College," 1–5.

19. Zlotocha, "A 'Blue Shirt' UW for Milwaukee," 84–110.

20. University of Wisconsin System, "University of Wisconsin Student Statistics, Fall 2014-15 Headcount Enrollment," 1.

21. Wisconsin Technical College System Board, "An Overview of the Wisconsin Technical College System," 3.

22. Milwaukee Area Technical College, "MATC Fast Facts," 1.

23. Richards, "Wisconsin Graduation Rate Rises While MPS' Edges Down."

24. Carl and Kappelman, "Post-Graduation Plans," 1.

25. University of Wisconsin–Madison Academic Planning and Institutional Research, *Data Digest 2014–2015*, 1.

26. Milwaukee Area Technical College, "College Enrollment," 2–3.

27. Wisconsin Technical College System, "Fact Book 2014," 3.

28. Calculations are based on inflation adjusted state appropriations per FTE and tuition revenue per FTE at UW–Milwaukee over time, using data provided by UW–Milwaukee.

29. Torinus, "Can Ray Cross Reposition the UW System?" Many familiar with Wisconsin higher education readily acknowledge that UW–Milwaukee has long been treated as a stepchild in the UW System, just as Milwaukee Area Technical College is treated as a stepchild in its region. See, Day, Allen, and Henken, "Milwaukee Area Technical College's Fiscal Condition."

30. Zlotocha, "A 'Blue Shirt' UW for Milwaukee," 93–95.

31. Committee for Undergraduate Recruitment, Admissions, and Financial Aid, "CURAFA Report to the University Committee," 3–10; and Savidge, "Regents Give UW-Madison OK to Enroll More Out-of-State Students."

32. University of Wisconsin System, "Student Statistics, Fall 2014–15."

33. University of Wisconsin System, "Report on Remedial Education in the UW System," 24.

34. Center for Urban Education, "Partners in Achieving Equity."

35. University of Wisconsin System, "Retention and Graduation: 2013–14," 5–25.

36. In contrast, UW–Milwaukee enrolled 2,119 white students that year and retained 1,534 for a second year of college (for a retention rate of 72%, compared to 66% for Pell recipients). Ibid., 22–25.

37. Ibid., 19-20.

38. Milwaukee Area Technical College, "Student Retention Trends," 3; and "Milwaukee Area Technical College, "Student Persistence," 2.

39. Milwaukee Area Technical College, "Transforming Lives," 28.

40. Author's calculations using U.S. Department of Education, "Integrated Postsecondary Education Data System Data Center."

41. Institute for College Access and Success, "Private Loans," 1.

42. Twenty percent of students who enter loan repayment after leaving Milwaukee Area Technical College default on their federal loan within three years, and 5.6 percent of students from UW–Milwaukee do as well. Data from 2012 come from author's calculations using U.S. Department of Education, "Integrated Postsecondary Education Data System Data Center."

43. U.S. Department of Labor, *Geographic Profile of Employment and Unemployment 2013*, 199, and *Geographic Profile of Employment and Unemployment 2009*, 199.

44. This difference was statistically significant ($p < .05$).

45. U.S. Department of Education, "Title IV Program Volume Reports: AY 2013–2014 Campus-Based Program Data by School."

46. In 2011, shortly after José completed his associate degree, President Obama signed into law the Consolidated Appropriations Act, which limited to students to twelve semesters of Pell Grant eligibility during their lifetime. This change affected all students regardless of when or where they received their first Pell Grant, and there were no exceptions.

47. Abdul-alim, "Dropouts Tell No Tales."

48. U.S. Department of Housing and Urban Development, *Barriers to Success*, 6.

49. For further reading, see Levine, *Ain't No Trust*; Edin and Lein, *Making Ends Meet*; and Soss, Fording, and Schram, *Disciplining the Poor*.

Chapter 9

1. For further reading, see Hoeft, *The Bingo Queens of the Oneida*.

2. While "it takes a village" is best known in the United States as title of a book by Hillary Clinton, a presidential candidate at the time of this writing, Clinton drew inspiration from an African proverb.

3. This is slightly lower than the University of Wisconsin System's bachelor's degree completion rate over six years, which in 2008–9 (for students entering six years earlier) was reported as 55 percent. University of Wisconsin System, "Retention and Graduation," 1.

4. Unfortunately we do not (as of the time this book was written) have data on total debt accumulated over time.

5. This process is called displacement and is regulated by federal law. For a detailed description of the mechanics of how this occurred with regard to students in this study, please see Goldrick-Rab et al., "Reducing Income Inequality in Higher Education."

6. The full details can be found in ibid.; and Anderson and Goldrick-Rab, "Impact of a Private Need-Based Grant Program on Beginning Two-Year College Students."

Chapter 10

1. Goldrick-Rab and Kendall, *F2CO Redefining College Affordability*, 7.
2. Stratford, "Debt-Free and (Mostly) Detail-Free"; and Alexander, "College Too Expensive?"
3. Baum, "Myth."
4. Tucker, "Getting More Low-Income Students into College Isn't about the Money."
5. For further reading, see Piven and Cloward, *Regulating the Poor*; and Schram, *Praxis for the Poor*.
6. Huelsman, "The Affordable College Compact," 3.
7. Page, Bartels, and Seawright, "Democracy and the Policy Preferences of Wealthy Americans," 59.
8. Scholzman, Verba, and Brady, *The Unheavenly Chorus*, 117–46.
9. For further reading, see Armstrong and Hamilton, *Paying for the Party*; Jacob, McCall, and Stange, "College as Country Club"; and Weisbrod, Ballou, and Asch, *Mission and Money*.
10. Tilly, *Durable Inequality*, 145–67; and Lucas, "Effectively Maintained Inequality," 1642–90.
11. For further reading, see McMahon, *Higher Learning, Greater Good*.
12. "@saragoldrickrab I think of loans as 'financial band-aids' . . . over a bullet hole" (C. Cady [ClareCady], Twitter post, February 5, 2014, https://twitter.com /ClareCady/status/431179014213795834); "@saragoldrickrab technically, yes. But I don't think loan amounts should be included in financial aid amounts because it's deceptive" (N. Daoud [ninascia], Twitter post, February 5, 2014, 9:03 P.M., https://twitter.com/ninascia/status/431118487843377152); and "@sara-goldrickrab Good grief no. Neither is work/study, that's a job/paycheck. The lies we tell ourselves . . ." (D. Bush [DebBush1], Twitter post, February 5, 2014, 9:23 P.M., https://twitter.com/DebBush1/status/431123539723165696).
13. For further reading, see Cheston, "Pell-Running"; Field, "Education Department Chases 'Pell Runners' Who Threaten Aid Program"; McClusky, "Higher Math"; Nelson, "Two Pell Grants?"; Terkel, "Rep. Denny Rehberg"; and Institute for College Access and Success, "Pell Grant Provisions Prevent Student Abuse."
14. For further reading, see Bruch, Feree, and Soss, "From Policy to Polity"; Soss, Fording, and Schram, *Disciplining the Poor*; and Schram, *Words of Welfare*.

15. For further reading on targeted programs, see Gilens, *Why Americans Hate Welfare*; and Sawhill, "Target Aid to Students Most Likely to Succeed."

16. Attacks on federal loan programs come from both the Left and the Right. For examples, see Dynarski, "PLUS Loans Are Not Student Aid"; Republican National Committee, "Republican Platform"; Kertscher, "Ron Johnson Is against All Government-Assisted Student Loans"; and Vedder, "End U.S. Student Loans."

17. U.S. Department of Education, "Shopping Sheet," 1.

18. National Association of Student Financial Aid Administrators, "President Obama."

19. Kelchen and Goldrick-Rab, "Accelerating College Knowledge," 199–232.

20. Scott, "Universities Test 'Tuition Guarantees' to Reduce Debt."

21. Truth in Tuition Act of 2010.

22. Institute for College Access and Success, "House FY13 Budget Increases Uncertainty and Complexity"; and Katsinas et al., "The Impact of New Pell Grant Restrictions on Community Colleges," 9–10.

23. Price et al., "Public Benefits and Community Colleges," 15.

24. Goldrick-Rab, Broton, and Frank, "Single Stop USA's Community College Initiative."

25. For further reading on the Angel Fund, see Geckeler et al., "Helping Community College Students Cope with Financial Emergencies," 39–65.

26. For further reading, see Dachelet and Goldrick-Rab, "Emergency Aid Programs for College Success."

27. Lower-Basch, "Goals for TANF Reauthorization," 5; and Shaw et al., *Putting Poor People to Work*, 78–86.

28. For further reading on two-generation models, see Carlson, "Campus Child Care, a 'Critical Student Benefit,' Is Disappearing"; King, Chase-Lansdale, and Small, eds., *Two Generations, One Future*; and Mosle, Patel, and Stedron, *Top Ten for 2Gen*.

29. Lower-Basch and Lee, "College Student Eligibility," 1–3; and Broton and Goldrick-Rab, "Public Testimony on Hunger in Higher Education."

30. College and University Food Bank Alliance, "Our Members."

31. Leos-Urbel et al., "Not Just for Poor Kids," 89; and Broton and Goldrick-Rab, "Public Testimony on Hunger in Higher Education," 4–9.

32. Goldrick-Rab and Broton, "To Cut Costs, College Students Are Buying Less Food and Even Going Hungry."

33. For further reading, see Gillborn and Youdell, *Rationing Education*.

34. Goldrick-Rab, Kelchen, and Hosch, "Information, Accountability, and College Costs."

35. Association of Community College Trustees, "Eligibility Changes to Income Protection Allowance."

36. Scott-Clayton, "A Jobs Program in Need of Reform."

37. For further reading, see Setzer and O'Sullivan, "A Federal Work Study Reform Agenda"; Scott-Clayton and Minaya, "Should Student Employment be Subsidized?"; and Goldrick-Rab, "Testimony to Advisory Committee on Student Financial Assistance."

38. See Huelsman, "The Affordable College Compact."

39. Hull, "The Path Least Taken," 3.

40. National Association of State Student Grant and Aid Programs, *42nd Annual Survey Report on State-Sponsored Student Financial Aid*, 8.

41. See Katsinas et al., "The Impact of New Pell Grant Restrictions on Community College."

42. Alexander et al., "Maintenance of Effort," 1–8.

43. See Kirshstein and Hurlburt, "Revenues."

44. Goldrick-Rab and Kolbe, "Rethinking State Support for Higher Ed."

45. National Association of State Student Grant Programs, *44th Annual Survey Report on State-Sponsored Student Financial Aid*, 3–8.

46. Education Commission of the States. "50 States Policy Database."

47. Baum, Elliott, and Ma, *Trends in Student Aid: 2014*, table 1.

48. Burd, "The Out-of-State Student Arms Race," 3–4.

49. Burd, "Merit Aid Madness."

50. Burd, "The Out-of-State Student Arms Race," 2.

51. Heller, "Merit Aid and College Access," 2–3.

52. Ibid., 5.

53. For further reading on these studies, see Heller and Marin, eds., *State Merit Scholarship Programs and Racial Inequality*; and Cornwell and Mustard, "Georgia's HOPE Scholarship and Minority and Low-Income Students," 77–100.

54. See Cornwell and Mustard, "Merit-Based College Scholarships and Car Sales," 77–100.

55. Ingles and Dalton, *High School Longitudinal Study of 2009*, 5; and Looney and Yannelis, "A Crisis in Student Loans?" 12–16.

56. Haskins, "Education and Economic Mobility," 6.

57. Goldrick-Rab and Kendall, *F2CO Redefining College Affordability*, 6.

58. Ibid., 5–14; and Oreopoulos and Petronijevic, "Making College Worth It," 41–65.

59. Bettinger et al., "The Role of Application Assistance and Information in College Decisions," 1205–42.

60. *Chattanooga Times Free Press*, "Gov. Haslam Urges High School Seniors to Apply for Tennessee Promise"; and Dynarski, "Rising Inequality in Postsecondary Education."

61. See Goldrick-Rab et al., "Reducing Income Inequality in Higher Education."

62. Archibald, Feldman, and McHenry, "A Quality-Preserving Increase in Four-Year College Attendance," 295.

63. Philbrick, *City School Systems in the United States*, 105.

64. Goldin and Katz, *The Race between Education and Technology*, 158–66.

65. I am advocating for "incremental universalism," a phrase borrowed from Sanford Schram, to whom I am indebted for great inspiration. See Schram, *After Welfare*.

66. Bernanke, "National and Regional Economic Overview."

67. There are many proposals for how to do this, including a proposal from 2016 presidential candidate Bernie Sanders. Here are two: Goldrick-Rab and Kendall, *F2CO Redefining College Affordability*; and Samuels, *Why Public Higher Education Should Be Free*.

68. Schram, *After Welfare*, 24; Skocpol, "Sustainable Social Policy"; and Wilson, *When Work Disappears*, 156–57.

69. Some of the best insights into how to improve public higher education are found in the following volumes: Bailey, Jaggers, and Jenkins, *Redesigning America's Community Colleges*; Crow and Dabars, *Designing the New American University*; Folbre, *Saving State U*; Kuh et al., *Using Evidence of Student Learning to Improve Higher Education*; and Newfield, *Unmaking the Public University*.

70. Associated Press, "Commissioner: New Funding Saves Big College Tuition Hike"; Indiana University Newsroom, "Indiana University to Freeze Undergraduate Tuition for Hoosier Residents Attending IU Bloomington"; and Fain, "Boom Budget in California."

71. National Council on State Legislatures, "Performance-Based Funding for Higher Education"; and Fingerhut and Kazis, *Tying Funding to Community College Outcomes*.

72. Woodhouse, "Funding Woes"; and Bidwell, "The 'New Normal' of Higher Ed Funding."

73. For further reading, see Behrman and Stacey, *The Social Benefits of Education*; Johnson, "Are Public Subsidies to Higher Education Regressive?"; and Wolfe and Haveman, "Social and Nonmarket Benefits from Education in an Advanced Economy."

74. Jaschik, "Higher Learning, Greater Good."

75. See Carruthers and Fox, "Aid for All."

76. *Chattanooga Times Free Press*, "Gov. Haslam Urges High School Seniors."

77. Ibid.

78. Fain, "Free Community College Catches On."

79. Campaign for Free College Tuition, "Making Free College Tuition a Reality."

80. Goldrick-Rab, "Free College Plan Will Help, Not Hurt, Low-Income Students."

81. Office of Senator Tammy Baldwin, "Sens. Baldwin, Booker and Rep. Scott Introduce America's College Promise Act."

82. Renfro and Armour-Garb, "The History of Open Admissions and Remedial Education," 20–22.

83. Attewell, Domina, and Levey, *Passing the Torch*, 185–201.

84. Leonhardt, "College for the Masses."
85. For further reading, see Kelly and Goldrick-Rab, *Reinventing Financial Aid.*
86. Konczal, "Could We Redirect Tax Subsidies to Pay for Free College?"; and Weissman and Lindemann, "The Cost of Making Our Public Colleges Tuition Free."
87. Lumina Foundation, *A Stronger America through Higher Education,* 2.
88. Johnson et al., *With Their Whole Lives Ahead of Them,* 1–52.
89. Wilde, "The Soul of Man under Socialism," 4.
90. For further reading, see Reese, *The Origins of the American High School.*

Appendix 1

1. Cumulative grade point averages in the book are reported for the most recent term when the student was enrolled.
2. Goldrick-Rab et al., "Reducing Income Inequality in Higher Education."
3. Dynarski, Hemelt, and Hyman, "The Missing Manual," 9.
4. Although the Wisconsin Technical College System (WTCS) participates in the National Student Clearinghouse, they do not participate in clearinghouse's DegreeVerify service, which tracks student degree completion regardless of where the student graduates. Data were therefore unavailable on degrees earned outside the WTCS for the 1,252 students in the sample who started at a WTCS institution. In particular, the reported rates of bachelor's degree completion among two-year college students are limited to the 248 students in the sample attending two-year branch campuses in the University of Wisconsin System.
5. Financial constraints unfortunately prevented the entire WSLS sample from being resurveyed in fall 2009. The sample for the second-year survey consisted of responders to the first-year survey who were verified Wisconsin residents and who were born in 1985 or later.
6. Eight WSLS participants declined to participate in further surveys and were therefore excluded from the survey sample for the third survey.
7. Stevenson et al., "What Are the Odds?" 1–23
8. Edin and Lein, "Work, Welfare and Single Mothers' Economic Survival Strategies," 254–55.
9. Three other graduate students also assisted with follow-up interviews.
10. Goldrick-Rab, Broton, and Frank, "Single Stop USA's Community College Initiative."
11. Creswell and Clark, *Designing and Conducting Mixed Methods Research,* 7–17.
12. Bryman, "Integrating Quantitative and Qualitative Research," 111.
13. Creswell and Clark, *Designing and Conducting Mixed Methods Research,* 77–81
14. All quantitative comparisons I discuss in the book are statistically significant at $p < .05$ or better.
15. Miles and Huberman, *Qualitative Data Analysis: An Expanded Sourcebook,* 12.

Appendix 2

1. Western Interstate Commission for Higher Education, *Knocking at the College Door*, 113.
2. University of Wisconsin System, "What Is the UW System."
3. Wisconsin Technical College System, "Our Story."
4. Author's calculations using U.S. Department of Education, "Integrated Postsecondary Education Data System."
5. Higher Educational Education Aids Board, *Wisconsin State Student Financial Data for 2008–2009*, 24–29.
6. Wisconsin Legislative Fiscal Bureau, "Student Financial Aid," 9.
7. University of Wisconsin System, "Higher Education Fact Sheet," 1.
8. University of Wisconsin System, "Student Statistics Fall 2014–15 Headcount Enrollment – Undergraduate Students by Institution," 1.
9. Wisconsin Technical College System, "Fact Book 2014," 2–3.
10. Author's calculations using U.S. Department of Education, "Integrated Postsecondary Education Data System."
11. Ibid.
12. Wisconsin Association of Independent Colleges and Universities, "WAICU Facts."
13. College of Menominee Nation, "Quick Facts 2015–2016," 6.
14. Author's calculations using U.S. Department of Education, "Integrated Postsecondary Education Data System."
15. Ibid.; and University of Wisconsin System, "Higher Education Fact Sheet," 2.
16. University of Wisconsin System, "Retention and Graduation: 2011–12," 23.
17. University of Wisconsin System, "Retention and Graduation: 2013–14," 7.
18. University of Wisconsin System, "Higher Education Fact Sheet," 1.
19. Author's calculations using U.S. Department of Education, "Integrated Postsecondary Education Data System."
20. Wisconsin Legislative Fiscal Bureau, "Student Financial Aid," 9.
21. Ibid, 10.
22. Wisconsin Legislative Fiscal Bureau, "University of Wisconsin System Overview: [2009]," 18.
23. Wisconsin Legislative Fiscal Bureau, "Wisconsin Technical College System Overview: [2009]," 5.
24. Wisconsin Legislative Fiscal Bureau, "University of Wisconsin System Overview: [2015]," 19, and "Wisconsin Technical College System Overview: [2015]," 5.
25. Dresser, Rogers, and Navot, *The State of Working Wisconsin 2010*, 11.
26. Ibid, 25.
27. Center on Wisconsin Strategy, "The State of Working Wisconsin 2014," 3.
28. Reed and Cochrane, *Student Debt and the Class of 2013*, 5.
29. Reed and Cheng, Student Debt and the Class of 2008, 4.

30. University of Wisconsin System, "Student Statistics, Fall Full-Time Equivalent Enrollment," 1.

31. Wisconsin Legislative Fiscal Bureau, "University of Wisconsin System Overview: [2015]"; and "Wisconsin Technical College System Overview," 5.

32. Author's calculations using Wisconsin Information System for Education Data Dashboard.

33. Western Interstate Commission for Higher Education, *Knocking at the College Door*, 113.

34. Center on Wisconsin Strategy, "The State of Working Wisconsin 2014," 9, 27–28.

References

Note: multiple references by a single author are arranged alphabetically by title rather than chronologically.

Abdul-alim, J. 2013. "Dropouts Tell No Tales." *Washington Monthly Magazine*, September–October.

Abramovitz, M. 1999. *Regulating the Lives of Women: Social Welfare Policy from Colonial Times to the Present*. New York: South End Press.

Acebo, C., S. S. Davis, K. B. Herman, and M. A. Carskadon. 1991. "Undergraduate Sleep Patterns: Evidence of Adaptation over Time." *Sleep Research* 20:111.

Ackert, L. F., N. Charupat, B. K. Church, and R. Deaves. 2006. "An Experimental Examination of the House Money Effect in a Multi-Period Setting." *Experimental Economics* 9:5–16.

Alexander, C., and A. Haley-Lock. 2015. "Underwork, Work Hour Insecurity, and a New Approach to Wage and Hour Regulation." *Industrial Relations*, January, 695–716.

Alexander, F. K., T. Harnisch, D. Hurley, and R. Moran. 2010. "Maintenance of Effort: An Evolving Federal-State Policy Approach to Ensuring College Affordability." *Journal of Education Finance* 36 (1): 76–87.

Alexander, K., D. Entwisle, and L. Olson. 2014. *The Long Shadow: Family Background, Disadvantaged Youth, and the Transition to Adulthood*. New York: Russell Sage Foundation.

Alexander, L. 2015. "College Too Expensive? That's a Myth." *Wisconsin State Journal*, July 6.

Allegretto, S. A., and K. Filion. 2011. "Waiting for Change: The $2.13 Federal Subminimum Wage." Briefing Paper 297. Economic Policy Institute, Washington, DC.

Alon, S. 2009. "The Evolution of Class Inequality in Higher Education: Competition, Exclusion, and Adaptation." *American Sociological Review* 74 (5): 731–55.

American College Health Association. 2014. *American College Health Association–National College Health Assessment II: Undergraduate Students Reference Group Data Report Spring 2014.* Hanover, MD: American College Health Association.

Anderson, D. M., and S. Goldrick-Rab. 2016. "Impact of a Private Need-Based Grant Program on Beginning Two-Year College Students." Wisconsin HOPE Lab White Paper, University of Wisconsin–Madison.

———. 2016. "The Wisconsin Grant: Overview and Recommendations for Evaluation." Policy Report of the Wisconsin HOPE Lab, University of Wisconsin–Madison.

Angier, N. 2013. "The Changing American Family." *New York Times,* November 25.

Annie E. Casey Foundation. 2014. *Race for Results: Building a Path to Opportunity for All Children.* Kids Count Policy Report. Baltimore, MD: Annie E. Casey Foundation. http://www.aecf.org/m/resourcedoc/AECF-RaceforResults-2014.pdf.

Archibald, R. B., and D. H. Feldman. 2011. *Why Does College Cost So Much?* Oxford: Oxford University Press.

Archibald, R. B., D. H. Feldman, and P. McHenry. 2015. "A Quality-Preserving Increase in Four-Year College Attendance." *Journal of Human Capital* 9 (3): 265–97.

Armstrong, E. A., and L. T. Hamilton. 2013. *Paying for the Party: How College Maintains Inequality.* Cambridge, MA: Harvard University Press.

Arria, A. M., J. M. Behen, D. Eisenberg, and S. Goldrick-Rab. 2014. "Connections between Mental Health and Academic Outcomes." Panel discussion held at the 2014 Depression on College Campuses Conference. University of Michigan, Ann Arbor, March 13. https://www.youtube.com/watch?v=mpBVi9irggc.

Arum, R., and J. Roksa. 2011. *Academically Adrift: Limited Learning on College Campuses.* Chicago: University of Chicago.

———. 2011. "Your So-Called Education." *New York Times,* May 14.

Ashiabi, G. 2005. "Household Food Insecurity and Children's School Engagement." *Journal of Children and Poverty* 11 (1): 3–17.

Associated Press. 2015. "Commissioner: New Funding Saves Big College Tuition Hike." *Washington Times,* May 21.

Association of Community College Trustees. n.d. "Eligibility Changes to Income Protection Allowance." http://www.acct.org/files/legacy/pdf/pell%20eligibility%20IPA%20one%20pager.pdf.

Astin, A. W. 1993. *What Matters in College? Four Critical Years Revisited*. San Francisco: Jossey-Bass.

Attewell, P., S. Heil, and L. Reisel. 2012. "What Is Academic Momentum? And Does It Matter?" *Educational Evaluation and Policy Analysis* 34 (1): 27–44.

Attewell, P., D. E. Lavin, T. Domina, and T. Levey. 2009. *Passing the Torch: Does Higher Education for the Disadvantaged Pay Off across the Generations?* New York: Russell Sage Foundation.

Babcock, P., and M. Marks. 2010. "The Falling Time Cost of College: Evidence from Half a Century of Time Use Data." NBER Working Paper no. 15954. National Bureau of Economic Research, Cambridge, MA.

Bady, A., and M. Konczal. 2012. "From Master Plan to No Plan: The Slow Death of Public Higher Education." *Dissent* (fall). http://www .dissentmagazine.org/article/from-master-plan-to-no-plan-the-slow-death -of-public-higher-education.

Bailey, M. J., and S. Dynarski. 2011. "Inequality in Postsecondary Education." In *Wither Opportunity?* ed. G. Duncan and R. Murnane, 117–32. New York: Russell Sage Foundation.

Bailey, T. R., S. S. Jaggars, and D. Jenkins. 2015. *Redesigning America's Community Colleges: A Clearer Path to Student Success*. Cambridge, MA: Harvard University Press.

Baird, S., F. H. G. Ferreira, B. Ozler, and M. Woolock. 2013. "Relative Effectiveness of Conditional and Unconditional Cash Transfers for Schooling Outcomes in Developing Countries: A Systematic Review." *Campbell Systematic Reviews*, vol. 9, no. 8.

Barnett, E. A., R. H. Bork, A. Mayer, J. Pretlow, H. Wathington, and M. J. Weiss. 2012. "Bridging the Gap: An Impact Study of Eight Developmental Summer Bridge Programs in Texas." NCPR Report. National Center for Postsecondary Research, Columbia College, New York. http://www .postsecondaryresearch.org/i/a/document/NCPR-BridgingtheGapBrief .pdf.

Barrow, L., and C. E. Rouse. 2013. "Financial Incentives and Educational Investment: The Impact of Performance Based Scholarships on Student Time Use." NBER Working Paper no. 19351. National Bureau of Economic Research, Cambridge, MA.

Bastedo, M. N., and O. Jaquette. 2011. "Running in Place: Low-Income Students and the Dynamics of Higher Education." *Educational Evaluation and Policy Analysis* 33 (3): 318–39.

Baum, S. 2012. "Myth: College Is Unaffordable for All but the Rich." American Council on Education, Washington, DC. http://www.acenet.edu/the -presidency/columns-and-features/Pages/Myth-College-Is-Unaffordable -for-All-but-the-Rich.aspx.

Baum, S., D. C. Elliott, and J. Ma. 2014. *Trends in Student Aid: 2014.* College Board. https://secure-media.collegeboard.org/digitalServices/misc /trends/2014-trends-student-aid-report-final.pdf.

Baum, S., and Johnson, M. 2015. *Student Debt: Who Borrows Most? What Lies Ahead?* Washington, DC: Urban Institute.

Baum, S., and J. Ma. 2014. *Trends in College Pricing: 2014.* College Board. https://secure-media.collegeboard.org/digitalServices/misc/trends/2014 -trends-college-pricing-report-final.pdf.

Baum, S., J. Ma, M. Pender, and D. Bell. 2015. *Trends in Student Aid: 2015.* College Board. http://trends.collegeboard.org/sites/default/files/trends -student-aid-web-final-508-2.pdf.

Baum, S., and K. Payea. 2012. *Trends in Student Aid: 2012.* College Board. http://trends.collegeboard.org/sites/default/files/student-aid-2012-full -report.pdf.

Baum, S., and S. Schwartz. 2006. *How Much Debt Is Too Much? Defining Benchmarks for Manageable Student Debt.* College Board. April 20. http:// research.collegeboard.org/sites/default/files/publications/2012/9 /researchinreview-2006-12-benchmarks-manageable-student-debt.pdf.

Baylor, E. 2014. "State Disinvestment in Higher Education Has Led to an Explosion of Student-Loan Debt." Center for American Progress, December 3. https://www.americanprogress.org/issues/higher-education/report /2014/12/03/102407/state-disinvestment-in-higher-education-has-led-to -an-explosion-of-student-loan-debt/.

Behrman, J. R., and N. Stacey, eds. 1997. *The Social Benefits of Education.* Ann Arbor: University of Michigan Press.

Belenky, G., N. J. Wesensten, D. R. Thorne, M. L. Thomas, H. C. Sing, D. P. Redmond, et al. 2003. "Patterns of Performance Degradation and Restoration during Sleep Restriction and Subsequent Recovery: A Sleep Dose-Response Study." *Journal of Sleep Research* 12 (1): 1–12.

Benson, A., R. Esteva, and F. Levy. 2015. "Dropouts, Taxes and Risk: The Economic Return to College under Realistic Assumptions." Working Paper, Department of Urban Studies and Planning, MIT, Cambridge, MA. http://dusp.mit.edu/sites/dusp.mit.edu/files/attachments/publications /California%20Paper%20for%20Circulation.pdf

Bergeron, D., and A. Flores. 2015. "College for All: Improving College Access and Degree Attainment through an Early Guarantee of Federal Financial Aid." Center for American Progress, May 6. https://www.americanprogress .org/issues/higher-education/report/2015/05/06/112518/improving -college-access-and-degree-attainment-through-an-early-guarantee-of -federal-financial-aid/.

Bernanke, B. S. 2007. "National and Regional Economic Overview." Speech presented at Presentation of the Citizens of the Carolinas Award, Char-lotte, NC, November 29. http://www.federalreserve.gov/newsevents/speech/bernanke20071129a.htm.

Bettinger, E. 2004. "How Financial Aid Affects Persistence." In *College Choices: The Economics of Where to Go, When to Go, and How to Pay for It*, ed. C. Hoxby, 207-238. Chicago: University of Chicago Press.

Bettinger, E. P., B. T. Long, P. Oreopoulos, and L. Sanbonmatsu. 2012. "The Role of Application Assistance and Information in College Decisions: Results from the H&R Block FAFSA Experiment." *Quarterly Journal of Economics* 127 (3): 1205–42.

Bidwell, A. 2014. "Can Ending Student Loans Improve Outcomes?" *U.S. News and World Report*, October 1.

———. 2015. "The 'New Normal' of Higher Ed Funding: Students Footing the Bill." *U.S. News and World Report*, April 13.

Bigler, P. J., and M. A. Carskadon. 1990. "The Sleep/Wake Patterns of College Students across a Semester." *Sleep Research* 19:113.

Binder, M., K. Krause, C. Miller, and O. Cerna. 2015. "Providing Incentives for Timely Progress toward Earning a College Degree: Results from a Perfor-mance Based Scholarship Experiment." MDRC Working Paper. MDRC, New York. http://www.mdrc.org/publication/providing-incentives-timely -progress-toward-earning-college-degree.

Bird, K., and B. L. Castleman. 2014. "Here Today, Gone Tomorrow? Investi-gating Rates and Patterns of Financial Aid Renewal among College Fresh-men." EdPolicyWorks Working Paper. EdPolicyWorks, University of Vir-ginia, Charlottesville. http://curry.virginia.edu/uploads/resourceLibrary /25_Bird_Financial_Aid_Renewal.pdf.

Bittman, M. 2015. "No Justice, No . . . Anything." *New York Times*, May 13.

Bound, J., M. F. Lovenheim, and S. Turner. 2012. "Increasing Time to Bacca-laureate Degree in the United States." *Education Finance and Policy* 7 (4): 375–424.

Bowen, W. G., M. M. Chingos, and M. S. McPherson. 2009. *Crossing the Finish Line: Completing College at America's Public Universities*. Princeton, NJ: Princeton University Press.

Bozick, R. 2007. "The Changing Role of Family Income and Ability in De-termining Educational Achievements." *Sociology of Education* 80 (July): 261–85.

———. 2007. "Making It through the First Year of College: The Role of Students' Economic Resources, Employment, and Living Arrangements." *Sociology of Education* 80 (3): 261–85.

Brooks-Gunn, J., and G. J. Duncan. 1997. "The Effects of Poverty on Children." *Children and Poverty* 7 (2): 55–71.

Broton, K., V. Frank, and S. Goldrick-Rab. 2014. "Safety, Security and College Attainment: An Investigation of Undergraduates' Basic Needs and Institutional Response." Wisconsin HOPE Lab, University of Wisconsin–Madison. http://wihopelab.com/publications/APPAM.Draft.10.28.2014.pdf.

Broton, K., and S. Goldrick-Rab. 2014. "The Problem of College Students without Reliable Housing." Scholars Strategy Network, Cambridge, MA. http://www.scholarsstrategynetwork.org/brief/problem-college-students-without-reliable-housing.

———. 2015. "Public Testimony on Hunger in Higher Education." Wisconsin HOPE Lab, University of Wisconsin–Madison. http://wihopelab.com/publications/Hunger_Testimony_Broton_Goldrick-Rab_2015.pdf.

Broton, K., S. Goldrick-Rab, and J. Benson. 2016. "Working for College: The Causal Impacts of Financial Grants on Undergraduate Employment." Educational Evaluation and Policy Analysis. Published electronically March 23. https://www.researchgate.net/publicaton/299400059 Working_for_College_The Causal_Impacts_of_Financial_Grants_on_Undergraduate_Employment.

Brown, M., A. Haughwout, D. Lee, M. Mabutas, and W. van der Klaauw. 2012. "Grading Student Loans." *Liberty Street Economics* (blog). March 5, Federal Reserve Bank of New York. http://libertystreeteconomics.newyorkfed.org/2012/03/grading-student-loans.html#.VqKiiPkrJD8.

———. 2014. "Measuring Student Debt and its Performance." Federal Reserve Bank of New York Staff Report no. 668.

Brown, M., A. Haughwout, D. Lee, J. Scally, and W. van der Klaauw. 2015. "Looking at Student Loan Defaults through a Larger Window." *Liberty Street Economics* (blog), February 19. Federal Reserve Bank of New York. http://libertystreeteconomics.newyorkfed.org/2015/02/looking_at_student_loan_defaults_through_a_larger_window.html#.ViQYIe1Vikp.

Brown, M., J. K. Scholz, and A. Seshadri. 2009. "A New Test of Borrowing Constraints for Education." *Review of Economic Studies* 79:511–38.

Bruch, S. K., M. M. Feree, and J. Soss. 2010. "From Policy to Polity: Democracy, Paternalism, and the Incorporation of Disadvantaged Citizens." *American Sociological Review* 75 (2): 205–26.

Bryan, E., and B. E. Simmons. 2009. "Family Involvement: Impacts on Post-Secondary Educational Success for First-Generation Appalachian College Students." *Journal of College Student Development* 50 (4): 391–405.

Bryman, A. 2006. "Integrating Quantitative and Qualitative Research: How Is It Done?" *Qualitative Research* 6 (1): 97–113.

Burd, S. 2013. "Merit Aid Madness." *Washington Monthly*, September–October.

———. 2015. "The Out-of-State Student Arms Race: How Public Universities

Use Merit Aid to Recruit Nonresident Students." New America Foundation, Washington, DC.

———. 2013. "Undermining Pell: How Colleges Compete for Wealthy Students and Leave the Low Income Behind." New America Foundation, Washington, DC.

Burdman, P. 2005. "The Student Debt Dilemma: Debt Aversion as a Barrier to College Access." Research Paper no. CSHE.13.05. University of California, Berkeley.

Burton, L. 2007. "Childhood Adultification in Economically Disadvantaged Families: A Conceptual Model." *Family Relations* 56 (4): 329–45.

Busteed, B., and S. Kafka. 2015. "Most Americans Say Higher Education Not Affordable." Gallup, April 16.

Byndloss, D. C., R. Coven, Y. Kusayeva, C. Johnston, and J. Sherwin. 2015. *In Search of a Match: A Guide for Helping Students Make Informed College Choices.* MDRC Report. MDRC, New York. http://www.mdrc.org/sites /default/files/in_search_for_a_match.pdf.

Cady, C. L. 2014. "Food Insecurity as a Student Issue." *Journal of College and Character* 15 (4): 265–72.

Campaign for Free College Tuition. 2015. "Making Free College Tuition a Reality." http://www.freecollegenow.org/making_free_college_tuition _a_reality.

Campbell, C., and N. Hillman. 2015. *A Closer Look at the Trillion: Borrowing, Repayment, and Default at Iowa's Community Colleges.* Association of Community College Trustees, Washington, DC. http://www.acct.org/files /Publications/2015/ACCT_Borrowing-Repayment-Iowa_CCs_09-28 -2015.pdf.

Carey, K. 2012. "'Academically Adrift': The News Gets Worse and Worse." *Chronicle of Higher Education,* February 12.

Carl, B., and K. Kappelman. 2012. *Post-Graduation Plans, Postsecondary Enrollment Trends, and College Readiness among MPS Seniors.* Research Brief, Milwaukee Public Schools, Milwaukee, WI.

Carlson, S. 2015. "Campus Child Care, a 'Critical Student Benefit,' Is Disappearing." *Chronicle of Higher Education,* May 18.

Carpenter, B. 2001. "Sleep Deprivation May Be Undermining Teen Health." *Monitor on Psychology* 32 (9): 42.

Carruthers, C. K., and W. F. Fox. 2015. "Aid for All: College Coaching, Financial Aid, and Post-Secondary Persistence in Tennessee." Working Paper no. 2015-06. Department of Economics, University of Tennessee. http://web .utk.edu/~ccarrut1/Carruthers_Fox_May2015b.pdf.

Carskadon, M. A. 2002. *Adolescent Sleep Patterns: Biological, Social and Psychological Influences.* Cambridge: Cambridge University Press.

————. 2002. *Inside the Teenage Brain: Interviews. Frontline.* http://www.pbs .org/wgbh/pages/frontline/shows/teenbrain/interviews/carskadon.html.

Carskadon, M. A., and S. S. Davis. 1989. "Sleep-Wake Patterns in the High-School-to-College Transition: Preliminary Data." *Sleep Research* 18:113.

Castleman, B. L., and B. T. Long. 2012. "Looking beyond Enrollment: The Causal Effect of Need-Based Grants on College Access, Persistence, and Graduation." NBER Working Paper no. 19306. National Bureau of Economic Research, Cambridge, MA.

Castleman, B. L., S. Schwartz, and S. Baum. 2015. *Decision Making for Student Success: Behavioral Insights to Improve Access and Persistence.* New York: Routledge Press.

Center for Economic Development, University of Wisconsin–Milwaukee. 2010. *The Economic State of Milwaukee, 1990–2008.* https://www4.uwm.edu /ced/publications/milwecon_2010.pdf.

————. 1998. *The Economic State of Milwaukee: The City and the Region.* https://www4.uwm.edu/ced/publications/milwecon_2010.pdf.

Center for Urban Education. 2012. "Partners in Achieving Equity—University of Wisconsin System." Rossier School of Education, University of Southern California. http://cue.usc.edu/partners/university_of_wisconsin_system _uws.html.

Center on Wisconsin Strategy. 2014. *The State of Working Wisconsin 2014.* http://www.cows.org/_data/documents/1647.pdf.

Cha, P., and R. Patel. 2010. "Rewarding Progress, Reducing Debt: Early Results from the Performance-Based Scholarship Demonstration in Ohio." MDRC Report. MDRC, New York. http://www.mdrc.org/publication /rewarding-progress-reducing-debt.

Chaluda, A. 2015. "Do Cash Transfers Increase the Wellbeing of Children? A Review of the Literature." Report prepared by Supporting Transformation by Reducing Insecurity and Vulnerability with Economic Strengthening Program. https://www.microlinks.org/sites/default/files/resource/files /STRIVE_Cash_Transfer_lit_review_final2015.pdf.

Chaparro, M. P., S. S. Zagloul, P. Holck, and J. Dobbs. 2009. "Food Insecurity Prevalence among College Students at the University of Hawai'i at Manoa." *Public Health Nutrition* 12 (11): 2097–2103.

Chattanooga Times Free Press. 2015. "Gov. Haslam Urges High School Seniors to Apply for Tennessee Promise." October 6. http://www.timesfreepress .com/news/local/story/2015/oct/06/haslam-urges-seniors-apply -tennessee-promise/328936/.

Cheston, D. 2013. "Pell-Running: Taxpayers Lose $1 Billion or More a Year to Fraudulent Use of Pell Grants." Commentaries, February 26. John William

Pope Center. http://www.popecenter.org/commentaries/article.html?id =2811.

Chetty, R., N. Hendren, E. Saez, and P. Kline. 2014. "Where Is the Land of Opportunity? The Geography of Intergenerational Mobility in the United States." *Quarterly Journal of Economics* 129(4): 1553-1623.

Child Trends Data Bank. 2015. "Births to Unmarried Women." http://www .childtrends.org/?indicators=births-to-unmarried-women.

Chopra, R. 2013. "Student Debt Swells, Federal Loans Now Top a Trillion." Consumer Financial Protection Bureau. http://www.consumerfinance.gov /newsroom/student-debt-swells-federal-loans-now-top-a-trillion/.

Clinton, H. 2007. "Remarks on Student Activism at Wellesley College." Speech delivered on November 1. The American Presidency Project. http://www.presidency.ucsb.edu/ws/?pid=77072.

Cramer, K. J. 2016. *The Politics of Resentment: Rural Consciousness in Wisconsin and the Rise of Scott Walker*. Chicago: University of Chicago Press.

Clydesdale, T. 2008. *The First Year Out: Understanding American Teens after High School*. Chicago: University of Chicago Press.

Cohen, P. 2015. "Middle Class, but Feeling Economically Insecure." *New York Times*, April 10.

Coleman-Jensen, A., C. Gregory, and A. Singh. 2014. *Household Food Security in the United States in 2013*. Report no. 173. Economic Research Service, U.S. Department of Agriculture, Washington, DC. http://www.ers.usda .gov/media/1565415/err173.pdf.

College and University Food Bank Alliance. 2013. "Our Members." Last updated December 10, 2015. http://www.cufba.org/member-info/.

College Board Advocacy and Policy Center.2013. *Rethinking Pell Grants*. College Board. http://media.collegeboard.com/digitalServices/pdf/advocacy /policycenter/advocacy-rethinking-pell-grants-report.pdf.

College of Menominee Nation. 2015. "Quick Facts 2015–2016." http://www .menominee.edu/uploadedFiles/CMN/Development/quick_facts.pdf.

Committee for Undergraduate Recruitment, Admissions and Financial Aid. 2013. "CURAFA Report to the University Committee." University of Wisconsin–Madison. https://wiscape.wisc.edu/docs/WebDispenser /wiscapedocuments/curafa-ideal-class-report.pdf?sfvrsn=2.

Complete College America. 2013. "The Power of 15 Credits: Enrollment Intensity and Postsecondary Student Achievement." http://www .completecollege.org/docs/CCA%20Intensity%20Brief-April3.pdf.

———. 2013. "State Financial Aid Programs and Full-Time Attendance". Policy Brief. http://www.completecollege.org/pdfs/2013-10-14-state-aid.pdf.

———. 2011. "Three Policies to Reduce Time to Degree." http://www

.completecollege.org/docs/Three%20Policies%20to%20Reduce%20Time%20to%20Degree%20-%20Nate%20Johnson.pdf.

Corcoran, M. E., and A. Chaudry. 1997. "The Dynamics of Childhood Poverty." *Children and Poverty* 7 (2): 40–54.

Cornwell, C., and D. B. Mustard. 2004. "Georgia's HOPE Scholarship and Minority and Low-Income Students: Program Effects and Proposed Reforms." In *State Merit Scholarship Programs and Racial Inequality*, ed. D. E. Heller and P. Marin, 77–100. Cambridge, MA: Civil Rights Project at Harvard University.

———. 2007. "Merit-Based College Scholarships and Car Sales." *Education Finance and Policy* 2 (2): 133–51.

Cottom, T. M. 2016. *Lower Ed: How For-Profit Colleges Deepen Inequality in America*. New York: The New Press.

Council of Economic Advisers. 2014. *The Economics of Early Childhood Investments*. http://permanent.access.gpo.gov/gpo43212/the_economics_of_early_childhood_investments.pdf.

Creswell, J., and V. Clark. 2011. *Designing and Conducting Mixed Methods Research*. Thousand Oaks, CA: Sage Publications.

Crow, M. M., and W. B. Dabars. 2015. *Designing the New American University*. Baltimore, MD: Johns Hopkins University Press.

Cunningham, A. F., and D. A. Santiago. 2008. *Student Aversion to Borrowing: Who Borrows and Who Doesn't*. Report by Institute for Higher Education Policy and Excelencia in Education. Institute for Higher Education Policy, Washington, DC. http://www.ihep.org/sites/default/files/uploads/docs/pubs/studentaversiontoborrowing.pdf.

Dachelet, K., and S. Goldrick-Rab. 2015. "Emergency Aid Programs for College Success." Wisconsin HOPE Lab Working Paper, University of Wisconsin–Madison.

Dadgar, M. 2012. "The Academic Consequences of Unemployment for Students Enrolled in Community College." CCRC Working Paper no. 46. Community College Research Center, Columbia University, New York.

Dannenberg, M., and M. Voight. 2013. "Doing Away with Debt: Using Existing Resources to Ensure College Affordability for Low and Middle-Income Families." Education Trust, Washington, DC. http://edtrust.org/wp-content/uploads/2013/10/Doing_Away_With_Debt.pdf.

Darolia, R. 2014. "Working (and Studying) Day and Night: Heterogeneous Effects of Working on the Academic Performance of Full-Time and Part-Time Students." *Economics of Education Review* 38:38–50.

Darolia, R., C. Koedel, P. Martorell, K. Wilson, and F. Perez-Arce. 2015. "Do Employers Prefer Workers Who Attend For-Profit Colleges? Evidence from a Field Experiment." *Journal of Policy Analysis and Management* 34 (3): 881–903.

Davis, J. 2012. *School Enrollment and Work Status: 2011.* U.S. Census Bureau, American Community Survey Briefs. https://www.census.gov/prod /2013pubs/acsbr11-14.pdf.

Day, D., V. Allen, and R. Henken. 2010. "Milwaukee Area Technical College's Fiscal Condition: Growing Demand, Shrinking Resources." Public Policy Forum, Milwaukee, WI. http://publicpolicyforum.org/sites/default/files /MATCFiscalCondition.pdf.

Delaney, J. A. 2014. "The Role of State Policy in Promoting College Affordability." *Annals of the American Academy of Political and Social Science* 655 (1): 56–78

Dynarski, S., and D. Deming. 2009. "Into College, Out of Poverty? Policies to Increase the Postsecondary Attainment of the Poor." NBER Working Paper no. 15387. National Bureau of Economic Research, Washington, DC.

Deming, D. J., C. Goldin, and L. F. Katz. 2011. "The For-Profit Postsecondary School Sector: Nimble Critters or Agile Predators." NBER Working Paper no. 17710. National Bureau of Economic Research, Cambridge, MA.

———. 2013. "For-Profit Colleges." *Future of Children* 23 (1): 137–63.

Deming, D. J., N. Yuchtman, A. Abulafi, C. Goldin, and L. F. Katz. 2014. "The Value of Postsecondary Credentials in the Labor Market: An Experimental Study." NBER Working Paper no. 20528. National Bureau of Economic Research, Cambridge, MA.

DeParle, J. 2012. "Two Classes, Divided by 'I Do.'" *New York Times,* July 14.

DeSimone, J. S. 2008. "The Impact of Employment during School on College Student Academic Performance." NBER Working Paper no. 14006. National Bureau of Economic Research, Cambridge, MA.

DesJardins, S. L., B. P. McCall, M. Ott, and J. Kim. 2013. "A Quasi-Experimental Investigation of How the Gates Millennium Scholars Program Is Related to College Students' Time Use and Activities." *Educational Evaluation and Policy Analysis* 32 (4): 456–75.

Desmond, M., and R. Turley. 2009. "The Role of Familism in Explaining the Hispanic-White College Application Gap." *Social Problems* 56 (2): 311–34.

Desrochers, D. M. 2014. "Labor Intensive or Labor Expensive? Changing Staffing and Compensation Patterns in Higher Education." Delta Cost Project, February Issue Brief. American Institutes for Research. http:// www.deltacostproject.org/sites/default/files/products/DeltaCostAIR _Staffing_Brief_2_3_14.pdf.

Deverey, S. n.d. "Promoting College Affordability and Limiting Over-Borrowing." White Paper. National Council of Higher Education Resources. http://c.ymcdn.com/sites/www.ncher.us/resource/collection /3906FBDA-E100-4C41-B678-885A90AEF105/05_White_Paper --Promoting_College_Affordability_-_FINAL.pdf.

Dick, A. W., and A. S. Edlin. 1997. "The Implicit Taxes from College Financial Aid." *Journal of Public Economics* 65 (3): 295–322.

DiMaggio, P., and J. Mohr. 1985. "Cultural Capital, Educational Attainment, and Marital Selection." *American Journal of Sociology* 90 (6): 1231–61.

Donatante, B. 2013. "Why Millennials Can't Grow Up." *Slate.* http://www .slate.com/articles/health_and_science/medical_examiner/2013/12 /millennial_narcissism_helicopter_parents_are_college_students_bigger _problem.html.

Douglass, J. A. 2007. *The Conditions for Admission: Access, Equity and the Social Contract of Public Universities.* Palo Alto, CA: Stanford University Press.

Dresser, L., J. Rogers, and E. Navot. 2010. *The State of Working Wisconsin 2010.* Center on Wisconsin Strategy, University of Wisconsin–Madison. http:// www.cows.org/_data/documents/1112.pdf

Dubas, J. S., and A. C. Petersen. 1996. "Geographical Distance from Parents and Adjustment during Adolescence and Young Adulthood." *New Directions for Child and Adolescent Development* 71:3–19.

Duncan, G. J., K. Magnuson, and E. Votruba-Drzal. 2014. "Boosting Family Income to Promote Child Development." *Future of Children* 24 (1): 99–120.

Dynarski, S. 2014. "An Economist's Perspective on Student Loans in the United States." ES Working Paper Series, September. Brookings Institution, Washington, DC. http://www.brookings.edu/~/media/research /files/papers/2014/09/economist_perspective_student_loans_dynarski /economist_perspective_student_loans_dynarski.pdf.

———. 2014. "PLUS Loans Are Not Student Aid." *The Cranky Analyst* (blog). http://susandynarski.blogspot.com/2014/04/plus-loans-are-not-student -aid.html.

———. 2014. "Rising Inequality in Postsecondary Education." Social Mobility Memo, February 13. Brookings Institution, Washington, DC. http:// www.brookings.edu/blogs/social-mobility-memos/posts/2014/02/13 -inequality-in-postsecondary-education.

———. 2015. "Why Students with Smallest Debts Have the Larger Problem." *New York Times,* August 31.

Dynarski, S. M., S. W. Hemelt, and J. M. Hyman. 2013. "The Missing Manual: Using National Student Clearinghouse Data to Track Postsecondary Outcomes." NBER Working Paper no. 19552. National Bureau of Economic Research, Cambridge, MA.

Dynarski, S., and J. Scott-Clayton. 2013. "Financial Aid Policy: Lessons from Research." NBRR Working Paper no. 18710. National Bureau of Economic Research, Cambridge, MA.

———. 2014. "There Is a Simpler Way for Students to Apply for Financial Aid." *New York Times,* June 20.

Dynarski, S., and M. Wiederspan. 2012. "Student Aid Simplification: Looking Back and Looking Ahead." *National Tax Journal* 65 (1): 211–34.

Eagan, K., E. B. Stolzenberg, J. J. Ramirez, M. C. Aragon, M. R. Suchard, and S. Hurtado. 2014. "The American Freshman: National Norms Fall 2014." Higher Education Research Institute, University of California, Los Angeles.

eCampus News. 2015. "Will Further State Higher-Ed Funding Cuts Hinder Economic Innovation?" April 21. http://www.ecampusnews.com/funding /state-highered-funding-785/.

Economic Policy Institute. 2014. "College Wage Premium, by Gender, 1973– 2013." The State of Working America. http://stateofworkingamerica.org /chart/swa-wages-figure-4n-college-wage-premium/.

Edin, K., and M. Kefalas. 2011. *Promises I Can Keep: Why Poor Women Put Motherhood before Marriage*. Berkeley: University of California Press.

Edin, K., and L. Lein. 1997. *Making Ends Meet*. New York: Russell Sage Foundation.

———. 1997. "Work, Welfare and Single Mothers' Economic Survival Strategies." *American Sociological Review* 63 (2): 253–66.

Education Commission of the States. n.d. "50-State Policy Database." http:// statefinancialaidredesign.org/state-financial-aid-database/.

Ehrenberg, R. G., and D. R. Sherman. 1987. "Employment While in College, Academic Achievement and Postcollege Outcomes." *Journal of Human Resources* 22 (1): 1–23.

Eisenberg, D., E. Golberstein, and S. E. Gollust. 2007. "Help-Seeking and Access to Mental Health Care in a University Student Population." *Medical Care* 45 (7): 594–601.

Ensign, R. L. 2012. "How Not to Blow It with Financial Aid: Common Mistakes Parents and Students Make When Seeking Help with College Costs." *Wall Street Journal*, September 10.

Equifax. 2015. "Different Credit Scores: Why Are There Different Credit Scores?" Last updated March 18, 2015. https://help.equifax.com/app /answers/detail/a_id/21/~/different-credit-scores

Erickson, J. 2014. "The Middle-Class Squeeze: A Picture of Stagnant Incomes, Rising Costs, and What We Can Do to Strengthen America's Middle Class." Center for American Progress. https://www.americanprogress.org /issues/economy/report/2014/09/24/96903/the-middle-class-squeeze/.

Evans, B. 2013. "SMART Money: Do Financial Incentives Encourage College Students to Study Science?" Working Paper. http://cepa.stanford.edu /sites/default/files/Evans%20Job%20Market%20Paper.pdf.

Evans, B. A. 2015. "Public Testimony on Hunger in Higher Education." Wisconsin HOPE Lab, University of Wisconsin–Madison. https://hungercommis

sion.rti.org/Portals/0/SiteHtml/Activities/WrittenTestimony/Written
/NCH_Written_Testimony_Brooke_Evans.pdf.

Fain, P. 2015. "Boom Budget in California." *Inside Higher Ed*, March 15.

———. 2015. "Free Community College Catches On." *Inside Higher Ed*, July 9.

Fastweb. 2011. "Profile of Pell Grant Recipients Quick Reference Guide."
http://www.finaid.org/educators/ProfileofPellGrantRecipients.pdf.

Federal Education Budget Project. 2015. "Background and Analysis: Federal
Student Loan Default Rates." New America Foundation, Washington, DC.

Feldman, B. 2012. "Why You Should Take Out Student Loans for College."
ReadyForZero (blog). October 3. http://blog.readyforzero.com/why-you
-should-take-out-student-loans-to-pay-for-college/.

Field, K. 2011. "Education Department Chases 'Pell Runners' Who Threaten
Aid Program." *Chronicle of Higher Education*, August 28.

File, T., and C. Ryan. 2014. *Computer and Internet Use in the United States: 2013*.
American Community Survey Reports, ACS-28. Washington, DC: U.S.
Census Bureau.

Fingerhut, E., and R. Kazis. 2012. *Tying Funding to Community College Outcomes: Models, Tools, and Recommendations for States*. Boston: Jobs for the
Future.

Finkelmeyer, T. 2010. "Is College Still Worth It?" *Cap Times*, July 21. http://
host.madison.com/ct/news/local/education/university/is-college-still
-worth-it/article_4758d0d7-7459-50d6-bade-41ec17f58ffd.html.

Flanagan, C., A. Fuligni, and A. Schulenberg. 1993. "Residential Setting and
Parent-Adolescent Relationships during the College Years." *Journal of Youth
Adolescence* 22 (2): 171–89.

Folbre, N. 2010. "The Retirement Zone: Losing Means-Tested Benefits." *New
York Times*, March 22.

Folbre, N. 2010. *Saving State U: Fixing Public Higher Education*. New York: The
New Press.

Fortelny, G., and M. Parkinson. 2014. "FAFSA and Application Processing
System Update." Prepared for 2014 Federal Student Aid Training Conference for Financial Aid Professionals. https://www.isac.org/dotAsset
/e5fd41e4-5f29-493e-9eb5-060827f24879.pdf.

Foster, J. B. 2006. "The Household Debt Bubble." *Monthly Review*, vol. 58, no. 1.

Freudenberg, N., L. Manzo, H. Jones, A. Kwan, E. Tsui, and M. Gagnon.
2011. "Food Insecurity at CUNY: Results from a Survey of CUNY Undergraduate Students." Healthy CUNY Initiative, City University of New
York. http://www.gc.cuny.edu/CUNY_GC/media/CUNY-Graduate
-Center/PDF/Centers/Center%20for%20Human%20Environments
/cunyfoodinsecurity.pdf.

Friend, R. C. 2014. "Death Knell for Pell: A Taxpayer's Justification for Pulling

the Plug." California Policy Center. http://californiapolicycenter.org
/death-knell-for-pell-a-taxpayers-justification-for-pulling-the-plug/.

Fuligni, A. J., and S. Pedersen. 2002. "Family Obligation and the Transition to
Young Adulthood." *Developmental Psychology* 38:856–68.

Fuligni, A. J., G. J. Rivera, and A. Leininger. 2007. "Family Identity and the
Educational Progress of Adolescents from Asian and Latin American Back-
grounds." In *Contesting Stereotypes and Creating Identities: Social Categories,
Social Identities, and Educational Participation*, ed. A. Fuligni. New York:
Russell Sage Foundation Press.

Fuligni, A. J., V. Tseng, and M. Lam. 1999. "Attitudes toward Family Obligations among American Adolescents with Asian, Latin American, and European Backgrounds." *Child Development* 70:1030–44.

Gaines, A., C. A. Robb, L. L. Knol, and S. Sickler. 2014. "Examining the Role
of Financial Factors, Resources and Skills in Predicting Food Security
Status among College Students." *International Journal of Consumer Studies*
38 (4): 374–84.

Gault, B., L. Reichlin, and S. Roman. 2014. "College Affordability for Low Income Adults: Improving Returns on Investment for Families and Society."
Lumina Foundation. https://www.luminafoundation.org/files/publications
/ideas_summit/College_Affordability_for_Low-Income_Adults.pdf.

Gault, B., Reichlin, L., Reynolds, E., and Froehner, M. 2014. "Campus Child
Care Declining Even as Growing Numbers of Parents Attend College."
Institute for Women's Policy Research, Washington, DC.

Geckeler, C., C. Beach, M. Pih, and L. Yan. 2008. "Helping Community College Students Cope with Financial Emergencies: Lessons from the Dreamkeepers and Angel Fund Emergency Financial Aid Programs." MDRC
Report. MDRC, New York. http://knowledgecenter.completionbydesign
.org/sites/default/files/336%20Geckeler%20Beach%202008.pdf.

Gehl, R. 2013. "Pell Grant Abuse Widespread." *Downtrend.com* (blog). http://
downtrend.com/robertgehl/pell-grant-abuse-widespread.

Geiger, R. L. 2010. "Postmortem for the Current Era: Change in American
Higher Education, 1980–2010." Working Paper no. 3. Center for the Study
of Higher Education, Pennsylvania State University, Philadelphia.

Geronimus, A. R., J. Bound, and L. J. Neidert. 1995. "On the Validity of Using
Census Geocode Characteristics to Proxy Individual Socioeconomic Char-
acteristics." NBER Working Paper no. 189. National Bureau of Economic
Research, Cambridge, MA.

Gilbert, C., and D. E. Heller. 2010. "The Truman Commission and Its Impact
on Federal Higher Education Policy from 1947 to 2010." Paper presented
at the Association for the Study of Higher Education Annual Conference,
Indianapolis, IN, November 19.

Gilens, M. 1999. *Why Americans Hate Welfare: Race, Media, and the Politics of Antipoverty Policy*. Chicago: University of Chicago Press.

Gilford, T. T., and A. Reynolds. 2011. "My Mother's Keeper: The Effects of Parentification on Black Female College Students." *Journal of Black Psychology* 37:55–77.

Gillborn, D., and D. Youdell. 1999. *Rationing Education*. New York: Open University Press.

Glynn, S. J. 2012. "Families Need More Help to Care for Their Children." Fact Sheet: Child Care, Center for American Progress. https://www.americanprogress.org/issues/labor/news/2012/08/16/11978/fact-sheet-child-care/.

Goldin, C., and L. F. Katz. 2010. *The Race between Education and Technology*. Cambridge, MA: Harvard University Press.

Goldrick-Rab, S. 2006. "Following Their Every Move: How Social Class Shapes Postsecondary Pathways." *Sociology of Education* 79 (1): 61–79.

———. 2015. "Free College Plan Will Help, Not Hurt, Low-Income Students." *Talkpoverty.org* (blog). February 24. http://talkpoverty.org/2015/02/24/free-college-plan/.

———. 2015. "Testimony to Advisory Committee on Student Financial Assistance." *Sara Goldrick-Rab* (blog). September 11. https://medium.com/@saragoldrickrab/testimony-to-advisory-committee-on-student-financial-assistance-a5f9c10d473a.

Goldrick-Rab, S., and K. Broton. 2015. "To Cut Costs, College Students Are Buying Less Food and Even Going Hungry." *The Conversation*, September 25. http://theconversation.com/to-cut-costs-college-students-are-buying-less-food-and-even-going-hungry-47975.

Goldrick-Rab, S. and K. Broton. 2015. "Hungry, Homeless, and in College." *New York Times*, December 4.

Goldrick-Rab, S., K. Broton, and D. Eisenberg. 2015. "Hungry to Learn: Addressing Food and Housing Insecurity among Undergraduates." White Paper. Wisconsin HOPE Lab, University of Wisconsin–Madison. http://wihopelab.com/publications/Wisconsin_HOPE_Lab_Hungry_To_Learn.pdf

Goldrick-Rab, S., K. Broton, and V. M. Frank. 2014. "Single Stop USA's Community College Initiative." Implementation Assessment. Wisconsin HOPE Lab, University of Wisconsin–Madison. http://wihopelab.com/projects/SSUSA-Implementation-Assessment.pdf.

Goldrick-Rab, S., K. Broton, and C. Gates. 2013. "Clearing the Path to a Brighter Future: Addressing Barriers to Community College Access and Success." Report prepared for the Association of Community College Trustees and Single Stop.

Goldrick-Rab, S., D. N. Harris, and P. A. Trostel. 2009. "Why Financial Aid Matters (or Does Not) for College Success: Toward a New Interdisciplinary Perspective." In *Higher Education: Handbook of Theory and Research*, vol. 24, ed. John C. Smart, 1–45. Berlin: Springer.

Goldrick-Rab, S., R. Kelchen, D. Harris, and J. Benson. 2016. "Reducing Income Inequality in Higher Education: Experimental Evidence on the Impact of Financial Aid on College Completion." *American Journal of Sociology*, vol. 121, no. 6 (forthcoming).

Goldrick-Rab, S., R. Kelchen, and B. Hosch. 2015. "Information, Accountability, and College Costs: The Need for Standardized Living Cost Calculations in Higher Education." Policy Brief 15-01. Wisconsin HOPE Lab, University of Wisconsin–Madison.

Goldrick-Rab, S., R. Kelchen, and J. Houle. 2014. "The Color of Student Debt: Implications of Federal Loan Program Reforms for Black Students and Historically Black Colleges and Universities." Working Paper. Wisconsin HOPE Lab, University of Wisconsin–Madison.

Goldrick-Rab, S., and N. Kendall. 2014. *F2CO Redefining College Affordability: Securing America's Future with a Free Two-Year College Option.* April. http://www.wihopelab.com/publications/Redefining_College_Affordability.pdf.

———. 2015. "The Real Price of College." College Completion Series: Part Two. The Century Foundation. https://tcf.org/content/report/the-real-price-of-college.

Goldrick-Rab, S., and T. Kolbe. 2015. "Rethinking State Support for Higher Ed." *Inside Higher Ed*, September 28.

Goldrick-Rab, S., J. Minikel-Lacocque, and P. Kinsley. 2011. "Managing to Make It: The College Trajectories of Traditional-Age Students with Children." Working Paper 1, Wisconsin Financial Aid Study, University of Wisconsin–Madison. http://www.wiscaid.org/documents/appam_parentpaper_wiscaid.pdf.

Goldrick-Rab, S., and F. Pfeffer. 2009. "Beyond Access: Explaining Social Class Differences in College Transfer." *Sociology of Education* 82 (2): 101–25.

Goldrick-Rab, S., L, Schudde, and J. Stampen. 2014. "Creating Cultures of Affordability: Can Institutional Incentives Improve the Effectiveness of Financial Aid?" In *Reinventing Student Aid for the 21ˢᵗ Century*, ed. A. Kelly and S. Goldrick-Rab, 191–206. Cambridge, MA: Harvard University Press.

Goldrick-Rab, S., and K. Sorenson. 2010. "Unmarried Parents in College." *Fragile Families* 20 (2): 179–203.

Goldring, C. 2004. "Family and Collective Remittances to Mexico: A Multi-Dimensional Typology." *Development and Change* 35 (4): 79–84.

Goldstein, J. 2012. "How the Poor, the Middle Class and the Rich Spend Their Money." *Planet Money*. National Public Radio. August 1. http://www.npr.org/sections/money/2012/08/01/157664524/how-the-poor-the-middle-class-and-the-rich-spend-their-money.

Gould, E. 2012. "High-Scoring, Low-Income Students No More Likely to Complete College Than Low-Scoring, Rich Students." *Working Economics* (blog). March 9. Economic Policy Institute. http://www.epi.org/blog /college-graduation-scores-income-levels/#sthash.LbT9vNw1.dpuf.

Gould, E., and T. Cooke. 2015. "High Quality Child Care Is Out of Reach for Working Families." Economic Policy Institute. http://www.epi.org /publication/child-care-affordability/.

Grace, F. 2004. "Help for Sleep-Deprived Students." *CBS News*. April 19. http://www.cbsnews.com/stories/2004/04/19/health/main612476 .shtml.

Graham, H. D. 2011. *The Uncertain Triumph: Federal Education Policy in the Kennedy and Johnson Years*. Chapel Hill: University of North Carolina Press.

Green, J., and J. Densley. 2014. "Pell Grant Fraud Awareness: White-Collar Crime Challenges." *FBI Law Enforcement Bulletin*. February. https://leb .fbi.gov/2014/february/pell-grant-fraud-awareness-white-collar-crime -challenges.

Grigsby, M. 2009. *College Life through the Eyes of Students*. Albany, NY: SUNY Press.

Gurda, J. 1999. *The Making of Milwaukee*. Madison: University of Wisconsin Press.

Haley-Lock, A. 2012. "The Structural Contexts of Low-Wage Work: Restaurant Employment Practices across Firm Geography, Size, and Ownership Status." *Journal of Poverty* 16:447–68.

Haney-Lopez, I. 2014. *Dog Whistle Politics: How Coded Racial Appeals Have Reinvented Racism and Wrecked the Middle Class*. Oxford: Oxford University Press.

Harvard Energy and Facilities. 2015. "Dorm Crew." http://www .energyandfacilities.harvard.edu/facilities-services/dorm-crew.

Haskins, R. 2008. "Education and Economic Mobility." In *Getting Ahead or Losing Ground: Economic Mobility in America*, ed. J. Isaacs, I. V. Sawhill, and R. Haskins, chap. 8. [Washington, DC]: Brookings Institution.

Haughwout, A., D. Lee, J. Scally, and W. van der Klaauw. 2015. "Student Loan Borrowing and Repayment Trends, 2015." Press Briefing Presentation, Federal Reserve Bank of New York. https://www.newyorkfed.org /medialibrary/media/newsevents/mediaadvisory/2015/Student-Loan -Press-Briefing-Presentation.pdf

Haushofer, J., and J. Shapiro. 2013. "Household Response to Income Changes: Evidence from an Unconditional Cash Transfer Program in Kenya." Princeton University Publication, Princeton, NJ.

Hearn, J. C., and J. M. Holdsworth. 2004. "Federal Student Aid: The Shift from Grants to Loans." In *Public Funding of Higher Education: Changing*

Contexts and New Rationales, ed. E. P. St. John and M. D. Parsons, 40–74. Baltimore, MD: Johns Hopkins University Press.

Heller, D. E. 2006. "Merit Aid and College Access." Paper presented at the Symposium on the Consequences of Merit-Based Student Aid, Wisconsin Center for the Advancement of Postsecondary Education, Madison, March 1.

Heller, D. E., and P. Marin, eds. 2004. *State Merit Scholarship Programs and Racial Inequality.* Cambridge, MA: Civil Rights Project at Harvard University.

Hicks, E. 2015. "Inequality, Nonlinearity, and the College Experience: An Investigation of Reverse Transfer in the American Higher Education System." PhD diss., University of Iowa.

Higher Educational Aids Board. 2012. *Report of the 2012 Commission on Financial Aid Consolidation and Modernization.* Madison: State of Wisconsin Higher Educational Aids Board.

Higher Education Aids Board. 2010. *Wisconsin State Student Financial Data for 2008–2009.* Board Report #10–19. Madison: State of Wisconsin Higher Educational Aids Board. http://www.heab.state.wi.us/docs/board/0910/rep1019.pdf.

Hillman, N. 2014. "College on Credit: A Multi-Level Analysis of Student Loan Default." *Review of Higher Education* 37 (2): 169–95.

———. 2014. "Differential Impacts of College Ratings: the Case of Education Deserts." Working Paper, Educational Leadership and Policy Analysis, University of Wisconsin–Madison. https://news.education.wisc.edu/docs/WebDispenser/news-connections-pdf/crp---hillman---draft.pdf?sfvrsn=6.

Hiltonsmith, R. 2015. "Pulling up the Higher Ed Ladder: Myth and Reality in the Crisis of College Affordability." Demos, New York. http://www.demos.org/publication/pulling-higher-ed-ladder-myth-and-reality-crisis-college-affordability.

Hiltonsmith, R., and T. Draut. 2014. "The Great Cost Shift Continues: State Higher Education Funding after the Recession." Demos, New York. http://www.demos.org/publication/great-cost-shift-continues-state-higher-education-funding-after-recession.

Hoeft, M. 2014. *The Bingo Queens of the Oneida: How Two Moms Started Tribal Gaming in Wisconsin.* Madison: Wisconsin Historical Society Press.

Horn, L. J., and A. G. Malizio. 1998. *Undergraduates Who Work: National Postsecondary Student Aid Study, 1996.* NCES 98-084. [Washington, DC]: U.S. Department of Education, Office of Educational Research and Improvement, National Center for Education Statistics.

Hout, M. 2012. "Social and Economic Returns to College Education in the United States." *Annual Review of Sociology* 38:379–400.

Hoxby, C., and C. Avery. 2013. "The Missing "One-Offs": The Hidden Supply of High-Achieving Low-Income Students." Brookings Paper on Economic Activity, Spring. Brookings Institution, Washington, DC.

Huelsman, M. 2014. "The Affordable College Compact: A Federal-State Partnership to Increase State Investment and Return to Debt-Free Public Higher Education." Demos, New York. http://www.demos.org/publication/affordable-college-compact.

———. 2015. "The Debt Divide: The Racial and Class Bias Behind the "New Normal" of Student Borrowing." Demos, New York. http://www.demos.org/publication/debt-divide-racial-and-class-bias-behind-new-normal-student-borrowing.

Huff, R. P. 2004. "Research Corner: The Evolution of the Process of Allocating Federal Campus-Based Student Financial Aid to Postsecondary Education Institutions." *Journal of Student Financial Aid* 34 (2): 35–42.

Hughes, R., I. Serebryanikova, K. Donaldson, and M. Leveritt. 2011. "Student Food Insecurity: The Skeleton in the University Closet." *Nutrition and Dietetics* 68 (1): 27–32.

Hull, J. 2014. "The Path Least Taken: At a Glance." Center for Public Education, Alexandria, VA.

Hunt, R. 2015. "How to Fix the Student Loan Mess." *CNBC*, September 21. http://www.cnbc.com/2015/09/21/how-to-fix-the-student-loan-mess-commentary.html.

Hutcheson, P. A. 2011. "Goals for United States Higher Education: From Democracy to Globalisation." *History of Education: Journal of the History of Society* 40 (1): 45–57.

———. 2002. "The 1947 President's Commission and the National Rhetoric on Higher Education Policy." *History of Higher Education Annual: 2002*, ed. Roger L. Geiger, 91–109. New Brunswick, NJ: Transaction Publishers.

———. 2007. "Setting the Nation's Agenda for Higher Education: A Review of Selected National Commission Reports, 1947–2006." *History of Education Quarterly* 47 (3): 359–67.

Indiana University Newsroom. 2015. "Indiana University to Freeze Undergraduate Tuition for Hoosier Residents Attending IU Bloomington." Press release. May 20. http://news.iu.edu/releases/iu/2015/05/tuition-freeze-undergraduate.shtml.

Ingles, S. J., and B. Dalton. 2013. *High School Longitudinal Study of 2009, First Follow-up: A First Look at Fall 2009 Ninth-Graders in 2012*. NCES Publication no. 2014-360. Washington, DC: National Center for Education Statistics, U.S. Department of Education. http://nces.ed.gov/pubsearch.

InsideHigherEd. 2015. "Parents Are Saving Less for College." April 29. https://www.insidehighered.com/quicktakes/2015/04/29/parents-are-saving-less-college.

Institute for College Access and Success. 2014. "Data Show No Evidence of 'Over-Borrowing' at Community Colleges: Colleges Don't Need More Authority to Limit Student Aid Options." July 12. http://ticas.org/sites/default/files/Over-borrowing_at_community_colleges.pdf.

———. 2012. "House FY13 Budget Increases Uncertainty and Complexity in the Financial Aid Process for Students with Family Incomes over $20,000." Fact sheet. July 15. http://ticas.org/sites/default/files/legacy/files/pub/Auto-zero_EFC_rollback_in_House_FY13_Budget_07-15-12.pdf.

———. 2011. "Pell Grant Provisions Prevent Student Abuse." July 18. http://ticas.org/sites/default/files/legacy/files/pub/Protections_against_Pell_abuse_one-pager_July_18-_updated.pdf.

———. 2014. "Private Loans: Facts and Trends." June. http://ticas.org/sites/default/files/pub_files/private_loan_facts_trends.pdf.

———. 2014. "Quick Facts about Student Debt." March 31. http://ticas.org/content/pub/quick-facts-about-student-debt.

———. 2009. "Student Debt and the Class of 2008." The Project on Student Debt. http://ticas.org/sites/default/files/pub_files/classof2008.pdf.

Jack, A. 2016. "Same Folks Different Strokes: Class, Culture, and the New Diversity at Elite Colleges and Universities." PhD diss., Harvard University, Cambridge, MA.

Jacob, B., B. McCall, and K. M. Stange. 2013. "College as Country Club: Do Colleges Cater to Students' Preferences for Consumption?" NBER Working Paper no. 18745. National Bureau of Economic Research, Cambridge, MA.

Jaschik, S. 2009. "Higher Learning, Greater Good." *Inside Higher Ed.* April 21 https://www.insidehighered.com/news/2009/04/21/mcmahon.

Jenkins, D., T. Leinbach, P. M. Crosta, D. Prince, and D. Whittaker. 2006. "Using Census Data to Classify Community College Students by Socio-economic Status and Community Characteristics." CCRC Research Tools no. 1. Community College Research Center, Columbia University, New York.

Jiang, Y., M. Ekono, and C. Skinner. 2015. "Basic Facts about Low-Income Children: Children Aged 12 through 17 Years, 2013." National Center for Children in Poverty Columbia University, New York.

Johnson, D. S., T. M. Smeeding, and B. B. Torrey. 2005. "Economic Inequality through the Prisms of Income and Consumption." *Monthly Labor Review* 128 (4): 11.

Johnson, J., J. Rochkind, A. N. Ott, and S. DuPont. n.d. *With Their Whole Lives Ahead of Them: Myths and Realities about Why So Many Students Fail to Finish College.* A Public Agenda Report for the Bill & Melinda Gates Foundation. New York: Public Agenda. http://www.publicagenda.org/files/theirwholelivesaheadofthem.pdf.

Johnson, N. 2014. "College Costs, Prices and the Great Recession." Lumina Issue Paper. Lumina Foundation, Indianapolis, IN. https://www
.luminafoundation.org/files/publications/issue_papers/College_Costs
_Prices_and_the_Great_Recession.pdf.

Johnson, W. R. 2006. "Are Public Subsidies to Higher Education Regressive?" *Education Finance and Policy* 1 (3): 288–315.

Johnston, D. C. 2015. "Income Inequality: 1 Inch to 5 Miles." Tax Analysts, February 25. http://www.taxanalysts.com/www/features.nsf/Articles
/C52956572546624F85257B1D004DE3FC.

Joyce, A. 2014. "How Helicopter Parents Are Ruining College Students." *New York Times*, September 2.

Jyoti, D. F., E. A. Frongillo, and S. J. Jones. 2005. "Food Insecurity Affects School Children's Academic Performance, Weight Gain, and Social Skills." *Journal of Nutrition* 135 (12): 2831–39.

Kahn, L. B. 2010. "The Long-Term Labor Market Consequences of Graduating from College in a Bad Economy." *Labor Economics* 17 (2): 303–16.

Kalenkoski, C. M., and S. W. Pabilonia. 2010. "Parental Transfers, Student Achievement, and the Labor Supply of College Students." *Journal of Population Economics* 23 (2): 469–96.

Katsinas, S. G., J. E. Davis, J. N. Friedel, J. P. Koh, and P. D. Grant. 2012. "The Impact of New Pell Grant Restrictions on Community Colleges: A Three State Study of Alabama, Arkansas, and Mississippi." Education Policy Center Report, University of Alabama, Tuscaloosa.

Katz, M. B. 2013. *The Undeserving Poor: America's Enduring Confrontation with Poverty*. Oxford: Oxford University Press.

Kearney, M. S., B. Hershbein, and E, Jacome. 2015. "Profiles of Change: Employment, Earnings, and Occupations from 1990–2013." *Up Front* (blog). Brookings Institution, Washington, DC. http://www.brookings.edu/blogs
/up-front/posts/2015/04/21-employment-earnings-occupations-profiles
-from-1990-to-2013-kearney-hershbein.

Kelchen, R. 2014. "Exploring Trends and Alternative Allocation Strategies for Campus-Based Financial Aid Programs." Working Paper. Department of Education Leadership, Management and Policy, Seton Hall University, South Orange, NJ.

———. 2015. "Financial Need and Aid Volatility among Students with Zero Expected Family Contribution." *Journal of Student Financial Aid* 44 (3): 179–201.

———. 2015. "Is 'Overborrowing' for College an Epidemic?" *Kelchen on Education* (blog). May 20. https://kelchenoneducation.wordpress.com/2015
/05/20/is-overborrowing-for-college-an-epidemic/.

———. 2014. "A Longitudinal Analysis of Student Fees: The Roles of States and Institutions." Working Paper. Department of Education Leadership, Management and Policy, Seton Hall University, South Orange, NJ.

Kelchen, R., and S. Goldrick-Rab. 2015. "Accelerating College Knowledge: A Fiscal Analysis of a Targeted Early Commitment Pell Grant Program." *Journal of Higher Education* 86 (2): 199–232.

Kelchen, R., B. J. Hosch, and S. Goldrick-Rab. 2014. "The Costs of College Attendance: Trends, Variation, and Consistency in Institutional Living Cost Allowances." Working Paper. Wisconsin HOPE Lab, University of Wisconsin–Madison.

Kelly, A. P., and S. Goldrick-Rab. 2014. *Reinventing Financial Aid: Charting a New Course to College Affordability.* Cambridge, MA: Harvard University Press.

Kena, G., L. Musu-Gillette, J. Robinson, A. Rathbun, Z. Wang, J. Zhang, S. Wilkinson-Flicker, and E. E. Valez. 2015. *The Condition of Education 2015.* NCES publication no. 2015-144. Washington, DC: U.S. Department of Education, National Center for Education Statistics. http://nces.ed.gov /pubsearch.

Kertscher, T. 2015. "Ron Johnson Is against All Government-Assisted Student Loans, U.S. Senate Rival Russ Feingold Says." PolitiFact Wisconsin, June 19. http://www.politifact.com/wisconsin/statements/2015/jun/19/russ -feingold/ron-johnson-against-all-government-assisted-studen/.

Keyes, S. 2012. "Rep. Virginia Foxx on People with Student Loans: 'I Have Very Little Tolerance' for Them." Think Progress, April 13. http:// thinkprogress.org/education/2012/04/13/464154/foxx-tolerance -student-loans/.

King, C., P. L. Chase-Lansdale, and M. Small, eds. 2013. *Two Generations, One Future: An Anthology from the Ascend Fellowship.* Washington, DC: Ascend at the Aspen Institute. https://www.dropbox.com/s/se9i606hmnurc54 /Anthology_Final.pdf?dl=0.

Kinsley, P., and S. Goldrick-Rab. "Making the Grade: The Academic Side of College Life among Financial Aid Recipients." Working Paper. Wisconsin HOPE Lab, University of Wisconsin–Madison.

Kinsley, P. M. 2014. "The Pull of Home: Family Dynamics and the Initial College Experiences of Low-Income Undergraduates." PhD diss., University of Wisconsin–Madison.

Kirshstein, R. J., and S. Hurlburt. 2012. "Revenues: Where Does the Money Come From?" A Delta Data Update, 2000–2010. American Institutes for Research, Washington, DC.

Kochhar, R., and Fry, R. 2014. "Wealth Inequality Has Widened along Racial, Ethnic Lines since End of Great Recession." Pew Research Center, Washington, DC.

Kohn, M. L. 1963. "Social Class and Parent-Child Relationships: An Interpretation." *American Journal of Sociology* 68 (4): 471–80.

Konczal, M. 2011. "Could We Redirect Tax Subsidies to Pay for Free College?" *Next New Deal* (blog). Roosevelt Institute. December 20. http://rooseveltinstitute.org/rortybombcould-we-redirect-tax-subsidies-pay-free-college/.

Kreuger, P. M., and E. M. Friedman. 2009. "Sleep Duration in the United States: A Cross-Sectional Population-Based Study." *American Journal of Epidemiology* 169 (9): 1052–63.

Kuh, G. D., T. M. Cruce, R. Shoup, J. Kinzie, and R. M. Gonyea. 2008. "Unmasking the Effects of Student Engagement on First-Year College Grades and Persistence." *Journal of Higher Education* 79 (5): 540–63.

Kuh, G. D., S. O. Ikenberry, N. A. Jankowski, T. R. Cain, P. T. Ewell, P. Hutchings, and J. Kinzie. 2015. *Using Evidence of Student Learning to Improve Higher Education.* San Francisco: Jossey-Bass.

Kutz, M., J. McNerney, H. Badger, J. Cameron, E. McMeen, A. Richards, B. Sugarman, and R. Wiita. 2014. "Meet Us in the Middle: Affordability for the Working Student." Report of the ASUW Student Debt Reduction Working Group. Associated Students of the University of Washington, Seattle.

Lambert, M. T. 2014. *Privatization and the Public Good: Public Universities in the Balance.* Cambridge, MA: Harvard Education Press.

Lambert, S. J., P. J., Fugiel, and J. R. Henly. 2014. "Precarious Work Schedules among Early-Career Employees in the U.S.: A National Snapshot." Research Brief. Employment Instability, Family Well-Being, and Social Policy Network, University of Chicago.

———. 2014. "Schedule Unpredictability among Early Career Workers in the U.S. Labor Market: A National Snapshot." Research Brief. Employment Instability, Family Well-Being, and Social Policy Network, University of Chicago.

Lambert, S. J., A. Haley-Lock, and J. R. Henly. 2012. "Schedule Flexibility in Hourly Jobs: Unanticipated Consequences and Promising Directions." *Community, Work and Family* 15 (3): 293–315.

Lareau, A. 2011. *Unequal Childhoods: Class, Race, and Family Life*, 2nd ed., with an update a decade later. Berkeley: University of California Press.

Lauff, E., E. M. Christopher and S. J. Ingels. 2014. *Education Longitudinal Study of 2002: A First Look at 2002 High School Sophomores 10 Years Later.* NCES 2014-363. U.S. Department of Education. Washington, DC: National Center for Education Statistics. http://nces.ed.gov/pubsearch.

Leonhardt, D. 2015. "College for the Masses." *New York Times*, April 24.

Leos-Urbel, J., A. E. Schwartz, M. Weinstein, and S. Corcoran. 2013. "Not Just for Poor Kids: The Impact of Universal Free School Breakfast on Meal

Participation and Student Outcomes." *Economics of Education Review* 36:88–107.

Leuven, E., H. Oosterbeek, and B. van der Klaauw. 2010. "The Effect of Financial Rewards on Students' Achievement: Evidence from a Randomized Experiment." *Journal of the European Economic Association* 8 (6): 1243–65.

Levine, J. 2013. *Ain't No Trust*. Berkeley: University of California Press.

Levy, F., L. Mishel, and J. Bernstein. 1996. *Running in Place: Recent Trends in U.S. Living Standards*. Collingdale, PA: Diane Publishing Company.

Lewin, T. 2014. "Most College Students Don't Earn a Degree in 4 Years, Study Finds." *New York Times*, December 1.

Light, Audrey. 1998. "Estimating Returns to Schooling: When Does the Career Begin?" *Economics of Education Review* 17 (1): 31–45.

Lindsay, P. M. 2015. "Attending to Attendance." *Chronicle of Higher Education*, February 4.

Lindsay, T. K. 2014. "Two Years after College, Too Many Grads Are Still 'Adrift.'" *The Hill* (blog). October 1. http://thehill.com/blogs/pundits -blog/education/219352-two-years-after-college-too-many-grads-are-still -adrift.

Lindsley, K., and C. King. 2014. "Food Insecurity of Campus-Residing Alaskan College Students." *Journal of the Academy of Nutrition and Dietetics* 114 (9): A94.

Lino, Mark. 2014. *Expenditures on Children by Families, 2013*. Miscellaneous Publication no. 1528-2013. Alexandria, VA: Center for Nutrition Policy and Promotion, U.S. Department of Agriculture. http://www.cnpp.usda.gov /sites/default/files/expenditures_on_children_by_families/crc2013.pdf.

Livingston, G. 2014. "Fewer Than Half of U.S. Kids Today Live in a 'Traditional' Family." Fact Tank, December 22. Pew Research Center. http:// www.pewresearch.org/fact-tank/2014/12/22/less-than-half-of-u-s-kids -today-live-in-a-traditional-family/.

Logan, J. R., and B. J. Stults. 2011. "The Persistence of Segregation in the Metropolis: New Findings from the 2010 Census." Census Brief prepared for US2010 Project. http://www.s4.brown.edu/us2010/Data/Report/report2.pdf.

Lohfink, M. M., and M. B. Paulsen. 2005. "Comparing the Determinants of Persistence for First-Generation and Continuing-Generation Students." *Journal of College Student Development* 46 (4): 409–28.

Looney, A., and C. Yannelis. 2015. "A Crisis in Student Loans? How Changes in the Characteristics of Borrowers and in the Institutions They Attended Contributed to Rising Loan Defaults." Brookings Paper on Economic Activity. Brookings Institution, Washington, DC.

Loss, C. P. 2012. *Between Citizens and the State: The Politics of American Higher Education in the 20th Century*. Princeton, NJ: Princeton University Press.

Lower-Basch, E. 2013. "Goals for TANF Reauthorization." TANF Policy Brief.

Center for Law and Social Policy, Washington, DC. http://www.clasp.org /resources-and-publications/files/TANF-Reauthorization-Goals.pdf.

Lower-Basch, E., and H. Lee. 2014. "College Student Eligibility." SNAP Policy Brief. Center for Law and Social Policy, Washington, DC. http://www .clasp.org/resources-and-publications/publication-1/SNAP-Policy-Brief _College-Student-Eligibility-Update.pdf.

Lucas, S. R. 2001. "Effectively Maintained Inequality: Education Transitions, Track Mobility, and Social Background Effects." *American Journal of Sociology* 106 (6): 1642–90.

Lumina Foundation. 2015. *A Stronger America through Higher Education*. Indianapolis, IN: Lumina Foundation.

Luzer, D. 2011. "The Lie about Pell Grants, the 'Welfare of the 21st Century.'" *Washington Monthly*, April 5.

Lythcott-Haims, J. 2015. *How to Raise an Adult: Break Free of the Overparenting Trap and Prepare Your Kid for Success*. New York: Henry Holt and Co.

Ma, J., S. Baum, M. Pender, and D. Bell. 2015. *Trends in College Pricing: 2015*. College Board. http://trends.collegeboard.org/sites/default/files/trends -student-aid-web-final-508-2.pdf.

MacDonald, I. H., R. Malatest, R. Assels, R. Baroud, L. Gong, L. Bernstein, and C. Price. 2009. *FINAL Impacts Report: Foundations for Success Project*. Report prepared by R. A. Malatest and Associates, Ltd., for the Canada Millennium Scholarship Foundation. Ottawa: Canada Millennium Scholarship Foundation.

Mai, M. 2014. "Hunger in Higher Education: Food Insecurity among Wisconsin Low-Income Undergraduates." Master's Thesis, University of Wisconsin–Madison.

Marcus, J. 2015. "Confusing Financial Aid Letters Leave Students, Parents Adrift." nprEd: How Learning Happens, National Public Radio. May 7.
———. 2014. "Taxpayer-Funded Aid Program Benefits Richer Students." *Hechinger Report*, January 1.

Maroto, M. E., A. Snelling, and H. Linck. 2014. "Food Insecurity among Community College Students: Prevalence and Association with Grade Point Average." *Community College Journal* 39 (6): 515–26.

Martin, R. 2009. "UW System's Growth Agenda for Wisconsin." Presentation by University of Wisconsin System, February 9. https://www .wisconsin.edu/news/download/news_documents/2009/february_2009 /GrowthAgendaActionSteps.pdf.

Mayer, A. K., R. Patel, and M. Gutierrez. 2015. "Four-Year Effects on Degree Receipt and Employment Outcomes from a Performance-Based Scholarship Program in Ohio." MDRC Working Paper. MDRC, New York. http://www.mdrc.org/publication/four-year-effects-degree-receipt-and -employment-outcomes-performance-based-scholarship.

McCluskey, N. 2008. "Higher Math." *Washington Times*, July 31.

McDonald, M., and P. Brady. 2014. "The Plural of Anecdote Is Data (Except for Student Debt)." Hamilton Place Strategies. http://www.hamiltonplacestrategies.com/sites/default/files/newsfiles/Media%20coverage%20of%20student%20debt_1.pdf.

McMahon, W. W. 2009. *Higher Learning, Greater Good*. Baltimore, MD: Johns Hopkins University Press.

McMillion, R. 2004. *The Role of Work and Loans in Paying for an Undergraduate Education: Observations from the 2003–2004 National Postsecondary Student Aid Study (NPSAS)*. TG Research and Analytical Services. Texas Guaranteed Student Loan Corporation, Round Rock, TX.

Mettler, S. 2014. *Degrees of Inequality: How the Politics of Higher Education Sabotaged the American Dream*. New York: Basic Books.

———. 2005. *Soldiers to Citizens: The G.I. Bill and the Making of the Greatest Generation*. Oxford: Oxford University Press.

Miles, M., and A. Huberman. 1994. *Qualitative Data Analysis: An Expanded Sourcebook*. Thousand Oaks, CA: Sage Publications.

Miller, C., M. Binder, V. Harris, and K. Krause. 2011. *Staying on Track: Early Findings from a Performance-Based Scholarship Program at the University of New Mexico*. MDRC Report. MDRC, New York. http://www.mdrc.org/sites/default/files/full_511.pdf.

Miller, H., and Goldrick-Rab, S. 2015. "Making Sense of Transitions: An Examination of Transfer among Economically Disadvantaged Undergraduates." Presented at 2015 meetings of the American Educational Research Association, Chicago, April 16–20.

Miller, N. L., and L. G. Shattuck. 2005. "Sleep Patterns of Young Men and Women Enrolled at the United States Military Academy: Results from Year 1 of a 4-Year Longitudinal Study." *Sleep* 28 (7): 837–41.

Mills, M. 2014. "Study Finds Working and Paying for College Nearly Impossible." *USA Today*, April 15.

Milwaukee Area Technical College. 2014. "MATC Fast Facts: Data from 2013–14 Fiscal Year." http://www.matc.edu/discover_matc/upload/2013-2014_Fast_Facts.pdf.

———. 2014. "College Enrollment." http://www.matc.edu/administration/upload/MATC_Dashboard_FY2014-College-Enrollment.pdf.

———. 2014. "Student Persistence." http://www.matc.edu/administration/upload/MATC_Dashboard_FY2014-Students-Persistence.pdf.

———. 2014. "Student Retention Trends." http://www.matc.edu/administration/upload/MATC_Dashboard_FY2014-Student-Retention.pdf

———. 2013. "Transforming Lives: 2013 Annual Report." http://www.matc.edu/discover_matc/upload/2013_AnnualReport.pdf.

Milwaukee Business Journals. 2007. "Domtar to Close Wisconsin Mill, Cut 500 State Jobs." December 13.

Milwaukee Department of City Development. 2003. *2000 City of Milwaukee Urban Atlas: Summary of Population and Housing Characteristics Based on the 2000 U.S. Census.* Milwaukee: Department of City Development, Long Range Planning Division.

Mitchell, J. 2013. "Panel Calls for Overhauling Student Grants." *Wall Street Journal,* April 9.

———. 2013. "Student-Aid Scams Targeted by Schools, Government." *Wall Street Journal,* June 23.

———. 2014. "Student Loans Entice Borrowers More for Cash Than a Degree: Low-Cost Debt Proves a Draw for Some Caught Up in Weak Job Market." *Wall Street Journal,* March 2.

Mitchell, M., V. Palacios, and M. Leachman. 2014. "States Are Still Funding Higher Education below Pre-Recession Levels." Center on Budget and Policy Priorities, Washington, DC. http://www.cbpp.org/sites/default /files/atoms/files/5-1-14sfp.pdf.

Moore, R. L., A. H. Studenmund, and T. Slobko. 1991. "The Effect of the Financial Aid Package on the Choice of a Selective College." *Economics of Education Review* 10 (4): 311–21.

Mortensen, T. 2014. "Financial Barriers to Higher Education by Parental Income and Institutional Level/Control, 1990 to 2012." Postsecondary Education Opportunity Paper no. 263. May. Washington, DC: Pell Institute for the Study of Opportunity in Higher Education.

———. 2014. "State, Local and Federal Fiscal Support for Higher Education per $1000 of State Personal Income, FY1961 to FY2014." Postsecondary Education Opportunity, spreadsheet. May. Washington, DC: Pell Institute for the Study of Opportunity in Higher Education.

———. 2015. "State Investment and Disinvestment in Higher Education, 1969–2015." Postsecondary Education Opportunity Paper no. 260. February. Washington, DC: Pell Institute for the Study of Opportunity in Higher Education.

———. 2011. "Time Use of Full-Time College Students Ages 18 to 24 Years, 2003 to 2009." Postsecondary Education Opportunity Paper no. 223. January. Washington, DC: Pell Institute for the Study of Opportunity in Higher Education.

Mortimer, J. 2003. *Working and Growing Up in America.* Cambridge, MA: Harvard University Press.

Mosle, A., N. Patel, and J. Stedron. 2014. *Top Ten for 2Gen: Policy Ideas and Principles to Advance Two-Generation Efforts.* Ascend at the Aspen Institute, Washington, DC.

Mullainathan, S., and Shafir, E. 2013. *Scarcity: Why Having Too Little Means So Much*. New York: Picador Press.

Murphy, J. M., C. A. Wehler, M. E. Pagano, M. Little, R. E. Kleinman, and M. S. Jellinek. 1998. "Relationship between Hunger and Psychological Functioning in Low-Income American Children." *Journal of the American Academy of Child and Adolescent Psychiatry* 37 (2): 163–70.

Muthén, L. K., and B. O. Muthén. 2012. *Mplus: Statistical Analysis with Latent Variables: User's Guide*. Los Angeles: Muthén & Muthén.

Nam, Y., D. Hamilton, W. A. Darity, and A. E. Price 2015. "Bootstraps Are for Black Kids: Race, Wealth, and the Impact of Intergenerational Transfers on Adult Outcomes." Research Brief. Insight Center for Economic Development. http://www.insightcced.org/wp-content/uploads/2015/07/Bootstraps-are-for-Black-Kids-Sept.pdf.

National Association of Student Financial Aid Administrators. 2014. "The Campus-Based Formula." NASFAA Task Force Report. NASFAA, Washington, DC.

———. 2012. "Debt Load and Overborrowing." Annotated Bibliography. NASFAA, Washington, DC. https://www.nasfaa.org/uploads/documents/debt_annotated_bib.pdf.

———. 2014. "Developing the Cost of Attendance, in Preparation for NCAA Rule Changes." NASFAA Updates, Monograph 24. NASFAA, Washington, DC.

———. 2014. *Financial Aid for Unaccompanied Homeless Youth: A Survey Report*. Washington, DC: NASFAA. http://www.naehcy.org/sites/default/files/dl/fafsa-survey-report.pdf.

———. 2015. "President Obama: Feds to Allow Use of Prior-Prior Year Income Data on the FAFSA Starting in 2017–18 School Year." Press release. September 13. http://www.nasfaa.org/ppy_nasfaa_press_release.

———. 2015. *2015 Administrative Burden Survey*. http://www.nasfaa.org/uploads/documents/ektron/f5fdae89-a23f-4572-9724-15e5a9f614d2/0d73bf4cd48a43a6a9414b6ec1a6ab9d2.pdf.

National Association of State Student Grant and Aid Programs. 2013. *44th Annual Survey Report on State-Sponsored Student Financial Aid*. file:///C:/Users/zipt/Downloads/NASSGAP_Report_12-13%20(1).pdf.

———. 2011. *42nd Annual Survey Report on State-Sponsored Student Financial Aid*. file:///C:/Users/zipt/Downloads/NASSGAP_Report_10-11.pdf.

National Center for Education Statistics. 1900s–. *National Postsecondary Student Aid Study NPSAS*. Washington, DC: National Center for Education Statistics, Office of Educational Research and Improvement, U.S. Department of Education.

National Center for Public Policy and Higher Education. 2003. "Five National

Trends." http://www.highereducation.org/reports/losing_ground_up
/national_trends.shtml

National Council on State Legislatures. 2015. "Performance-Based Funding
for Higher Education." July 31. National Council on State Legislatures,
Denver, CO. http://www.ncsl.org/research/education/performance
-funding.aspx.

National Scholarship Providers Association. 2013. "Impact of Award Displace-
ment on Students and Their Families: Recommendations for Colleges,
Universities, Policymakers and Scholarship Providers." White Paper.
September 16. National Scholarship Providers Association, Boulder, CO.
https://scholarshipproviders.org/Content/Content/6/Documents
/NSPA%20Impact%20of%20Award%20Displacement%209.2013.pdf.

Nelson, L. 2015. "Our Greedy Colleges." *Vox*, August 12.

———. 2013. "Two Pell Grants?" *Inside Higher Ed*, April 9.

———. 2015. "Pell Grant Program Overview." http://atlas.newamerica.org
/federal-pell-grant-program.

Newfield, C. 2008. *Unmaking the Public University: The Forty Year Assault on
the Middle Class*. Cambridge, MA: Harvard University Press.

Newman, K. S. 2012. *The Accordion Family: Boomerang Kids, Anxious Parents,
and the Private Toll of Global Competition*. Boston: Beacon Press.

New York Times. 1874. "College Education." November 26.

———. 1907. "Students Who Fight Their Way through College." February 24.

New York University Faculty against the Sexton Plan. 2015. *The Art of the
Gouge: How NYU Squeezes Billions from Its Students and Where That Money
Goes*. NYUFASP, New York. http://cs.nyu.edu/faculty/davise/NYU2031
/GougeMcNallyJackson.pdf.

Noah, T. 2013. "Everyone's a Queen: The Republicans' Rapidly Expanding
Definition of Welfare." *New Republic*, April 1.

Novack, J., and S. Fitch. 2009. "When Work Doesn't Pay for the Middle
Class." *Forbes*, September 17.

O'Brien, R. L., and D. S. Pedulla. 2010. "Beyond the Poverty Line." *Stanford
Social Innovation Review* (fall).

Office of Senator Tammy Baldwin. 2015. "Sens. Baldwin, Booker and Rep.
Scott Introduce America's College Promise Act to Make Higher Education
More Accessible and Affordable." Press release. July 8. http://www.baldwin
.senate.gov/press-releases/baldwin-americas-college-promise-act-to-make
-higher-education-more-accessible-and-affordable-.

Oreopoulos, P., and U. Petronijevic. 2013. "Making College Worth It: A
Review of Research on the Returns to Higher Education." NBER Working
Paper 19053. National Bureau of Economic Research, Cambridge, MA.

Oreopoulos, P., T. Von Wachter, and A. Heisz. 2006. "The Short- and Long-

Term Career Effects of Graduating in a Recession" *American Economic Journal: Applied Economics* 4 (1): 1–29.

Orszag, J. M., P. R. Orszag, and D. M. Whitmore. 2001. "Learning and Earning: Working in College." Commissioned by Upromise, Inc. https://www.brockport.edu/career01/upromise.htm.

Orszag, P. R., and T. J. Kane. 2003. "Higher Education Spending: The Role of Medicaid and the Business Cycle." Brookings Policy Brief Series no. 124. Brookings Institution, Washington, DC.

Page, B. I., L. M. Bartels, and J. Seawright. 2013. "Democracy and the Policy Preferences of Wealthy Americans." *Perspectives on Politics* 11 (1): 51–73.

Paris, K. A. 1985. *A Political History of Vocational, Technical, and Adult Education in Wisconsin*. Madison: Wisconsin Board of Vocational, Technical, and Adult Education.

Pascarella, E. T., and C. Blaich. 2013. "Lessons from the Wabash National Study of Liberal Arts Education." *Change: The Magazine of Higher Learning* (March–April).

Pascarella, E. T., and P. T. Terenzini. 2005. *A Third Decade of Research*. Vol. 2 of *How College Affects Students*. San Francisco: Jossey-Bass.

Patel, R., L. Richburg-Hayes, E. de la Campa, and T. Rudd. 2013. "Performance-Based Scholarships: What Have We Learned? Interim Findings from the PBS Demonstration." MDRC Policy Brief. MDRC, New York. http://www.mdrc.org/sites/default/files/pbs_what_have_we_learned.pdf.

Patel, R., and I. Valenzuela. 2013. *Moving Forward: Early Findings from the Performance-Based Scholarship Demonstration in Arizona*. MDRC Report. MDRC, New York. http://www.mdrc.org/sites/default/files/Moving_Forward_FR_0.pdf.

Patton-López, M. M., D. F. López-Cevallos, D. L. Cancel-Tirado, and L. Vazquez. 2014. "Prevalence and Correlates of Food Insecurity among Students Attending a Midsize Rural University in Oregon." *Journal of Nutrition Education and Behavior* 36 (3): 209–14.

Pawasarat, J., and L. M. Quinn. 2013. "Wisconsin's Mass Incarceration of African American Males: Workforce Challenges for 2013." Employment Training Institute, University of Wisconsin–Milwaukee. https://www4.uwm.edu/eti/2013/BlackImprisonment.pdf.

Payment Accuracy. n.d. "High-Error Programs." https://paymentaccuracy.gov/high-priority-programs.

Pell Institute for the Study of Opportunity in Higher Education and Penn-AHEAD. 2015. *Indicators of Higher Education Equity in the United States: 45 Year Trend Report*. Rev. ed. Pell Institute for the Study of Opportunity in Higher Education, Washington, DC; PennAHEAD, Philadelphia. http://

www.pellinstitute.org/downloads/publications-Indicators_of_Higher
_Education_Equity_in_the_US_45_Year_Trend_Report.pdf.

Perna, L. W. 2010. "Understanding the Working College Student." *Academe* 96 (4): 30–33.

Petrilli, M. 2013. "Pell Grants Shouldn't Pay for Remedial College." *Bloomberg Business*, April 30.

Pew Charitable Trusts. 2012. "Pursuing the American Dream: Economic Mobility across Generations." July 9. Pew Charitable Trusts Economic Mobility Project. http://www.pewtrusts.org/en/research-and-analysis /reports/0001/01/01/pursuing-the-american-dream.

Pew Research Center. 2014. *The Rising Cost of Not Going to College.* http://www .pewsocialtrends.org/files/2014/02/SDT-higher-ed-FINAL-02-11-2014.pdf.

Pew Research Center for the People and the Press. 2014. "January 2014 Political Survey, Final Topline." http://www.people-press.org/files/legacy -questionnaires/1-30-14%20Iraq%20and%20Afghanistan%20Topline %20for%20Release.pdf.

Pfeffer, F. T., S. Danziger, and R. F. Schoeni. 2013. "Wealth Disparities before and after the Great Recession." *Annals of the American Academy of Political and Social Science* 650 (1): 98–123.

Philanthropy News Digest. 2007. "Fund for Wisconsin Scholars Establishes $175 Million Endowment for Scholarships." December 19. http://philanthropy newsdigest.org/news/fund-for-wisconsin-scholars-establishes-175-million -endowment-for-scholarships.

Philbrick, J. D. 1885. *City School Systems in the United States: Issues 1–3.* Washington, DC: Government Printing Office.

Pike, G. R., and G. D. Kuh. 2005. "First- and Second-Generation College Students: A Comparison of Their Engagement and Intellectual Development." *Journal of Higher Education* 76 (3): 276–30.

Piketty, T. 2014. *Capital in the Twenty-First Century.* Cambridge, MA: Harvard University Press.

Piven, F. F., and R. Cloward. 1993. *Regulating the Poor: The Functions of Public Welfare.* New York: Vintage Books.

Planty, M, W. Hussar, T. Snyder, G. Kena, A. KewalRamani, J. Kemp, K. Bianco, and R. Dinkes. 2009. *The Condition of Education 2009.* NCES 2009-081. National Center for Education Statistics, Institute of Education Sciences, U.S. Department of Education. Washington, DC.

Porter, E. 2013. "The Measure of Our Poverty." *Economix* (blog). *New York Times*, September 20. http://economix.blogs.nytimes.com/2013/09/20 /the-measure-of-our-poverty/?_r=0.

President's Commission on Higher Education. 1947. *Higher Education for American Democracy.* Vols. 1–6. Washington, DC: Government Printing Office.

————. 1947. *Higher Education for American Democracy*. Vol. 2. New York: Harper & Brothers Publishers.

Preston, M. 2006. "The Most 'Representative' State: Wisconsin." "The Morning Grind," July 27. CNN. http://www.cnn.com/2006/POLITICS/07/27/mg.thu/index.html?eref=aol.

Price, D., M. Long, S. S. Quast, J. McMaken, and G. Kioukis. 2014. "Public Benefits and Community Colleges: Lessons from the Benefits Access for College Completion Evaluation." Final Evaluation Report. OMG Center for Collaborative Learning, Philadelphia. http://www.equalmeasure.org/wp-content/uploads/2014/12/BACC-Final-Report-FINAL-111914.pdf.

Raver, C. C., A. L. Roy, and E. Pressler. 2014. "Struggling to Stay Afloat: Dynamic Models of Poverty-Related Adversity and Childhood Outcomes." In *Families in an Era of Increasing Inequality*, ed. P. R. Amato, A. Booth, S. M. McHale, and J. Van Hook, 201–12. Cham, Switzerland: Springer International Publishing.

Redden, E. 2008. "Many Community Colleges Opt Out of Loan Program." *Inside Higher Ed*, April 17.

Reed, M., and D. Cheng. *Student Debt and the Class of 2008*. The Project on Student Debt, Institute for College Access and Success. http://files.eric.ed.gov/fulltext/ED509357.pdf.

Reed, M., and D. Cochrane. 2014. *Student Debt and the Class of 2013*. The Project on Student Debt, Institute for College Access and Success. http://ticas.org/sites/default/files/legacy/files/pub/classof2013.pdf.

Reese, W. J. 1999. *The Origins of the American High School*. New Haven, CT: Yale University Press.

Renfro, S., and A. Armour-Garb. 1999. "The History of Open Admissions and Remedial Education at the City University of New York." Chap. 3 of *Open Admissions and Remedial Education at the City University of New York*. [New York]: [Office of the Mayor]. http://www.nyc.gov/html/records/rwg/cuny/html/admissions.html.

Republican National Committee. 2015. "Republican Platform: Renewing American Values." https://gop.com/platform/renewing-american-values/#Item17.

Resnikoff, N. 2014. "The Hunger Crisis in America's Universities." "Climbing Out," August 8. MSNBC. Last updated September 3, 2014. http://www.msnbc.com/msnbc/the-hunger-crisis-americas-universities.

Richards, E. 2015. "Wisconsin Black Suspension Rate Highest in U.S. for High Schools." *Milwaukee Journal Sentinel*, March 1.

————. 2014. "Wisconsin Graduation Rate Rises while MPS' Edges Down." *Milwaukee Journal Sentinel*, May 8, 2014.

Richburg-Hayes, L., T. Brock, A. LeBlanc, C. Paxon, C. E. Rouse, and L. Barrow. 2009. "Rewarding Persistence: Effects of a Performance-

Based Scholarship Program for Low-Income Parents." MDRC Report. MDRC, New York. http://www.mdrc.org/sites/default/files/rewarding _persistence_fr.pdf.

Richburg-Hayes, L., R. Patel, T. Brock, E. de la Campa, T. Rudd, and I. Valenzuela. 2015. "Providing More Cash for College: Interim Findings from the Performance-Based Scholarship Demonstration in California." MDRC Report. MDRC, New York.

Ripley, A. 2015. "The Upwardly Mobile Barista." *Atlantic Magazine*, May.

Robinson, J., and D. Cheston. 2012. "Pell Grants: Where Does All the Money Go?" Pope Center Series on Higher Education. John William Pope Center for Higher Education Policy, Raleigh, NC. http://www.johnlocke.org /acrobat/pope_articles/pell_report_final.pdf.

Rosas, M., and F. A. Hamrick. 2002. "Postsecondary Enrollment and Academic Decision-Making: Family Influences on Women College Students of Mexican Descent." *Equity and Excellence in Education* 35 (1): 59–69.

Saez, E., and G. Zucman. 2014. "Exploding Wealth Inequality in the United States." Washington Center for Equitable Growth, Washington, DC. http://equitablegrowth.org/exploding-wealth-inequality-united-states/.

———. 2014. "Wealth Inequality in the United States Since 1913: Evidence from Capitalized Income Tax Data." NBER Working Paper no. 20625. National Bureau of Economic Research, Cambridge, MA.

Salam, R. 2012. "If You're Going to Accept Direct Loans and Pell Grants, You Should Tell Us If Students Are Actually Learning Something." *National Review*, February 7.

Sallie Mae Corporation. 2014. *How America Pays for College: Sallie Mae's National Study of College Students and Parents.* http://news.salliemae.com /files/doc_library/file/HowAmericaPaysforCollege2014FNL.pdf.

Samuels, R. 2013. *Why Public Higher Education Should Be Free: How to Decrease Cost and Increase Quality at American Universities.* New Brunswick, NJ: Rutgers University Press.

Sanchez, B. 2006. "Makin' It in College: The Value of Significant Individuals in the Lives of Mexican American Adolescents." *Journal of Hispanic Higher Education* 5 (1): 38–67.

Savidge, N. 2015. "Regents Give UW–Madison OK to Enroll More Out-of-State Students." *Wisconsin State Journal*, October 10.

Sawhill, I. V. 2015. "Make Pell Grants Conditional on College Readiness." Social Mobility Memo, October 20. Brookings Institution, Washington, DC. http://www.brookings.edu/blogs/social-mobility-memos/posts /2015/10/20-conditional-pell-grants-sawhill.

———. 2014. "Target Aid to Students Most Likely to Succeed." *EducationNext*, vol. 14, no. 2.

Schneider, B. 2005. "Social Capital in Action: Alignment of Parental Support in Adolescents' Transition to Postsecondary Education." *Social Forces* 84 (2): 1181–1206.

Schoeni, R. F., and K. Ross. 2005. "Material Assistance from Families during the Transition to Adulthood." In *On the Frontier of Adulthood*, ed. R. A. Settersten, F. F. Furstenberg, and R. G. Rumbaut, 396–416. Chicago: University of Chicago Press.

Scholzman, K. L., S. Verba, and H. E. Brady. 2012. *The Unheavenly Chorus: Unequal Political Voice and the Broken Promise of American Democracy.* Princeton, NJ: Princeton University Press.

Schram, S. 2000. *After Welfare: The Culture of Postindustrial Social Policy.* New York: New York University Press.

———. 2002. *Praxis for the Poor: Piven and Cloward and the Future of Social Science in Social Welfare.* New York: New York University Press.

———. 1995. *Words of Welfare: The Poverty of Social Science and the Social Science of Poverty.* Minneapolis: University of Minnesota Press.

Schuck, P. H., and R. J. Zeckhauser. 2006. *Targeting in Social Programs: Avoiding Bad Bets, Removing Bad Apples.* Washington, DC: Brookings Institution.

Schudde, L., and J. Scott-Clayton. 2014. "Pell Grants as Performance-Based Aid? An Examination of Satisfactory Academic Progress Requirements in the Nation's Largest Need-Based Aid Program." Center for Analysis of Postsecondary Education and Employment Working Paper. Community College Research Center, Teachers College, Columbia University, New York.

Scott, D. 2013. "Universities Test 'Tuition Guarantees' to Reduce Debt." *Governing the States and Localities*, February 12.

Scott-Clayton, J. 2011. "The Causal Effect of Federal Work-Study Participation: Quasi-Experimental Evidence from West Virginia." *Educational Evaluation and Policy Analysis* 33 (4): 506–27.

———. 2011. "A Jobs Program in Need of Reform." *New York Times*, September 9.

Scott-Clayton, J., and V. Minaya. 2015. "Should Student Employment be Subsidized? Conditional Counterfactuals and the Outcomes of Work-Study Participation." *Economics of Education Review*, in press.

Selingo, J. J. 2014. "The Rich Get Richer in Higher Ed: 40 Colleges Hold Two-Thirds of the Wealth, and Growing." *Washington Post*, April 24.

Setzer, R., and R. O'Sullivan. 2014. "A Federal Work Study Reform Agenda to Better Serve Low-Income Students." Young Invincibles. September 22. http://younginvincibles.org/a-federal-work-study-reform-agenda-to-better-serve-low-income-students/.

Shapiro, D., A. Dundar, P. K. Wakhungu, X. Yuan, and A. Harrell. 2015.

"Transfer and Mobility: A National View of Student Movement in Postsec-ondary Institutions, Fall 2008 Cohort." National Student Clearinghouse Signature Report no. 9. https://nscresearchcenter.org/signaturereport9/.

Shapiro, T. M., T. Maschede, and S. Osoro. 2014. "The Widening Racial Wealth Gap: Why Wealth Is Not Color Blind." In *The Assets Perspective*, ed. R. Cramer and T. Williams, 99–122. New York: Palgrave Macmillan.

Shaw, K. M, S. Goldrick-Rab, C. Mazzeo, and J. Jacobs. 2006. *Putting Poor People to Work: How the Work-First Idea Eroded College Access for the Poor.* New York: Russell Sage Foundation.

Skocpol, T. 1990. "Sustainable Social Policy: Fighting Poverty without Poverty Programs." *The American Prospect* (summer).

Sloane, W. 2013. "Lunch for 9 Million?" *Inside Higher Ed*, December 20.

Smith, J. 2013. "$2.2 Million in Grants Awarded to Area College Students Who Quit or Failed." *WECT News*, November 20.

Soss, J., R. C. Fording, and S. F. Schram. 2011. *Disciplining the Poor: Neoliberal Paternalism and the Persistent Power of Race.* Chicago: University of Chicago Press.

Stack, C. B. 1974. *All Our Kin.* New York: Harper & Row.

Stack, C. B., and L. M. Burton. 1993. "Kinscripts." *Journal of Comparative Family Studies* 24 (2): 157–70.

Stange, K. 2015. "Differential Pricing in Undergraduate Education: Effects on Degree Production by Field." *Journal of Policy Analysis and Management* 34 (1): 107–35.

Stern, D., and Y.-F. Nakata. 1991. "Paid Employment among U.S. College Students: Trends, Effects, and Possible Causes." *Journal of Higher Education* 62 (1): 25–43.

Stevens, M. L., E. A. Armstrong, and R. Arum. 2008. "Sieve, Incubator, Temple, Hub: Empirical and Theoretical Advances in the Sociology of Higher Education." *Annual Review of Sociology* 34:127–51.

Stevenson, J., J. Dykema, K. Cyffka, L. Klein, and S. Goldrick-Rab. 2012. "What Are the Odds? Lotteries versus Cash Incentives—Response Rates, Cost and Data Quality for a Web Survey of Low-Income Former and Current College." Paper presented at the 67th annual meeting of the American Association for Public Opinion Research, Orlando Florida, May 18.

Stinebrickner, R., and T. R. Stinebrickner. 2003. "Working during School and Academic Performance. *Journal of Labor Economics* 21 (2): 473–91.

Stratford, M. 2015. "Debt-Free and (Mostly) Detail-Free." *Inside Higher Ed*, June 19.

———. 2015. "GOP Would Freeze Pell." *Inside Higher Education*, March 18.

———. 2014. "Higher Ed Cuts in GOP Budget." *Inside Higher Ed*, April 2.

Stuber, J. M. 2011. *Inside the College Gates: How Class and Culture Matter in Higher Education.* Lexington Books.

Suárez-Orozco, C., and Suárez-Orozco, M. 1995. *Transformations: Immigration, Family Life, and Achievement Motivation among Latino Adolescents*. Palo Alto, CA: Stanford University Press.

Substance Abuse and Mental Health Services Administration. 2014. *Results from the 2013 National Survey on Drug Use and Health: Summary of National Findings*. NSDUH Series H-48, HHS Publication no. (SMA) 14-4863. Rockville, MD: Substance Abuse and Mental Health Services Administration.

Swartz, T. T., M. Kim, M. Uno, J. Mortimer, and K. B. O'Brien. 2011. "Safety Nets and Scaffolds: Parental Support in the Transition to Adulthood." *Journal of Marriage and Family* 73 (2): 414–29.

Swift, A. 2014. "Americans Rely Less on Credit Cards Than in Previous Years." Gallup, April 25. http://www.gallup.com/poll/168668/americans-rely-less-credit-cards-previous-years.aspx.

Taylor, P., R. Kochhar, R. Fry, G. Valesco, and S. Motel. 2011. "Wealth Gaps Rise to Record Highs between Whites, Blacks and Hispanics." Pew Research Center, Washington, DC.

Terkel, A. 2011. "Rep. Denny Rehberg: Pell Grants Are Becoming 'The Welfare of the 21st Century.'" *Huffington Post*, April 1.

Thaler, R. H., and E. J. Johnson. 1990. "Gambling with the House Money and Trying to Break Even: The Effects of Prior Outcomes on Risky Choice." *Management Science* 36 (6): 643–60.

Thelin, J. R. 2013. *A History of American Higher Education*. Baltimore, MD: Johns Hopkins University Press.

Tighe, Kathleen. 2013. "Student Aid Fraud." Interview by Pedro Echevarria, August 29. C-SPAN. http://www.c-span.org/video/?314776-6/student-aid-fraud.

Tilly, C. 1998. *Durable Inequality*. Berkeley: University of California Press.

Tinto, V. 1993. *Leaving College: Rethinking the Causes and Cures of Student Attrition*. Vol. 2. Chicago: University of Chicago Press.

———. 2007. "Research and Practice of Student Retention: What Next?" *Journal of College Student Retention* 8 (1): 1–19.

Torinus, J. 2015. "Can Ray Cross Reposition the UW System?" *Urban Milwaukee*, April 2.

Truth in Tuition Act of 2010. 2010. H.R. 4546. 111th Cong.

Tucker, S. M. 2014. "Getting More Low-Income Students into College Isn't about Money, It's about the Curriculum." *Forbes*, March 4.

Turley, R. N. L. 2009. "College Proximity: Mapping Access to Opportunity." *Sociology of Education* 82 (2): 126–46.

Turley, R. N. L., and G. Wodtke. 2010. "College Residence and Academic Performance: Who Benefits from Living on Campus?" *Urban Education* 45 (4): 506–32.

Turner, S. 2004. "Going to College and Finishing College: Explaining Different Educational Outcomes." In *College Choices: The Economics of Where to Go, When to Go, and How to Pay for It,* ed. M. Hoxby, 13–62. Chicago: University of Chicago Press.

U.S. Census Bureau. 2015. "American Community Survey." Last revised June 22, 2015. https://www.census.gov/programs-surveys/acs/about.html.

U.S. Census Bureau. 2015. "2009–2013 5-Year American Community Survey."

U.S. Congress, Joint Economic Committee. 2015. *The Economic Exposure of Federal Credit Programs: Hearing Before the Joint Economic Committee, Congress of the United States,* 114th Congress, 1st sess., June 17. (Testimony of Jason Delisle, Director, Federal Education Budget Project.)

———. 2015. *Financing Higher Education: Exploring Current Challenges and Potential Alternatives.* September 30. (Testimony of Andrew P. Kelly, Resident Scholar and Director, Center on Higher Education Reform, American Enterprise Institute.)

U.S. Department of Education. 2013. "Access Matters." http://files.eric.ed.gov/fulltext/ED553377.pdf.

———. 2015. "Completing the FAFSA." *Ed Review Newsletter.* http://www2.ed.gov/news/newsletters/edreview/2015/0109.html#2.

———. 2013. "Digest of Education Statistics." National Center for Education Statistics, Washington, DC. https://nces.ed.gov/programs/digest/.

———. 2013. "Federal Pell Grant Program End-of-Year Report." Office of Postsecondary Education. http://www2.ed.gov/finaid/prof/resources/data/pell-2013-14/pell-eoy-2013-14.html.

———. n.d. "Federal versus Private Loans." Federal Student Aid, U.S. Department of Education. https://studentaid.ed.gov/sa/types/loans/federal-vs-private.

———. n.d. "How Much Can I Borrow?" Federal Student Aid. https://studentaid.ed.gov/sa/types/loans/subsidized-unsubsidized#how-much.

———. n.d. "Integrated Postsecondary Education Data System Data Center." National Center for Education Statistics. https://nces.ed.gov/ipeds/datacenter/Default.aspx.

———. 2015. "Questions and Answers: Financial Aid and Undocumented Students." http://blogs.nvcc.edu/financialaid/files/2015/10/financial-aid-and-undocumented-students-1.pdf.

———. n.d. "Shopping Sheet for Information for Financial Aid Professionals." Office of Federal Student Aid. https://www.ifap.ed.gov/eannouncements/attachments/ShoppingSheetTemplate20152016.pdf.

———. 2015. "Title IV Program Volume Reports: 2013–2014 Award Year Campus-Based Program Data by School." https://studentaid.ed.gov/sa/about/data-center/student/title-iv.

————. 2011. *Trends in High School Dropout and Completion Rates in the United States: 1972–2009*. NCES 2012-006. U.S. Department of Education. Washington, DC: National Center for Education Statistics. http://nces.ed .gov/pubsearch.

————. 2014. "2013–2014 Federal Pell Grant Program End-of-Year." http:// www2.ed.gov/finaid/prof/resources/data/pell-2013-14/pell-eoy-2013-14 .html.

U.S. Department of Education, Office of the Inspector General. 2013. *Semi-annual Report to Congress, No. 66: October 1, 2012–March 31, 2013*. https:// www2.ed.gov/about/offices/list/oig/semiann/sar66.pdf.

U.S. Department of Housing and Urban Development. 2015. *Barriers to Success: Housing Insecurity for U.S. College Students*. Office of Policy Development and Research. http://www.huduser.gov/portal/periodicals/insight /insight_2.pdf.

U.S. Department of Labor. 2014. "Changes in Basic Minimum Wages in Non-Farm Employment under State Law: Selected Years 1968 to 2013." U.S. Department of Labor, Washington, DC. http://www.dol.gov/whd/state /stateMinWageHis.htm.

————. 2013. *Geographic Profile of Employment and Unemployment, 2013*. Bureau of Labor Statistics. Bulletin 2780. http://www.bls.gov/opub/gp/pdf /gp13full.pdf.

————. 2009. *Geographic Profile of Employment and Unemployment, 2009*. Bureau of Labor Statistics. Bulletin 2748. http://www.bls.gov/opub/gp /pdf/gp09full.pdf.

U.S. Department of Labor, Bureau of Labor Statistics. 2015. "Labor Force Statistics from the Current Population Survey." Last modified October 8. http://www.bls.gov/cps/cps_htgm.htm.

U.S. Government Accountability Office. 2014. *Higher Education: State Funding Trends and Policies on Affordability*. GAO Publication no. GAO-15–151. http://www.gao.gov/assets/670/667557.pdf.

U.S. Senate Committee on Health, Education, Labor and Pensions. 2014. "Alexander: 'College More Affordable than Most Students Think.'" March 27. Press release. http://www.help.senate.gov/chair/newsroom/press /alexander-college-more-affordable-than-most-students-think.

————. 2015. "Alexander: If Colleges Share in the Risk of Student Loan Defaults, They Can Help Reduce Overborrowing—and the Cost of College." May 20. Press release. http://www.help.senate.gov/chair/newsroom/press /alexander-if-colleges-share-in-the-risk-of-student-loan-defaults-they-can -help-reduce-overborrowingand-the-cost-of-college.

University of Maryland University College. 2012. *10 Great Ways to Pay for Your Education: Discover Affordable Financial Options that Work within Your*

Budget. https://www.pdffiller.com/en/project/47621468.htm?form_id=
13572069.

University of Wisconsin Foundation. 2013. *Connecting People, Inspiring Ideas:
2013 University of Wisconsin Foundation Annual Report on Stewardship*.
https://www.supportuw.org/wp-content/uploads/annual_report_13.pdf.

University of Wisconsin–Madison Academic Planning and Institutional
Research. 2015. *Data Digest 2014–2015*. https://apir.wisc.edu/datadigest
/201415Digest/dd15_web.pdf.

University of Wisconsin–Milwaukee Office of Assessment and Institutional
Research. 2014. *Fact Book 2013–14*. http://www4.uwm.edu/acad_aff
/assessment/factbook/fb1314.pdf.

University of Wisconsin System. 2014. *Fact Book 13–14: A Reference Guide to
University of Wisconsin System Statistics and General Information*. https://
www.wisconsin.edu/download/publications(2)/Fact-Book.pdf.

———. 2015. "Higher Education Fact Sheet." Office of Policy Analysis and
Research. https://www.wisconsin.edu/reports-statistics/download
/educational_statistics/Higher_Education_Facts.pdf.

———. 2014. "Minutes of the Regular Meeting of the Board of Regents of
the University of Wisconsin System." June 5. https://www.wisconsin.edu
/regents/download/meeting_materials/2014/june_5-6/June-5,-2014
-Minutes.pdf.

———. 2012. "Report on Remedial Education in the UW System: Demographics, Remedial Completion, Retention, and Graduation September 2012."
https://www.wisconsin.edu/reports-statistics/download/educational
_statistics/2012-Remedial-Report_final.pdf.

———. 2010. "Retention and Graduation: 2011–12." Informational Memo-
randum. Madison, University of Wisconsin System.

———. 2015. "Retention and Graduation Rates." https://www.wisconsin.edu
/reports-statistics/download/educational_statistics/ret-grad.pdf.

———. 2014. "Retention and Graduation: 2013–14." Informational Memo-
randum. https://www.wisconsin.edu/reports-statistics/download
/educational_statistics/informational_memoranda/rg13-14.pdf.

———. 2015. "Student Statistics, Fall 2014–15: Headcount Enrollment—
Undergraduate Students." https://www.wisconsin.edu/reports-statistics
/download/student_statistics_/2014-15/pdf/r_b305_c_tot.pdf.

———. 2015. "Student Statistics, Fall 2014–15: Headcount Enrollment—
Undergraduate Students by Institution." https://www.wisconsin.edu
/reports-statistics/download/student_statistics_/2014-15/pdf/r_b300
_tot.pdf.

———. 2015. "Student Statistics, Fall Full-Time Equivalent Enrollment—
Undergraduate Students by Institution." https://www.wisconsin.edu

/reports-statistics/download/student_statistics_/2014-15/pdf/r_a600
_tot.pdf.

———. 2015. "University of Wisconsin Student Statistics, Fall 2014–15 Headcount Enrollment by Race/Ethnicity and Classification." https://www
.wisconsin.edu/reports-statistics/download/student_statistics_/2014-15
/pdf/r_b108_tot.pdf.

———. 2015. "What Is the UW System." https://www.wisconsin.edu/about
-the-uw-system/.

———. n.d. "Wisconsin State Appropriations and Tuition, Redbook Budget
– Exhibit II." https://secure.uwsa.edu/redbook-2014-15/book1/pages
/003.html.

UWM Foundation, Inc., and Affiliates. 2014. *Consolidated Financial Statements
and Supplementary Information*. Milwaukee: UWM Foundation. http://
uwmfdn.org/getdoc/73efbf27-73d5-4d62-9fb2-fcaa2db4bff8/78665-6-14
-UWM-Foundation.aspx.

Van Dongen, H. P., G. Maislin, J. M. Mullington, and D. F. Dinges. 2003. "The
Cumulative Cost of Additional Wakefulness: Dose-Response Effects on
Neurobehavioral Functions and Sleep Physiology from Chronic Sleep
Restriction and Total Sleep Deprivation." *Sleep* 26:117–26.

Van Dyke, R., B. Little, and C. Callender. 2005. "Survey of Higher Education
Students' Attitudes to Debt and Term-Time Working and Their Impact on
Attainment." Higher Education Funding Council for England, Bristol.

Vedder, R. 2012. "End U.S. Student Loans, Don't Make Them Cheaper."
Bloomberg View, June 17.

———. 2012. "Federal Student Aid, and Unintended Consequences." *Impri-
mis*, vol. 41, nos. 5–6.

Venator, J., and R. V. Reeves, 2015. "Three Reasons College Matters for Social
Mobility." Social Mobility Memo, February 6. Brookings Institution, Washington, DC. http://www.brookings.edu/blogs/social-mobility-memos
/posts/2015/02/06-college-education-equity-reeves.

Walpole, M. 2003. "Socioeconomic Status and College: How SES Affects College Experiences and Outcomes." *Review of Higher Education* 27 (1): 45–73.

Ware, M., E. Weissman, and D. McDermott. 2013. "Aid Like a Paycheck: Incremental Aid to Promote Student Success." MDRC Policy Brief. MDRC,
New York.

Washington Post. 2015. "The CNN Democratic Debate Transcript, Annotated."
October 13.

Waterman, S. J. 2012. "Home-Going as a Strategy for Success among Haudenosaunee College and University Students." *Journal of Student Affairs
Research and Practice* 49 (2): 193–209.

Weatherly, J. N., A. Derenne, and H. K. Terrell. 2010. "College Students

Discount Money 'Won' More Than Money 'Owed.'" *Psychological Record* 60:463–72.

Wei, C., and P. Skomsvold. 2011. "Borrowing at the Maximum: Undergraduate Stafford Loan Borrowers in 2007–08." NCES 2012–161. National Center for Education Statistics, U.S. Department of Education, Washington, DC.

Weisbrod, B. A., J. P. Ballou, and E. D. Asch. 2010. *Mission and Money: Understanding the University*. Cambridge: Cambridge University Press.

Weissman, J., and A. Lindemann. 2014. "The Cost of Making Our Public Colleges Tuition Free: $0." *MoneyBox* (blog), *Slate*, December 9. http://www.slate.com/blogs/moneybox/2014/12/09/the_cost_of_making_our_public_colleges_tuition_free_0.html.

Western Interstate Commission for Higher Education. 2008. *Knocking at the College Door: Projections of High School Graduates: Projections of High School Graduates by State and Race/Ethnicity 1992–2022*. Boulder, CO: Western Interstate Commission for Higher Education. http://wiche.edu/info/publications/knocking_complete_book.pdf.

Wightman, P., R. Schoeni, and K. Robinson. 2010. "Familial Assistance to Young Adults." Working Brief. University of Michigan, Ann Arbor.

———. 2012. "Familial Financial Assistance to Young Adults." National Poverty Center Working Paper Series no. 12-10. http://npc.umich.edu/publications/u/2012-10%20NPC%20Working%20Paper.pdf.

Wilde, O. 1891. "The Soul of Man under Socialism." Marxists Internet Archive. https://www.marxists.org/reference/archive/wilde-oscar/soul-man/.

Williams, W. E. 2012. "Too Much College." Unpublished Paper. George Mason University, Fairfax, VA. http://econfaculty.gmu.edu/wew/articles/12/TooMuchCollege.htm.

Wilson, W. J. 1997. *When Work Disappears: The World of the New Urban Poor*. New York: Vintage.

Wine, J., N. Janson, and S. Wheeless. 2011. *2004/09 Beginning Postsecondary Students Longitudinal Study (BPS:04/09) Full-scale Methodology Report* (NCES 2012-246). National Center for Education Statistics, Institute of Education Sciences, U.S. Department of Education, Washington, DC. http://nces.ed.gov/pubsearch.

Wine, J. S., and J. A. Riccobono. n.d. *National Postsecondary Student Aid Study*. RTI International, Education Studies Division, Chicago. http://www.bls.gov/cex/hhsrvywrkshp_wine.pdf.

Winterrowd, E. 2014. "Annual Report 2013–2014: Results from the Client Information Form and Learning Outcomes Satisfaction Survey." University of Wisconsin System Counseling Impact Assessment Committee. University of Wisconsin System, Madison, WI.

Wisconsin Association of Independent Colleges and Universities. 2015. "WAICU Facts." www.waicu.org/research/waicu-facts.

Wisconsin Council on Children and Families. 2011. *Race to Equity Report: A Baseline Report on the State of Racial Disparities in Dane County.* http://racetoequity.net/dev/wp-content/uploads/WCCF-R2E-Report.pdf.

Wisconsin HOPE Lab. 2015. "What We're Learning: FAFSA." Data Brief 15-02. Wisconsin HOPE Lab, University of Wisconsin–Madison.

————. 2015. "What We're Learning: Satisfactory Academic Progress." Data Brief 15-01. Wisconsin HOPE Lab, University of Wisconsin–Madison.

————. 2016. "What We're Learning: Student Financial Contributions to Families—a Data Update from the Wisconsin HOPE Lab." Data Brief 16-01. Wisconsin HOPE Lab, University of Wisconsin–Madison.

Wisconsin Information System for Education Data Dashboard. http://wisedash.dpi.wi.gov/Dashboard/portalHome.jsp.

Wisconsin Legislative Fiscal Bureau. 2015. "Student Financial Aid." Informational Paper 34. http://legis.wisconsin.gov/lfb/publications/informational-papers/documents/2015/34_student%20financial%20aid.pdf.

————. 2009. "University of Wisconsin System Overview: [2009]." Informational Paper 36. Wisconsin State Legislature, Legislative Fiscal Bureau, Madison.

————. 2015. "University of Wisconsin System Overview: [2015]." Informational Paper 32. Wisconsin State Legislature, Legislative Fiscal Bureau, Madison. http://legis.wisconsin.gov/lfb/publications/informational-papers/documents/2015/32_uw%20overview.pdf.

————. 2009. "Wisconsin Technical College System Overview: [2009]." Informational Paper 35. Wisconsin State Legislature, Legislative Fiscal Bureau, Madison.

————. 2015. "Wisconsin Technical College System Overview: [2015]." Informational Paper 31. Wisconsin State Legislature, Legislative Fiscal Bureau, Madison. http://legis.wisconsin.gov/lfb/publications/informational-papers/documents/2015/31_wtcs.pdf.

Wisconsin Technical College System. 2014. "Fact Book 2014: 2012–13 and 10-year trend." WTCS, Madison, WI. http://www.wtcsystem.edu/wtcsexternal/cmspages/getdocumentfile.aspx?nodeguid=3879c9ef-7e83-4f74-8517-f43d34041700.

Wisconsin Technical College System. 2015. "Our Story." http://www.wistechcolleges.org/wisconsins-colleges/our-story.

Wisconsin Technical College System Board. 2015. "An Overview of the Wisconsin Technical College System." http://www.wtcsystem.edu/wtcsexternal/cmspages/getdocumentfile.aspx?nodeguid=3879c9ef-7e83-4f74-8517-f43d34041700.

Witte, J. W., and B. Wolfe. 2009. "Is University of Wisconsin Education Becoming More Elite? A Partial Answer." Working Paper, no. 2009-005. La Follette School of Public Affairs, University of Wisconsin–Madison.

Wolfe, B. L., and R. H. Haveman. 2002. "Social and Nonmarket Benefits from Education in an Advanced Economy." *Proceedings from Federal Reserve Bank of Boston* 47 (June): 97–142.

Wolff, E. N. 2010. "Recent Trends in Household Wealth in the United States: Rising Debt and the Middle-Class Squeeze—an Update to 2007." Working Paper Series no. 159. Levy Economics Institute, Bard College, Annandale-On-Hudson, NY.

Woodhouse, K. 2015. "Funding Woes." *Inside Higher Ed*, May 5.

Yang, D. 2011. "Migrant Remittances." *Journal of Economic Perspectives* 25 (3): 129–52.

Ydstie, J. 2011. "Why Some Men Earn Less Than They Did 40 Years Ago." *Weekend Edition*, National Public Radio, September 17. http://www.npr.org/2011/09/17/140554967/median-male-workers-income-lower-than-in-1973.

Zelizer, V. 1997. *The Social Meaning of Money: Pin Money, Paychecks, Poor Relief, and Other Currencies*. Princeton, NJ: Princeton University Press.

Zlotocha, S. 2009. "A 'Blue Shirt' UW for Milwaukee: Making the Case for the University of Wisconsin–Milwaukee, 1948–1956." *e.polis* 3:84–110.

Index

Focal group students' pseudonyms are indexed by first name (e.g., Chloe).

Page numbers followed by the letter *f* indicate a figure; those followed by the letter *t* indicate a table.